Reading Diagnosis and Instruction: A C–A–L–M Approach

SUSAN MANDEL GLAZER
Rider College

LYNDON W. SEARFOSS
Arizona State University

 PRENTICE HALL, Englewood Cliffs, New Jersey 07632

Library of Congress Cataloging-in-Publication Data

GLAZER, SUSAN MANDEL.
  Reading diagnosis and instruction.

  Includes bibliographies and index.
  1. Reading (Elementary) 2. Language arts (Elementary) 3. English language—Study and teaching (Elementary) I. SEARFOSS, LYNDON W. II. Title.
LB1573.G515   1988   372.4   87-25910
ISBN 0-13-755810-4

Editorial/production supervision and
  interior design: *Edith Riker*
Manufacturing buyer: *Margaret Rizzi*
Cover design: *Photo Plus Art*
Cover and interior photos: *Joseph Kowal*

© 1988 by Prentice-Hall, Inc.
A Division of Simon & Schuster
Englewood Cliffs, New Jersey 07632

All rights reserved. No part of this book may be
reproduced, in any form or by any means,
without permission in writing from the publisher.

Printed in the United States of America

10 9 8 7 6 5 4 3 2 1

ISBN 0-13-755810-4

Prentice-Hall International (UK) Limited, *London*
Prentice-Hall of Australia Pty. Limited, *Sydney*
Prentice-Hall Canada Inc., *Toronto*
Prentice-Hall Hispanoamericana, S.A., *Mexico*
Prentice-Hall of India Private Limited, *New Delhi*
Prentice-Hall of Japan, Inc., *Tokyo*
Simon & Schuster Asia Pte. Ltd., *Singapore*
Editora Prentice-Hall do Brasil, Ltda., *Rio de Janeiro*

CONTENTS

PREFACE   *xi*

1
FRAMEWORK FOR DIAGNOSIS   *1*

    What Is Reading?   2
    How Do We Assist Students Who Do Not Learn to Read Well?   3
    Diagnostic Propositions   4
    The C-A-L-M Approach to Diagnosis versus
      Traditional Procedures   6
    Summary   8
    Questions to Ponder   8
    Reference   8
    Suggested Reading   9

2
DIAGNOSTIC VARIABLES 10

Effective Learning Environments *12*
Oral and Written Language Fluency *13*
Physical Factors *18*
Self-Esteem and Self-Confidence *21*
Concluding Remarks on Diagnostic Variables *22*
Differences Between C-A-L-M and Medical Model *22*
Summary *23*
Questions to Ponder *24*
References *24*
Suggested Reading *24*

3
ASSESSING CLASSROOM ENVIRONMENTS: THEORY AND METHODS 25

The Ethnographic Perspective *27*
Aspects of Classroom Environment *32*
Collecting Classroom Environment Data *41*
Summary *42*
Questions to Ponder *42*
References *43*
Suggested Reading *44*

4
ORAL LANGUAGE FLUENCY   46

    Oral Language Variables *48*
    Assessing Oral Language Fluency *49*
    C-A-L-M Informal Procedures *54*
    Instructional Strategies for Enhancing Oral Language *71*
    Summary *78*
    Questions to Ponder *79*
    References *79*
    Suggested Reading *81*

5
WRITTEN LANGUAGE FLUENCY   *82*

    What Do We Measure? *83*
    Assessing Written Language Fluency *85*
    Assessing Various Elements *102*
    Guiding Students to Improve Written Language Fluency *109*
    Using Literature to Guide Students to Write *112*
    Summary *113*
    Questions to Ponder *114*
    References *114*
    Suggested Reading *115*

6
READING COMPREHENSION AND RETENTION 116

Overview of Comprehension Theories *117*
What Do We Assess to Determine Comprehension Ability? *122*
Formal/Standardized Assessment Tools for Analyzing
   Text Comprehension *122*
Informal Tools for Assessing Comprehension *126*
C-A-L-M Assessment Procedures in
   Interactive Settings *180*
Summary *189*
Questions to Ponder *190*
References *190*
Suggested Reading *194*

7
COMPREHENSION OF THE WRITTEN CODING SYSTEM 196

Awareness and Comprehension of Print *197*
Vocabulary Development *206*
Word Recognition Strategies in Classroom and Clinic Settings *211*
Strategies for Teaching Use of Context *218*
Spelling Development *220*
Decoding or Word-Identification Skills *230*
Teaching Strategies for Decoding Development *237*
Summary *238*
Questions to Ponder *238*
References *239*
Suggested Reading *241*

8

PHYSICAL FACTORS AFFECTING LANGUAGE LEARNING *243*

Physical Factors *244*
Visual Factors *246*
Auditory Factors: Hearing or Acuity *257*
Allergies *264*
Nutrition *269*
Alcohol and Drug Abuse *272*
Perceptual and Neurological Factors *274*
Summary *281*
Questions to Ponder *281*
References *282*
Suggested Reading *284*

9

PROCEDURES FOR CLASSROOM DIAGNOSIS *287*

Linking Diagnostic Questions, Variables, and Procedures *291*
Organizing and Reporting Diagnostic Information *293*
Sample Classroom Diagnosis Report *293*

10 PROCEDURES FOR CLINICAL READING DIAGNOSIS 307

Referral System *308*
Cursory Screening *318*
Clinical Diagnosis *326*
Sample Case Report: Long Form *330*
Special Note on the Long-Form Report *347*
Sample Case Report: Short Form *348*
Summary *354*
References *355*

Appendix A
SUGGESTED LITERATURE FOR DIAGNOSIS AND INSTRUCTION 357

Helping Children Develop Oral and Written Language Fluency *358*
Wordless Books *359*
Alphabet Books to Help Children Understand the Relationship Between Alphabetic Writing and Speech *360*
Books to Help Children Develop Oral and Written Language Fluency Using Different Forms of Language Expression *361*
Books to Help Children Develop Reading Comprehension by Presenting Common Experiences and/or Ideas *365*
Books Dealing with Disabilities and/or Handicapping Conditions *373*

Appendix B

LIST OF FORMAL TESTS AND INFORMAL ASSESSMENT INSTRUMENTS   *380*

    Formal Tests   *380*
    Informal Tests   *386*
    List of Publishers and Addresses   *388*

INDEX   *391*

PREFACE

Reading Diagnosis and Instruction: A C–A–L–M Approach was created for graduate students enrolled in courses in diagnosis and instruction, in communication arts & reading. The text is also appropriate for undergraduate students who have had several courses in reading foundations and methods. And, in-service professionals will find the text resourceful as well. The materials in the text are the results of interactions with "real" students and teachers working together in the Reading/Language Arts Clinic at Rider College, Lawrenceville, New Jersey.

The first two chapters discuss philosophy and variables important for continuous assessment and change in instructional practices in classrooms and clinics. The next six chapters describe the variables and approaches to diagnostic and instructional procedures. Chapters 9 and 10 describe applications of the procedures described throughout the text and include several case reports. These case studies should serve as models for students who are learning about interpreting and reporting behavioral observations.

Appendix A includes a list of annotations describing literature for children and young adults that can be used for diagnosis and instruction. Appendix B consists of a select annotated listing of formal and informal tests with appropriate uses for these.

The materials in the text were developed based on the point of view that communication is the most important human variable for success in life. The effectiveness of that communication determines, in great part, the quality of life a person leads. Interactions resulting from communication affects achievements. As they interact with students, teachers observe the processes used as well as the language products resulting from communication. The processes and products are evaluated using various testing mechanisms, some informal, but many of which are standardized. The results of such evaluations usually determine grade placement, curriculum choices, and instructional strategies. Such evaluations often seriously affect teachers' more general, less formal perceptions of students' abilities to communicate using oral and written language in response to reading and listening. And, teachers' perceptions toward students help students develop feelings about themselves. Students then develop self-esteem and confidence—or do not—based on evaluations in classrooms and clinics.

It is clear, then, that the obligations of professionals responsible for observing and evaluating reading and language behaviors are ominous. The "fate" of students' schooling rests in the hands of these professionals. Inappropriate interpretations of behavior or evaluations based on minimal knowledge of communication processes could result in personal and academic failures for students.

GOALS AND PURPOSES

This manuscript is an attempt to discuss diagnosis and instruction of reading and related behaviors considering:

1. Reading, writing, oral language (listening and speaking), and thinking as integrated processes
2. Diagnostic and instructional procedures as inseparable and ongoing
3. Several environments in which literacy activities occur as valid settings for both diagnosis and instruction
4. All printed materials, including literature, text, periodicals, and others as materials appropriate for assessing students' reading abilities
5. Current research and literature that stresses reading as a language process.

Our purposes are simple. We want to suggest productive ways to:

- Discover students' strengths and needs
- Enhance students' self-esteem by encouraging them to work toward building their strengths
- Help them to learn about how they construct and share ideas effectively
- Help students and their teachers hypothesize and predict appropriate instructional strategies for achieving success when interacting with text, both oral and written.

The text, based on current literature in our field, has a commonsense notion. This should bring the diagnostic process used in classrooms and clinics "down to earth." We hope that the information and tone help educators eliminate the "one-session" testing notion that says, "This score tells all about the student's reading ability. We can make decisions about grade placement and instruction based on this score. We can predict how the student will respond to reading activities in all content areas." Most important, we hope that the text directs professionals to ask again and again, "What am I doing to create positive change in students? How do I need to adjust the environment, including instruction, to meet student's needs?"

AN INVITATION TO GROW

This text is a departure from many written about diagnosis and instruction. We encourage you to read our ideas and compare them to the ideas and approaches of the other professionals in reading and language arts. We invite you to use the ideas in this text and add to them by incorporating our notions about assessing and guiding reading and related behaviors. We have grown from our interactions with children, graduate students, and parents. We have grown, too, as we interacted to create this volume. We urge you also to become actively involved with language; as you learn how to grow, so will your students.

ACKNOWLEDGEMENTS

As authors, we know that this text could not have been created without the help and support of many people. We acknowledge all of our professional colleagues at Arizona State University and Rider College, our friends, and families, and we mention a few. The children, graduate students, teachers, and parents of the Reading/Language Arts Clinic at Rider College were the major sources for much of the text's content. The environments and many of the procedures described evolved from interactions with these wonderful people. Susan Willig and Shirley Chlopak at Prentice Hall believed in us and provided guidance for making this book a reality. Edie Riker, our production editor, provided "hand holding" directions through the entire production process. Penelope Denton's expertise helped us conceptualize the classroom as a complex learning and living environment for teachers and students. Gloria B. Smith, Rider College, and Cynthia Mershon Hickman, West Windsor-Plainsboro Regional School District, New Jersey, compiled two outstanding appendices. Lesley Mandel Morrow, Rutgers University, contributed the oral language transcription in Chapter 4. Diane Curry's ethnographic notes in Chapter 6 were part of a research project carried out at Rider College. Photographs were taken by Joseph Kowal, Carriage Studios, Morrisville, Pennsylvania. We thank Geraldine Holley, Helen Hudzina, Deborah Monroe, Wanda Guarino, and Celeste Thatcher of the Rider College Word Processing Center. We acknowledge John Ruess, Jr., Buz Cofrances, and Kathleen J. Frankel for their assistance in collecting literature and sharing ideas related to several chapters.

Marris Cutting is recognized for contributing ideas to worksheets in Chapter 6. Proofreading for content by Louise Beste, Phyllis Fantauzzo, Lorraine M. Sieben, and Michael Welborn helped to refine the text. Carole Nicolini of the Reading/Language Arts Clinic at Rider College, provided emotional, editorial, and management support for both of us during the four-year project.

We appreciate the comments of the reviewers: Jerome Niles, Virginia Polytechnic Institute & State University; Barbara C. Palmer, Florida State University; Donne E. Alvermann, University of Georgia; and James F. Baumann, Purdue University.

A very special thanks to Margaret Cagney, friend and colleague at Glassboro State College, New Jersey, for bringing us together. Our professional lives would not be manageable without the unconditional support and friendship of Richard M. Glazer and Ernest L. Cofrances, III. Finally, we thank each other for the healthy and creative interactions in all of our joint projects.

SMG
LWS

1

FRAMEWORK FOR DIAGNOSIS

What Is Reading?

How Do We Assist Students Who Do Not Learn to Read Well?

Diagnostic Propositions

The C–A–L–M Approach to Diagnosis versus Traditional Procedures

Summary

Questions to Ponder

Reference

Suggested Reading

The explosion of research on language processing which has marked the past decade has produced a diverse and rich body of information. The framework for diagnosis and instruction presented in Chapter 1 is derived from this literature. To provide a means of organizing and presenting our framework for diagnosis, we pose two simple questions and explore answers to each:

What is reading?
How do we assist students who do not learn to read well?

WHAT IS READING?

Reading is receiving ideas, experiences, feelings, emotions, and concepts. It is an activity that permits one to gain vast knowledge. When reading, we can live and travel vicariously and become acquainted with people and events of the past that have shaped our worlds. Reading creates for us mental maps of events so that ideas can be transmitted from the mind of one, the author, to the mind of another—the receiver/reader.

Humans read even before encountering print. They read faces and sound vibrations; they read the thrust of the wind on their skin; they read the intriguing language of animals. It was not until humans invented a symbol system to record, in words, the ideas that emanate from human minds and souls that reading problems began. Interpreting the written "squiggles" that represent thoughts seems to create difficulties for some people. These difficulties, we believe, are not "reading problems," but rather, they may represent problems with the coding system itself or with the pedagogy designed to help students learn to read. Actual problems with reading are often quite complex and misunderstood. Experts have difficulty agreeing what reading problems are, how to assess them, and how to assist students who have reading difficulties.

We believe that young children's eagerness to learn to read is based on their belief that being able to read opens wonderful worlds of experiences. Students must experience the excitement of "breaking the code," realizing that when they read ignorance is shed. This is the power of literacy and the excitement of the reading experience. When young children and adults achieve literacy, which permits the reception and expression of ideas and feelings, the result is joy and personal fulfillment. Diagnosis and diagnostic procedures, therefore, must be broad and flexible in order to discover what reading is for each student—and when each student does it well.

HOW DO WE ASSIST STUDENTS WHO DO NOT LEARN TO READ WELL?

If we view reading as an activity that encourages initiation into new worlds, then reading assessment and pedagogical practices to assist students who are not reading well take on unique parameters. When we ask "What is reading?" we must look at individual students in many environments and observe strengths and needs. Observing them as whole individuals who are unique dominates the diagnostic process. Noting multiple reactions and responses and interpreting recorded observations in several settings seems to be a reasonable approach for discovering students' strengths and needs. Interpretations of these observations should result in meaningful suggestions for students' learning. Keen sensitive observers, like good researchers, find data that help to explain student performance and permit predictions of future student behaviors. *Thus, a purpose for diagnosis seems to be directing educators to instructional change.*

Changes in instructional practices should result after observing students reading and composing in classroomlike settings, when they are involved in multiple and varied instructional and recreational reading activities. The process of diagnosing strengths in multiple environments as well as instructional settings over time reflects our model. Reviewing observation notes, video and audio recordings, materials produced by students, and then asking questions about data collection provides information about each student's performance. Accumulating materials and reviewing them helps us look for consistencies or inconsistencies in behaviors. Once notes on students' behaviors are gathered and reviewed, decisions concerning further diagnosis and instructional needs in reading and writing can be made by teachers, diagnosticians, parents, and students themselves. As Gillet and Temple (1982, p. 8) suggest, "diagnosis is a process requiring decisions made by people, not instruments."

DIAGNOSTIC PROPOSITIONS

Diagnosis is involved, ongoing, cumulative, and time consuming. A thorough diagnosis should result in a picture of each student's language behaviors. The model for diagnosis we propose is labeled C–A–L–M for *c*ontinuous *a*ssessment of *l*anguage *m*odel. It provides a paradigm for collecting information to form tentative hypotheses about students' abilities and needs. The following propositions underlie the C–A–L–M diagnostic model described in this text.

1. Diagnosis is asking questions. A child and parents came into a clinic, distressed, frustrated, and quite dismayed. Mark had just received a report card indicating that his reading performance was poor. Accusations spurted from the parents, attributing failures to the classroom teacher's behavior and inappropriate instruction and materials for teaching Mark to read. A sharp-tongued interchange between parents then began, each blaming the other for the problems. Mark stood by calmly, head down, quiet and probably bewildered by the confusion that was initiated as a result of one report card. Accusations, uncomfortable feelings, and hostility were present. No one asked Mark questions about the situation; parents did not ask questions of the clinical personnel and parents did not ask questions of each other. *No one asked, "How can we help Mark to solve the problem?"*

To assume that simply asking questions solves reading problems is unrealistic. Asking questions, however, begins an open-ended approach to diagnosis. Questions allow the use of alternative procedures for teaching and further testing. Questions redirect the diagnostician to reevaluate data in order to look for alternatives for determining needs. Questions guide observers to look and relook at students in many situations. Asking questions begins and concludes the diagnostic process. *Questions should always be asked with one major goal in mind: "How can we help the student?"*

2. Diagnosis is observing learners in many language situations. We recall one mother's turmoil when she learned of her child's score on a year-end standardized reading test. The observed test score after a three-hour paper and pencil testing session was the determining factor for the child's academic placement for the next year. This does not make sense to us. Children read in many situations. They read labels on containers, instructions for games, comic books, text books, joke and game books, and advertisements. Determining the focus for instruction should result after observation of reading and other language behaviors in multiple settings.

3. Diagnosis is assessment over time. A sensible assessment of any situation takes time. When we determine the quality of a restaurant, that occurs over time. We may visit that restaurant often and eat different foods. We inquire about the chef or cook, the baker, the proprietor. We observe the decor, the service, and the personable nature of the employees. We want the service, food, employees, and atmosphere to be consistent so we can predict our experience in that restaurant on our next visit. Observing a student's reading and writing abilities is similar to observing the quality of a restaurant. We observe the student many times. We watch the student's use of language skills during different times of the day and throughout the school year. We observe the student's response to language on the playground, in reading groups, in the lunchroom, with the art, math, music teachers, and in all other instructional settings. We watch the student perform in formal as well as informal evaluation sessions. As we would continuously visit a restaurant, we continuously watch the student. Evaluation of the restaurant must occur continuously over time, for we would be leery of recommending it to a friend without tasting its products for more than a few times. Evaluation of a student's reading and writing must occur over time, too.

4. Diagnosis is restating questions. Initial questions begin the observation process as we will discuss in detail in later chapters. They direct and focus the efforts of the diagnosticians. Observing over time answers some questions, but often proves others to be irrelevant. Some questions will seem inappropriate after initial observations. Looking at field notes and assessing data provokes the development of new questions.[1] When reviewing field notes, trends may be observed; for example: Why do we see one student understanding information when reading out loud, but not silently? Why does another student retain the information when read to? As one reads field notes and analyzes and interprets observational data, questions occur. Restating questions, dis-

---

[1] The term "field notes" is borrowed from anthropology. These are written accounts of behavior, free from evaluative terms. Further discussion of field notes is found in Chapter 3.

garding irrelevant ones, and creating new ones are essential activities for diagnosing students' reading behaviors. Noticing consistencies or inconsistencies in language behaviors, questioning and then requestioning, all provide supportive information for pedagogical change.

THE C–A–L–M APPROACH TO DIAGNOSIS VERSUS TRADITIONAL PROCEDURES

For many years, it has been the practice to use a medical model, also referred to as a diagnostic/prescriptive model, for describing reading and other language behaviors. Diagnostic practitioners favoring this model usually test students to discover "abnormalities" for which some course of treatment or learning prescription is then applied. The purpose of the application is to bring the student "back to normal." Students assessed in such a medical manner view themselves in this light and think: "Gosh, I have something wrong with me and they will find out what it is and then make it better." More often than not this model creates more problems than it solves, for it works under the assumptions that:

1. Standardized testing, under controlled conditions, replicates all reading behaviors in all situations and therefore can be used for placement and for the development of instructional procedures.
2. A single set of procedures can help us become informed about a student's performance.
3. Formal testing can determine abilities of all students.
4. The learning problems lie within the learner.
5. The purpose of diagnosis is to find a label to categorize problem readers for placement.

The use of the medical model in diagnosis and instruction suggests to students that they learn how to read the way they are assessed, one skill at a time. It suggests, too, that when a series of subskills are placed together and mastered, students will be able to read. It subtly forces us to conclude erroneously that there is only one instructional method, one set of materials, one setting, and one set of formal tests needed to solve reading and other literacy problems. We do not mean to suggest that single variables such as formal tests do not contribute to the holistic picture of the language learner. What we do believe, however, is that much data are needed in order to draw tentative conclusions about children's success or failures with reading. The test score and subscores are only one small part of the total diagnostic evaluation. If the evaluation is continuous and ongoing, testing, too, should be continuous. Diagnosis of reading and other language abilities must include as many observations and assessments of a student's interactions with print as possible. Fundamental to such a diagnosis are the propositions stated thus far in Chapter 1.

Diagnosis is

1. Asking initial questions about student performance in language activities
2. Observing students continuously in many language situations and asking initial questions
3. Observing and assessing students over time
4. Restating questions after observations for more definitive clarification of student needs, and beginning the process again.

The C–A–L–M model visually presented in Figure 1–1 suggests that observations must occur over time. Time permits the collection of cumulative data in many reading environments. These environments, found in most school settings as described in Table 1–1 occur when people, materials, space, and language come together to communicate. Initial diagnostic questions are general, but as data are collected they become specific and, therefore, narrow. New questions are broad, but are again narrowed in this ongoing process as additional data are collected and reviewed. The continuous nature of this process respects learner growth and change, environmental differences, and teacher styles. Information collected is both quantitative and qualitative. The diagnostician's ability to devise a synthesis of all types of data describes the skill we hope each reader of this text will acquire.

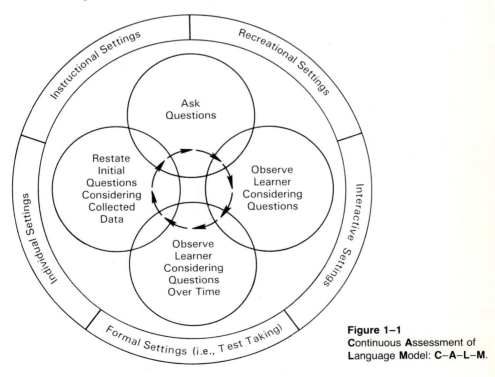

Figure 1–1
Continuous Assessment of Language Model: C–A–L–M.

Table 1–1 Reading Environments

SETTING	DESCRIPTION
Instructional	Large and small group gatherings when one provides instructional intervention. Leader may be teacher, clinician, special teacher, or student
Individual	One-to-one interaction and deliberate intervention focusing on literacy activities. Interactors may be student and professional, aide or peer.
Formal (i.e., test taking)	Group assessment procedures including standardized and informal assessment tools administered in formal setting. Structured for assessment purposes.
Interactive	Small group work, peer to peer, with academic goal.
Recreational	Reading, assigned or unassigned, which occurs without direction—in lunchrooms, on playgrounds, on the bus or in a car, or in other noninstructional settings.

SUMMARY

This chapter explained a framework for diagnosis focusing on two questions:

1. What is reading?
2. How do we assist students who do not learn to read well?

We view the diagnostic process as an ongoing one, resulting in changes in instructional procedures. Continuous observation using formal and informal tools describes to a great extent the activities of a skilled diagnostician.

QUESTIONS TO PONDER

1. Write some words or terms you believe describe the authors' view of the reading process. Compare your view of the reading process with that of the authors.
2. How has this chapter caused you to question your views of diagnosis?
3. What differences exist between the medical model of diagnosis and the C–A–L–M for clinic and classroom procedures?

REFERENCE

Gillet, J. M. & Temple, C. (1982). *Understanding reading problems,* Boston: Little, Brown.

SUGGESTED READING

Gilmore, P. & Glatthorn, A. (1982). *Children in and out of school.* Washington, DC: Center for Applied Linguistics. See articles by Mehan; Cazden; McDermott & Hood.

Huey, E. B. (1908). *The psychology and pedagogy of reading.* New York: Macmillan. A classic account of the reading process. Insightful, intuitively modern in theory, and well written.

Jennings, F. G. (1982). *This is reading.* New York: Plenum Publishing Company. (Originally published by Teachers College, Columbia University, 1965.) Jennings' skills as a writer help to share descriptions of the reading process humanly and practically.

Levine, K. (1982). Functional literacy: Fond illusions and false economies. *Harvard Educational Review, 52,* 249–266. Levine provides a critique of existing notions about literacy.

Moffett, J. (1983). *Teaching the universe of discourse* (2nd ed.). Boston: Houghton Mifflin Company. Sketches a pedagogical theory of discourse that provides a firm rationale for curriculum development.

Smith, F. (1978). *Reading without nonsense.* New York: Teachers College, Columbia University. "It is difficult to make reading impossible," begins this very readable, enchanting description of the reading process.

Snow, C. E. (1983). Literacy and language: Relationships during the preschool years. *Harvard Educational Review, 53,* 165–189. Snow explores characteristics of parent–child interactions which support language acquisitions.

Wiener, M. & Cromer, W. (1967). Reading and reading difficulty: A conceptional analysis. *Harvard Educational Review, 37,* 620–643. Classic article which examines common issues and flaws in the many definitions of reading in the 1950s and 1960s. These flaws were reflected in diagnostic instruments and procedures developed during the same period.

2

DIAGNOSTIC VARIABLES

Effective Learning Environments

Oral and Written Language Fluency

Physical Factors

Self-Esteem and Self-Confidence

Concluding Remarks on Diagnostic Variables

Differences between C–A–L–M and Medical Model

Summary

Questions to Ponder

References

Suggested Reading

The work of a diagnostician is like that of a detective. It involves finding the pieces of a diagnostic puzzle and watching it take shape. This four-step process begins with questions and proceeds to the collection of data, which is evaluated in response to initial questions. Finally, new questions are formulated and the process begins again. Continuously collecting observational data about students' performance in language learning activities provides a broad picture of growth and change. This ongoing process provides the examiner with information that describes each student's strengths and needs and provides substantial data for the development of instructional strategies to meet individual needs.

Diagnostic Process

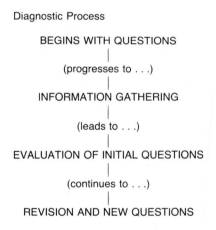

This chapter answers the question: What do we diagnose? We diagnose variables that affect language learning and fluency. These include:

1. Effective learning environments;
2. Oral language fluency;
3. Written language fluency;
4. Comprehension and retention of text content;
5. Comprehension of the written coding system;
6. Physical factors; and,
7. Self-esteem.

EFFECTIVE LEARNING ENVIRONMENTS

Learning environments are learning tools for students and teachers. Observations of students as they function in and amongst tables, chairs, books, and other materials should guide teachers to predict student behaviors. Environmental arrangements may help one student to function effectively and a second to fail. Huxley said it so eloquently:

> In no other species are the differences between individuals so great as in the human race.... On top of all the temperamental and anatomical differences ... are differences in biochemical make-up and differences in general ability and special gifts ... differences so great that they can almost be regarded as differences not in degree, but in kind. To herd all these dissimilar creatures into one classroom and to subject them all to the same kind of intellectual, emotional, and ethical training seems, on the surface of it, absurd. (1967, p. 70)

Failure to adjust learning environments to meet individual needs results in rigid instructional practices and prescribed content. Rigid, teacher-centered learning environments result in consequences described in the following fable.

Once upon a time, the animals decided they must do something heroic to meet the problems of "A New World." So they elected a school board consisting of a bear, a badger, and a beaver. The school board hired a porcupine as a teacher. The curriculum consisted of running, climbing, swimming, and flying. To make it easier to administer the curriculum, all the animals took all the subjects.

The duck was excellent in swimming, in fact better than his instructor; but he made only passing grades in flying and was very poor in running. Since he was slow in running, he had to stay after school and also drop swimming in order to practice running. This was kept up until his web feet were badly worn and he was only average in swimming.

The squirrel was excellent in climbing until she developed frustration in the flying class, where her teacher made her start from the ground up instead of the treetop down. She also developed a "charley horse" from overexertion, and then got a C in climbing and a D in running.

The eagle was a problem child and was disciplined severely. In the climbing class he beat all the others to the treetop, but insisted on using his own way to get there.

The rabbit started at the top of the class in running but had a nervous breakdown because of so much extra work in swimming.

At the end of the year an abnormal eel that could swim exceedingly well, and also run, climb, and fly a little, had the highest average and was valedictorian.

The prairie dogs stayed out of school and fought the tax levy because the administration would not add digging and burrowing to the curriculum. They apprenticed their child to a badger and later joined the groundhogs to start a successful private school. And so the school was closed, much to the relief of all the forest people.

It behooves us to notice each student's abilities and interests. Furthermore, it seems logical that all students can get to the "top" in something, but not in the same manner. If we expect carbon-copied children then we will, in fact, have perceptual-impaired dyslexic, alexic, dysgraphic, emotionally disturbed students at all ages and stages, and in all schools. If we expect all students to learn subjects the same way, then students will always have problems.

ORAL AND WRITTEN LANGUAGE FLUENCY

Fluency in language can best be described as the ability to demonstrate the use of meaningful language to make things happen to gain control of the world. Language fluency develops biologically and grows with environmental interactions. Fluency means using language to effectively influence our environments. Commands, for example, help the speaker get things that are wanted; tone of voice sets a mood and elicits responses. Dialogues with colloquial expressions and reduced syntactic structures personalize and make intimate otherwise formal or pedantic conversations.

Marie Clay and Don Holdaway are among those who have pioneered the concept of control using language. These researchers and others have found that children learn early how to use language to control their environments. Words and phrases joined by tones, stress, pitch, and juncture create meaning. Language controls are described in Table 2-1.

These six types of language controls are acquired (learned) during the early years of life. Observing a child's oral language behavior tells much about the language environment of the home, previous school experiences, and experiences with peers. Using one of these language forms in one situation does not mean that the same form is easily used in another. A child may voluntarily say to a friend, "I want that toy, now!" That same language form may be taboo

Table 2-1 Types of Language Controls

LANGUAGE EXPRESSION	TYPES OF LANGUAGE CONTROL
Dum-dee, dum-dee, dum-dee, dum A fat cat with a hat who ate a rat and sat on the bat. (Patterning)	The *playful, fun kinds of language* children use helps them gain control over language for functional use. This form also provides a fun-frolic language model, which creates happy feelings about words.
Why? What's that?	*Investigation language* allows children to question and thus control. Preschoolers say "Why" all the time. Children in the early school years say, "How do you do it?" and everyone says, "What's that?" Sometimes children are not even requesting a response. They question to gain attention.
Give me that! Come here! Do it! Stop that!	*Commands or orders* are charges from speakers that demonstrate controls. How others respond to children's commands determines how they learn to use language forms to control their worlds.
The grass is green. There are lots of birds flying. It's raining now. See three cars.	*Descriptive language* helps children represent observed phenomena in concrete ways. Children bring reality to abstractions using meaningful language.
I feel sick. My stomach hurts. I'm cold. My feelings are hurt, and I want to cry. I don't like you!	*Language that describes abstract feelings and human emotions* is learned in the early years. This language builds interdependencies, interpersonal relationships, and tells about the speakers' ability to share abstractness.
How are you? Do you want it? Tell me about it? How do you feel?	*Language that encourages dialogue for human interaction* requires responses. This builds friendships, companionships, and more, such as—later on—business relationships.

in a classroom setting. A child would not say, "I want that assignment and I want to do it now." Modifications of language forms are learned by youngsters as a result of experiences. It is important that children learn to modify language for school, peer, and other human interactions. Multiple language experiences help children develop the ability to:

1. Have *fun* with language and play with it.
2. Use language as *an investigative tool* to find out about the world.
3. Create *commands* or orders to control situations.
4. Describe *concrete phenomena*.
5. Express *feelings and emotions* through language.
6. Use language to *create interdependent/interactive situations*.

How to observe and encourage students' use of those language forms in oral and written formats will be described in Chapters 4 and 5.

Comprehension and Retention of Text Content

Perceptions are individual realities of objects, events, and ideas in the world. The only reality, according to some, is individual reality. Perceptions are realized through the senses. A sensory stimulus generates the retrieval or recall of summaries of events, ideas, experiences stored in memory. Looking at the moon shining in the sky and thinking about its glowing light is reality. Knowing that scientists have observed that the moon is large, very dark, and uneven, and that its glow belongs to the sun is abstract, and in a way, unreal, for we have not observed these phenomena. We want to believe that the moon is smooth, lovely to look at, and warm, for that is our "visual perception" of the moon—that is what appears to be real. Further, we can predict that the moon will appear tomorrow similar to the way it appeared today.

Perceptions can also be described as predictions. When we hear a siren, we can predict that it is probably a fire engine or an ambulance. We can predict that rain has come when we hear soft drops on the window pane. We have heard rain before and have developed "auditory perceptions" that help us predict what is occurring. We can predict someone's mood when we look at a face with a snarled frown. We can "guess" that the frown means the person is upset, uneasy, disturbed, perturbed, or sick. How do we know these things? We have stored in our memories perceptions about the world based on our memories of experiences or *schemata*. We learn to predict and hypothesize, taking educated guesses about current situations based on schemata stored away in our brain.

Stored information about ideas and concepts is necessary for fluent reading. These schemata include information about:

How language works (spelling, decoding, syntactic structures)
Content or facts
Strategies for remembering and organizing information
Appropriate behaviors in reading and writing activities
Classroom, teacher, and parent goals.

Learners comprehend and retain information when there is interest, need, and relevance. Because comprehension and retention depend on the ability to sense, find, and demand meaning, one must organize information for retention to take place. The human mind strives for organization. Demands for recall made in school require that students organize data as it is delivered—whether from text to learner, teacher to learner, or media or peers to learner. The "momentary" need to remember is *short-term memory*. When there is little interest or desire to recall, the short-term memory empties itself, providing space for new information. This memory behavior effectively handles emotional responses for its owner by forgetting painful data and retaining that which offers rewards. Our concerns are those frequent situations in school were content is preselected for students. How do we guide students to recall when interest is reduced? How do we convince them that recalling this information is important?

We must understand, first, that in school it is the short-term memory that is taxed. This facility has limited capacity. We know that the memory can hold only five to seven items of information for short periods of time. In order to keep information for longer periods it must be rehearsed. Think, for a moment, about remembering telephone numbers or zip codes without writing them down. We rehearse them by saying the numbers over and over again. To recall content, the mind groups or clusters information in bunches. Five to nine "bunches" of information can be recalled. For example, the word *reading* has seven letters. If presented letter by letter, there are seven discrete letters to recall:

R–E–A–D–I–N–G

If presented as a single cluster or whole word there is only one item, *reading*, which leaves room for approximately six more. So, it makes sense to deliver information by "bunching" it into content units that are related to something pleasurable and meaningful to each student. Students will hold information from reading and listening in short-term memory if they can connect meaning already in their memories to it. If they can't, the material is usually discarded and forgotten.

The key to success in most classrooms is the ability to instantaneously recall appropriate information in response to requests made by teachers and peers. Frank Smith (1982) sums up the memory puzzle with one word—*organization*—which is important for both short-term and long-term memory. Short-term memory sometimes holds isolated ideas as information data. Long-term memory has a storage system, or structure for related data. This structure or schema, if we could see it, might look like boxes, files, bunches of information, each labeled to fit individual situations. Students develop strategies for keeping information forever. Long-term memory requires organized storage. A file box or bunch of information would be pulled out of memory when the appropriate action, key, or stimuli is activated.

Each human's ideas are stored and organized in unique ways. The human mind has a need to organize information in order to keep a sense of balance, especially in school.

Students learn quickly the importance of selecting appropriate responses in each given situation to achieve successful interactions in school and with peers. The diagnostician observes students' responses (perceptions of the world) to note how closely related each response is to the realities (expected behaviors). Strategies for guiding students to function effectively in a variety of settings within environments can then be recommended.

Comprehending the Written Coding System

The ability to read and write depends a great deal on one's comprehension (understanding) that print corresponds with ideas, events, and feelings. Conceptual understanding of the mechanics of print, understanding that each word represents an object, feeling, series of events, empowers students for literacy. It is impossible, even with our broad collection of literature, to determine how and when children learn these ideas. We do know that language play and rehearsal of words and phrases through sight and sound seem to help children understand the written coding system. The incident which follows relates this well.

A mother came to us to discuss her child's reading ability. A three year old who accompanied the parent that day became restless after twenty minutes of discussion. Pulling on her mother's skirt, she said:

> "Mommy put your coat on,
> Mommy put your coat on,
> Mommy put your coat on,
> Let's go home."

Obviously, from the repetitive nature and phrasing, the child had heard and rehearsed a nursery rhyme such as:

> Polly put the kettle on,
> Polly put the kettle on,
> Polly put the kettle on,
> Let's all have tea.

She had "caught" the cadence, the rhythm of language, and reproduced the phrases using the syntactic format as structure for her own words. How does this happen? We are not sure. We do know that understanding words in print first requires delightful experiences, such as a child hearing the nursery rhyme.

If the child sees the repetitive lines, "Polly put the kettle on," and notes similarities in print, the child discovers a match in printed data. That child will also observe that oral language repeats, as does the visual aspect of the written code that represents the language rhyme. Matching speech to print requires noting similarities and differences between oral and written language codes.

PHYSICAL FACTORS

The abilities to see, hear, attend to tasks, and demonstrate motor control for tasks such as writing represent physical factors.

Seeing

Although visual deficits are as frequent among reading failures as nonreading failures (Emas, 1962), historically, impaired vision has been associated with reading disabilities (Robinson, 1946).[1] The ability to see clearly at far-point targets (the chalkboard, for example), the ability to fuse the image the eye brings to the brain, recognition of colors, and the ability to move the eyes from left to right (ocular motility) comprise the visual skills that, if impaired, are potential causes of reading failures.

Hearing

Students who cannot hear face problems in reading if learning to read depends on oral recitation and instruction. The teacher's use of oral directions, instructional activities, and evaluations of student performance based on teacher's oral activities determine the significance of each student's deficits. Deficiencies based on physiological concerns include pitch (frequency) of sounds, or how high or low the sound seems, and loudness (decibel counts). These seem to affect one's ability to read.

[1] Helen Robinson's 1946 report of problems in reading states that 63.3 percent of all pupils who had reading problems had some kind of visual difficulty. Researchers, however, have argued among themselves as to the exact percentage of disabled readers who exhibit visual problems.

Auditory acuity (hearing) and discrimination problems, often grouped together, are quite different. Although discrimination activities are often referred to as hearing deficiencies, memory span—seldom studied in conjunction with auditory discrimination abilities—should be considered instead. In this text, hearing loss refers *only* to the physical aspects of acuity.

Attending to Task

Students who move about in their seats, procrastinate, and end a school day without completing assignments receive labels which include hyperactive or inattentative. Such "labels" usually describe behaviors referred to as neurological disorders, implying brain damage. However, reading failures rarely result from brain damage (Bond and Tinker, 1973). Hyperactivity and inattentive behaviors often result when students are expected to sit in seats in an orderly, teacher-controlled fashion. Students who do not conform to these restrictive behavioral controls find life in school difficult. To survive, some manage to receive special placement in less restrictive environments. But when quiet, immobile, stern posture prevails as the expected mode of behavior in classrooms, attending and sitting become important physical activities that affect reading behaviors. Many students, when required to sit still or keep quiet, may find it difficult to concentrate on curriculum content since they must focus on the expected body behavior. Diagnosticians should determine the degree to which a classroom organization requires these behaviors. If classroom organization factors are important then they ought to become part of the diagnosis.

Motor Control

The student's ability to write, throw a ball, cut with scissors or knife, and use eating utensils confidently demonstrates control in small muscles in hands and feet. This control is important for reading and writing. These muscles should be able to control fingers for holding and grasping pencils, pens, crayons, and felt-tipped markers. Development of small muscles in the eyes helps the beginning reader develop directionality control.

For years, discussions concerning small muscle development have included the following terms (Harris & Hodges, 1981):

> Lateral dominance or laterality
> Directional confusion
> Crossed dominance
> Mixed dominance.

Laterality or lateral dominance. Often referred to as cerebral dominance, it "is the awareness of the left and right sides of one's body, plus the ability to name them correctly and to project consistently the concept of left and right to the environment" (Harris & Hodges, 1981, p. 174).

Directional confusion. A weakness or nonexistent ability to perceive spatial orientation characterizes directional confusion. It also includes an uncertainty or inconsistency in left-right directions or movements, as in attempting to read or write English from right to left (Harris & Hodges, 1981, p. 90).

Cross dominance. Motor preferences are not always confined to one side. The cross dominance theory states that unless all of one's motor preferences are unilateral, such as right-handed, right-eyed, and right-footed, neurological development is incomplete or immature (Harris & Hodges, 1981, p. 75). (Research has failed to support this theory as a cause of reading failure).

Mixed dominance. This is the apparent failure to establish consistent cerebral hemispheric superiority. Mixed cerebral dominance is one theory used to account for language and speech disorders (Harris & Hodges, 1981, p. 199).

These terms, many of them used interchangeably, provide students of reading and language arts with the vocabulary commonly used to describe atypical behaviors. Interestingly, research results concerning laterality have reported relationships between consistent use of one hand for writing and success in reading (Shearer, 1968), and others have found no significant relationships between students who will switch pencils and pens from the left to the right hand and their writing and reading ability (Cohen & Glass, 1968, p. 345). *Because of conflicting research findings and the vague use of terms it seems reasonable to assume that diagnosing laterality is dubious and unwarranted.* It seems important, however, to study students' motor adroitness and the consistency of this adroitness in many literacy activities.

Nutrition

Good health and success in school seem to be linked. Children with special health problems are often faced with reading disabilities, although few of these problems seldom cause reading failure. A child who is not well nourished, who has mineral and vitamin deficiencies, will suffer from fatigue, which may result in a lack of desire to become involved with anything but sleep and food. Poor teeth, allergies, the common cold will distract students. Energies to survive physical deficits may dominate so that learning suffers. Pertz and Putnam (1982) stress the need for teachers to become aware of the relationships of diet to learning. They indicate that research shows that a highly nutritional breakfast results in improved student attention in morning classes. Robinson's (1946) early study demonstrated that nutrition was indeed a causal factor in reading success and failures. When possible, the lay public and physicians must observe students' food habits and general health, for these play major roles in success in reading and writing.

Other Factors

Educators have found it difficult to classify physical variables related to reading acquisition. Often factors that are reported as physical abilities would better be classified elsewhere. Neurological factors are an example of these. Terms such as dyslexia,[2] dysgraphia,[3] minimal brain dysfunction,[4] and alexia[5] are labels used to describe various problems in reading or writing. These terms may be descriptive labels for neurological deficits; they may be related to the way students organize ideas and transform these into oral or written language codes; they may be related to the mental processes that involve communication skills. They are, however, definitive in nature and often used to secure special placement for students. Special instruction is meritorious, but labeling for placement usually results in labeling for life. When effective instructional procedures are used, and success achieved, labels do not have purpose and should be discarded.

SELF-ESTEEM AND SELF-CONFIDENCE

Have you noticed students whose heads are down when walking, who sit in the back of the classroom never looking up, and who rarely participate in discussions? They often say, "I can't do it," "I'm not smart," "I don't know," "I forgot," or shrug their shoulders in an unknowing manner when asked to respond to questions. Most of the these students have probably met with failure.

Students who have low self-esteem fear error and thus avoid trial. But in order to perfect a task of any kind, a student must try—and fail, if necessary—until change, that is, *learning* occurs.

---

[2]Dyslexia is a term that will be discussed later, but for now, it can be defined as "a medical term for alexia, partial, but severe inability to read." Word blindness is used in its place at times (Harris & Hodges, 1981, p. 95).

[3]Dysgraphia "a mild form of apraxis involving difficulty in producing handwriting because of disease [or] injury to the brain" (Harris & Hodges, 1981, p. 95).

[4]Minimal brain dysfunction (MBD) is "a label of hypothetical nature used to explain the course of a learning disability, based on soft signs rather than on clear evidence of brain damage" (Harris & Hodges, 1981, p. 198).

[5]Alexia is "the complete inability to read; specifically a form of aphasia in which the visual modality is disabled, yet reasonable vision, intelligence, and language functions, other than reading, are intact" (Harris & Hodges, 1981, p. 10).

The student with positive self-esteem and confidence has been praised for trying, erring, and trying again. Students who feel in control of their learning take the responsibility for understanding that failure is part of the learning process. Fluent readers demonstrate feelings of self-worth, an interest and desire to read, and have the confidence to sustain efforts required to gain control over reading and writing. How to assess and observe students' feelings about themselves in the learning environment plus the strategies for guiding students to become self-confident and independent learners are discussed in each chapter. We include this variable with others, and not independently, since self-esteem affects all responses to stimuli in and out of schools.

CONCLUDING REMARKS ON DIAGNOSTIC VARIABLES

Diagnosing these and other variables creates confusion for us, since we aspire to observations of students as "whole" human beings. It is almost impossible, however, to study human behavior "holistically" since we, as humans, tend to focus on one idea at a time.

We hear, speak, read, or write with a purpose in mind which is general but individually focused on specifics. While observing student behaviors we tend to record data with a focus on one behavior at a time. To overcome completely the split, segmented, subskill approach to diagnosis, therefore, is unreasonable and impractical. However, if we can be trained to synthesize and organize assessment data, then language and thought can be unified. We may begin by understanding exactly what each assessment tool is supposed to measure.

DIFFERENCES BETWEEN C–A–L–M AND MEDICAL MODEL

The C–A–L–M diagnostic framework differs from the medical model. It behooves us, therefore, to compare the variables as stated in this chapter to a traditional diagnostic outline.

In the traditional diagnostic procedure, the student's work is usually diagnosed with one testing instrument, resulting in a score. In the C–A–L–M procedures, continuous observations, continuous informal testing, as well as some use of formal procedures comprise the diagnosis.

All student behaviors and responses to tests, materials, peers, and adults are observed, recorded, and evaluated continuously to arrive at a "well-rounded" view of the learner. Table 2–2 illustrates the differences in diagnostic models.

Table 2–2 C–A–L–M versus the Medical Model

C–A–L–M APPROACH	MEDICAL MODEL APPROACH
1. Thought processes and language competence play interactive roles when one constructs meaning. These components are viewed together.	1. Emphasis centers on making meaning from graphic symbols. Word identification is emphasized.
2. Students work with whole ideas—stories, poems, etc.—moving from generalizations to specifics.	2. Instructional procedures begin with letters, then words, then sentences. Lessons proceed from parts and move to wholes. Ideas move from specifics to generalizations.
3. Comprehension is viewed as a *process*. Language clues are used by readers to search their memory. Stimuli generate acceptable student responses, based on respect for individual perceptions.	3. Comprehension is viewed as a *product*, resulting from students' ability to call words correctly and offer expected responses. Personal perceptions of ideas are usually irrelevant.
4. In reading instruction, ideas rather than printed words alone are important. Meanings of language, sounds of language, and grammatical structures of language are considered together when observing students.	4. Reading instruction is viewed as a strategy guiding students to translate graphic symbols in oral language.
5. As the reader becomes skilled, graphic information is less important. Clues for meaning, from readers' perceptions, take precedent.	5. Written language is subservient to oral language.
6. Diagnostic procedures investigate students' strengths and needs, resulting in the most effective pedagogical procedures and learning styles.	6. Diagnostic procedures result in recognition of deficits, labels, and grade levels.
7. Actions resulting from diagnosis are tentative since both diagnostic and instructional procedures are continuous and ongoing educational procedures.	7. Actions resulting from diagnosis are prescriptive and definitive, since assessment is scheduled and conducted by prescription.

SUMMARY

The C–A–L–M approach to diagnosis is four-pronged. Those who practice assessment using this model: (1) question, (2) collect data, (3) evaluate that data considering initial questions, and (4) restate questions, based on collected information and answered questions. Environments, oral and written language fluency, perceptions, understanding the written language coding system, physical factors, and self-concept must be diagnosed. The C–A–L–M framework demands that diagnosticians assess materials, environments, and instructional personnel, as well as students.

QUESTIONS TO PONDER

1. How many of the types of language controls can you observe watching:
   a. children playing?
   b. a card game?
   c. people at a cocktail party?
2. Why do you suppose the importance of physical factors to reading are minimized in this text?
3. How does the definition of "perception" in this chapter differ from other definitions found in the literature in the field of reading?
4. How do our definitions and explanations of variables alter your current views of children in the reading and language process?

REFERENCES

Bond, G. L., & Tinker, M. A. (1973). *Reading disabilities: Their diagnosis and correction*. New York: Appleton-Century-Crofts.
Cohen, A., & Glass, G. G. (1968). Lateral dominance and reading ability. *Reading Teacher, 21*, 343–348.
Emas, T. H. (1962). Physical factors in reading. *Reading Teacher, 15*, 427–432.
Harris, T. L., & Hodges, R. E. (Eds.). (1981). *A dictionary of reading*. Newark, DE: International Reading Association.
Huxley, A. (1967). Human potentialities. *Psychology Today, 1*, 69–78.
Pertz, D. L., & Putnam, L. (1982). What is the relationship between nutrition and learning? *Reading Teacher, 35*, 702–706.
Robinson, H. (1946). *Why pupils fail in reading*. Chicago: University of Chicago Press.
Shearer, E. (1968). Physical skills and reading backwardness. *Educational Research, 10*, 197–206.
Smith, F. (1982). *Reading without nonsense* (2nd ed.). New York: Teachers College Press.

SUGGESTED READING

Gentile, L. M., Kamil, M. L., & Blanchard, J. S. (1983). *Reading research revisited*. Columbus, OH: Charles E. Merrill. Original research articles with commentaries and critiques related to research in reading provide students with an in-depth discussion of historical and contemporary research topics.
Smith, F. (1982). *Understanding reading* (3rd ed.). New York: Holt Rinehart & Winston. This text offers the reader an understanding of a psycholinguistic analysis of learning to read and the reading process. Ideas are presented clearly and simply.
Smith, F. (1983). *Essays into literacy*. Exeter, NH: Heinemann Educational Books. A variety of the best essays of Frank Smith on reading and writing are included in this collected volume.

3

ASSESSING CLASSROOM ENVIRONMENTS
THEORY AND METHODS

The Ethnographic Perspective

Aspects of Classroom Environment

Collecting Classroom Environment Data

Summary

Questions to Ponder

References

Suggested Reading

Classroom environments are the major variable in the C–A–L–M model. The intent of this chapter, therefore, will be to explain the environmental factors that contribute to a descriptive definition of the classroom. Our classrooms and clinics include those where deliberate instruction results in planned and unplanned learning. Ideas presented in this chapter and in other sections of the text for assessing the student in instructional settings will be better understood if classroom environments are viewed as complex, social settings. We ask:

> What is classroom environment?
> What factors create the environment in a classroom?
> How can classroom factors be observed, assessed, and improved?

Recent researchers have begun laying the foundation to explain the nature of classroom life. The heart of this new wave of research reflects the view that classrooms are environments with interactive, emerging social processes occurring for many reasons over time. Notions of context, time, and nonverbal behaviors are now studied by researchers interested in describing and defining the classroom environment. John Withall, an early writer in this area of research, suggested studies consider seeking answers to these questions:

1. What is the relationship between climate and the quality of the learning that occurs in a classroom?
2. To what extent is the climate in a given classroom a function of the personality of the teacher?
3. To what extent do peer-group relationships influence the classroom climate? (1949, p. 361)

Delamont, nearly thirty years later, suggested that:

> The classroom relationship of teacher and pupils is seen as a joint act—a relationship that works, and is about doing work. The interaction is understood as the daily "give-and-take" between teachers and pupils. The process is one of *negotiation*—an on-going process by which everyday realities of the classroom are constantly defined and redefined. (1976b, p. 25)

Thus emerges the viewpoint, that classroom environments are built daily by the participants in them and in school. The classroom is an interactional setting that is *created* by students, teachers, the principal, all participants and factors inside and outside the classroom. This complexity of classroom environments can be adequately described and evaluated only when multidimensional instruments are used. Ethnographic methodology is probably most appropriate for describing complex classroom environments. Ethnographic procedures and implications for teachers shall be our focus.

THE ETHNOGRAPHIC PERSPECTIVE

Ethnography involves the discovery of systems of meaning from the viewpoint of people within a given culture (Spradley, 1979, 1980). Field anthropologists have used ethnographic methods in their studies of societies. Recently, however, educational researchers have begun to examine the concept of schooling as a form of culture. In attempting to follow this concept, educators have adopted some new perspectives for approaching schools and classrooms as cultures.

The teacher as classroom ethnographer acts simultaneously as a participant and observer within the culture of school and classroom. One view occurs from the inside as participant and simultaneously another view comes from the outside as observer. Hence the term "participant observer." The nature of such an approach is nonexperimental. In other words, behavioral variables are not defined prior to entering the classroom. In fact, variables can be explained only after the ethnographer's immersion into daily living in the classroom. The ethnographic methods of participant observation and interviewing provide a naturalistic approach for observing and assessing the classroom environment.

In the effort to collect valid and reliable data, teachers as observers need to enter the learning environment with as open a mind as possible. Preconceived notions about students and their performance must be recognized and set aside for the moment. Observations are carried out and data collected in three stages: (1) orientation to the setting, (2) reconnoitering, and (3) the hypothesis-testing stage (Spindler, 1982; Guthrie and Hall, 1984).

During the setting orientation stage, referred to by Spindler as the reconnaissance phase, the teacher-observer surveys the field. Preobservational data is collected from such sources as medical and school records. Initially, the observer will only describe behavior.

A second stage in the observation process, called reconnoitering, occurs by interacting with actual informants. The teacher begins to form relationships with the student(s) and others who impact on the student's performance including special teachers, parents, grandparents, babysitters, and so forth. During this phase the teacher/observer narrows the focus of the data collection to those elements that seem most influential on student learning. At this point questions or notions about expected behaviors develop. These are referred to as *hypotheses*.

After initial data about students and the environment are collected, questions are then developed and answered utilizing data from additional observations over time. This is the hypothesis-testing stage.

If, for example, one observes a student who seems impatient in one kind of environment that is set up with a rigid furniture arrangement, then one might hypothesize and test the following:

- With a more casual furniture arrangement, the student may develop "wait time" and relax when working.
- He will have flexibility to move around the working area and can complete activities by sitting, standing, or squatting away from his desk;
- He will be able to interact with a "buddy" (fellow student) during work period.

Considering the above hypothesis, additional observations would be made. Such "hypothesized" behavior changes would be accepted or rejected based on observable data.

Relationship to C–A–L–M

Review of the C–A–L–M approach and these ethnographic stages demonstrates similarities. Both models require the observer to be part of the environment, as a participant in activities. Activities are observed by this observer-participant based on questions, either stated formally, or in one's mind. Once data is collected, hypotheses are developed by the ethnographer and observations are continued; irrelevant questions are discarded with C–A–L–M, and new ones, based on previous observations, are developed. The C–A–L–M procedures and those derived from ethnography rely on varied sorts of data collected over time.

Procedures for Participant Observation

Participant observation requires one to collect data by: (1) direct observation of events; (2) the maintenance of field notes; (3) casual conversations; (4) formal and informal interviewing; and, (5) mappings and the collection of documents. The participant-observer describes what is happening, how the events are organized, and what people have to know in order to participate in these events.

Most action among people is constituted by sets of organizing principles. Daily human interactions, however, usually occur spontaneously as patterns of conduct. We learn about these interactions, attitudes, values, modes, and sets of organizing principles by observing and recording observations of the interactions in environments consciously.

Ultimately, the participant-observer interprets these observations, noticing patterns of social organization. Let us examine participant-observer procedures more closely.

Orientation. To begin, the teacher-observer surveys the field. Preobservational data is collected from medical and school records. The observer might be considered part of a treasure hunt looking for links in the puzzle that guides descriptions of behavior with one goal: finding effective learning strategies for students.

Direct observation. The participant-observer begins *focusing observations* on student behaviors and the classroom environments created each day. As we described, this is the reconnoitering stage, the time in which the teacher begins to form relationships with students and others who affect each student's performance. The teacher-observer narrows the focus of the investigation to those elements that seem most influential. In other words, the teacher discards irrelevant or peripheral data. During each observation, information is written into field notes and might be tape recorded.

Field notes. Field notes, written daily, consist of classroom observations written down in a shorthand or telegraphic manner and then transcribed to fuller versions for coding and interpretive purposes. Bogdan and Taylor (1975) estimate that observers can spend approximately six hours transcribing notes for each hour of observation out in the field. Field note information includes dates, times, places of observations, and diagrams of the classroom settings. Interactions are objectively described. People, specific settings, direct quotations, and nonverbal communications depict classroom ambience.

Figure 3–1 Sample Field Notes

Date: February 11, 1987
Time: 11:32 A.M. to 12:15 P.M.
Place: A fifth grade classroom in New Jersey

Michael, age nine, was the focus of the field notes. His inconsistent behavior forced the teacher to have a trained graduate student take field notes. The teacher, sometimes referred to as "Susan" in the notes, was observing students as they completed a writing assignment in which they were expected to explain how to set a table. She was moving about the classroom, noting students' needs and serving as consultant to children when necessary. The notes of the graduate student were as follows:

11:32   Looked through books. Looked in desk. Said "I can't find mine. Where the heck is mine?" Kept looking through books. Looked over at the teacher when she said she wanted their attention. Drummed fingers on the desk. Told me it may be sticky on the floor because someone threw up.
11:35   Sat on floor. Tied left shoe when teacher began talking. Looked around. Took off shoe. Looked in shoe. Put shoe on. Tied shoe. Looked around when kids were responding.
11:37   Untied right shoe. Took off right shoe. Watched Susan. Fixed sock. Put on shoe. Tied shoe. Looked up at Susan when tying shoe. Looked at kids. Alternated tying shoe and looking at Susan.

Figure 3–1 *Continued*

11:40	Smiled at boy who responded. Smiled after response. Alternated between looking at boy talking and what Susan was doing. Folded arms in front of him. Said "That's good enough," when Susan buttoned her jacket.
11:42	Rocked back and forth when Susan began talking. Sat back and put knees together. Made comment to another boy. Rocked back and forth. Watched Susan write on board. Scratched back. Drummed hands on floor. Looked to floor. Put hands near face. Looked over at me.
11:45	Talked to boy about flies ("zapped them"). Said "It's purple." Looked at finger. Said "Table for two." Wrote with left hand.
11:46	Wrote one line without looking up. Wrote second and third lines without looking up. Wrote fourth line without looking up. Erased. Wrote fifth line (wiped mouth with hand). Did not look up. Wrote sixth line without looking up.
11:48	Looked over at me. Wrote another line. Shook head slightly. Said "Hmm"—finger by mouth. Erased. Looked up. Looked at arm. Rubbed arm. Looked and listened to boy next to him. Swatted flies. Commented on what he had written.
11:50	Looked up. Wrote another line. People next to him were talking. Did not look up—continued writing. Looked over at Susan. Continued writing. Erased. Scratched neck. Read over list. Added another sentence.
11:52	People talking next to him. Did not look up. Said to neighbor "I'm on eleven already". Looked over to Susan when she began talking. Scratched neck. Continued writing. Continued writing without looking up when Susan was talking to group that had finished. Looked over once. Turned paper over. Continued writing. Did not look up. Swatted flies. Continued writing. Did not look over when Susan was talking.
11:54	Put down pencil. Sighed. Told friend "I have thirteen." Went over to group. Stood up, then sat down. Bit fingernail when Susan was explaining. Went back to table. Said he forgot pencil. Started playing with friend's truck.
11:56	Playing without friends at desk. Came over when Susan called. Gave back truck. Said to friend "I'll switch." Said to Jacob "You done." Worked with Jacob.
11:58	Said "I set mine for two people." Knocked over cup with knives. Went back to desk with two spoons. Put spoons in desk. Joined Jacob.
12:00	Listened as Jacob read his list. Flipped his pencil. Said "Read it to me." Followed Jacob's directions. Brought one chair and put plate way on edge. Directions read "Put plate on edge of table." Threw cup up and down. When he put the cup on top of the plate, Jacob went back to edit his papers.
12:02	Looked over at other group. Took spoon and pretended it was a slingshot. Tore off edge of his paper and put it in his mouth. Said (to three boys) that he got thirty-five cents a week allowance. Flipped spoon up and down. Crawled under counter. Watched two boys "set their table." Said "rats" when he thought they had done something wrong. Pretended to eat.
12:04	Took two forks and put them on top of one another. Hit paper with spoon. Susan was talking now to group. He continued talking to four other boys, playing games with fork and spoon. When other boys joined larger group, he did, too. Crawled to other side of group.
12:06	Sat slightly apart from group in the rear. Flipped paper with fork. Susan sat down beside him. Put his paper behind him. Flipped pencil up and down. Watched Susan. Flipped pencil.
12:08	Looked back at his paper. Poked hole in his paper with pencil (gently). Looked at Susan. Picked up paper. Put down paper. Looked at clock. Looked at wrist. Looked at Susan. Looked at wrist. Looked at girl behind him. Put out leg. Knelt. Picked up paper. Looked at another group.
12:10	NOTE: He did this when Susan said there would only be time for one more group to share what they had written. Stood up and walked over to desk. Put down paper on desk. Walked back to group, but paused and started batting flies. Standing apart from group. The teacher motioned him to join group. Squatted behind the teacher. Looked at Susan. Raised hand twice but was not called on. Smiled at friend. Rocked back and forth. Tapped legs with hands.

Field notes are the foundations for conceptualizing classroom structures. One can form hypotheses about students' strengths and needs based on field notes. Interviewing techniques add clarification and substantiate implications assumed from field notes.

The Ethnographic Interview

Students and teachers have *their* moments for revealing particularly useful bits of information. The teacher as interviewer-observer must develop an intuitive sense of "when the time is right" while collecting information through informal as well as formal interviews.

Informal interview procedures. Informal interviews can just happen in the course of daily classroom living. There are no specific outcomes sought. Since the informal nature of the interview adds a great deal to data collection, the teacher-interviewer might decide to avoid formality. Responses are qualitative since they are solicited in an unsystematic manner.

It is important to investigate through informal interviews, the social, as well as educational attitudes of students and adults. Thus, interviews may occur in the school corridor, in the classroom, on the playground, or in the supermarket. The teacher-interviewer must make some decisions, however, about the following:

1. How much information is needed outside the school setting in order to discover the student's needs?
2. Which persons in the student's life ought to be interviewed?

We believe that everyone involved with students on a regular basis should be interviewed including parents, grandparents, special teachers, babysitters, even sales persons in local stores. Although these interviews are open-ended and spontaneous, some general questions might serve as a guide in the interview process:

1. Tell me about _____ (student's name).
2. What do you like best about _____ (student's name)?
3. What would you like to see change about _____ (student's name)?

Be sure to *listen* in order to learn about students. Watch the informant's facial expressions in order to gather information expressed by body language. Uncomfortable attitudes about a student that seem negative may not be stated, but would be implicitly expressed in body language. Hesitation or a wince, for example, could give the interviewer information.

Data collected from informal, "on the spot" interviews should be recorded when possible, on tape, or in a notebook. The interpretations are intuitive and classified as "hunches" and can be compared to the more formal data.

Formal interview procedures. Unlike informal interviews, formal interviewing requires structure. The formal interview procedures have structured elements that include:

1. Demographic data (name, age, ethnic affiliation, birth date, place of birth, residence);
2. Social position and academic status;
3. Working conditions (how the informant interacts with the student(s);
4. Location of interaction and time; and
5. Exact nature of interaction with student over time.

Questions developed are based on notions that reveal significant elements related to student learning problems. The interviewing process begins with key persons in students' lives. Formal interviews are restrictive since informants respond to predetermined, structured interview schedules. Data gathered in the formal interview are quantifiable since they are systematically arranged and collected.

Questions developed for the formal interview are specific to persons in student's lives and settings. These include questions about:

1. Environment (space) in which interview takes place or the environment in which the student interacts with individuals;
2. The person(s) being interviewed (actors);
3. The activity or set of activities related to the person;
4. The objects that are included in the activities (physical things);
5. The set of activities that the person carries out with the student (events);
6. The sequence of events that take place over time (related activities);
7. The goal(s) set for the student and the person involved;
8. The emotions felt and expressed (feelings).

Infinite numbers of questions can be formulated and posed in a formal interview. However, by using the eight dimensions above, many social and academic situations can be described. Responses to these questions can be considered in an interrelated framework. Table 3–1 provides sample questions for each setting.

ASPECTS OF CLASSROOM ENVIRONMENT

We have explored the ethnographic perspective that includes research methods of participant observation and interviewing. In particular we have seen how observing and interviewing involve the teacher as classroom ethnographer/diagnostician.

Table 3-1 Parallel Questions: Formal Interviews Conducted by a Diagnostician

ENVIRONMENT(S) (SPACE)	PERSONS (ACTORS)	ACTIVITIES	OBJECTS	EVENTS	EVENTS OVER TIME	GOALS	EMOTIONS (FEELINGS)
QUESTIONS TO STUDENT							
Describe the place in which you work *(the person in question)*.	Describe what *(person)* is like.	Describe all the activities you do when you work with *(person)*.	Describe all of the objects you use when you work with *(person)*.	Describe the usual things that happen when you work with *(person)*.	Describe changes you have noticed about *(person)* since you've worked with him/her.	What do you think you can accomplish when you work with *(person)*?	How do you feel about *(person)*?
QUESTIONS TO TEACHER(S)							
Describe the place in which you work (interact) with *(the student)*.	Describe all of the persons who work with you and *(student)*.	Describe all of the activities you do with *(student)*.	Describe the objects you and *(student)* use. How do each of you use those? (same ways? different ways?)	Describe the usual things that happen when you work with *(student)*.	Describe changes you have noticed since you first began working with *(student)*.	What do you want to see *(student)* achieve?	How do you feel about *(student)* when you work together?

Now we turn to examining factors in the learning process that constitute classroom environment:

1. Physical environment
2. Interactional organization in the classroom
3. Classroom power and group influence
4. Student expectations of teachers
5. Student attitudes
6. Student knowledge
7. Student performance and competence
8. Personal classroom history

Physical Environment

In her portrait of the classroom environment, James, speaking as a teacher, wrote:

> Teaching is an art, and the classroom is the canvas on which the painting grows... Although the rooms all start out basically alike, they soon reflect the personality of the teacher and take on an individuality of their own. (1969, pp. 30–31)

She described some of the decisions made by teachers that serve to set up classroom environments. For example, teachers decorate rooms and bulletin boards. The ways in which space is used certainly serves to create an effect in a classroom. Teachers also arrange furniture in the school environment. By lining desks in straight rows, for example, a teacher can create a formal atmosphere. Less teacher-centered arrangements, such as large circles or smaller clusters of desks, allow students to face each other and consequently provide means for more socializing and the exchanging of ideas.

Observations by James, Adams, and Biddle (1970) and Loughlin and Suina (1982) demonstrated that students' seating positions in a class affected the extent to which teachers interact with students. These researchers showed how teachers conversed more with students seated on a V-shaped wedge through the middle of the classroom, thus providing less contact with students seated at the back or sides of the room.

Delamont (1976a) also explained how teaching styles can affect the physical settings teachers create in their classrooms. She described factors such as the ways in which teachers make space available to students, the amount of light and air in the room, or the number of living things, plants or animals, nurtured by the teacher.

Therefore, a *quick first glance at a classroom can, and usually does, reveal subtle messages about what goes on inside regarding the interactions between students and teachers*. Physical classroom environment factors serve as substantive descriptions of life in the classroom. Loughlin and Suina (1982) offer a conceptual framework and practical guidance for structuring classroom environment (see Suggested Reading).

Interactional Organization in the Classroom

Teachers arrange classroom furniture and create a particular environment through such things as bulletin board displays. However, they also structure classroom life on another level of the relationship between home and school. The microethnographic research of Schultz, Florio, and Erickson (1982) explored home–school discontinuity in communication and its affects on students and teachers, both socially and academically. The research thrust was aptly stated:

> That children act in ways that are judged appropriate at home, yet inappropriate at school, impresses us as important for understanding some sources of children's misbehavior in school, especially in the early grades. It also im-

A relaxed environment encourages interaction with books.

presses us with the need to understand more fully children's socialization into communicative traditions at home and at school, traditions that may be mutually congruent or incongruent. (Schultz, Florio, & Erickson, 1982, p. 91)

Their findings pointed to the fact that students may interpret what is happening in their language classes in terms of the norms for participation used at home. While the behavior may be appropriate at home, during the language arts lesson it is considered to be inappropriate and the student receives negative feedback from the teachers.

Research of this type demonstrates the need for teachers to understand the interface between home and school communication structures. This awareness could help teachers to renegotiate the interactional environment in classrooms and help them accommodate the communicative styles students bring with them to school. They could, for example, be more explicit with students when explaining class content or assignments (Nelson, 1985).

Classroom Power and Group Influence

A stereotypic view of classroom interaction places the teacher as *the* authority in control of decision making. A more realistic perspective, however, focuses on transactional interchanges between the person demonstrating leadership and those who accept it. Leadership, defined as behavior that influences others, is performed by both teachers *and* students, satisfying human striving for power.

Leadership functions in the classroom are shared and performed by all group members. In a sensitive analysis of the ways that students influence each other, Furlong (1976) argued that students are in a continuous state of adjusting their behavior to one another so that interaction changes across different situations within relatively short spans of time. These interactions transfer meanings symbolically to the rest of the class and are supported by such behavior including smiling or laughter. The following description showed an interaction set in operation:

> When Mrs. Alan comes in, Carol and Diane are missing: She asks where they are. Angela says they were in the last lesson.
> Angela: "Them lot are outside, Miss."
> Mrs. Alan goes out and sends in Carol and Diane who enter, laughing loudly, and start to sit down. They are followed in by Mrs. Alan who shouts, "Stand at the front." They continue to laugh and look round the room, though less confidently than before. Other class members are no longer laughing with them and Carol's and Diane's eyes rove round the room, but come into contact with no one in particular. (Furlong, 1976, p. 28)

In similar ways, power and influence shift in the classroom. We might observe then that classroom power is shared among students and with the teacher in ways that are developed by classroom participants through covert as well as explicit actions. (See Chapter 4 for assessing language in interactive settings).

Student Expectations of Teachers

Just as the issues of power among students and teachers are relevant to an understanding of classroom environment, so are the expectations of how another person will behave in the classroom arena of social action.

In discussing an interactionist model for students' expectations of their teachers, Nash found:

> Within every classroom there is a high consensus of opinion among teachers and pupils about the relative abilities of the members of the class. It is suggested that these findings support the interactionist theory that children are continually engaged in forming a self-concept and in developing consistent patterns of behavior appropriate to this self-concept. The firmer these patterns of behavior become the more unshakeable the perceptual models of them held by others will be, and the more power their expectations will have in confirming the actor's behavior. (1976, p. 85)

Nash explained how findings regarding students' expectations about "good" and "bad" teachers are not just descriptions of whether or not students like or dislike teachers. More important, these views formulate the rules of conduct that students construct for teachers. These expectations develop a normative function in which students transform "what teachers generally say and do into customary rules for all their teachers to follow" (1976, p. 65). The impact of student expectancies on teacher behavior should be of particular interest for observation and diagnosis of language performance.

Student Attitudes

Historically, classroom environment research has focused heavily on the demonstration of teacher attitudes and teaching styles (see, for example, Bennett & Jordan, 1975; Brophy & Good, 1974; Jackson, 1968). Much less energy and journal space have been allotted to examing student attitudes as a valid source for assessing classroom environment. An essential part of understanding classroom learning lies in this untapped resource.

Attitudes are not necessarily a reflection of what people *actually* do. They are ways of thinking or expressing feelings and opinions *about* what people do. By exploring student attitudes the teacher-researcher gains insight into how students themselves define classroom encounters. Knowledge of students' perceptions may help teachers make more meaningful interpretations of student actions while learning.

At this time, there are no "tried-and-true" methods available for eliciting attitudinal data from students regarding their lives in school. In an ethnographic description of classroom interaction, Denton (1983) demonstrated that small group interviewing would facilitate student willingness to talk about their positive as well as negative attitudes toward teachers, student teachers, and peers. Denton's conclusion that student attitudes reflect a view that classroom performance is an interactional process, lends further support for observing and interviewing students about attitudes in school.

Student Knowledge

Students acquire and know about other facets of the school environment. Simply stated, they are "schoolwise."

Delamont observed that students spend as much time sizing up teachers as the teachers spend "talking" about students:

> Apart from her success at creating a learning atmosphere, and her adherence to her role specifications, pupils judge teachers by clues picked up from their personal fronts. Clearly many of the characteristics Goffman (1971) suggests as significant aspects of the personal front are important in school: physical appearance, clothing, age, sex, race, speech and the paralinguistic features of posture, gesture and the like. Some of these things are very obvious in schools. (1976b, p. 76)

Attractiveness and the dimensions of age and marital status are used to categorize teachers. For students, age seems directly related to the number of years' experience a teacher has had in the classroom, rather than a function of being chronologically younger or older. Among girls, Delamont found well-developed perspectives about marital status, summarized in these comments:

> She's married and usually a married one has more understanding . . . married teachers tend to be more sort of placid and not get all angry. Being married is associated with having a happy life outside school. (1976a, p. 79).

Students are interested in the private as well as the school lives of teachers and the principal. The "sizing-up process" is continuous and serves a cohesive function in the classroom environment.

Student Performance and Competence

Students' effective participation in the classroom environment is necessary as part of mastering academic content. Effective participation is not just a matter of learning things or *knowing*. It also involves *showing* this knowledge to the teacher and to other students.

Ethnographic research suggests there is a "hierarchy of contexts" (McDermott, 1979). Mehan (1980) implied that effective participation in the classroom depends on recognizing various contexts and produces appropriate behavior in each context. Mehan explained how this process occurs:

> Different contexts impose different constraints on students' actions in that certain ways of speaking and certain ways of behaving are normatively enforced in each context. These constraints may vary from event to event, from phase to phase within an event, and from interactional sequence to interactional sequence within an event's phase. These constraints require that students engage in active interpretive work to make sense of constantly shifting social circumstances. (1980, p. 72)

Research of this type demonstrates that classroom environment is indeed multidimensional. Students are influenced by teachers and vice versa as they all mutually construct classroom environments.

Personal Classroom History

Along with the participants in any classroom setting, there exists history in the making. It is personal history in that it uniquely applies to a specific group of students and a teacher as a result of their interactions over time. Facets of classroom life are embedded in humor, in subtle references to "significant" events, and in taxonomies of characteristic foibles established among the classroom participants.

In their long-term participant observational studies, Walker and Adelman noted how jokes were a part of things that observers did not "get" initially:

> For example, during one lesson the teacher was listening to the boys read through short essays that they had written for homework on the subject of "Prisons." After one boy, Wilson, had finished reading out his rather obviously skimped piece of work the teacher sighed and said rather crossly:
> *Teacher:* Wilson, we'll have to put you away if you don't change your ways and do your homework. It that all you've done?
> *Boy:* Strawberries, strawberries, (laughter).
> When we asked why this was funny, we were told that one of the teacher's favorite expressions was that their work was "Like strawberries—good as far as it goes, but it doesn't last nearly long enough." Here we want to use the incident because it seems to us that it dramatizes and highlights an important quality in the way talk is used to communicate meanings in long-term situations. (1976, pp. 138–139)

Information of this sort cannot be gleaned by short-term quantitative research. As the familiar cliche states, "You had to be there." The teacher-researcher *does* have to be there over considerable amounts of time to gain access to the shared meanings that create the environment with students.

Figure 3–2 Assessing the Classroom Environment

	YES	NO
PHYSICAL ENVIRONMENT		
Are bulletin boards visually attractive?	___	___
. . . used for instruction?	___	___
. . . prepared by students?	___	___

Is student work displayed in the classroom?
___ Frequently ___ Somewhat ___ Not much

How are student desks arranged?
___ Rows ___ Circle ___ Clusters ___ Other

	YES	NO
Are desks arranged so students can see chalkboards?	___	___
Are there plants or animals in the classroom?	___	___
Is the classroom well ventilated?	___	___
. . . adequately lighted?	___	___
. . . clean and orderly?	___	___

INTERACTIONAL ENVIRONMENT

	YES	NO
Are purpose(s) and importance of activities explained to students initially?	___	___
Are different teaching methods used?	___	___

___ Drill ___ Explanation ___ Demonstration
___ Discussion ___ Simulation ___ Problem-solving

	YES	NO
Are directions and explanations clearly stated?	___	___
Are directions and explanations restated using different words and modes when students do not understand?	___	___
Are student responses encouraged?	___	___

Is feedback given?
___ Frequently ___ Sometimes ___ Rarely
___ Positive and helpful ___ Negative ___ Both

What types of nonverbal feedback are evident?
___ Little or none ___ Smiles ___ Frowns
___ Physical contact ___ Other (list)

Are students on tasks when required to complete work?
___ Some ___ Most ___ Few ___ Varies

SOCIAL ENVIRONMENT

	YES	NO
Are different size groups used?	___	___

___ Whole ___ Small ___ Triads/pairs

Is peer tutoring organized and used for instruction?	___ ___
Are classroom rules defined?	___ ___
. . . displayed?	___ ___
. . . reviewed as needed?	___ ___
Are consequences for rule violations defined?	___ ___
. . . clear to students?	___ ___
Do students monitor classroom behavior?	___ ___
Are student opinions and attitudes elicited? How?	___ ___
___ Journal writing	
___ Whole class discussion	
___ Individual conferences	
Is decision making teacher-centered?	___ ___
. . . teacher- and student-centered?	___ ___
Is enthusiasm for learning communicated to students?	___ ___
Is mutual respect evident in the classroom?	___ ___
Is there humor, laughter in the classroom?	___ ___
Are students responsible for routine tasks?	___ ___

The checklist in Figure 3–2 serves as a starting place to help classroom and clinic teachers identify some significant environment factors that can improve the overall classroom learning environment.

COLLECTING CLASSROOM ENVIRONMENT DATA

You will recall that ethnography can be defined as "the work of describing a culture, with the central aim focusing on understanding a way of living" (Spradley, 1980, p. 3). This definition is based on the belief that each culture—therefore each learning environment, including classrooms and clinics—has unique ways of assigning meaning to human behavior (Guthrie & Hall, 1984).

Perceptions of the classroom and clinic environments vary for each student who works and lives there. As diagnosticians we need to observe students in order to understand their social and cognitive behaviors. We could ask, "How does a student perceive learning in a classroom or clinic environment?" Ethnographic methods provide us with ways to systematically record and collect data which focus on: (1) grasping the student's point of view; (2) describing life both in and out of the classroom; and, (3) understanding how students construct their interactions to perform and succeed in school.

One collects data by watching, writing about the events, and by tape-recording events in the student's learning environment. Such recorded events provide perspectives and insights into students' behaviors. Data collected over time provide the teacher-researcher with an understanding of the many different interrelationships that students encounter as they read and write. Original goals and intentions for instruction in relationship to student performance may change as a result of observations.

Observational notes serve as valuable diagnostic tools for answering questions about student performance in both the classroom and clinic. The focus and extent of these observations may vary depending on time-available data. *Classroom teachers will probably have limited time for extended diagnosis of individual students, so selecting the most needy students is essential.*

SUMMARY

In preparing classroom and clinical diagnoses, teachers need to observe students over time. As participant-observers, teachers and diagnosticians look multidimensionally at student activities and interactions with materials, peers, and concepts. In their role as classroom ethnographers, they begin to question assumptions and expectations made about students and the effectiveness of certain strengths and materials on learning. Extended observations help us observe student behavior, discovering the rules each develops while learning. Rules in students' minds guide them to predict responses in future learning activities.

Daily observations are important for assessing students' strengths and needs. As teacher-researcher, the teacher or diagnostician must become as objective as possible in data collection, analysis, and interpretation.

Interviews provide the opportunity to ask questions that tell something about perceptual differences: "Is there something in a student's background that has inhibited reading performance? Are environments, including the people in charge of instruction, ineffective for students?" Interviews also guide teacher-researchers to respond to questions about student's performance in multiple environments. Observations over time and comparisons of observational and interview data are additional tools for assessing classroom environments. As we investigate complexities in the learning environment, we arrive at a more comprehensive understanding of individual student performance in a particular classroom or clinic setting.

QUESTIONS TO PONDER

1. Define and discuss *classroom environment?*
2. What are two primary ethnographic methods? In what ways are these methods useful to teachers?

3. How has your concept of "classroom environment" changed after reading this chapter?
4. How do social interactions affect the classroom learning environment?

REFERENCES

Adams, R. S., & Biddle, B. J. (1970). *Realities of teaching.* New York: Holt, Rinehart & Winston.
Bennett, S. N., & Jordan, J. (1975). A typology of teaching styles in primary schools. *British Journal of Educational Psychology, 45,* 20–28.
Bogdan, R. C., & Biklen, S. K. (1982). *Qualitative research for education: An introduction to theory and methods.* Boston: Allyn & Bacon.
Bogdan, R. C., & Taylor, S. J. (1975). *Introduction to qualitative research methods.* New York: John Wiley & Sons.
Brophy, J. E., & Good, T. L. (1974). *Teacher–student relationships.* New York: Holt, Rinehart & Winston.
Cohn, M. (1981). Observations of learning to read and write naturally. *Language Arts, 58,* 549–555.
Deborah, J. (1969). *The taming: A teacher speaks.* New York: McGraw-Hill.
Delamont, S. (1976a). Beyond Flander's fields: The relationship of subject matter and individuality to classroom style. In M. Stubbs & S. Delamont (Eds.), *Explorations in Classroom Observations* (pp. 101–131). New York: John Wiley & Sons.
Delamont, S. (1976b). *Interaction in the classroom.* London: Methuen & Company.
Denton, P. (1983). *A community in learning: An ethnographic description of classroom interaction.* Unpublished doctoral dissertation, Arizona State University.
Furlong, V. (1976). Interaction sets in the classroom: Towards a study of pupil knowledge. In M. Stubbs & S. Delamont (Eds.), *Explorations in Classroom Observation* (pp. 23–44). New York: John Wiley & Sons.
Goffman, E. (1971). *The presentation of self in everyday life.* Harmondsworth, England: Penguin.
Guthrie, L. F. & Hall, W. S. (1984). Ethnographic approaches to reading research. In P. D. Pearson (Ed.), *Handbook of Reading Research* (pp. 91–110). New York: Longman.
Herndon, J. (1971). *How to survive in your native land.* New York: Simon & Schuster.
Jackson, P. W. (1968). *Life in classrooms.* New York: Holt, Rinehart & Winston.
Kohl, H. R. *The open classroom: A practical guide to a new way of teaching.* New York: A New York Review Book.
Loughlin, C. E., & Suina, J. H. (1982). *The learning environment: An instructional strategy.* New York: Teachers College, Columbia University.
McDermott, R. P., & Roth, D. The social organization of behavior: Interactional approaches. *Annual Review of Anthropology, 7,* 321–345.
Mehan, H. (1980). The competent student. *Anthropology and Education Quarterly, 11,* 131–152.
Nash, R. (1976a). Pupil's expectations of their teachers. In M. Stubbs & S. Delamont (Eds.), *Explorations in Classroom Observations* (pp. 83–98). New York: John Wiley and Sons.
Nash, R. (1976b). *Teacher expectations and pupil learning.* Boston: Routledge & Kegan-Paul.
Nelson, N. W. (1985). Teacher talk and child listening: Fostering a better match. In C. S. Simon (Ed.), *Communication Skills and Classroom Success* (pp. 65–102). San Diego: College-Hill Press.

Peterson, P., Wilkinson, L. C., & Hallinan, M. (Eds.). (1984). *The social context of instruction: Group organization and group processes*. New York: Academic Press.

Schmuck, R. A., & Schmuck, P. A. (1979). *Group processes in the classroom*. Dubuque, IA: W. C. Brown.

Schultz, J. J., Florio, S., & Erickson, F. (1982). Where's the floor? Aspects of the cultural organization of social relationships in communication at home and in school. In P. Gilmore & A. Glatthorn (Eds.), *Children in and out of School: Ethnography and education* (pp. 88–123). Washington, DC: Center for Applied Linguistics.

Silberman, C. (1970). *Crisis in the classroom*. New York: Random House.

Simon, C. S. (Ed.). (1985). *Communication skills and classroom success: Assessment of language-learning disabled students*. San Diego: College-Hill Press.

Spindler, G. (Ed.). (1982). *Doing the ethnography of schooling: Educational anthropology in action*. New York: Holt, Rinehart & Winston.

Spradley, J. P. (1979). *The ethnographic interview*. New York: Holt, Rinehart & Winston.

Spradley, J. P. (1980). *Participant observation*. New York: Holt, Rinehart & Winston.

Stubbs, M. & Delamont, S. (Eds.). (1976). *Explorations in classroom observation*. New York: John Wiley and Sons.

Walker, R., & Adelman, C. (1976). Strawberries. In M. Stubbs & S. Delamont (Eds.), *Explorations in classroom observation* (pp. 133–172). New York: John Wiley and Sons.

Withall, J. (1949). The development of a technique for the measurement of social–emotional climate in classrooms. *Journal of Experimental Education, 17,* 347–361.

SUGGESTED READING

Bogdan, R. C., & Biklen, S. K. (1982). *Qualitative research for education: An introduction to theory and methods*. Boston: Allyn & Bacon. This volume provides a thorough description of qualitative research tools, applications to fieldwork, as well as analysis after data collection.

Cohn, M. (1981). Observations of learning to read and write naturally. *Language Arts, 58,* 549–555. Anecdotal observations of a parent/teacher that demonstrate the developmental nature of children's oral and written language. This article sets forth the implication that if "developmental learning" can be successful at home, it should certainly be successful when children start school.

Loughlin, C. E., & Suina, J. H. (1982). *The learning environment: An instructional strategy*. New York: Teachers College, Columbia University. Comprehensive, practical resource guide for structuring the learning environment. Discusses organization of space, arranging learning materials, environmental problem solving, and how the classroom environment can support students with special needs.

Peterson, P., Wilkinson, L. C., & Hallinan, M. (Eds.). (1984). *The social context of instruction: Group organization and group processes*. New York: Academic Press. From a sociological, sociolinguistic, and process–product perspective, this text addresses the issue of how student grouping can respond effectively to student diversity. Student achievement, social skills, and motivation can be dependent on how teachers organize instructional groups.

Simons, C. S. (Ed.). (1985). *Communication skills and classroom success: Assessment of language-learning disabled students*. San Diego: College-Hill Press. A comprehensive examination of communication problems and assessment strategies for helping children develop improved classroom performance. A source for demonstrating how classroom performance is affected by an individual's communication skills.

Stubbs, M., & Delamont, S. (Eds.). (1976). *Explorations in classroom observation.* New York: Wiley. An edited volume of articles on classroom ethnographic research. Researchers examine classroom interaction environments utilizing ethnographic methods and highly descriptive data.

4

ORAL LANGUAGE FLUENCY

Oral Language Variables

Assessing Oral Language Fluency

C–A–L–M Informal Procedures

Instructional Strategies for Enhancing Oral Language

Summary

Questions to Ponder

References

Suggested Reading

There is perhaps no greater accomplishment than learning to use language. Language, some believe, is essential for thinking. If one believes this statement, then one accepts the notion that language, used fluently, liberates us to reason, to be independent in thought, and to internalize experiences in personal ways. As Jerome Bruner wrote:

> In effect, language provides a means, not only for representing experience, but also for transforming it . . . Once the child has succeeded in internalizing language as a cognitive instrument, it becomes possible for him to represent and systematically transform the regularities of experience with far greater flexibility and power than before. (1964, p. 4)

We therefore ask the following questions:

- How does each of us control our worlds using oral language?
- What can be done to help students who do not seem to gain control of their lives through oral language?

The answers to these questions are not easy. We know that there is a strong interdependence between language and cognition or thought. Lindfors (1980) helps us answer these questions by stressing the interactive nature of language and thinking in intellectual development and learning in school. She wrote:

> The very act of expressing our thought through language often "nails it down" for us. As adults we are all aware of this in our own experience. We understand better, have a better grip on a difficult concept, once we have struggled to put it into words, once we have written a paper about it or tried to explain it to someone else. So for children, giving expression to their developing concepts can help to strengthen those very concepts (as well as make it possible for them to receive feedback relating to those developing concepts—feedback mainly through language, of course). (1980, p. 13)

Understanding that one's language affects others and helps us control our lives is probably not understood by most youngsters or adults. Halliday (1973) suggests that children learn language when they learn its functions. Youngsters, for example, will learn to say the words "socks" and "shoes" before the words "hat" and "coat." They act upon the first, put them on before putting on their coats or hats. Language learning results from a need to function. Language is unlikely to be learned in situations where it has no apparent utility.

Children learn functions of language and control their worlds. Many writers have classified language functions, (Halliday, 1973; Dale, 1976; Gillet & Temple, 1982; Moffett, 1983). All classification systems group language functions illustrating that communication permits one to establish sets of relationships among sender, receiver, and a message (Moffett, 1983, p. 5). The messages sent and received by human beings are recorded from thoughts to language. When students have problems reading fluently they are in a sense having problems with "languaging their thoughts" using the coding system necessary for sharing their lives. This justifies observing oral language in school environments before and with other variables.

Languaging refers to oral behaviors. How a student explains experiences is "languaging." We ask, Does the student "language" fluently enough for others to understand his or her experiences? Collecting samples of students' oral language then transcribing, evaluating, and comparing these with several oral transcriptions over time is a way to describe fluency.

In the past the focus for description of language and research has been on the visible part of language: the sound system (phonology), the grammar (syntax), and the vocabulary. Relationships between and among language forms referred to as *semantic* and *pragmatic variables* seem more significant since they represent the interactive processes necessary for effective communication. It is difficult to measure semantic and pragmatic variables in language, since these require long observations and an analysis of how students use language to control situations. It seems easier, for example, to determine whether children use inflectional endings (*s, es*) than it is to determine whether their commands, requests, or descriptions result in actions based on intended or unintended goals. The problem seems to lie in determining how to collect concrete evidence of language fluency in oral form, how to observe effective or ineffective oral language use, and how to reduce the data collection to meaningful conditions.

ORAL LANGUAGE VARIABLES

A student's command over oral language depends on the ability to manipulate the variables of oral language. Among these variables are elements of vocabulary and syntax, which are used to cohesively organize information appropriately for the audience. Cohesive control usually results when language elements are placed in appropriate forms. This results in effective oral communication. These forms include *description, narration, explanation,* and *reasoning.* The interaction of oral language variables guides fluency and can be assessed through continuous observation. Interconnections between and among controls, elements, and forms of language are illustrated in Figure 4–1.

The various language controls are created by using language elements (word vocabulary, syntactic structure, and story structure) forming organized

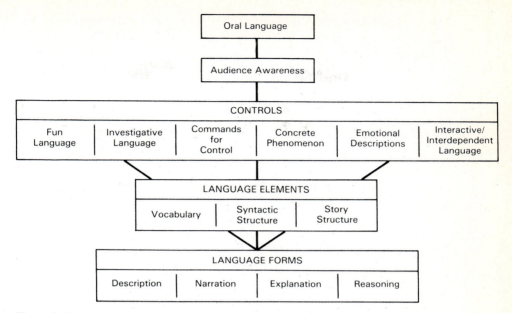

Figure 4-1

sentences to impart "story." All of the elements are manipulated for the purpose of communicating with an audience. Language forms—description, narration, explanation, and reasoning—are available arrangements for communication. The more data accumulations—such as test scores, note reviews, and interview interpretations—the more reliable the diagnostic generalizations become. Oral language assessment cannot be limited to single measures of oral vocabulary or single measures of oral syntax. In the next section, we describe tools for measuring oral language in a variety of settings. This approach is consistent with the C–A–L–M approach to diagnosis.

ASSESSING ORAL LANGUAGE FLUENCY

We begin by using tools permitting data collections to accumulate in several environments over periods of time. Our goal for you is the production of a case report that presents students' language abilities in:

- Recreational settings
- Instructional settings
- Formal test-taking settings
- Individual settings
- Peer interactive settings.

The case reports use data from:

1. Formal tests
2. Published informal procedures
3. C–A–L–M procedures.

Formal Tests for Assessing Oral Language

Many formal tests have been constructed to assess oral language behavior. Several are described in Table 4–1 (see pp. 52–53). The functions of each instrument and the age and level for which the tests are recommended are also included.

Published Informal Procedures

Several informal measures have been developed to assess oral language. They are used:

- To sharpen observational skills, by focusing attention on specific language variables in oral production
- To permit professionals to predict future performance, for instructional placement and selection of appropriate curriculum materials.

We have selected these informal measures:

The Syntactic Complexity Formula. Botel, Dawkins, and Granowsky, 1972.
Record of Oral Language and Biks and Gutches. Clay, Gill, Glynn, McNaughton, and Salmon, 1983.
Way with Words. Kovac and Cahir, 1981.
Oral Language Evaluation. Silvaroli, Skinner, and Maynes, 1985.

The Syntactic Complexity Formula, originally designed to assess written language, has been used successfully to determine the complexity of oral language behavior (Glazer & Morrow, 1978). This instrument, developed by Botel and Granowsky (1972), provides a scoring system for determining element complexity. The levels of complexity are based on research findings which suggest that the more frequently a structure is used, the easier it is to process. A level of complexity is offered, not a grade equivalent. The recording system is a bit complex, but very descriptive for learning about the sentence structure used by students. It is the basis upon which the checklist to assess oral language maturity (figure 4–3) was developed.

Record of Oral Language includes forty-two selected sentences which Clay rates from difficult to easy. These represent syntactic structures. The test administrator says the sentence and asks that the student repeat it. The responses are matched with the original and deviations are recorded. These are labeled as: "suggestions or omissions," "transposition," "additions," "contractions." Clay and associates found in several studies that information received about students' oral language production in repetition is valuable. The repetitive use of some structures indicates control of those language structures, elements, and processes. Results from responses to forty-two repetitions should demonstrate trends in rule usage, indicating strengths and needs in oral language production.

After reviewing the materials, it is clear that Clay has found the complexity of syntax to be important in determining the level of development of oral language.

Way With Words suggests that the examiner use a tape recorder to record language stimulated from questions on various topics, including: emotional acceptance—such as likes and dislikes, physical attractiveness, and teacher preference; competence—such as capabilities at school work and in sports; power—such as leadership and teacher preference. Responses to the questions are recorded in writing by the examiner. Evaluation focuses on the language as it demonstrates the student's ability to become interactively involved with another. Questions answered include:

> Is the student aware of the way a particular social or academic situation is reflected through oral language?
> Can the student use appropriate language forms in different situations (syntactic structures) to help the listener know that he/she understands interactions?

The guide provides samples which should help the examiner-teacher understand the meaning of responses with respect to students' views of language power, competence, and emotional responses.

Oral Language Evaluation enables teachers "to quickly establish a beginning oral language level in either English or Spanish" (p. 4). It yields an instructional level and provides activities to help the student develop oral language. Since specific descriptions of language are unavailable, these authors have established their own language continuum or model which they believe is the way oral language develops. These are represented in the diagram below:

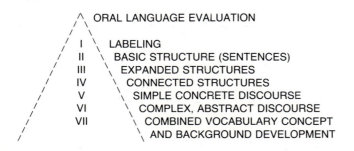

TABLE 4-1 Formal Tests To Assess Oral Language Behavior

TEST	PURPOSE AND LEVEL OF ASSESSMENT	DESCRIPTION
Assessment of Children's Language Comprehension, by Rochana Foster, Jane Giddan, Joel Stark. Consulting Psychologists Press, 1972. Administrator: Speech pathologist, reading specialist, or psychologist.	To test receptive language difficulties in young children. (Ages 3 to 7)	Test consists of a core vocabulary of fifty common words that are combined into two-, three-, and four-word phrases. Child points to appropriate picture in response to words read by examiner.
Carrow Elicited Language Inventory, by Elizabeth Carrow-Woolfolk. Teaching Resources, 1974. Administrator: Speech pathologist, psychologist, reading specialist.	To measure grammatical structure. (Ages 3 to 7)	The child is asked to repeat fifty-two oral stimuli. Responses recorded on audiotape, and transcribed and scored.
Cognitive Abilities Test: Multilevel Edition, Form 3, by Robert L. Thorndike and Elizabeth P. Hagen. Riverside Publishing Company, 1978. Administrator: Reading specialist, teacher.	To test verbal-quantitative and nonverbal-cognitive abilities. (Grades 3 to 12)	This test includes three subtests. We are concerned *only* with the first subtest, which includes: verbal, vocabulary, sentence completion, verbal classification, verbal analogies.
Developmental Sentence Analysis, by Laura L. Lee. Northwestern University Press, 1974. Administrator: Speech pathologist, psychologist, reading specialist.	A system designed to qualify syntactic development in young children. (Ages 2 to 6 and 11 months)	A normative speech sample is taken by taped interview and analyzed by scoring the presence of various grammatical forms, including: pronouns, personal pronouns, main verbs, secondary verbs, negative conjunctions, interrogative reversals, and questions.

Peabody Picture Vocabulary Test. Devised by Lloyd M. Dunn and Leota M. Dunn. American Guidance Service, 1981. Administrator: Reading specialist, psychologist.

Screens receptive vocabulary or verbal ability. (Ages 2½ to 40)

Screens by using a series of plates. Student is asked to select picture that illustrates stimulus word spoken by examiner.

Test for Auditory Comprehension of Language, by Elizabeth Carrow-Woolfolk. Teaching Resources, 1973. Administrator: Speech or language pathologist, psychologist, reading specialist.

Designed to measure auditory comprehension of language elements: syntax, morphology, and vocabulary in English or Spanish. (Ages 3 to 6)

One hundred and one stimulus pictures, each containing three line drawings, are shown to the student who is expected to choose a picture from a choice of three.

Test of Language Development, by Phyllis L. Newcomer and Donald D. Hammill. Pro-Ed, 1982. Administrator: School psychologist, reading specialist, speech therapist.

Test assesses semantic, syntactic, and phonological components of children's language. (Ages 4 to 8 and 11 months)

Eight subtests assess picture vocabulary, oral vocabulary, grammatical understanding, sentence imitation, grammatical completion, word articulation, and word discrimination.

Wechsler Adult Intelligence Scale (WAIS) (1981), *Wechsler Intelligence Scale for Children*—Revised (WISC–R) (1974), *Wechsler Preschool and Primary Scale of Intelligence* (WPPSI) (1967). by David Wechsler. Administrator: Psychologist.

Tests are designed to assess intellectual functioning ability to cope with the world, to guide placement decisions. (Ages 16 to 75, ages 6 to 16, and ages 4 to 6½, respectively)

All have several subtests. For purposes here we are interested in those that assess: information, picture completion, vocabulary, picture arrangement, sentences, and digit span, (short-term memory behavior, visual imagery).

Stanford-Binet Intelligence Scale, Fourth Edition, by Robert L. Thorndike and Elizabeth P. Hagen. Riverside Publishing Company, 1986. Administrator: Psychologist

Assesses mental ability for placement decisions. (Ages 2 to adult)

Concerned *only* with subtests assessing verbal fluency/vocabulary, and judgment and reasoning.

These levels are evaluated from low to high (I to VII). Earliest levels are described as lowest and include simple syntactic structures, whereas the highest include complex syntactic structures. The authors pose the question, "Is language fluency maintained when abstract thoughts are included in a story with an extended vocabulary based on background and conceptual development?"

These instruments provide information about oral language in a systematic, descriptive way. They provide *beginning* points for instruction while defining specific elements of language and discourse.

C–A–L–M INFORMAL PROCEDURES

Our tools for assessing oral language were selected because they comply with this text's model of oral language, C–A–L–M. The activities included in the following sections and in Figures 4–2, 4–3, and Table 4–2 should help to provide data about controls, elements, and forms. Some will allow observation of several simultaneously.

Before presenting C–A–L–M procedures, let us recall that, traditionally, measurements of language fluency are dispersed among several professional fields of study. This dispersement can best be viewed in the chart following:

VARIABLE	TYPE OF TESTS WHICH INCLUDE VARIABLE	
Vocabulary	Reading tests	Measure sight vocabulary, meaning, words in context.
	Writing tests	Assess word usage, spelling, isolated word meanings.
Syntactic complexity	Writing tests	Assess thematic maturity, sentence complexity, sentence structure, knowledge of grammar (parts of speech).
Organization	Intelligence tests	Assess order comprehension (common sense about things and ideas).
	Reading tests	Assess ability to sequence, ability to find main story theme, ability to sequence story events.
Audience awareness		Seldom if ever assessed directly; is alluded to when effectiveness of prose is measured in tests of written language. (i.e., Stanford Writing Test–Test of Written Language).

An alternate route to gathering and sorting data about students' language fluency requires that we look at questions about student performance. Therefore, in the C–A–L–M system, we begin by sorting questions into categories considering controls, elements, and forms of oral language performance.

Assessments of oral language using C–A–L–M must be limited to transcriptions of one student in one setting at a time. We must, however, recommend that several samples from each student working in activities that generate oral language in (1) individual, (2) instructional, (3) interactive, and (4) recreational environments be analyzed with C–A–L–M tools in order to gain a broad picture of oral language behavior.

Use the guidelines for materials, directions, and procedures to collect students' oral language productions. Once language is collected, transcripts can be analyzed using C–A–L–M assessment tools.

General Guidelines for Collecting Oral Language Samples

Materials.

1. Have a tape recorder available for recording language in individual, instructional, interactive, recreational, and formal (test-taking) environments.
2. Provide books without words, so students can tell the story in their own words. (See Appendix A for wordless picture books.)
3. Provide interesting objects—seashells, toys, games, rocks, and so on—to stimulate oral language from students.
4. Sometimes animals—rabbits, gerbils, mice—provide stimulation for students to talk when other objects or books do not. Provide animals in the classroom for those students who need live stimuli.

Directions for collecting samples in formal settings (individual and instructional).

1. Place the tape recorder in an out-of-the way place and turn it on to play/record. Be sure that the tape provides sufficient time to record the language produced in the formal setting.
2. Individual and instructional oral language may be encouraged by:
   a. asking the student to tell a story from a wordless picture book
   b. asking the student to describe an object
   c. asking the student to read and retell what he or she has read
   d. the examiner telling a personal incident and then asking that the student do the same.
3. Once the language is recorded, transcribe the text. It is important to transcribe both the student's language and the teacher's.

Directions for collecting samples in informal settings (interactive and recreational).

1. Place the tape recorder in an out-of-the-way place and turn it on to play/record. Be sure that the tape provides time to record all of the language that is produced during the interactions.
2. Collect several recordings of oral language during interactive activities and during recreational times.
3. Transcribe the oral language from the tape to written form and analyze it using C–A–L–M tools.

Checklists found in this chapter should be used to answer questions concerning student's oral language behavior. The descriptions you write on the checklists should provide insights so that instructional changes can be made to guide students to produce language effectively.

Remember, for example, when you collect data concerning oral controls, you are *not* interested in comparing language performance across controls. You are *only* concerned with discovering the controls that seem to be used most effectively by each student. This will give you an indication of which language controls are used effectively by each student so that you can help each individual student make things happen in his or her environment. *You can, for example, match books to students who use similar controls.* This should help them express their desires, goals, and lives more effectively. Appendix A includes a discussion of the controls and recommended usage for many books to assist you in matching students and materials.

Procedures for assessing oral language controls. The checklist presented in Figure 4–2 is designed to guide the assessment of oral language controls.

Procedures for assessing language elements. Loban's (1963) suspicion that sentence length does not adequately measure language maturity and complexity has directed researchers to collect oral language samples and transcribe them in *T-units* defined as:

> a unit whose total length . . . contains . . . one main clause with all of the subordinate clauses attached to it . . . each unit grammatically capable of being terminated with a capital letter and a period. (Hunt, 1965, p. 20–21)

Terminable or *T-unit segmentation* provides a means to solve the problem of sentence length as a variable of oral language complexity, since numbers of words are not sufficient information to determine difficulty (Glazer & Morrow, 1978). For example, in a clinical setting, we are interested in gathering oral language samples from students and then transcribing these in order to observe frequency and kind of use of structures. These observations indicate language flexibility and, usually, understanding (Glazer, 1973, Ruddell, 1963).

Figure 4–2 Assessing Oral Controls

QUESTION	YES	NO	NEED MORE DATA
FUN LANGUAGE Does the student mimic and play with oral language creating stories, poems, and nonsense words?			
INVESTIGATIVE LANGUAGE Does the student ask "Why"? Does the student notice specifics and ask, "What's that?" Does the student demonstrate curiosity for learning by asking, 　　"How do you do that?" 　　"Show Me!"			
LANGUAGE TO CONTROL COMMAND FOR CONTROL Does the student command or direct this demonstration with 　　phrases including: 　　"Give me that ———." 　　"Come here ———." 　　"You do it, now."			
CONCRETE PHENOMENA Does the student describe things using objectives and 　　comparisons?			
EMOTIONAL DESCRIPTIONS Does the student say, for example, 　　"I hurt." 　　"That feels sad." 　　"I feel lonely."			
INTERDEPENDENT/INTERACTIVE LANGUAGE Does the student encourage conversation by saying: 　　"You tell me." 　　"What do you think?"			

We have chosen to assess syntax, since we believe that this permits us to learn about students' ability to structure words and phrase their vocabulary into meaningful units. Implicit in our assessment model is "holistic observation." Holistic units include observations of language controls which are determined by syntactic structures, but even more by the words, vocabulary, used to create these controls. It seems appropriate here, to look at the whole sample guided by the following findings from research. Table 4–2 summarizes the difficulty of processing various syntactic elements and sentence structures. This historical summary supports our notion of syntactic flexibility and diversity as measures of maturity in oral language usage. To date we have found no recent research to cause us to reject these findings.

Table 4–2 Developmental Trends in Oral Language Syntax

FORM	EXAMPLE	RESEARCH
Sentence Structures		
Subject-verb (Also includes noun clause of dialogue)	He runs. She said.	Eighty percent of all oral language patterns represented by these structures. (O'Donnell, Griffin, & Norris, 1967; Strickland, 1962)
Subject-verb adverb	He runs quickly. She runs home. They run in the morning.	
Subject-verb-object	I see the horse.	Used often but less frequently than con-constructions above. (O'Donnell, Griffin, & Norris, 1967)
Subject-*to be* verb form complement	The girl is happy.	
Subject-verb-infinitive	The dog likes to play.	
Subject-verb-object compliment	They made her sad.	Used infrequently in oral form. (Sauer, 1970)
Subject-verb-indirect object-object	They gave him the candy.	
Possessive	The girl's toy	Used increasingly between ages 8 through 10. (Hunt, 1965)
Explicit negative	n't, not, no, etc.	Explicit negative *Not* considered difficult or hard to process. (Just & Carpenter, 1971)
Implicit negative	some of the time seldom few scarcely a minority	Difficult to process and seldom used. (Gaer, 1969; Just & Carpenter, 1971)
Adverbials of time	I ate lunch later.	Used in the earlier years, with declined use in latter school grades. (Hunt, 1965, p. 133)
Adverbials of place	I eat lunch at home.	
Adverbials of manner	I eat lunch quickly. I ski cautiously.	Use of this structure increases with maturity. (Hunt, 1965)
Models	shall, should, might, may, probably—infer tentativeness	Increased use of models indicates maturity and the use of tentativeness helps us detect a sense of understanding. (Loban, 1963)

Table 4–2 Continued

FORM	EXAMPLE	RESEARCH
Coordinates, including *and, but, or, so,* etc.	I went to the store and I got an apple but it was rotten.	Coordinate *and* is not difficult, however, the use of others increases with maturity in both reading and writing. (Hunt, 1965; O'Donnell, Griffin, & Norris, 1967; Robertson, 1968; Stoodt, 1972)
Participles as gerunds as well as nominals.	Skiing is my favorite sport. Frightened, the boy ran home.	Form is usually found in the language of the mature speaker. (Loban, 1963; Goodman, 1969)
Clauses used as subjects.	How she works is her business.	Found in language of older students. (Bormuth, 1969)
Deletions resulting in relative clauses.	The boy who I know lives in Ohio.	Deletions resulting in relative clauses are difficult. (Fagan, 1970) Deletions in general indicate some maturity in expressive language. (Fagan, 1971)
Pronoun usage	Tony gave her the ball.	Generally difficult to process. (Goodman, 1969)
Adverbials placed at the beginning of sentences.	In school I ate lunch.	Generally, when used at the beginning, are more difficult to process than if used at sentence endings—especially adverbials of manner. (Ruddell, 1963; Bormuth, 1969; Strickland, 1962)
Passive forms	The boy was hit by the ball. The girl was frightened.	Difficult to produce and understand for children as well as adults. (Coleman, 1965; Gaer, 1969).

The information and research on developmental trends in oral language syntax presented in Table 4–2 should assist you in making clinical diagnoses. The information can also be applied as you use the checklist in Figure 4–3 to assess your students' maturity in oral language. If students speak in a non-standard form, convert oral language transcriptions into standard English for assessment purposes. The checklist is a modification of one developed by Morton Botel and Alvin Granowsky (1972).

Oral language samples you collect over time from each student should provide information demonstrating changes reflecting growth. For example, uses of elements and kernel (simple) sentences might vary and increase. If noticeable inflexibility or lack of additions, deletions, or rearrangements of elements exist, or if lack of increased content vocabulary is noticed, referral

Figure 4–3 Checklist to Assess Oral Language Maturity

E = easy
LE = less easy
MD = moderately difficult
D = difficult

SYNTACTIC ELEMENTS	NUMBER OF TIMES ELEMENT APPEARS IN ORAL LANGUAGE.

SENTENCE PATTERNS

1. (E) *Subject-verb* (*adverbial*)   He ran. He ran home.   _____
2. (E) *Subject-verb-object*   I hit the ball.   _____
3. (E) *Subject-be-complement* (noun, adjective, adverb)   He is good.   _____
4. (E) *Subject-verb-infinitive*   She wanted to play.   _____
5. (LE) *Subject-verb-indirect object-object*   I gave her the ball.   _____
6. (LE) *Subject-verb-object-complement*   We named her president.   _____

SIMPLE TRANSFORMATIONS

1. (E) *Interrogative* (including tag-end questions)   You did it, didn't you?   _____
2. (E) *Exclamatory*   What a game!   _____
3. (E) *Imperative*   Go to the store.   _____

COORDINATE CLAUSE JOINED BY "AND"

He came and he went.   _____

NOUN MODIFIERS

1. (LE) *Adjectives*   big, smart   _____
2. (LE) *Possessive*   man's, Mary's   _____
3. (LE) *Quantitative determiners*   all, many, one   _____
4. (LE) *Predeterminers*   some of, none of, twenty of   _____
5. (LE) *Participles* (in the natural adjective position)   *crying* boy, *scalded* cat   _____
6. (LE) *Prepositional phrase*   The boy on the bench . . .   _____

OTHER MODIFIERS

1. (LE) *Adverbials* (including prepositional phrases when they do not immediately follow the verb in the SVAdverbial pattern)   The boy ran to the store *down the street*.   _____
2. (LE) *Modals*   should, would, must, ought to, dare to, etc.   _____
3. (LE) *Negatives*   no, not, never, neither, not, n't   _____
4. (LE) *Set expressions*   once upon a time, many years ago, etc.   _____
5. *Infinitives* (when they do not immediately follow the verb in a SVInfinitive pattern.)   I wanted her *to play*.   _____

6. (LE) *Gerund* (when used as a subject)   *Running* is fun.   _____

COORDINATES

1. (LE) *Coordinate clause* (joined by but, for, so, or, yet)   I will do it *or* you will do it.   _____
2. (LE) *Deletion in coordinate clauses*   John swims *and* Mary swims, becomes John and Mary swim.   _____
3. (LE) *Paired coordinate* (both . . . and)   *Both* Bob did it *and* Bill did it.   _____

(MD) *Passive*   I was hit by the ball. I was hit.   _____
(MD) *Paired conjunction* (neither . . . nor, either . . . or)   *Either* Bob will go *or* I will.   _____
(MD) *Dependent clauses* (adjective, adverb, noun)   I went before you did.   _____
(MD) *Comparatives* (as . . . as, . . . -er than, same . . . as, more . . . than)   He is bigger than you.   _____
(D) *Participles* (-ed or -ing forms not used in the usual adjective position)   *Running,* John fell. The cat, *scalded,* yowled.   _____
(D) *Infinitives as subject*   *To sleep* is important.   _____
(D) *Appositives* (when set off by commas)   John, *my friend,* is here.   _____
(MD) *Conjunctive adverbs* (however, thus, nevertheless, etc.)   *Thus,* the day ended.   _____
(D) *Clauses used as subject*   *What he does* is his concern.   _____
(D) *Absolutes*   *The performance over,* Mr. Smith lit his pipe.   _____

OTHER

1. *Non-sentence expressions*   ah, you see, etc.   _____

to a language specialist at a hospital or center for neurological studies may be in order. Child study teams, which may include a psychologist, psychiatrist, and learning disability specialist, may also be consulted since minimal syntactic flexibility accompanied by limited vocabulary might result from situations in a student's life causing emotional disturbances. Limited intelligence may also play a part in restricted language.

Oral Language Analysis: A Sample

The language sample assessed in Figures 4–4 and 4–5 was elicted from a six-year-old boy. A picture book was the stimulus for language and the interview was tape recorded. This sample demonstrates data collection processes and suggested reporting procedures.

Figure 4–4 Oral Language Sample Segmented Into T-Units

Name <u>Michael</u>　　Age <u>6</u>　　Grade <u>1</u>　　Sex <u>Male</u>　　T-units <u>13</u>

1　　　　　　　　　　　2　　　　　　　3
(He is brushing his teeth) (he is eating) (he's getting dressed) (and he is gonna play cowboys and
　　　　　　　　　4　　　　　　　5　　　　　　6
indians) (he is reading a book) (he's pretending he is a doctor with a fake patient) (he's pretending
　　7　　　　　　8　　　　　　　9　　　　　　10
that he is a cowboy) (and he's playing Indians) (he's pretending he is a sheriff) (and he caught a man)
　　　　　11　　　　　　　　　12　　　　　　13
(and now he's gonna put him in the jailhouse) (a genie came out of the bottle) (and he is very happy).

The following chart demonstrates the syntactic analysis

T-UNIT	ELEMENT	EVALUATION	SENTENCE OF LENGTH OF T-UNIT
1. He is brushing his teeth	Subject be (is) object	Easy	5
2. He is eating	Subject-*be*-verb	Easy	3
3. He's getting dressed	Subject-*be*-complement	Easy	3
4. And he is gonna play cowboys and indians	Coordinate Subject-*be*-Infinitive object plus deletion	Easy Easy	8
5. He is reading a book	Subject-*be*-complement (Obj.)	Easy Easy	5
6. He's pretending he is a doctor with a fake patient	Subject-*be*-complement Dependent clause Adverb clause Adjective addition	Easy Moderately difficult Less easy	10
7. He's pretending that he is a cowboy	Subject-*be*-complement Dependent clause	Less easy Easy Less easy	7
8. And he's playing Indians	Coordinate Subject-*be*-complement (Obj.)	Easy Easy	4
9. He's pretending he is a sheriff	Subject-*be*-complement Dependent clause	Easy Moderately difficult	7
10. And he caught a man	Coordinate Subject-verb-object	Easy Easy	5

11. And now he's gonna put him in the jailhouse	Coordinate Adverb time at beginning Subject-verb-infinitive-indirect object	Easy Easy Less Easy	10
12. A genie came out of the bottle	Subject-verb Adverbial	Easy	7
13. And he is very happy	Coordinate Subject-*be*-complement-Adjective Qualifier	Easy Easy Easy	5

Figure 4–5 Assessment of Michael's Oral Language Maturity

E = easy
LE = less easy
MD = moderately difficult
D = difficult

SYNTACTIC ELEMENTS	NUMBER OF TIMES ELEMENT APPEARS IN ORAL LANGUAGE.
SENTENCE PATTERNS	
1. (E) *Subject-verb (adverbial)* He ran. He ran home.	2
2. (E) *Subject-verb-object* I hit the ball.	1
3. (E) *Subject-be-complement* (noun, adjective, adverb) He is good.	10
4. (E) *Subject-verb-infinitive* She wanted to play.	
5. (LE) *Subject-verb-indirect object-object* I gave her the ball.	0
6. (LE) *Subject-verb-object-complement* We named her president.	0
SIMPLE TRANSFORMATIONS	
1. (E) *Interrogative* (including tag-end questions) You did it, didn't you?	
2. (E) *Exclamatory* What a game!	
3. (E) *Imperative* Go to the store.	
COORDINATE CLAUSE JOINED BY "and"	
He came and he went.	5

Figure 4–5 Continued

NOUN MODIFIERS

1. (LE) *Adjectives* big, smart
2. (LE) *Possessives*   man's, Mary's
3. (LE) *Quantitative determiners*   all, many, one
4. (LE) *Predeterminers*   some of, none of, twenty of
5. (LE) *Participles* (in the natural adjective position) *crying* boy, *scalded* cat
6. (LE) *Prepositional phrase*   The boy *on the bench* . . .

OTHER MODIFIERS

1. (LE) *Adverbials* (including prepositional phrases when they do not immediately follow the verb in the SVAdv. pattern) ____2____
2. (LE) *Modals*   should, would, must, ought to, dare to, etc.
3. (LE) *Negatives*   no, not, never, neither, not, n't
4. (LE) *Set expressions*   once upon a time, many years ago, etc.
5. (LE) *Infinitives* (when they do not immediately follow the verb in a SVInfinitive pattern.)   I wanted her *to play*.
6. (LE) *Gerund* (when used as a subject)   *Running* is fun.

COORDINATES

1. (LE) *Coordinate clause* (joined by but, for, so, or, yet)   I will do it *or you will do it*.
2. (LE) *Deletion in coordinate clauses*   John swims and Mary swims becomes John and Mary swim.
3. (LE) *Paired coordinate* (both . . . and)   *Both* Bob did it *and* Bill did it.

(MD) *Passive*   I was hit by the ball. I was hit.
(MD) *Paired conjunction* (neither . . . nor, either . . . or)   *Either* Bob will go *or* I will.
(MD) *Dependent clauses* (adjective, adverb, noun)   I went before you did. ____3____
(MD) *Comparatives* (as . . . as, -er than, same . . . as, more . . . than)   He is bigger than you.
(D) *Participles* (-ed or -ing forms not used in the usual adjective position)   *Running,* John fell. The cat, *scalded,* yowled.
(D) *Infinitives as subject*   *To sleep* is important.
(D) *Appositives* (when set off by commas)   John, *my friend,* is here.
(MD) *Conjunctive adverbs* (however, thus, nevertheless, etc.)   *Thus,* the day ended.
(D) *Clauses used as subject*   *What he does* is his concern.
(D) *Absolutes*   *The performance over,* Mr. Smith lit his pipe.

OTHER

1. *Non-sentence expressions*   ah, you see, etc.

Figure 4–5 summarizes Michael's oral language productions that are described in Figure 4–4. Reviewing the number of syntactic elements used, as well as frequency of use permits diagnosticians to develop a descriptive evaluation similar to the one included below, which describes Michael's oral language fluency.

Michael's Language Evaluation

Michael's language sample indicates that he uses elements of language that are *easy* and *less easy* to process. Longer T-units in the sample reflect some flexibility and variability (see Figure 4–4). Unit number 6, for example, includes additional elements that are *less easy* and *moderately difficult*. This is true also for T-unit numbered 11. The variability begins after the first five T-units. This probably indicates that Michael "warms up" to the stimulus after initial verbal responses, thus contributing more descriptive and elaborate language. The variety of kernel sentence usage is expected. All are "easy to process." The use of the coordinate "and" is also expected behavior, since young children string isolated ideas together in oral language using "and."

Michael's language is objective and include elements describing concrete phenomona. Pronouns refer to main characters in the story. "He" (the pronoun used) is probably a subsitute for the name of the main character. The present tense is used consistently throughout the sample, demonstrating a reflective oral style (Moffett, 1983).

The only language controls used in this sample by Michael are those that are concrete. Michael described, throughout, what was in the pictures. There are no commands, no emotional descriptions, no intent to act or provoke interactions or interdependence by using inference. His vocabulary seems weighted with nouns and adjectives. Again, concrete objects are noted. From this sample, it cannot be determined if Michael is aware of an audience (who is listening). There seems to be a lack of sense of story organization except that which the stimulus (a picture book) provokes. A summary of the information generated from the analysis follows.

Summary of Michael's Oral Language

Controls: Concrete phenomena
Elements–Vocabulary:
    Words and phrases are nouns and adjectives representing concrete phenomona objects.
Syntactic structures most frequently used:
    Subject-verb
    Subject-verb *to be*-adjectives
    Subject-verb-object

Organization:
    Story line is controlled by picture order
Audience awareness:
    Unclear concerning student's intent

Interactive Settings: Assessing Language Effectively

Since language requires interaction, it seems important to notice not just the controls but also the setting, and the activities that encourage language production during interactions. Therefore, interactive situations must be observed and assessed. Assessing oral language in interactive settings requires observing and analyzing transcriptions resulting from discussions. This challenging diagnostic procedure requires time, experience, and knowledge about oral as well as body language behaviors.

Much can be learned about student's language performance in interactive conversation. Questions focus therefore, as follows:

1. Does the student begin the talking?
2. Does the student use language "like the teacher's"? Similar? Different?
3. Does the student respond to context after someone else initiates the discussion?
4. Are new ideas generated and syntactic variations used to express these?
5. Does vocabulary seem appropriate for exchanging ideas effectively?

Procedures. Follow these guidelines for collecting language in an interactive setting:

1. Develop a clinical or small group setting that resembles a relaxed environment. Provide:
    A small table with objects on it, or
    A small section of a book corner where books are reviewed and selected.
   The environment should be familiar to the students.
2. Place a tape recorder in the room. Explain your purposes to the student. Say, I want to understand how you think by listening to how you talk to each other; I want to find out what interests you; I want to find out where you need to build skills.
3. Record several different oral language interactions with different individuals interacting with the student being diagnosed.

A sample interaction. The following is a sample interactive dialogue between Michael, age six, and Lisa, age eight. The dialogue will then be recorded on various summary sheets (see Figures 4–6 and 4–7).

Figure 4–6 Sample Summary Sheet: Language Controls for Michael, Age 6

	STUDENT (MICHAEL)		INTERACTOR (LISA)	
CONTROL	FREQUENCY OF T-UNITS	CONTENT	FREQUENCY OF T-UNITS	CONTENT
Fun language	0		0	
Investigative controls	1	Response to Lisa's	2	Requesting information
Commands for control	1	Response to Lisa's	1	Response to story in a state of need
Concrete phenomena	2	Response to Lisa's questions	1	Offers age: "I am 8."
Emotional descriptions	0		1	Makes closure on activity
Interactive/Interdependence language	0		3	2—Requests information 1—Responds to Michael

Comments: Michael did not initiate language. All language was in response to Lisa.

Setting: A small room, with a wordless picture book on the table.
Two children: Michael, age six, and Lisa, age eight.
Time of Day: 10:00 A.M.
Duration of time spent in room together: 20 minutes.

The children were asked to sit at the table. Both sat down, smiled at each other, without exchanging oral language for approximately four minutes. The numbers following each line of dialogue match the numbers for each student in Figure 4–7.

LISA: Hello. (1. nonsentence)
MICHAEL: (Looks up at Lisa, but does not respond.) (0)
LISA: Do you konw what we are supposed to do? (2. S-V-adv)
MICHAEL: (Shrugs shoulders and puts head down, looking at tale). (0)
LISA: How old are you? (3. S-V-adj)
MICHAEL Six (1. other)
LISA: I'm eight. (4. S-V-adj)
MICHAEL: So what. (2. exclamation)

Figure 4–7 Sample Assessment of Element: Syntax

Student's Name: Michael
Date: 3-12-87
Age: 6
Setting: Small room: 2 chairs and table
Interactor: Lisa

LANGUAGE SAMPLE: MICHAEL

T-UNITS	LENGTH	ELEMENT ADDITIONS						
		ADJ.	ADV.	POSS.	NEG.	INFIN.	DEP. CLAUSE	OTHER
1. Other	1							
2. Exclamation	2							
3. S-V-obj	4		1					
4. Other	2		1					
5. S-*be*-adv	4							
6. S-V-IO	5							
7. S-V-adv	4							
8. S-V-inf	5		1					

LISA: (Walks around to the book on the table. Picks it up and looks at it.) Boy, this is big. (5. S-*be*-adj)

MICHAEL: Yeah. Yeah, I saw it already. (3. S-V-obj)

LISA: You did? (6. S-V)

MICHAEL: Yeah, yesterday. (4. other)
A lady was here. (5. S-*be*-adv)
She asked me the story. (6. S-V-IO)

LISA: Oh. (0) (Pause; thumbs through book, takes it around to the table side, as if to sit next to Michael. Begins to tell story, as if reading it to Michael.)

Figure 4–7 Continued

		LANGUAGE SAMPLE: LISA						
		ELEMENT ADDITIONS						
T-UNITS	LENGTH	ADJ.	ADV.	POSS.	NEG.	INF.	DEP. CLAUSE	OTHER
1. Non-sentence	1							
2. S-V-adv	9					1	1	
3. S-V-adj	4							Transformation
4. S-V-adj	3							
5. S-*be*-adj	4							
6. S-V	2							
7. S-V-obj	5							
8. S-V-obj	4							
9. S-V-obj	6							Exclamations

At completion of story:

    Lisa: Did you like the story? (7. S-V-obj)
    Michael: (Shrugs shoulders.) (0)
    Lisa: I liked the story. (8. S-V-obj)
    Michael: (Respnds after Lisa gets up and replaces book from the spot where she had taken it—this period of time approximately three minutes. (0) He takes book, and turns to the last page.) I didn't know that (7. S-V-adv) he went to sleep again. (8. S-V-inf)
    Lisa: Yeah, see the picture shows it. (9. S-V-obj)

Listening to one's own voice while reading helps oral fluency.

Summary Comments: In only one instance did Michael attempt to use language controls. That control was in the form of a statement. His last oral language production, "I didn't know that he went to sleep again," demonstrates that control. Information suggests that Michael will use investigative language in response to a stimulus (Lisa) probably more easily with a child then with an adult. The constructions, although minimal in number, were more complex than those used in individual assessment sessions. Additional collections of oral language noting these differences are recommended.

Figures 4–6 and 4–7 demonstrate the collection, analysis, and reporting procedures for language created in an interactive setting. The numbers correspond to T-units for each child. Michael's first T-unit (1) is "other"; Lisa's first T-unit (1) is a "nonsentence."

INSTRUCTIONAL STRATEGIES FOR ENHANCING ORAL LANGUAGE

One learns language and learns about life through language by interacting with others. The instructional strategies that are presented in Table 4–3 provide opportunities for enhancing oral language in meaningful, interactive settings.

Drama for Stimulating Oral Language

Drama can be useful in encouraging oral language interactions. In remedial oral language classrooms, drama is not a script; it is not training, or coaching to meet certain types of behavior as in a formal play. It is a way most people discover for themselves how to cope with new or unusual experiences—even unsettling ones. When a new experience, or one that provides discomfort, is anticipated, each of us tend to rehearse it in our minds by talking to ourselves about "how to solve the problem," how to act. We want time to rehearse beforehand what to say and how to use the body with appropriate gestures to help language express thoughts to an audience. We create drama for ourselves, therefore; we rehearse to explore feelings and experiences and to decrease anxiety so that we can gain control in different settings. Heathcote (Wagner, 1976) refers to this as evolved, not directed, drama activities for the reduction of anxiety and increase in oral language. For example, when "role playing," we act out decisions. These decisions are made based on individual perceptions of self in the world. Responses from an "audience" guide us to see, at least in part, how individual perceptions are received by groups—peers and adults alike. Students need responses in order to guide them to play "real roles" in life outside of school. Drama or role playing in classrooms, therefore, serves to develop healthy self-concepts to produce language. The more drama activities simulate life, the more comfortable students will be when they experience acted roles in society. It is essential that positive self-concepts concerning decisions about school events, both social and academic, be developed. The student with a healthy feeling about self will "perform" feeling capably important. Those whose self-concept is minimal will see themselves as incapable or unimportant and therefore perform accordingly (Quandt & Selznick, 1984, p. 1–2).

    The diagnostician who is able to skillfully observe students in groups acting roles in several settings can adjust environments in order to maximize each student's performance. Adjusting environments means:

> Placing students with peers whose language encourages group talk
> Placing students in environments (small area, with appropriate furniture and materials) that "push" each to talk—describe, explain, narrate, and even reason.

Table 4–3 Instructional Strategies to Enhance Oral Language

STRATEGY	PURPOSE	INTENDED AUDIENCE	PROCEDURES	AGE AND RATIONALE	SUGGESTED SETTING AND MATERIALS
Choral reading	Provides practice in oral fluency; Develops self-confidence by providing support system—a chorus. Builds in successful oral reading experiences because of group participation. Provides models for oral expression.	Large groups of all ages and stages; resembles church chorus singing or reading in unison.	1. Select short selection as a poem, fable, popular song. Selection is determined by age group. 2. Read the selection to students. If they can read, provide the text for them to follow as you read. 3. If nonreaders, read selection often, memorization can occur. 4. When students are not familiar with selection, read in *unison*. This is difficult, so be careful to listen for monotonous oral language. 5. Record group, and replay. 6. Encourage self-evaluation. 7. Begin again, and request modification of oral language based on evaluations.	Best for intermediate readers and adults. This technique relaxes the anxious student by providing oral support systems. All readers, poor and good, read together, and form a reading bond. Unmeasurable good feelings about self are created, particularly in poor readers. Enough choral reading develops a purpose for reading for meaning.	Size of rooms should reflect group size: Small informal circle on floor or in chairs; or large chorus type arrangement; informal; instructional; recreational.
Choral drama	Provides individual oral reading with support system. Develops "wait-time" when students permit others to participate. Select passages that include either: cumulative language; opportunities for dialogue reading; refrains. 2. Designate certain lines, or parts, to students. 3. Proceed as in choral reading strategy.	All levels; large and small groups.	*Refrains* provide a good beginning for choral reading. The leader can read the beginning and cue the entire group, or part, or one student to read the rest. Develops anticipatory skills, as well as providing a purpose for attending to the reading task. *Dialogue* gives students the opportunity to respond in what can resemble a question and answer format. This, too, holds attention to the text or oral language if memorized and gives purpose to all in the group. *Cumulative language* helps one hypothesize exactly what is next. This mnemonic device, used in choral reading, will help students develop the ability to anticipate oral language with confidence.	Same as rational for choral reading.	Setting: same as choral reading. *Materials:* books that repeat; examples include: *Little Red Riding Hood*, P. Galdone (illus) (McGraw-Hill, 1974); *Drummer Hoff*, E. Emberly (Prentice Hall, 1967); *She'll Be Comin' round the Mountain*, R. Quackenbush (Lippincott, 1973); *Giraffe and A Half*, Shel Silverstein (Harper Junior Books, 1964); *Are You My Mother?* P. Eastman (Random House, 1967).

Method	Audience	Purpose	Description	Examples/Materials
Echo reading (referred to in remedial situations as "neurological impress methods"; see Heckelman, 1969)	One-to-one only	To increase oral fluency in recitation and reading.	*For reading*: The reader sits slightly in front of the teacher. Both hold the book or reading material. Both read in unison; the teacher directs the voice into the student's ear, at close range. If necessary, the teacher reads a bit louder and a bit ahead of the student. As fluency is built and confidence gained, teacher can lower voice or lag behind student. *For oral language*: Same as above, but student *must* know poem, story, riddle, or other selection in order to build fluency.	Short stories, or poems, that have language that encourages fluency. Examples: *Seven Eggs*, M. Hooper (Harper & Row, 1985); *Rosie's Walk*, P. Hutchins (Macmillan, 1968); *If the Dinosaurs Came Back*, B. Most (Harcourt, Brace, Jovanovich, 1978)
Television or media reading (adapted from radio reading; see Greene, 1979, Searfoss 1975).	All	To communicate a message through oral reading; shares the communication by summarizing or restating message orally.	*Getting started*: Reader reads or shows pictures (can be slides); audience attends. Leader explains purpose for attending; to restate message, as on a news program. *Communicating the message*: Leader must convey message any way possible. So if reading, and word is unknown, may skip or substitute another. If using films, or photos, or pictures, add, or subtract those that enhance communication. *Checking for understanding*: Ask audience member to relate message; if clear, response is usually brief; reader/leader has shared message clearly. (Rotation of leader gives many a chance to produce oral language). *Clarifying an unclear message*: Leader/reader returns to materials—book, film, pictures, etc.—to clear up confusion in story as retold by audience member. Leader takes responsibility for unclear message—adjusts language (visual or oral) to fit audience.	Maximizes use of oral and visual sense modes. Exposes student to correct language immediately. After time, this reading pattern is "impressed" on the student's mind. Goal: to communicate message. Fosters the giver–receiver aspect of language, with freedom to restate, rework, retell, reread, without fear of failure. Books without words, including: *A Boy, A Dog, and A Frog*, M. Mayer (Dial, 1967); *Skates*, E. J. Keats (Watts, 1972); Scripts—television or radio—for solo reader; news reporting—descriptive, commentary etc.—are suggested; TV shows without sound; computer software—a picture story without words; 35mm slide show—no words.
The lap approach	Young children, ages 2 to 10.	Provides language in "loving" manner, to boost younger students to begin to generalize about the oral reading process. Aides, parents, teachers, students can do this with young children.	Find a quiet, intimate place in the classroom for you, the teacher, and one child to sit. Put child on your lap in a close position, next to you. Read the story or passage to student, running your hand under the line of print, encouraging the student to hold the book and do the same.	Hearing, using language in text in a "loving" way guides students to generalize about word and sentence structures, letter sounds, how stories are constructed. *Cat in the Hat*, Dr. Seuss (Beginner, 1968); *Foot Book* (Random House, 1968); *Hand, Hand, Fingers, Thumb*, A. Perkins (Random House, 1969).

73

Table 4-3 Continued

STRATEGY	PURPOSE	INTENDED AUDIENCE	PROCEDURES	AGE AND RATIONALE	SUGGESTED SETTING AND MATERIALS
Show and tell	To talk and show at the same time	All levels (small or large groups)	Bring group together. Give listeners time to examine the object shown—pass it around. Leave it on a table earlier for examination with sign so students know that they are expected to be familiar with object. Encourage an informal audience exchange so that students respond by asking *questions about the object only.* After a while, when routine is set, work with "shower and teller," to direct oral language. 1. Help student use "descriptive" language. 2. Help student explain a process—how something works, steps in the process, etc. 3. Help student narrate—tell a story: what happened first, next, and last. Be sure to practice with student before he/she performs for group. Audience can be guided with key words to direct questions for oratorical style. If student, for example, is asked to describe, audience cues for descriptive questions include: "How does it look? How does it feel? How does it smell? How do you use it?" Words for narration or questions include: "Tell me what happened first, next, last. What events occurred? What was the order of events?" Questions requiring explanation include: "What do you do first? What is the next step? What is last?"	Permits speaker to talk about loved subject, object, experience, usually in more knowledgeable way than the audience. Builds self-confidence.	Self-selected by students. "Real" reason for selection should be shared orally. Some reasons might include: "I like it," "I made it," "It is interesting," "My friend gave it to me."

Small group discussion	To create a climate for talking in an oral language exchange; to encourage participation in descriptive, explanatory, narrative discourse; to facilitate manipulation of ideas and "languaging" those thoughts. To provide opportunity to observe students' interactions in order to guide students to become flexible. (See rationale) in response performance.	All ages	Group five to nine students. This permits pairing. With remedial needs, limit group to three students. Groupings should be developed based on: students' age, interests, ability to control space and language. (If one student encourages another to speak, placement for those ought to be together.) Odd numbers of students seem best. (Moffett, 1983, p. 57) Language directors (from teacher to student to encourage interactions and flexible responses) include statements such as: Each of you tell about ———. Let's go around the table. I'll begin the talking. Tell how (explain) you do it; What is first (next, etc.). Begin the story and tell me the very first thing that happened (narration); How did it (she/he) look, act, etc.?	Four sorts of interactors usually exist in classrooms: the volunteer; the responder (will voluntarily respond when group request is made); the directed responder (answers only upon personal request); the "silent" student (almost never responds). Encourage responses from all.	People, the teacher, matched peers, are the "materials" to stimulate oral language. The teacher serves as the "intruder" to change behaviors to guide oral language output.

Selecting topics for role playing should be collaborative ventures. Brainstorming provides the vehicle for joint decision making in small and moderate sized groups. The generation of ideas by "storming one's brain" encourages students to observe possibilities without making judgments about those ideas. A scribe writes these ideas in front of the group on a chart or chalkboard, without comments or censorship, so that all "storms" are accepted. This activity provides information about student interests. Brainstorming supplies ideas for oral as well as written drama.

Brainstorming procedures for drama topics. Follow these guidelines to develop drama topics:

1. Draw a diagram (see Figure 4–8) on the chalkboard or chart and place the main topic at the focal point.
2. Ask the students to think of all the things that relate to the topic.
3. Fill in the responses as indicated in Table 4–4.

Heathcote (Wagner, 1976) recommends that once aspects or segments of an idea are developed, questioning should follow so that students can be guided to arrive at a particular moment when the essence of that experience is likely to be the most fully recognized. These questions help students to focus on the drama and direct oral language. Questions that help to focus drama include those that:

Seek student interests
Help define the moment of the drama
Encourage research in books or through interviews
Require specific information
Help to control the class for organization into the drama
Establish mood, belief, and disbelief.

Children with reading and other language problems need feelings of success. Drama provides built-in success for students and proof that success is achievable, thus creating good feelings. It moves each student away from self. Questions to stimulate drama about feelings about reading include:

- What do you do best in front of the group?
- How do you feel when you do the activity?
- Why do you feel good about an activity?
- Why do you feel uncomfortable about an activity? (Be specific.)

Conversing about problems stimulates oral discourse and allows students to release emotions that may hinder performance.

Table 4-4 Focusing Oral Language Drama

The following questions serve as models for the development of additional stimuli for oral language drama. These are based on the subject "Food," illustrated in Figure 4–8. Questions can be adapted to fit most content areas studied.

QUESTIONS ABOUT FOOD

Seeking student interests	What should we do a play about?
	What do we need for the play?
	How will we get the materials?
	What will we do with the materials when we get them?
	How many people should be eating?
	Who should be the focus (the cook, eaters, visitors, etc)?
	Where do we want the restaurant to be located?
	What will be the problem?
	What will be the "mistaken ingredient" that causes the people to leave the restaurant?
	How would you plan to get the people back to the restaurant?
	Who should be the character to do this?
	What happens to the person who eats the bad food?
Questions that define the moment	What is the time of day?
	What is the time of year?
	What will you be wearing to dinner?
	What will you be carrying?
	What do you think the atmosphere is like?
	At what point do you want to suggest that the food is bad?
Questions that require research or interviews with informed persons	What does a Spanish restaurant look like?
	What special ingredient would give a rancid taste even if it were not bad?
	How do Spanish cooks dress?
	What kind of special utensils would be needed to eat that special food?
	COURSE OF ACTION QUESTIONS:
Questions that help to control the group for organization into drama activities	Should this play happen now, in the past, or in the future?
	How many girls and boys should be in the play?
	Should the play be about helping the people who are sick from the food, or helping the chef who ruined the food? (point of view)
	Who should help the people (owner, customer, public health office)?
	BRANCHING ACTION QUESTIONS:
	How can we keep the cook from hearing the bad comments about the food?
	How can we look like very upset customers?
	How can we set the action so that we get mad at the owner for purchasing the wrong spices for the food?
	When do you want to stop the action?

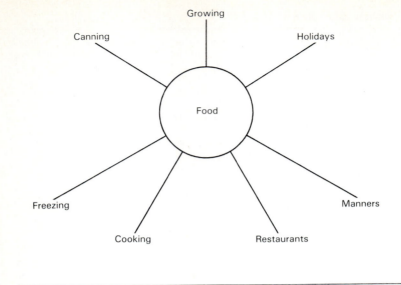

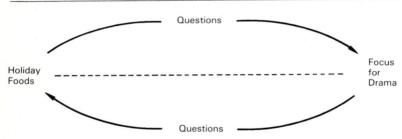

Figure 4–8

SUMMARY

We believe that oral language provides human beings with the ability to learn. Language itself is learned activity. Language becomes part of each human being. One learns language and learns about life through language by interacting with others. Language develops personally with each individual's view of the world. We become aware of our power over the world, using language subconsciously. This chapter has provided an overview of language learning and ways of recording, transcribing, and noticing changes in language performance over time. The implications set forth here and throughout this text about language learning are:

- Humans learn language as instinctively as they learn to eat.
- Language learning is unique to each individual and involves interaction which is necessary for practicing language usage.
- Language forms, elements, and controls are learned simultaneously with variations used when the need arises.
- Because language is human it requires interaction. The more interactive the language learner, the more sophisticated the language.
- Language learning is individual and cannot be evaluated by comparing one student to the other. We must compare each student's growth over time to note changes, variations, and elaborations.

QUESTIONS TO PONDER

1. Collect samples of adult oral language. Collect the same number of samples from children. Answer the following questions:
   a. How are the samples similar?
   b. How are they different?
2. When a child is fluent in oral language behaviors and has difficulty reading and writing, what sorts of variables do you need to consider to determine why the problem exists?
3. Find books that use the language control dominant with a selected child. Read the books, again and again, to that child. Do you notice the child using language from the texts? Is he/she repeating it? Is he/she using creative language following the author's text structures?
4. Collect oral language samples on tape, of students in: recreational settings; instructional settings; interactive settings. Then notice:
   a. changes, over time, in uses of syntactic elements;
   b. changes over time, in uses of sentence patterns;
   c. changes, over time, in density of syntax (added vocabulary, sentence combinings, element substitutions—that is, pronoun referents for nouns and noun phrases).
5. Ask yourself, what have I done to help create positive language changes in students' oral text?

REFERENCES

Bormuth, J., Manning, J., Carr, J., & Pearson, D. (1969 February). *Children's comprehension of between and within sentence syntactic structures*. Paper presented at the American Educational Research Association Conference, Los Angeles, CA.

Botel, M., & Granowsky, A. (1972). A formula for measuring syntactic complexity. *Elementary English, 49,* 513–516.

Bruner, S. J. (1964). The course of cognitive growth. *American Psychologist, 19,* 1–15.

Chomsky, N. (1975). *Reflections on language*. New York: Pantheon.

Clay, M. M., Gill, M., Glynn, T., McNaughton, T., & Salmon, K. (1983). *Record of oral language and Biks and Gutches*. Exeter, NH: Heinemann.

Coleman, E. B. (1965). Learning of prose written in four grammatical transformations. *Journal of Applied Psychology, 49,* 332–341.

Dale, P. (1976). *Language development: Structure and function* (2nd ed.). New York: Holt, Rinehart & Winston.

Eastman, P. D. (1967). *Are you my mother?* New York: Random House.

Emberley, E. (1967). *Drummer Hoff.* New York: Prentice-Hall.

Fagan, W. T. (1970). *The relationship between reading difficulty and the number of sentence transformations.* Unpublished doctoral dissertation, University of Alberta: Edmonton, Alberta.

Fagan, W. T. (1971). Transformations and comprehension. *Reading Teacher, 25,* 169–172.

Gaer, E. P. (1969). Children's understanding and productions of sentences. *Journal of verbal learning and verbal behavior, 8,* 289–294.

Galdone, P. (1974). *Little red riding hood.* New York: McGraw-Hill.

Gillet, J. W., & Temple, C. (1982). *Understanding reading problems.* Boston: Little, Brown.

Glazer, S. M. (1973). *A comparative analysis of syntax in some elementary grade reading materials.* Unpublished doctoral dissertation. University of Pennsylvania.

Glazer, S. M., & Morrow, L. M. (1978). The syntactic complexity of primary grade children's oral language and primary grade reading materials: A comparative analysis. *Journal of Reading Behavior, 10,* 200–202.

Goodman, K. S., & Burke, C. L. (1969). A study of oral reading miscues that result in grammatical retransformation: Final report (USOE study no. RR7-E-219). Detroit, MI: Wayne State University.

Greene, F. P. (1979). Radio reading. In C. Pennock (Ed.), *Reading comprehension at four linguistic levels* (pp. 104–107). Newark, DE: International Reading Association.

Halliday, M. A. (1973). *Explorations in the functions of language.* London: Edward Arnold.

Heckelman, R. G. (1969). A neurological-impress method of remedial reading instruction. *Academic Therapy, 4,* 277–282.

Hooper, M. (1985). *Seven eggs.* New York: Harper & Row.

Hunt, K. W. (1965). Grammatical structures written at three grade levels (NCTE research report no. 3). Champaign, IL: National Council of Teachers of English.

Hutchins, P. (1968). *Rosie's walk.* New York: Macmillan.

Just, M. A., & Carpenter, P. A. (1971). Comprehension of negatives with quantification. *Journal of Verbal Learning and Verbal Behavior, 10,* 244–253.

Keats, E. J. (1972). *Skates.* New York: Franklin Watts.

Kovac, C. & Cahir, S. (1981). *Away with words.* Washington, DC: Center for Applied Linguistics.

Lindfors, J. (1980). *Children's language and learning.* Englewood Cliffs, NJ: Prentice-Hall.

Loban, W. D. (1963). *The language of elementary school children* (NCTE research report no. 1). Champaign, IL: National Council of Teachers of English.

Mayer, M. (1967). *A boy, a dog, and frog.* New York: Dial.

Moffett, J. (1983). *Teaching the universe of discourse.* Boston: Houghton Mifflin.

Most, B. (1978). *If the dinosaurs came back.* New York: Harcourt Brace Jovanovich.

O'Donnell, R., Griffin, W. J., & Norris, R. C. (1967). Syntax of kindergarten and elementary school children: A transformational analysis. (NCTE research report no. 8). Champaign, IL: National Council of Teachers of English.

Perkins, A. (1969). *Hand, hand, fingers, thumb*. New York: Random House.
Quackenbush, R. (1973). *She'll be comin' round the mountain*. Philadelphia: J. B. Lippincott.
Quandt, I., & Selznick, R. (1984). *Self-concept and reading*. DE: International Reading Association.
Robertson, J. E. (1968). Pupil understanding of connections in reading. *Reading Research Quarterly, 3,* 387–417.
Ruddell, R. B. (1963). *An investigation of the effect of the similarity of oral and written patterns of language structures on reading comprehension*. Unpublished doctoral dissertation, Indiana University.
Saur, L. E. (1970). Fourth grade children's knowledge of grammatical structures. *Elementary English, 47,* 807–813.
Searfoss, L. W. (1975). Radio reading. *The Reading Teacher, 29,* 295–296.
Seuss, Dr. (1968). *Foot book*. New York: Random House.
Silvaroli, N. J., Skinner, J. T., & Maynes, R. (1985). *Oral language evaluation, teacher's manual* (2nd ed.). St. Paul, MN: EMC.
Silverstein, S. (1964). *A giraffe and a half*. New York: Harper Junior Books.
Smith, F. (1977). The use of language. *Language Arts, 54,* 638–644.
Stoodt, B. (1972). The relationship between understanding grammatical conjunctures and reading comprehension. *Elementary English, 49,* 502–504.
Strickland, R. (1962). *The language of elementary school children: Its relationship to the language of reading textbooks and the quality of reading of selected children*. Bloomington, IN: Bureau of Educational Studies and Testing.
Wagner, B. J. (1976). Dorothy Heath Cote, *Drama as a learning medium*. Washington, D.C.: National Educational Association.

SUGGESTED READING

Backlund, P., Gurry, J., Brown, K., & Jandt, F. (1980). Evaluating, speaking, and listening skill assessment instruments: Which one is best for you? *Language Arts, 57,* 621–627.
Genishi, C., & Dyson, A. (1984). *Language assessment in the early years*. Norwood, NJ: Albex.
Jaggar, A., & Smith-Burke, M. (Eds.). (1985). *Observing the language learner*. Newark, DE: International Reading Association.
Richgels, D. J. (1986). Grade school children's listening and reading comprehension of complex sentences. *Reading Research and Instruction, 25,* 201–219.
Tough, J. (1979). *Talk for teaching and learning*. London: Ward Lock Educational.

5

WRITTEN LANGUAGE FLUENCY

What Do We Measure?

Assessing Written Language Fluency

Assessing Various Elements

Guiding Students to Improve Written Language Fluency

Summary

Questions to Ponder

References

Suggested Reading

Written composition represents a form of fluency much like reading. Thus, we ask:

- How is fluency in writing related to fluency in reading?
- How do we assess written language fluency?
- How do we guide students to become fluent writers?

A rationale for understanding written composition as a process similar to reading is exemplified in the statement: "Both are acts of composing" (Tierney & Pearson, 1983). This strongly suggests that as readers interact with text, they are rewriting the author's language to create meaning so that they can make sense of the information. Readers are consciously or unconsciously composing meaning as they read. Therefore, Tierney and Pearson suggest, meaning exists in print, when the reader or writer places it there.

If students understand a text, we can assume that they have constructed meaning in the text authored by others for they—the students—have discovered ways to organize data. Organization of ideas using forms and structures of language helps the language receiver as well as the sender make thoughts available for others to inspect (Haley-James, 1982). Students learn to control ideas by delivering them in form—description, explanation, narration, and reasoning. They do this using the cognitive processes basic to every discipline (Squire, 1983). Students use prior knowledge as they read and write.

The belief that writing helps one read and reading helps one write justifies, for us, the process of assessing written language abilities through observation, testing, and interviews. We need to observe students' activities during all phases of the writing process.

WHAT DO WE MEASURE?

We assess those same variables observed in oral language behavior, but in an "upside down manner." This is demonstrated in Figure 5–1. Such a method of assessing seems appropriate since we start with the "whole piece of writing."

What Has Been Measured?

Because of previous notions about the writing process, composition has been measured in terms considering what students *cannot* accomplish. Such a paradigm for assessing writing disabilities has reinforced the anomalies syndrome

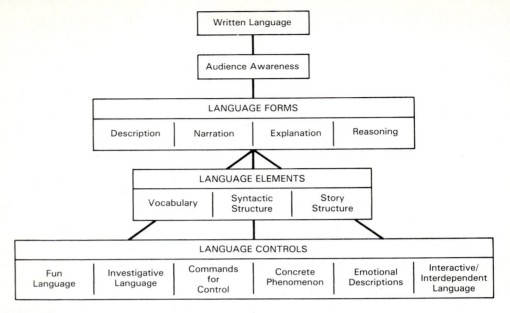

Figure 5–1

in which labels are frequently used including: agraphia (a loss of ability to produce handwriting because of disease or injury to the brain; specifically the loss of the motor and kinesthetic skills involved in writing); apraxia (the loss of the ability to make voluntary movements because of disease or injury to the brain resulting in disorders of production and sequencing of purposeful movements); dysgraphia (a mild form of apraxia involving difficulty in producing handwriting because of disease or injury to the brain). These anomalies result in problems related to physical factors; but do not usually interfere with thought processes. The ability to hold and manipulate a pen or pencil in order to hand write is physical. If we consider physical movements to be writing skills, then we must assume that they are prerequisites for composition. We agree, however, that they are prerequisites for the physical act of writing. Physical movements are *transcribing*, but not composing, skills.

Assessment of writing has in the past dealt with transcription abilities. The ladder effect in language learning had prevailed, and the steps to writing were assumed to be learning to listen first, talking next, reading, and then writing. But Ashton-Warner (1963) has clearly demonstrated that many children learn to write before they read. Writing is often the tool used by students to become readers. We are not sure which comes first, reading or writing, or even listening or speaking. We agree, however, that skills are learned interactively. The student may learn, for example, that a period means "stop" when seeing it in a sentence, not deliberately, but as a result of reading or hearing a poem that demands a drop in voice intonation.

The way writing was measured in the past also suggests that a student's "theory of life" is minimally important in compositions since transcriptions, or mechanical aspects, do not deal with interest or content. However, we know that students are motivated to produce and learn when there is interest—more than any other single factor. Measuring transcriptions without content analysis denies the power of this knowledge.

Measuring the content of written composition has its problems, however. There is a certain amount of security in assessment of those variables that are "on the page" and not related to unseen thoughts. Thus, we may never get beyond the surface level of assessment, and like diagnosticians of the past, we may continue to assess the results of thoughts, the transcriptions. We must, however, understand that we are *looking* at transcription, but will *consider ideas* by observing behaviors that lead the writer to the creation of text.

ASSESSING WRITTEN LANGUAGE FLUENCY

Information about students' written language fluency can be collected in:

1. Formal tests
2. Informal tests.

Formal Tests

Standardized tests of writing assess two types of skills: (1) knowledge of written conventions/mechanical skills—that is, punctuation, capitalization, word usage, spelling—as demonstrated in a paper-and-pencil test, usually in multiple-choice formats; (2) the student's ability to produce a sample of writing which is evaluated based on criteria for analyzing the use of specific elements. Descriptions of students' writing are restricted by the instruments that are used to evaluate them. The test descriptions in Table 5–1 should guide diagnosticians in selecting commercial materials for evaluation purposes. The fourth column notes those components of tests that can be described using the C–A–L–M model.

Informal Assessment Procedures

Informal procedures can be used for assessing growth in written language and to evaluate compositions. Observing students as they compose also helps us learn about students' strengths and needs. Developmental trends exist in writ-

Table 5–1 Descriptions of Writing Tests

TEST	DESCRIPTION	PURPOSE	C–A–L–M COMPONENTS ASSESSED
Test of Written Language (TOWL), Hamill & Larsen. PRO-ED, 1978.	Assesses word usage, style, and spelling. Illicits a writing sample based on three cartoons in a squence. Vocabulary sophistication, thought units, thematic maturity, and handwriting are measured. All variables are secured through transcription. Results reveal a scaled score used to make comparisons across subtests. Grade equivalent scores are used, but caution is indicated in interpretation by test authors. The Written Language Quotient offers an index of cognitive abilities across subtests.	To identify students who perform significantly poorer than peers; to trace students' strengths and needs in various writing abilities; to document progress in special writing programs; to conduct research in writing.	Vocabulary, Syntax, Organization or story sense
Stanford Writing Assessment Program, Gardner, Rudman, Karlsen, Merwin. The Psychological Corporation, 1983.	There are three parts to this program: primary, intermediate 1, and intermediate 2. In each, four kinds (forms) of writing are assessed: describing, narrating, explaining, and reasoning. These forms are observed and general merit, quantity and quality of ideas, effectiveness of organization, wording, syntactic structure, and mechanics are evaluated. A rating sheet is provided for each type and kind of writing. Several raters are requested to read and evaluate materials. Scores from 1 to 7 describe student performance.	To conduct schoolwide survey of students' writing abilities; to diagnose strengths and weaknesses in writing; to improve instruction through staff development and teaching suggestions.	Vocabulary Syntax Organization Forms: description narration explanation reasoning
The Picture Story Language Test (PSLT), Myklebust. Grune and Stratton, 1965.	Test includes a photograph of a young boy playing with miniature dolls and furniture. The student is asked to write the best story possible. The story is analyzed. There is no story sequence implied in the photo, therefore forcing the student to set direction for composition. Five levels of scoring are included.	Developed as a measure of effective written communication assessing quality of productivity, syntax, and abstract concreteness of content. Concerned with transcription aspects of writing without including variables such as handwriting and spelling.	Syntax Organization Forms: description explanation narration reasoning

ing as they do in speaking. We know that young children construct meaningful messages using symbols available to them from their environment and from their comprehension of print (Bissex, 1980; Clay, 1975; Harste, Burke, & Woodward, 1981). Research evidence to support the natural development of writing, similar to oral language development, is beginning to appear in the literature (Baghban, 1984; Bissex, 1980, Glazer, 1984). The natural "learning-to-write" process occurs when the learning environment supports students' early efforts to communicate thoughts in writing, even though the communication may be far from standard orthography. Students should be able to produce written language naturally when adults accept and support students' intent and when the setting encourages composition in a friendly, warm manner. Table 5–2, culled from several sources (Bissex, 1980; Glazer, 1980; Temple, Nathan, & Burris, 1982; Baghban, 1984; Hannan & Hamilton, 1984), is a chart describing developmental levels of writing. These are suggested to provide teacher-researchers with guidelines in order to compare student performance over time. The chart should be used cautiously, and as a guide for determining changes in stage of development, as each student grows.

The chart in Figure 5–2 should be used as a tool for assessing students' writing stages. The checklist *summarizes* data from observations; the following are tentative developmental stages through which most youngsters move.

Table 5–2 Developmental Stages of Writing

BEHAVIOR	IMPLICATION	ACTION TO BE TAKEN—TEACHER OR SPECIALIST
STAGE 1: PREWRITING STAGE		
Scribbles and draws and names these. Has no preconceived notion about what will evolve. Shows interest in words and letters.	The child is aware that print has meaning. Ideas can be communicated through pictures and words.	Paints, crayons, pencils, brushes, pens and markers, crafts for constructing objects, varieties of paper are important. Books with tapes and visuals (filmstrips) encourage written language. Books with "fun language" and predictable plots, alphabet books, books with language patterns (songs and rhyming books) are needed.
Demonstrates consciousness of self by drawing markings that resemble body movements. Preplanning does exist. Will often work on written project for longer periods of time (more than one sitting). Will describe creation orally when drawing. Letters are often included in drawing. Space relationships are surfacing and self-criticism begins.	Understands that adults communicate by writing. Needs adult recognition of written production. Values writing and needs to feel ownership.	Same as above.
Recognizes and reproduces letters. Knows sounds of some letters as illustrated by naming them. Writes words by inventing spellings. Recognizes that letters make words and words make sentences. Plays with spelling and sentence patterns.	The student is ready to represent thoughts in written form. Student is aware of conventions in the written coding system: Words are made from several letters. Each word is a unit. Several words are made from several units of letters placed together. The student is aware of sentence (syntactic form) structures. This is demonstrated when he/she places several word units together to represent thoughts. Student is hypothesizing and experimenting with the coding system by constructing words, phrases and sentences, demonstrating that there is a rule system already developed concerning written language construction.	Productions must be accepted without comment. Consideration of mechanical aspects, comments about spacing between words and spelling should occur with intention to guide students to use regular spelling conventions if appropriate and when possible. Plan the following: regular reading of books with regular spelling and sentence patterns (i.e., Dr. Seuss *Go Dog Go, Ten Apples up on Top*); individual conferences; having student tell you about the story; having student read story to you and see if you understand it—then retell it to student and ask the child to correct you. Make a folder for collecting students' writings. Encourage students to keep materials produced in the folder.

Table 5–2 Continued

BEHAVIOR	IMPLICATION	ACTION TO BE TAKEN—TEACHER OR SPECIALIST
STAGE 2: THE BEGINNING WRITER		
Begins to label drawings and caption pictures that are self-drawn. Writes long sentences using connectives—mostly "and."	Same as above.	Same as above.
Writes a list of sentences using the same pattern (i.e., I like a dog. I like ice cream. I like candy. I like to play.) Does not seem to be aware of a story line.	Has found a rule for constructing written text. Relies on familiar pattern for security. Is aware of syntactic forms for sharing ideas in a systematic fashion.	Read books developed in list format for students (see appendix A). Write lists of things.
Writes lists of sentences that include ideas as in above sample.	Uses list construction demonstrating that an awareness of structure (organization) is needed in composition.	Create lists of things and titles. Words or phrases should relate to topic of list (i.e., Halloween Things, Ice Cream Flavors, Summer Activities, etc.).
Writing includes consistent content but also demonstrates a graphic display, (consistent sentence or pattern). Graphic displays also include illustration. Is developing a sense of story.	Student understands that writing represents a written coding system and the code represents visual images, objects, and ideas.	Create text and ask youngster to illustrate. Read books that have pictures but no words (See appendix A.)
Content is full of personal experiences. Wants to share these with others.	Is developing power over written language and begins to demonstrate audience awareness.	Encourage diary writing (see Chapter 6). Read books to students that follow diary format.
Requests correct use of spelling and/or punctuation.	Understands that a consistent form is necessary for preparing text for an audience to read and comprehend.	Instruction in construction of language—particularly the coding system—is encouraged. (See Chapter 7.) Read books with regular and irregular spelling patterns (e.g., Dr. Seuss' *One Fish, Two Fish, Red Fish, Blue Fish* deals with "*ish*" spelling pattern). Play punctuation games.
Begins to overuse structures, based on rules of language (i.e., I wented or I goed.).	Student has internalized a rule (convention) and is using it.	Confer with student and encourage him/her to tell what is happening. This helps child understand protocols used for producing written language.
Writing increases in length daily.	Is aware that writing must be structured with a beginning, middle, and an end, and in sequence.	Student is becoming a writer. May profit from story sense activities. See Chapters 6 and 7.

Table 5–2 Continued

BEHAVIOR	IMPLICATION	ACTION TO BE TAKEN—TEACHER OR SPECIALIST
Begins to demonstrate concern for legibility of handwriting. Might say "Can you read this?" or may erase, or cross out, or begin again on a new sheet of paper.	Is aware of audience beyond immediate environment.	Same as above. Will need more individual time and peer teaming for beginning editing development, rewriting, etc.
STAGE 3: THE EMERGENT WRITER		
Writes (1) to inform other, (2) to persuade, (3) to command, (4) to question (uses variety of language controls).	Is aware, probably unconsciously, that written language can control environment.	Instruction is recommended for (1) understanding purposes for writing and (2) appropriate form usage to meet purposes.
Uses many words and phrases, in several content areas. Begins to use a variety of syntactic structures, including sentence additions and rearrangements, deletions, and substitutions.	Writes in oral language form, much like speaking.	Instruction in understanding the writing forms can be used across content.
May use dialogue as in a script. If given assignment, can focus thoughts through writing.	Is aware that forms help to transmit message. Is gaining confidence in using the written coding system.	

Assessing Forms in Written Composition

Written forms are determined by the author's intent. The composer asks "Who is my audience?" "What do I want to say?" "How will I organize the information to say it in order to pass it to the reader?" There are four forms used by writers: description, narration, explanation, and reasoning or persuasion.

Procedures for Description

When describing we draw a picture in writing. Effective description in fiction and nonfiction prose depends upon the author's ability to draw pictures using details. Think how you would describe, for example, your home. Do you take a mental walking tour beginning at the entrance and moving through, stopping to describe the most important rooms first and in most detail? Most of us do. We move visually through space, situations, and even text materials describing information in detail. We organize information in a map-like way. The effectiveness of description depends on several factors including order of information, consistency of the information ordered, and comprehensiveness of details (Stahl, 1974).

Oral composition can be transcribed to create written text.

How can we assess students' "mental walking tours?" To begin, collect writing samples over a period of one month or more. Writing samples must be compositions whose topics have been created by students.

Students, when relaxed, will begin to select topics without guidance. Once students write their compositions, select two or three, evaluate them using the checklist in Figure 5–3, and determine the students' abilities to effectively "describe." Use the checklist and your synthesis of the information to draw interpretations.

The responses on the checklist should ideally be "Yes" to all questions. An effective descriptive composition should form a mental picture of the topic in one's mind. Assessing several student papers over time should demonstrate growth trends. Describing changes, by noting moves from the "No" to the "Yes" columns, offers a way of illustrating students' growth and needs.

Procedures for Narration

Narration, unlike description, requires an order in story, from beginning to end. Students must be aware of their audience in order to create effective narratives. Narratives created in natural settings are invented stories and

Figure 5–2 Checklist to Assess Child's Writing Stage

BEHAVIOR	YES	NO	NO EVIDENCE
STAGE 1: PREWRITING			
Scribbles without preconception			
Shows interest in words and letters			
Preplans writing and drawing projects			
Spends longer periods on these projects			
Emergence of space relationships and self-criticisms			
Recognizes and names letters			
Invents spelling			
STAGE 2: THE BEGINNING WRITER			
Labels drawings			
Makes listing of same-pattern sentences			
Develops a sense of story			
Includes personal experiences in writing			
Overuses structures			
Requests help with spelling, punctuation, and legibility			
STAGE 3: THE EMERGENT WRITER			
Writes with purpose			
Uses a variety of content for composition			
Can focus thoughts through writing			

Summary Statement: _____

Stage: _____

imaginative events. They may be student accounts of actual experiences. We know that it is best to secure writing samples that come naturally from children. Output in assigned writing is limited (Graves, 1983). So, narratives collected for diagnostic purposes must be those written by students in climates that relax them so that they write naturally. These exist when:

1. Writing is part of a daily recreational activity—as in diary or journal writing.
2. Writing used to express personal ideas is valued highly.
3. Writing occurs spontaneously.

These conditions help students create self-initiated compositions.

Written Language Fluency 93

Figure 5–3 Assessing Descriptive Writing

DESCRIPTION OF VARIABLES	YES	NO	NEED MORE DATA
ORDER OF INFORMATION			
1. Does student order information explicitly? Uses numbers, ideas, or facts? Identifies order with letters (a,b,c,etc.)? Uses vocabulary such as "first, next, last"?			
2. Does student order information implicitly? Incorporates order intuitively, describing from most to least important elements? Describes according to size, (i.e., from largest to smallest)? Organizes according to distance (i.e., far to near)? Uses adjectives to generate order (e.g., the great, big, orange and black, creepy, crawly spider . . .)?			
INFORMATION CONSISTENCY			
3. Does the student remain on topic and in order? Are descriptive words synonymous throughout? Is distance between noun phrase and descriptor reasonable so information can be recalled easily? (e.g., Eleanor is a happy person. She likes people.)			
DETAILS			
4. Are details comprehensive? Are there several descriptors used for topic or idea description? Are descriptors words (i.e., large, happy, energetic)? Are descriptors phrases (i.e., extra long, just so-so, very hungry)? Is there a mixture of words and phrases that describes details?			
5. Does the student arrange information appropriately considering purpose and topic?			

COMMENTS AND INTERPRETATIONS: _____

Since we are interested in gaining information about students' narrative abilities when they write in natural, unassigned writing tasks, we must assume that the environment in which you observe students has a "built-in" free writing period. Narratives might appear in journals, as short stories, or in dialogues. If you need additional writing samples to demonstrate the students' abilities to write in narrative form, you might use the following story starters to secure a series of writing samples. Once you provide "starters," the sample must be classified as assigned writing.

- One evening I was walking on a road. All of a sudden I heard a loud bang, and crashes coming from somewhere in the distance. I was alone. I could not see far down the road. All of a sudden the sounds stopped.
- It all began with Dad saying, "Things are going to change around here."
- The cave was dark. The only light came from the opening. All of a sudden, a loud voice was heard, and darkness filled the cave.
- There were three teenagers who . . .
- John saw a large flash of what he thought was fire in the sky.
- There Tim was, all alone, without any money and nowhere near a telephone.
- Sally stood frozen stiff. Her hands began to perspire, her heart pounded in her chest, and she shook as she looked in the distance. Little did she dream that . . .

Use these and other story starters to collect writing samples when students have difficulty creating story independently. Assess the narrative with the guide in Figure 5–4.

Procedures for Explanation

When we explain we discuss actions. Details are included and all steps explicit. When one step is omitted, then the process of written explanation fails. This prose form often combines description as well as narration for effectiveness. Topics to encourage writing for assessing the students' ability to explain might include the following:

How to Set a Table
How to Play Chess
Directions to My Grandmother's House
How to Get to My Best Friend's House
How to Bake a Cake
How to Write a Research Paper
How to Ski
How to Earn Money
How to Maintain a Bicycle

Figure 5–4 Assessing Narrative Writing

	YES	NO	NEED MORE DATA
1. The student is writing to an audience. That audience is _____.			
2. The narrative has a main a. focus, or b. character.			
3. The narrative includes a series of related events about the focus character.			
4. The narrative includes a setting.			
5. The topic is carried throughout the narrative.			
6. If a story, events include: a. beginning b. ending c. middle series of events d. supporting characters.			

Comments and Interpretations: _____

_____

Collect samples as you would for descriptive or narrative writing. Use the checklist in Figure 5–5 to assess written explanations.

Procedures for Reasoning or Persuasion

Unlike description, narration, and explanation, reasoning and persuasion require that the author create new ideas. There is generally little or no concrete "imagery" in one's mind during prewriting. Often reasoning results from writers' imaginations and their ability to predict future events. If, for example, the student desires to persuade a parent that he/she should be permitted to drive the family's new car, reasoning must include probable parental reactions, ways to deal with reactions, several desirable alternatives, and—finally—effective persuasion.

Reasoning takes many forms. The most straightforward is problem solution. We suggest that you present students with problems to solve. Use the checklist in Figure 5–6 to guide observation. Suggested items to encourage composition follow:

Figure 5–5 Assessing Explanatory Writing

EXPLANATION	YES	NO	NEED MORE DATA
1. The student has explained information so that one can follow instructions.			
2. The language used: a. is clear, free from extraneous words b. explains consistently throughout.			
3. There is an obvious progression of order: a. project or process can be completed easily b. Reader knows when the end is near c. reader can move from the beginning to end without rereading.			

Comments and Interpretations: _____
(Note: All items in the list should be checked "Yes" if clarity exists in the explanation.)

- You are not doing well in school. What can you do to get out of going to school?
- You do not agree with our taxation system. How would you change it so that you might benefit?
- Convince your parents that you do not have to eat "good food," that you can grow eating junk food instead.
- Convince your parents that television watching helps you become a better student.
- You are convinced that the school year should be eight instead of ten months long. Convince the president of the school board to pass this rule.

The procedures for observing students' compositions are starting points. Develop further instruments using these as guides. There is a great need for the development of descriptive procedures for assessing writing forms. Use instruments cautiously and continue to add information to the checklists in order to define your students' writing abilities.

Quantitative Scoring of Written Language

We believe that descriptive analyses of written language provide insight into students' strengths. Collecting writing samples and using the evaluative tools provided in this text will assist you in producing some descriptive analyses.

Figure 5–6 Assessing Reasoning and Persuasion

REASONING/PERSUASION	YES	NO	NEED MORE DATA

1. The student:
   a. takes a point of view, and
   b. stays with it throughout the piece.
2. The student writes convincingly using:
   a. information from prior knowledge
   b. arguments that are supported with emotional descriptions
   c. arguments that are supported concretely.
3. The writer convinces the audience to believe the desired outcome.			

Comments and Interpretations: _____
(Note: The most efficient way to observe a student's ability to reason or persuade in written form is to ask yourself, "What is the student's purpose? Does that student accomplish that goal? Would you be convinced, if you were the reader, to take action as a result of the composition?")

We sometimes find it necessary, however, to use instruments that can also produce quantitative scores.

Traditionally, growth has meant higher scores. Therefore, we are including scoring systems so professionals can produce growth data based on scores and, simultaneously, produce descriptive analyses of changes over time.

Holistic Scoring Systems

Because the effectiveness of writing tasks depends on the composer's ability to manipulate syntax and word usage, idea expressions, coherence, and text organization, an overall or holistic scoring system seems appropriate. Holistic scoring attempts to provide a "whole" impression of the writer's ability to communicate ideas in response to an audience. Several scoring systems have emerged during the past decade.

The most widely used holistic evaluation systems score the general impressions of the evaluator. A second holistic approach focuses upon a set of criteria, but offers flexibility in the definition of score points. It is more stable than holistic scoring that depends solely upon raters' impressions.

The system we have selected is just one of many available systems. This system, developed by Greenhalgh and Townsend (1981),[1] derives its score by comparing writing samples with descriptions of expected behavior for each level, ranging from 0 through 4. These descriptions follow as presented by the authors.

0 = These papers are not scorable because they are blank or fail in other ways to respond to the assignment. They include:

- Papers that do not respond in any way to the required writing task regardless of how well organized and free from mechanical errors they may be
- Papers that respond only to the fact of the assignment (for example, "I hate this test!")
- Blank paper
- Papers that say "I don't know."
- Papers that copy or paraphrase assignments
- Papers that are illegible
- Papers written in a language other than English

1 = Papers that address the topic in a manner that does not demonstrate success with the task. These papers consider the verbal or visual cues in a marginal way. Responses may include the following:

- Narratives that are expressive in purpose instead of referential; that is, the writer attempts to relate a story and somewhere in that story the purpose is mentioned; episodes are narrated without sequence
- A referential response that classifies instead of narrates; that is, the writer simply lists the items pictured and tells what purpose each serves
- A referential response that falls into the category of "all I know about the topic"
- A referential response that simply describes the items observed
- A response using confused syntax resulting incoherence

2 = Papers that respond to the task, that is, they explain the steps or sequence in a skeletal or an inconsistent manner. These papers require the reader to infer a great deal and may often be confusing because of gaps in sequencing or because the information is poorly organized. These papers may include any or all of the following elements:

- A response in which the steps in a process or story are presented in a skeletal, bare fashion; there is little or no elaboration or detail requiring the reader to infer a great deal
- A process or story that may not be related in a straightforward sequence, skipping about leaving the reader confused

---

[1] Sections of article, "Evaluating students' writing holistically" reprinted with permission of the National Council of Teachers of English.

- A sequence in which there may be major gaps
- An explanation that may contain major inconsistencies
- A sample that may contain extraneous information that actually detracts from the effectiveness of the text; the writer may wander about and include too much additional information that causes the reader to lose sight of the main idea, wondering where the writer is going

3 = These papers do an effective job of explaining or story telling. Confusion, if any, is kept to a minimum and the reader would have to do very little inferring to follow the steps or story. These writers include details and elaboration not found in "2" papers that further aid the reader in visualizing through text. Some of the following elements may also be found in papers at this level:

- A straightforward sequential presentation, usually using words such as first, next, or then; there may be minor gaps in the explanation or procedures that are not stated clearly, but omissions can be readily inferred
- An explanation or description that goes a little beyond basic steps
- A response that includes a varied choice of words, specific details, or elaboration helping the reader visualize
- A response that may include material not essential to the explanation, such as including the explanation within the context of a narrative; but this material does not detract—or does so only in a minimal way—from the writer's accomplishing the stated purpose
- An explanation that shows the writer is aware of an audience through the inclusion of comments such as, "Do you understand so far?"

4 = Papers at this level are unified, well organized, and elaborated and the reader has to do virtually no inferring to visualize the process or story. Papers scored at this level contain all of the elements listed for the previous level; however, they are presented with greater clarity and consistency. These papers are characterized by the following elements:

- A response in which the writer clearly organizes and elaborates on the major steps or story so that the reader has no difficulty in following sequence
- An explanation that may go beyond the basic procedure or story line for the purpose of elaboration
- A response that includes an introductory comment ("I am going to tell you how") and/or a concluding comment ("And that's how I would do it"); Such comments indicate that the writer is aware of an audience, assumes that the reader has come to the text without prior knowledge.

The following writing activity and samples shown in the figures were assessed using the 0–4 scoring system described here. This activity can be used for students at all levels.

Activity for Soliciting Writing Sample for Holistic Scoring

Materials for "How to Set a Table."

> composition paper
> writing tools (pencils, pens, crayons, markers)
> paper or plastic dinner plates
> paper or plastic forks, knives, spoons
> paper napkins
> plastic or paper cups
> plastic or paper bowls

Purpose. To collect data in order to assess students' ability to explain, narrate, or describe to an audience how to carry out an activity.

Prewriting activity procedure. A prewriting activity is recommended. The examiner may put a coat, hat, briefcase, and other outer garments on a chair. Question to Students: I have to get ready to go to a meeting. I am about to put on the rest of my clothing. Someone tell me what to do.

As students begin to explain the directions, examiner must follow *exactly*. The purpose is to help students see that each step must be explained, thoroughly, in order for the listener to understand.

Instructions to students for writing activity. Say: "You are having company for the dinner. Many people. You want to set the table ahead of time and need help. Write directions for your friend, who has agreed to help, that will tell 'how to set the table.' Remember, this friend does not know how to set a table and has never done it before."

Examples of students' writing in response to this activity—as well as annotated evaluations of the writing—are presented in Figures 5–7, 5–8, 5–9.

Evaluation: Sample 1 (Figure 5–7) received a score of 1. The writer attends to the task, but in a skeletal way. The reader must infer a great deal about

Figure 5–7 Sample 1: How to Set A Table. Student: 13 Years, 9 Months; Grade 6

First I would go to the table a seat the people. Then I would put the plates down. the I would do the knifs a serewear. Then I would server food.

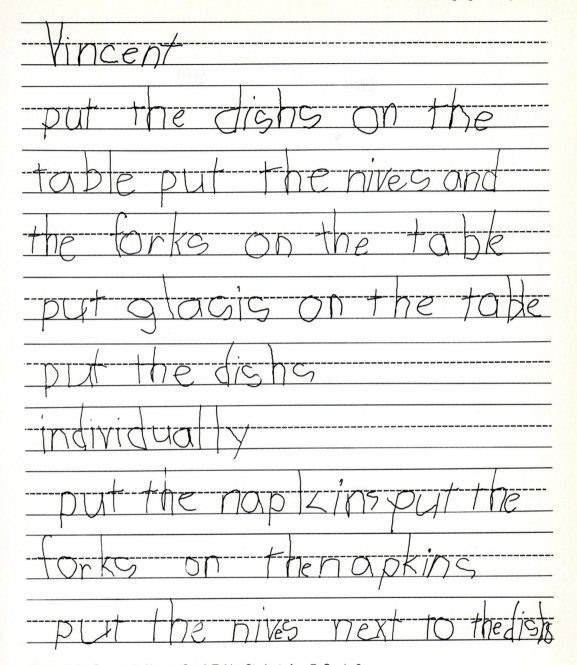

Figure 5–8 Sample 2: How to Set A Table. Student: Age 7; Grade 2

setting a table from this passage. The student seems to have a sense of order and timing, since there is a sequence of proposed events. Setting a table using these directions would be almost impossible. If this were written by a student in the early grades a higher score might be given. Considering the age and stage, a score of 1 seems appropriate.

Evaluation: Vincent's sample (Figure 5–8) has earned a score of 2. The run-on sentences without attention to capitalization at the beginning of each indicates lack of audience awareness. The score does indicate, however, that there is direction and focus. There is sequence, but little elaboration, providing a sense of order to the activity. Explanation exists minimally in narrative form.

Evaluation: Sample 3 (Figure 5–9) earned a score of 3+ since the author elaborates by preparing the audience for the activity. Third person (you) is used demonstrating awareness that the reader is being directed into action. Direction is given in narrative form, in sequence order. The author personalizes the explanation for the reader by using direct terms "Put the fork on your left." The detail concerning placement of objects provides adequate description. This paper includes everything but suggestions for completing the activity. If that were included, it would have earned a score of 4.

ASSESSING VARIOUS ELEMENTS

Empowered students construct well-managed prose and are aware, intuitively or consciously, that there must be relationships between the author and reader, the speaker and listener. If well-constructed, words, phrases, sentences, paragraphs, and larger units of discourse will "hang together" cohesively. Flexibility in use of elements determines success. Students must have, built into their memories, words and phrases and arrangements of these (syntactic structures) in order to be flexible writers.

To evaluate students' power to use elements flexibly, it seems appropriate for us to suggest that we examine elements separately. We agree that this seems to be a contradiction, for observing the "whole" composition is our goal. However, we can observe a prose piece using holistic scoring systems *first*, then look at elements, and finally synthesize all results evaluating students' ability to control elements to create a powerful "whole" piece of writing. When assessing students' writing, it is important to consider: syntactic structure, story structure, audience awareness (discussed in the next section), and vocabulary (discussed in a later chapter).

The density of syntax determines the intricateness of text. The sentence structure, arrangements, rearrangements, additions, deletions, and embeddings used by the writer reflect the ability of that writer to manipulate lan-

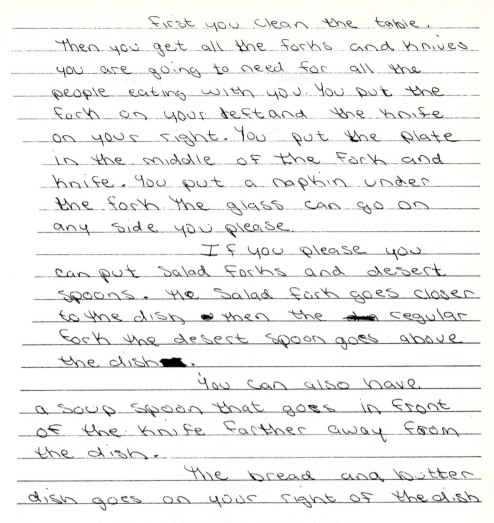

Figure 5-9 Sample 3: How to Set A Table. Student: 14 Years; Grade 8

guage effectively for communicating. The research review in Chapter 4 (pages 58–59) indicates how the developmental sophistication of element usage is determined. Syntax pulls elements together, unifying ideas. Additional questions follow which should help you further to observe syntactic complexity in written composition. These used in conjunction with Figure 4–3 in Chapter 4, will guide observations of written text.

- What syntactic elements does the student use to "tie" composition together?
- What syntactic changes are observed in student's writing over time?

- What indicates these changes?
- What syntactic changes are noted in writing that might result from interactions with literature (as the result of reading or hearing text)?

A series of samples of students' writing must be accumulated in order to assess changes in syntactic element use over time. These samples could be accumulated from the first week of school and periodically thereafter (weekly), so samples can then be compared. Analyzing written syntax should be conducted using procedures found on pages 60–65 of Chapter 4. Story structure and organization are discussed further in Chapter 6. Measuring tools are included.

Audience Awareness

Because the writer generally lacks physical and social surroundings when producing written communication, audience awareness must be built into the student's mind. This is difficult, for written communication lacks the para-

linguistic, postural, and natural cues that help the receiver of the language to establish meaning (Gumperz, Kaltzman, & O'Conner, 1983). These expressions are eliminated. The language therefore, must be intricate with syntatic and lexical elaboration to substitute for the lack of expressiveness in prose (Kreeft, 1984). Writers usually know that they are writing for someone else but the unskilled writer has little knowledge of how to do this deliberately (Kroll, 1978). Student writers must be able to guide themselves to create prose with a sense of what the reader will understand. There are a number of factors that make text appropriate for audience. In order to develop a sense of audience in text, the writer must be aware of the:

1. Appropriate vocabulary for the audience
2. Syntactic elements that make text effective
3. Logical order and sequence of events
4. Punctuation that carries messages universally
5. Details that help to impart information descriptively
6. Repetition of ideas in different forms—phrases, words, and structures—to communicate effectively with audience.

We ask the following questions about students' awareness of audience when assessing the developed skills in this element of composition:

- Is the student aware of the audience for which the prose is being written?
- What elements of writing (style, vocabulary, syntactic structures) does the student use to prepare the text for the appropriate audience?

Procedures for assessing audience awareness. It is important to understand that students, at certain ages, are egocentric and have difficulty writing for others. Piaget believes that children lose their gross egocentrism by the time they are seven or eight (Piaget, 1955). Kroll points out that while the total commitment to self begins to wane at these ages, refining egocentric behaviors continues throughout childhood and into adolescent years (1978). Once students can put themselves in the place of others, egocentric behaviors decline and students can play the roles of others in order to project ideas appropriate for the receiver of the communication. Moffett (1983) emphasizes the problems that occur when writers fail to allow for audience needs. Diagnosticians must be aware of the fact that it might be impossible to project for others until one can project away from self. Although age is a major factor in this element, stages of development determine readiness for audience writing. Even an adult writer can remain so egocentric that audience needs are ignored and details such as repetition, punctuation, and elaborated prose, for example, will only be included if the ego of the writer finds these necessary.

Evaluation of audience awareness will be based on inclusion of features necessary for communication to audiences at several distances. Moffett (1983) describes the audience distancing between speaker and audience, that is, between first and second person, as follows:

Reflection: Intrapersonal communication between two parts of one nervous system.
Conversation: Interpersonal communication between two people in vocal range.
Correspondence: Interpersonal communication between remote individuals or small groups with small personal knowledge of each other.
Publication: Interpersonal communication to a large anonymous group extended over space and time.

The scoring system in Figure 5–10 may be reproduced for each sample developed by students over time. Audience awareness includes effective use of all elements. The total, therefore, provides an overview of all elements of written

Figure 5–10 Scoring Audience Awareness

Audience Distancing level _____
(Select one: Reflection; Conversation; Correspondence; Publication, and write it on line above.)

	POOR								SUPERIOR
Paper addresses topic.	1	2	3	4	5	6	7	8	9	10
Vocabulary used carries message to audience. Includes various verb phrases, adverbials, and adjectives to aid interest. The words used meet the criteria necessary to fulfill the assignment.	1	2	3	4	5	6	7	8	9	10
Syntax is varied and inclusive: Each structure includes a kernel and supporting dependent elements. Additions, substitutions, deletions, rearrangements are used to add to interest to grammatical structure.	1	2	3	4	5	6	7	8	9	10
Organization seems logical and orderly. There are sufficient events (ideas) to support, clarify, reinforce message being delivered.	1	2	3	4	5	6	7	8	9	10
Punctuation markings add to the audience's perception of message delivered in an effective manner.	1	2	3	4	5	6	7	8	9	10
Details that help to describe ideas to an audience are relevant.	1	2	3	4	5	6	7	8	9	10
Repetition of words, ideas, sentence structures are used to communicate effectively with the intended audience.	1	2	3	4	5	6	7	8	9	10

Comments and Interpretations: _____

Total score: _____ Average: _____

language. This might be considered a form of holistic evaluation. We observe the whole piece of writing and derive an overall score.

As an example of how to use this system, let us look at the composition "Monsters" by eleven-year-old Stephi. The composition is presented in Figure 5–11 and evaluated in Figure 5–12. A look at the checklist rating Stephi's work illustrates this evaluation method.

Procedures for guiding students to awareness of audience. A group discussion seems to be the best way to begin instruction in audience awareness. The following questions must be considered when constructing your lesson:

- How old are these youngsters?
- What questions must I ask to guide them to be aware that when they write, they *must* consider their reader?

Figure 5–11 Stephi's Composition (Reprinted with Permission of Josephine and Joel Clark, Parents of Stephanie.)

> Stephi Clark
>
> Monsters
>
> Beyond the door is an whole bunch of monsters. The monsters try to scare me. One monster is hiding behind the door, all the sudden the monster jumps out. Their are about five monsters. Three of them are big. The other two monsters are very small. They are all purple. They are a very nice color. The monsters grabbed me. I pulled their claws away from my clothes and then I ran out of the tunnel, all the sudden, they were following me, but then I hid in a bunch of ~~bush~~ and they left and went into the tunnel. I then ran all the way home.

Written Language Fluency

Figure 5–12 Scoring Stephi's Composition

Audience Distancing Level: <u>mostly conversational</u>
Paper addresses topic requested by examiner. 8

Vocabulary used carries message to audience. Includes various verb phrases, adverbials, and adjectives to add interest. The words used meet the criteria necessary to fulfill assignment. 2

Syntax is varied, and inclusive: Each structure includes a kernel and some supporting elements. Additions, substitutions, deletions, rearrangements are used to add interest to grammatical structures. 3

Organization seems logical and orderly. There are sufficient events (ideas) to support, clarify, and reinforce message being delivered. 2

Punctuation markings add to the audience's perception of message in an effective manner. 5

Details that help to describe ideas to an audience are relevant. 3

Repetitions of words, ideas, sentence structures are used to communicate effectively with the intended audience. 2

Total score = 25 Average = 3.5

Comments: Stephi's audience awareness score is observed by adding the total scores and dividing by seven, the number of variables included in the scale. Her composition demonstrates a sense of audience awareness. She has used minimal syntactic variation, which has resulted in a rather "mundane" text. Thoughts are consistent with the monsters; but are presented in no logical order or in a sequence. Vocabulary is rather dry, with minimal use of additions or substitutions. There is a sense of awareness of appropriate format for sharing, since punctuation seems appropriate. The writer has used conversational form in most of the text. This is demonstrated by the use of past tense verb forms (I hid, I pulled, etc.). If additional samples demonstrate abilities described above it seems that the student needs to use strategies to develop sensitivity to audience by writing dialogue and presenting it to a live audience for rehearsal purposes.

The following are questions you can ask students to focus discussion and compositions.

Audience awareness activity. Ask questions of students as follows:

1. When you want something from your parents that they do not want you to have, how do you ask them?
2. If you disagree with something your teacher did, how would you convince her/him that he/she is wrong? What kinds of words would you use?

3. If you want to convince your priest, minister, or rabbi about a certain matter, what would you say to him/her?
4. How would you convince a friend that he/she should do something (play, go on a trip, etc.) with you?

Following the discussion help students to compare the language elements and tone used with each. Questions to guide them might include:

- How would your discussion with your parents be different from the one with your teacher?
- How would the discussion with your (minister, rabbi, priest) be different from the one with your parents (teacher, friend)?

If you wish, next have students write a response to one of the activity questions. Before students write, be sure that they indicate on their papers, the audience to whom the information is directed.

GUIDING STUDENTS TO IMPROVE WRITTEN LANGUAGE FLUENCY

Written language fluency can be encouraged using: (1) designated time periods for all in the environment to write, and (2) writing activities to stimulate reluctant writers.

Designated periods for writing should occur at the same time each day. During that time period all in the room—teachers and students—write. This is important, for working "next to" teachers and peers provides models for behavior important for the reluctant writer. Three to fifteen minutes daily is recommended. Begin with three and increase to fifteen minutes when appropriate. A relaxed, comfortable environment is necessary in order to help students write freely.

A number of *writing activities* can be used to stimulate reluctant writers. To guide students to compose descriptive, explanatory, or narrative prose, stimuli directed toward these writing forms must be available for students to select. Idea cards can be placed in the writing area for students. Guided selection should occur when students say "I don't know what to write." We recommend list-making and problem-solving activities for developing writing skills.

List-Making Activities

Procedures: Place idea cards in shoe boxes. Label each box "Ideas for Writing." Topics on cards should be three types: (1) ideas that are concrete in nature where students can observe and record lists of objects in the environment; (2)

ideas based on prior knowledge; and (3) ideas based on emotions and feelings generated by one's ideas about life. The list in Table 5–3 provides ideas. We have included the writing form and level imposed by the topic. However, only the idea should be written on a card—one on each.

Problem-Solving Activities

In this section are exmples of problem-solving activities for three different age groups.

Ages six through eleven:

1. You want to sleep at your friend's house. Your mother does not want you to. What will you say to convince her that it is O.K.? Give two reasons. Identify to whom you are writing.
2. You want a new bicycle. Your old one is not the right color. How will you convince your parents that it is important to have a bike in the newest color? Give two reasons. Who is your audience?
3. You think that you need an increase in your allowance. Give your parents three reasons for raising your allowance. Who are you convincing.?
4. Almost everyone in your class has a computer at home. Your parents do not want one. Try to convince them that it is important. Give at least two reasons why. Who are you asking?

The following is an example of an activity-problem and one student's solution:

You have a problem. You got a C on your first research paper in school. You do not think that you deserve it. What would you do? Give two alternatives.

Signed, *Miss Disturbed*

Dear Miss Disturbed,
 You have a problem. Here are two solutions. (1) Tell your teacher you did not receive the C. If that doesn't work then (2) ask if you can do the paper again. If that doesn't work, well, take the C. It isn't worth the effort.

Signed, *A Friend*

Table 5–3 Suggested Topics for List-Making Activities

IDEA	FORM	TYPE
Make a list of blue things you see here.	description	concrete
Make a list of your favorite things in this room.	description	concrete
Make a list of books in the room that you like.	description	concrete
Make a list of materials that you need for writing that are in this room now.	description	concrete
Make a list of things that you would like to have in this room, that are not here now.	description	prior experience
Make a list of things that you like to do when you are not in school.	description	prior experience
Make a list of things you did on your last vacation.	description	prior experience
Tell me how you got here today. Do it in a list format.	explanation	prior experience
List, in order, all the things that you do in one day.	description	prior experience
Tell me, in a list, how you would make one of the following: (1) a cake, (2) a doll house, (3) a model airplane.	explanation	prior experience or prior knowledge
Tell me, in a list, one of the following: (1) how to set a table; (2) how to earn money; (3) how to play checkers; (4) how to get to your house from here; (5) how to get a book out of the library.	explanation	prior experience or prior knowledge
Tell, in a list, how you feel when you think that you can't pass a test in school.	narration	prior knowledge and feelings
Use words to describe your best friend. Put them in a list. You can use phrases, if you want—that is, two or three words together.	description	feelings and concrete
Tell how you felt last time you had a birthday.	narration	feelings and prior knowledge
Tell how you feel when you get 100% on a school test. Describe your feelings in words, and put them in a list.	description/narration	feelings and prior knowledge
Tell, in a story form, about your trip to the circus (zoo, movies, your friend's house, your grandparent's home, etc). Do *not* use numbers in this composition. Write each idea, one after the other, like a story.	narration	prior knowledge
Tell a story about the time you had fun with your best friend.	narration	prior knowledge
Tell about the vacation your parents are planning.	narration	feelings based on ideas about life
Tell about your favorite television show. Tell what happened.	narration	prior knowledge
Tell how you think you would feel if you were an astronaut and flew in a space shuttle. What would happen?	narration	feelings
Tell about the last book you read. What happened?	narration	prior knowledge

Ages twelve through fourteen:

1. It is important to you to have your own paper route. Your parents think that it is dangerous because of the neighborhood. Give them three good reasons why it is not dangerous. Identify your audience.
2. Your class is going on an overnight trip, all expenses paid. Your mom is afraid to let you go. She does not trust the teacher alone with twenty-five twelve-year-olds. Convince her, with three reasons, that your teacher can keep twenty-five twelve-year-olds under control. To whom are you writing?
3. You just found out that on the reading achievement test, your score was one point below what you needed to be in the gifted group. Think of three ways to convince your teacher that you can do the advanced work. Who is your audience?
4. Your take-home test in social studies will not be ready on time. Convince your teacher that you *must* have an extension. Give at least three reasons. Who is your audience?

Ages fifteen and up:

1. Working a job is necessary if you want enough money for dates. The job you can get will force you to work from 7:00 P.M. to midnight. Your father is absolutely against this arrangement because he feels that you won't have time to do your homework. Develop a strategy for convincing him that you can do it. Include at least two reasons why it is possible. To whom are you writing?
2. You have a new boyfriend. Your mother does not like him. Give your mom three reasons why he is special. To whom are you writing?
3. You have a girlfriend that your parents do not like. They say she is "fast." Convince them that she is "fast" but in the right way. Tell three ways that you would prove this point. Who is your audience?
4. You have saved some money to buy your own car. You have enough for the down payment. Because you are seventeen, you need your parent's consent to purchase the automobile. Your father is against the purchase, and your mom is neutral. How will you convince them that they should let you have the car? Give at least two reasons. Who is your audience?

USING LITERATURE TO GUIDE STUDENTS TO WRITE

Models for writing behavior can result from listening to and reading literature. Several books, at the primary, intermediate, and advanced levels demonstrate list-making and problem-solving formats that use description, explanation, narration, and often reasoning and persuasion. The following are only a few of the many available for reading to students. Students, who are older, may read them to younger children. Of course, all books may be read by all students who are able to self-select and read them independently.

Books Written in a List Format

The Stupids Die by Harry Allard. Illustrated by James Marshall (Houghton Mifflin, 1981).
Mr. Gumpy's Outing by John Burningham (Harcourt Brace Jovanovich, Inc., 1971).
Aaron Awoke, an Alphabet Story by Marilee Robin Burton (Harper & Row, 1982).
Just Us Women by Jeannette Caines. Illustrated by Pat Cummings (Harper & Row, 1982).
I Never Win! by Judy Delton. Illustrated by C. Gilchrist (Carolrhoda Books, Inc., 1981).
Rosie's Walk by Pat Hutchins (Macmillan, 1968).
The Mystery of the Missing Red Mitten by Steven Kellogg (Children's Book Showcase, 1974).
Alexander and the Terrible, Horrible, No Good, Very Bad Day by Judith Viorst. Illustrated by R. Cruz (Atheneum Pubs., 1975).

Books Written in Problem-Solving Format

Avocado Baby by John Burningham (Thomas Y. Crowell, 1982).
The Little Fish that Got Away by Bernadine Cook. Illustrated by C. Johnson (William R. Scott, 1956).
Are You My Mother? by P. D. Eastman (Random House, Inc., 1960).
The Race Forever by R. A. Montgomery (Bantam Books, 1979).
The Cave of Time by Edward Pacard (Bantam Books, 1979).
Slimy's First Book of Puzzles and Games by Jim Razzi (Bantam Books, 1983).
Encyclopedia Brown and the Case of the Dead Eagles by Donald Sobol (Elsevier-Nelson, 1975).
Your Code Name is Jonah by Edward Pacard (Bantam Books, 1979).
Encyclopedia Brown Solves Them All by Donald Sobol (Scholastic Book Service, 1977).

SUMMARY

Written language presumes a recoding ability beyond oral language. It requires that students have the ability to use language forms—explanation, description, narration, and persuasion/reasoning—for language control. We have provided information about students' written language competence that guides you, the teacher, to observe forms first, to see the "whole" language unit. Once you identify form, other aspects such as syntactic structure and audience are also observed. We have included formal and informal assessment procedures for observing growth in written language fluency. Instructional strategies to guide and develop writers are included throughout.

QUESTIONS TO PONDER

1. Collect samples of adult written language. Collect the same number of samples from children. Answer the following questions:
   a. How are the samples similar?
   b. How are they different?
2. How can we guide students to improve written language fluency?
3. Keep a journal or list of all your writing for a week or so, than analyze several samples using some of the informal assessment procedures described in Chapter 5.

REFERENCES

Ashton-Warner, S. (1963). *Teacher*. New York: Bantam.
Baghban, M. (1984). *Our daughter learns to read and write: A case study from birth to three*. Newark, DE: International Reading Association.
Bissex, G. L. (1980). *Gyns at work: A child learns to write and read*. Cambridge, MA: Harvard University Press.
Clay, M. M. (1975). *What did I write?* Auckland, NZ: Heinemann.
Glazer, S. M. (1984, November). *The effects of dialogue journals on elements of student's writing: A longitudinal study*. Paper presented at the National Reading Conference, St. Petersburg, FL.
Glazer, S. M. (1980). *Getting ready to read*. Englewood Cliffs, NJ: Prentice-Hall.
Goodman, K. (1982). *Language and literacy: The selected writings of Kenneth S. Goodman* (Vol. 2). Boston: Rutledge & Kegan-Paul.
Graves, D. H. (1983) *Writing: Teachers and children at work*. Exeter, NH: Heinemann.
Greenhalgh, C., and Townsend, D. (1981). Evaluating students writing holistically. *Language Arts, 58,* 811–822.
Gumperz, J. J., Kaltman, H., & O'Connor, O. (1983). Cohesion in spoken and written discourse. In D. Tannen (Ed.), *Coherence in spoken and written discourse*. Norwood, NJ: Ablex.
Haley-James, S. (1982). Helping students learn through writing. *Language Arts, 59,* 726–731.
Hannan, E., & Hamilton, G. (1984). Writing: What to look for, what to do. *Language Arts,* 61, 364–366.
Harste, J., Burke, C, & Woodward, V. (1981). *Children, their language and world: Initial encounters with print*. NIE G-79-0121. Bloomington, IN: Indiana University.
Kreeft, J. (1984)). Dialogue writing—Bridge from talk to essay writing. *Language Arts,* 61, 141–150.
Kroll, B. M. (1978). Developing a sense of audience. *Language Arts,* 55, 828–831.
Moffett, J. (1983). *Teaching the universe of discourse*. Boston: Houghton Mifflin.
Piaget, J. (1955). *The language and thought of the child*. (M. Gabair, Trans.). New York: New American Library.
Smith, F. (1977). Reading like a writer: *Language Arts,* 60, 558–567.
Squire, J. R. (1983). Composing and comprehending: Two sides of the same basic process. *Language Arts. 60*(5), 581–589.

Stahl, A. (1974). A structural analysis of children's composition. *Research in the teaching of English, 8,* 184–205.

Temple, C. A., Nathan, R. G., & Burris, N. A. (1982). *The beginnings of writing.* Boston: Allyn & Bacon.

Tierney, R. J., & Pearson, P. D. (1983) Toward a composing model of reading. *Language Arts,* 60, 568–580.

SUGGESTED READINGS

Baghban, M. (1984). *Our daughter learns to read and write: A case study from birth to three.* Newark, DE: International Reading Association. This book is a readable, day-by-day account of the reading and writing development of a child from birth to age three.

Burrows, A. T., Jackson, D. C., & Saunders, D. O. (1965). *They all want to write* (3rd. ed.). New York: Holt, Rinehart & Winston. This is probably the first text written about composition that is sympathetic to our view of the process. Case studies are included which describe students' writing achievements.

Glazer, S. M. (1984, August/September). Liberating students to write. *Early Years,* pp. 67–69, 106–107. The article includes a plan and activities that stimulate the reluctant student to write. Information is focused for the elementary school but may be adapted for older students.

Graves, D. H. (1983). *Writing: Teachers and children at work.* Exeter, NH: Heinemann. This book is a readable guide for helping teachers to help children to write. Children's development in spelling, handwriting, and concepts are charted through descriptions of behaviors in writing and the classroom.

Mosenthal, P., Tamor, L, & Wamsley, S. A. (1983). *Research on writing: Principles and methods.* New York: Longman. This volume includes a series of theoretical and research articles explaining writing competence, evaluation systems, writing disabilities, and levels of inquiry in writing research. It is recommended for advanced students.

6

READING COMPREHENSION AND RETENTION

Overview of Comprehension Theories

What Do We Assess to Determine Comprehension Ability?

Formal/Standardized Assessment Tools for Analyzing Text Comprehension

Informal Tools for Assessing Comprehension

C–A–L–M Procedures

Summary

Questions to Ponder

References

Suggested Reading

In this chapter we will set a stage for understanding comprehension. Our focus is reading and comprehension from interactive, interdependent, linguistic, and cognitive points of view. The questions we pose are:

- What is comprehension?
- What do we assess to determine comprehension?
- How do we assess, guide, and improve students' abilities to comprehend?

OVERVIEW OF COMPREHENSION THEORIES

Substantial numbers of theorists have researched and defined comprehension processes (see, for example, Rumelhart, 1984; Tierney & Pearson, 1983; Smith, 1985; Rumelhart, 1977; Glazer, 1982; Rumelhart & Ortony, 1977). All agree that a person must possess the ability to understand in order to survive in our modern world. Current definitions of comprehension reflect today's research, which views learning in a holistic fashion. Educators consider the student, the environments in which the student works, the content, the student's prior knowledge, the text and content of the text the student is reading, and people in the environment. We evaluate the "whole" when observing language learning from text and lectures in school.

Notions about Comprehension

Previous notions about comprehension have resulted in narrow descriptions of the processes. One explanation proposed the notion that reading *must* be learned moving from symbols to sounds and from written words to spoken text in a prescribed order, one skill at a time. This explanation suggests that comprehension, thus learning, requires oral language production for evidence of reading and listening. The student retains facts and recalls them in a specific sequence upon request. When presented with appropriate stimuli, the student pulls from memory bits of information. However, this narrow view of comprehension and learning has resulted in comprehension difficulties in students. The student with problems usually responds with an alternate, unexpected response. The response is labeled an "error" and the student receives a "deficit" designation for school placement, expectations, and performance. The progressive "one-step-at-a-time" idea about learning assumes that when the student learns one skill, it is used to learn the next. If one "step" is learned inappropriately, or not at all, then the student falls behind and fails. This "product" or linear notion of comprehension requires recognition of facts learned and recalled in prescribed sequences. It implies that the same ideas and steps are important to all students in the instructional setting and, therefore, must be learned by all. Students' recall is assessed as comprehension and reported in values as quantities. The number of correct responses on tests often results in the assignment of a comprehension level and a grade equivalent. In the reading classroom the resulting reading grade denotes instructional placement.

Research efforts from 1970 to present focus heavily on the idea of comprehension processing (Rumelhart, 1977; Stanovich, 1980). Conclusions from these efforts stressed attention to task, encoding, inference, memory storage and retrieval, and their relationships to reading comprehension. These efforts were important and appropriate, for comprehension as a separate mechanism and process is nonexistent.

The resulting efforts of the many researchers cited in this chapter have unified a theory of cognitive processing as it relates to comprehension. Correct or incorrect responses on tests related to comprehension assessment are viewed in a broader way, considering the efforts of this unified cognitive processing theory. The work of the researchers mentioned throughout this chapter have convinced us that reading is a complex interactive process in which readers vary their focus from getting facts presented by an author to concentrating on predicting what the author's message ought to be (Pearson, 1984). We think that students who read well ask themselves, when they read and write, "What must I do with this information?" "What do I already know about it?" and "How much do I really care about learning this?" The many factors involved in reading comprehension behaviors force us to believe that we must look at the students' responses, but more important, attempt to find out how students process and retain information from reading, listening, and even writing.

The "how" of comprehension—how students control attention to task, how students process and use information to comprehend and recall, how students select and use strategies to elicit responses—rarely emerges as an assessed variable for reading comprehension. How each student interprets information based on prior experiences and knowledge rarely appears in a diagnostic report of reading comprehension. The lack of consideration of prior knowledge is best demonstrated in the following situation experienced by our niece when she was enrolled in first grade. Her responses to test-type reading activities placed her in the highest reading group with eight other "bright" youngsters. One day's lesson involved responses to a story on a worksheet presented to the children after reading the story from text. The selection focused on a child about to go to a birthday party. The illustration depicted a youngster in a starched, organdy dress with a large bow in her hair, wearing polished white party shoes. The child in the worksheet illustration was walking to the party when a large bus passed along side and splashed her starched dress with muddy water. The question following the illustration required that Stephanie mark the "face" which best described the child's feelings after the incident.

Stephanie marked the child with the smiling face. The correct response, according to the teacher's guidebook, was the sad face. That afternoon a note went to Stephanie's mother.

Dear Mrs. Brown,

     Stephanie seems to be developing a reading comprehension problem. Just to be safe, I am putting her in a lower reading group. This precaution is based on her work in school. She is making lots of mistakes in her workbook. I don't think she understands what she is reading.

Sincerely,

Mr. Pringle

Stephanie's mother questioned her child about her workbook responses. When she learned the content of the story, she made an appointment to see the teacher. She and Stephanie arrived, together, before school began one morning. Mrs. Brown questioned the teacher about speaking to Stephanie concerning the response on the worksheet. Mr. Pringle had not and Mrs. Brown questioned her daughter that moment. "Stephanie, tell me what you like to wear to parties," she asked. "Jeans, and that's all I ever wear when I go to my friend's house," Stephanie replied. "When do you wear a dress, Stephanie?" asked her mother. "Only when you make me wear one," came the assertive response. Without further conversation, Mr. Pringle agreed that Stephanie's response, based on her ideas about dressing for parties, seemed justified. "But," barked Mr. Pringle, "the answer is still wrong!" For Stephanie, the opportunity to change from a dress to blue jeans sparked an inner smile. Her perception of appropriate party clothing differed greatly from the author's. Mr. Pringle commented that although Stephanie does not wear dresses to parties, it was expected that she learn to respond in the "appropriate manner."

Who is correct? Was Stephanie's response wrong? Was the author wrong? Even more important, does Stephanie have a comprehension problem? If "product" resulting in predetermined responses is important then, yes, Stephanie has a comprehension deficit. But, if the child's perception of the world is considered, Stephanie responded appropriately. Prior knowledge and perceptions of experiences play important roles in the student's ability to predict appropriate responses to content in text materials. Because we consider individual perceptions important to comprehension processing, we must review the student's products. But more important, we must observe the student during the production process: We watch facial expressions, interactions with text materials, peers, and adults. All variables that intervene in the reading and writing influence student responses.

What Is Comprehension?

We agree with theorists and researchers of today, particularly those working in fields of cognitive psychology and socio- and psycholinguists (Goodman, 1985; Smith, 1983; Rumelhart, 1980), who suggest that reading comprehension is: (1) text understanding; (2) understanding that print represents ideas; (3) understanding that meaning in print is determined in great part by the sentence structure; and (4) unique to each individual since each has different ideas about things, events, and life.

When one processes printed information, one constructs meaning from text. The reader acts as an author, rewriting the author's information. This personalizes the text, for the reader brings prior knowledge and personal perceptions to form predictions about meaning. The text itself—the symbols and sounds one makes in response to symbols—serves only as instructions for the reader. These instructions represented by "squiggles" and sometimes graphics, photos, and illustrations, provide suggestions for understanding concepts and interrelationships between concepts within these instructions. Reading means making meaning in all reading behaviors. The successful reader in school makes meaning by matching minds with the text's author. This suggests that the reader makes sense of school text materials when communication coincides cognitively, experientially, and linguistically, creating semantic interactions between the sender (author of text) and the receiver (the reader) of information. The reader connects information from text and lecture to prior knowledge using the symbol system (print) that describes the information.

This chapter will focus on comprehension of texts read and heard. We assume, when discussing comprehension assessment, that the student knows that (1) print represents ideas and (2) that the student can use syntactic structures to help comprehend these ideas. Our discussion will focus on assessment respecting Pearson's and Johnson's (1978) explanation of the comprehension process. They state:

> Comprehension is building bridges between the new and the known ... Comprehension is active not passive; that is, the reader cannot help but interpret and alter what he reads in accordance with prior knowledge about the topic under discussion.... Comprehension involves a great deal of inference making. (p. 24)

In order for students to construct text meaning, each must possess abilities necessary for perceiving the author's intent. Simply speaking, the reader must possess the ability to: (1) make inferences, recognizing differences between these and facts; (2) relate prior knowledge to new data; and (3) anticipate (expect or predict) certain events to occur in certain sequences. Prior knowledge and inferencing ability guide student responses. Each student processes information to match content differently. This uniqueness seems best described as we recall the time a friend was invited to a formal dance. She had been dating a medical student whose life was quite casual. He had, like most medical students, limited financial resources. "Formal" to our friend at that time, meant anything but blue jeans. When she asked us what to wear, we recommended a full-length gown. "Gosh," she stated, "I thought a dress would be just fine." Perceptions, inferences, and expectations about formal attire resulted from her current life experiences. Our perception of "formal" was quite different. Ideas between us were inconsistent because our current lifestyles differed. Text comprehension, demonstrated by the response, reflected the available data. The example demonstrates the inconsistent or un-uniform variable in data processing for text comprehension. This inconsistency, obviously, occurs within each student because each possesses different interests and experiences. A student will attend to the reading task, attend to the story, attend to details, events, and sequence of ideas based on interests. The depth of comprehension, therefore, is different for one than for another based on students' interest in that content. Inconsistency in attention to text materials depends, too, on the value and morals often referred to as beliefs that each reader brings to the text. The beliefs one holds determine how one perceives materials in print. Stephanie's response to text illustrates how two different beliefs about one issue often result in an event which can alter one's life (in this case, demotion). And our friend's perception of "formal" might have caused embarrassment.

In addition to inferences guided by prior knowledge, expectations, and beliefs, one must be able to organize information in order to recall effectively. How well the reader remembers information depends on skillful organization of the materials. The ability to organize for "pulling out" appropriate information at just the right moment determines success or failure in testing environments. Readers who organize information differently than the test find information useless.

WHAT DO WE ASSESS TO DETERMINE COMPREHENSION ABILITY?

One of our biggest concerns throughout this text deals with validity of assessment results. We ask ourselves, over and over again, do assessment tools actually measure a particular behavior? Can one tool assess any behavior? If you beleive that almost all text comprehension depends upon each student's knowledge accumulations, perceptions and expectations, consideration—even mention—of product measurement particularly with one tool becomes scary.

When assessing comprehension, therefore, we measure many things using several tools. We look at the product of a series of manipulations which have occurred in the reader's mind. We measure: (1) prior knowledge about content; (2) prior knowledge about language and meaning; and (3) prior knowledge about the language in text materials. We measure one's ability to predict spontaneously about information. The ability to predict is probably the single most important skill in the comprehension process. It is dependent upon prior knowledge and also upon the reader's ability to access directly the mental phenomena or subjective consciousness used when processing ideas (Spiro, 1984, p. 75). If one is conscious of the processes used to understand text, if one can think out loud telling oneself what is going on in one's brain to help comprehension, one can deliberately put to use those skills that are successful (Brown, 1980; Collins, Brown & Larkin, 1980). The successful reader takes an "educated guess" and predicts and anticipates information appropriately. Such a student eliminates inappropriate alternatives to produce expected "guesses." We will attempt to assess the spontaneity of prediction, too.

FORMAL/STANDARDIZED ASSESSMENT TOOLS FOR ANALYZING TEXT COMPREHENSION

The information explosion in comprehension research has resulted in a series of assessment techniques (Farr & Carey, 1986). Formal evaluation tools often adopt these techniques as formats for comprehension test construction. These include: (1) multiple-choice tests, (2) cloze tests, (3) oral reading formats, and (4) oral and written recall. As you read the following, it is important to keep in mind that students, while taking tests, must process information using prior knowledge about many variables including the test's content and also their own test-taking experiences.

Multiple-choice tests. Multiple-choice test formats dominate commercial test materials. Comprehension tests that use multiple-choice formats usually provide the student with a short reading passage followed by several choice questions. These questions are designed to assess reading comprehension. The student is expected to read a passage and select the appropriate response from a series. This format assumes that the ability to predict or select responses based on reading passages has an element of universality. This concept makes us "think twice" about selecting a multiple-choice test for assessing students' reading comprehension. Farr and Carey (1986) recognize, as we do, that the assumption that "one answer" is correct is preposterous. Think about selecting only one color tie to wear with your blue blazer. Think, too, that if you select one other than the "prescribed color" you are wrong, and you will be ostracized from the occasion to which you wear that tie. This example should help you indeed, to decide that it is preposterous to prescribe a tie color as appropriate or inappropriate. It is, too, just as inappropriate to prescribe a single answer to a comprehension question. When test writers select responses to questions, they consider these limitations. There are conventionally predictable responses for most questions. But, think about the creative, spontaneous, flexible reader who finds the usual responses unusual and inappropriate. This reader goes beyond conventions and infers "incorrectly" when making test responses.

Our discussion suggests greater concerns, too. If we consider Spiro's (1984) notion of student protocols—what one thinks about when responding, and how one reaches that choice—multiple-choice formats alone are of little use. The language abilities of students, how they use syntax, vocabulary, and chunks of words to create meaning are not deliberately addressed either. These tests provide subscores and grade equivalents, and they provide standardized normed scores so that professionals may compare students in their schools with national achievements. These tests truly test the student's ability to take a test using this format—but they do not necessarily test the student's language ability.

Our society has become almost dependent on multiple-choice test formats. It is almost an American tradition. When you eat at some restaurants, for example, you will sometimes find a card that asks your opinion of the establishment. These often use multiple-choice formats for consumer responses. We are a "multiple-choice brainwashed" society selecting from prescribed choices, often accepting these as the only choices. Old habits are hard to break. The habit of multiple-choice tests to assess comprehension thrives in these United States. These serve their function as part of a total battery of assessment tools. When they are only one part of a total picture, they provide useful information about performance. The interpreter of data, the specialist, must determine the importance of data from multiple-choice tests in the comprehension processes.

Cloze procedure type tests. The cloze procedure, developed by Taylor in 1953, requires the student to supply words deleted from text. Test construction consists of systematic deletions; every *n*th word is left out. Every fifth word is the most frequently used formula. Examiners' interests focus on determining how often students supply accurate words.

Much conflicting research concerning the effectiveness of this procedure for assessing reading comprehension exists in the literature (Bormouth 1963, 1966, 1968; Rankin & Culhane, 1969). Farr and Carey (1986) see formidable limitations for using this type of testing tool to assess comprehension. Their main concern is the lack of clarity concerning exactly what cloze-type tests do measure. Content passages, for example, may require the student to use words that are general in nature and not specific to the area of study. Shanahan (1982) and Czira (1983) address the issue of intersentence-comprehension. They doubt the format's validity as a tool for measuring a student's ability to understand the relationships of sentences within test passages. Students with oral language behaviors that are different than standard form will probably have difficulty. Since, in the cloze test, reliance on syntactic word arrangements often provides students with clues for correct responses, the linguistically different speaker faces distinct disadvantages. Some researchers have found that the deletion format of the cloze creates a special form of anxiety in students (Page, 1976; Ganier, 1976; Carey, 1978). This anxiety, of course, can be tempered with training in using cloze formats before using the procedure for assessment purposes.

Cloze-type tests have been used for two general purposes: (1) to assess the student's use of context comprehension, and (2) to determine the student's reading level; that is, does the student read the materials demonstrating that he or she can handle similar materials independently or with instructional intervention? This ambivalent discussion demonstrates our confusion concerning the effective use of cloze to assess or even guide students in comprehending text materials.

Oral reading formats. "Read it out loud, to me, Jennifer, so I can see if you understand it." This request, made by teachers and parents alike, demonstrates the long and influential history that oral reading behavior has played in American reading instruction. Oral reading errors, or lack of errors, have formed the basis for most instruction in reading comprehension as well as phonics, word recognition, and vocabulary development. But the method of counting the number of errors as a means for determining text comprehension has been contested. Researchers have questioned, too, the relationship between oral and silent reading (Fields, 1960; Wells, 1950); and researchers still question this relationship without definitive conclusions. Spache (1976) suggests that the demanding nature of oral reading activities prevents the reader from adequately processing or reacting to ideas. He states that "the mechanical and

Oral reading is a format for assessing reading comprehension.

vocal demands of oral reading give almost no time for any depth of thinking as making judgments, in interpreting interrelationships of ideas, or in reading critically" (p. 121). The necessity of oral reading, for some, is obvious. For example, youngsters who need to hear themselves read in order to confirm what the eyes see, or beginning and remedial readers who need help keeping their place on the page must read out loud. The voice "anchors" their place.

Oral reading continues to remain a format for testing reading comprehension. It fills much instructional time as well.

The enormous numbers of tools availble for assessing comprehension confuses teachers and specialists. Appendix B of this text includes an annotated listing of selected standardized/formal devices for gaining insight into student's comprehension.

INFORMAL TOOLS FOR ASSESSING COMPREHENSION

The term "informal" means that tools rely heavily on interpretations of observations by skilled examiners. Informal tools employ a wider variety of formats, many more than formal-type tests, and yield more behaviors for observational purposes. The more behavior samples available for each student, the more likely we are to determine comprehension ability accurately. In addition to professional informal assessment, student self-evaluations help to create independent learners who can determine their successes. Multiple types of formats permit all those observing reading comprehension behavior to observe responses in several settings. Formats most often used in informal assessment include (1) commercially prepared tests, (2) teacher-made tests, (3) observational data—systematized and spontaneous, (4) checklists, and (5) anecdotal records. Several formats are appropriately used for both assessment and instruction. Earlier discussion reminds us that comprehension includes students' abilities to recall, predict, and use prior knowledge. It seems mind boggling for us to consider all of these variables. But we must. We cannot, however, have an individual assessment tool for each of the variables involved in the comprehension process. We can collect several samples of students' responses in several situations over time and determine most of these abilities using the samples. We agree that qualitative results play an important role in assessing performance. We insist that qualitative data be combined with quantitative results to form interpretations concerning students' reading comprehension abilities. The combination should provide a broader, more comprehensive picture of students' comprehension abilities.

Because our C–A–L–M approach to diagnosis requires continuous observation in several environments, the diagnostic process never really ends. When you report results of data collections you are sharing some information about the student's language productions. As soon as you share these, however, the information is somewhat outdated, because the student continually changes.

Guidelines for Selecting Informal Assessment Materials

The guide in Figure 6–1 should help in selecting tools and procedures for assessment. The checklist should serve as the summary tool for collecting data concerning assessment tools, times of observations, and student behaviors. Following the checklist, we will discuss several types of informal testing materials. The checklist can be applied to each type.

Figure 6–1 Assessment Materials Checklist

Variable Identification Coding System:
PK = Prior Knowledge   P = Perception   I = Inference   H = Hypothesis

Student _____ Teacher _____

ASSESSMENT FORMATS	YES	NO
Do assessment tools permit continuous observations?	_____	_____
Are tools appropriate for determining abilities to read several types of reading materials?	_____	_____
Does the material seem to be written so that the student can understand the text?	_____	_____
Is content familiar? (PK)	_____	_____

Tools used _____

Do assessment results indicate that student uses information from memory and incorporates it with new data? (PK)	_____	_____

Tools used _____

Do materials encourage the student to respond in expected ways? (P,PK,H)	_____	_____

Tools used _____

Does the format for response permit the student to retell information in his or her own words? (P,PK)	_____	_____

Tools used _____

Additional data concerning tools used for comprehension assessment

_____

_____

_____

List all tools for assessment and dates used _____

_____

The Informal Reading Inventory

The informal reading inventory (IRI) format originally developed by Betts (1957) has provided teachers and clinicians with information about students' oral and silent reading and vocabulary abilities for a long time. The format permits examiners to observe several types of behaviors. One can detect students' abilities to use prior knowledge and make predictions (or hypothesize) about content and word recognition skills. Diagnosticians can observe students' flexibility with the written coding system, as well. Many commercial IRI's are available; several of these are included in Appendix B.

Commercial IRIs. The comprehension section of commercial IRIs usually consists of passages corresponding in difficulty to text materials used for teaching reading from beginning levels through high school. Sets of questions generally follow each passage; these are designed to assess the student's ability to gain information from reading. Information is designated as literal or inferential. The checklist in Figure 6–2 should serve as a guide for selecting commercial IRI passages for oral and silent reading assessment, and for listening comprehension. The IRI you select should meet as many of the criteria listed in the checklist as possible.

Teacher-made IRIs. When selecting IRIs, those elements considered for constructing them are also those observed for selection. So, begin by referring to the checklist in Figure 6–2 as a guide for creating your own assessment tool. Proceed by determining your purpose for assessment. Do you want (1) to determine students' reading levels for instruction placement; or (2) are you interested in assessing students' knowledge as a result of reading text materials? Follow the steps suggested below to create an assessment tool that fits your needs.

Directions For Writing IRIs

1. For assessing ability to read texts select three and sometimes four passages from textbooks that students are expected to read. Passages designed for early readers should be approximately 100 words in length. Upper-level readers should use passages 200 words long. Passages should be self-contained and relay a complete message or story.
2. When determining grade level for reading or grade placement, select passages from a graded textbook series. A basal reading series is best. Be sure that passages are new for the student. If they have been read before, the element of spontaneity is lost.
3. Create questions for each passage. Be sure that questions cover most of the content contained in the text of each passage. Include the following kinds of questions:
    Those that ask for direct recall of information cited in the passage; for example:
       What is the passage about?

Figure 6–2 Elements of a Good IRI

	YES
Is information interesting to students?	_____
Does information "tap" prior knowledge?	_____
Is language in passages cohesive?	_____
• Are sentences clear?	_____
• Are pronouns used easily defined?	_____
• When one word is substituted for another, is the meaning the same and clear?	_____
• Are important words repeated often enough to help the reader keep the idea of the passage in short term memory?	_____
When you read the questions, are your responses similar to the expected response most of the time? (80 percent correct?)	_____
Does the language in the text sound appropriate for your students? Does it seem familiar?	_____
Are words in passages familiar for students?	_____
Do passages follow logical sequences?	_____
Are connectives used so that cause-effect passages are easily understood?	_____
When passages are descriptive, is language interesting, colorful—"rememberable"?	_____
Do passages contain information that is clearly factual?	_____
Do passages encourage students to hypothesize, predict, and infer?	_____
Do some questions assess students' prior knowledge?	_____
Do some questions expect students to "anticipate"?	_____
Do some questions encourage students to "retell" in their own words?	_____
Are there at least three different passages available at each grade/reading level?	_____

I will repeat some words (phrases) from the passage—what do you think of after you hear each?
Those that include the main idea (the most important idea in each passage); for example:
   Who is the passage about?
   What is the passage about?
   How does the title of the passage tell you what it is about?
Those that indicate awareness of a "logical sequence" of events in each passage; for example:
   What happened first, next, last?
Those that require recall of details; for example:
   When did it happen?
   Describe what it (her, him, they) looks like?
   How many were there?
Those that indicate awareness of story characters; for example:
   What made you believe that *(main character)* was happy, (sad, angry, devious, religious, etc.)?
Those that use prior knowledge, and knowledge from the passage, to hypothesize or infer ideas; for example:
   What do you suppose will happen next?
   Why do you think that (particular to passage) happened?
Those that demonstrate students' understanding of words used in passage; for example:
   If passage included word *frigid* and phrase *high as a kite*
   When have you been *frigid*?
   When are you *as high as a kite*?

Be sure that questions are simply stated and open-ended inviting personal opinions. Create questions that require inference and prediction. Questions should be straightforward. Ask questions in the order in which the information appears in each passage. Write questions that require independent responses. Dependency of one question on the next limits students' answers.

4. Make a teacher-copy and a student-copy of each passage. Passages typed in double-spaced format or printed on a near-letter quality computer printer are most readable.
5. Place passages in a folder or bookbinder in order of difficulty.
6. Develop some form of recording/summary sheet (see Figure 6–4 for a sample) for documenting student responses including oral reading behaviors and guided and unguided retellings.

Quantitative Scoring of Reading Passages

Commercial and teacher-made IRIs offer percentage scores as a means to help educators determine students' reading levels. Betts (1957) and others determined standards for setting criteria for these levels. Standards have varied little over the years. Most designate reading ability with three levels: (1) independent, which is the level at which a student can read without assistance; (2) instructional, which is the level a student can read when in instructional session; and (3) frustration, a level indicating the inability to read easily. We feel that students are often pushed to the frustration level, which defeats our purpose. Frustration leads to discomfort, thus negative attitudes toward reading behavior. Therefore, it is important that those involved in the evaluation process respect the emotions and self-concepts of students, particularly those with problems. Even in the assessment process, success is our goal. We recommend that students are "pushed" to read only as far as their instructional level; in this way, we can continue to build positive attitudes toward the reading process. The standards set by Betts, and later altered based on research (Powell, 1970; Powell & Dunkeld, 1971)—continue to provide appropriate guidelines for educators. The scoring and assessment procedures used in the past still apply to oral and silent reading, and to responses resulting from listening.

Traditionally, oral reading evaluations result from simply counting the number of incorrect responses, which include substitutions, omissions, reversals, repetitions, and insertions. Words or corrections supplied by the diagnostician are considered incorrect responses for the reader and fit in these categories. However, it seems that certain substitutions, insertions, and omissions do not interfere with students' text understanding. When you examine students and believe this is the case, such responses (or miscues) should not be counted as errors, thereby lowering the reading comprehension level. As Goodman says so well:

> It must be remembered that accurate recognition is not the major objective in reading. The goal is always meaning. Because even proficient readers make errors on unfamiliar materials, teachers must resist the temptation to meticulously correct all inconsequential mistakes. They must always ask whether a particular miscue really makes a difference. (1971, p. 14)

The coding system in Figure 6–3 is suggested for scoring IRI responses during oral reading behaviors. Take note of Goodman's advice, and think before marking an error. Ask yourself, "Did the error change the passage meaning?"

Administering the IRI

Administration of an IRI might be a scheduled procedure or one that happens in an environment that encourages continuous reading activities including informal responses. Descriptions of the procedures for administering IRIs formally can be found in manuals accompanying these tools.

Qualitative Scoring

When using C–A–L–M a number of variables should be considered. See Figure 6–4, which contains statements developed to guide your observations of students' use of prior knowledge, perceptions, and ability to infer or predict.

C–A–L–M Procedures

Our paradigm, *C*ontinuous *A*ssessment of *L*anguage *M*odel suggests that diagnosis of reading abilities occurs over time and in instructional, recreational, interactive, individual and formal-group test-taking, settings in and out of

Figure 6-3 Scoring IRI Responses

RESPONSE	Examples
QUANTIFIABLE	
Substitutions	Vera bought the shirt. [borrowed inserted above "bought"] (Insert substitution as student reads.)
Omissions	The shirt was a large <u>size</u> ten. (Underscore student's omissions.)
Reversals	Are you my mother? (Mark as shown.)
Repetitions	He brought a bicycle. [squiggly line under "He brought"] (Indicated with a squiggly line.)
False starts	He got a pinwheel. [gah-gah, he got written above] (Write false start attempts.)
Insertions	Give me the cookie. [chocolate chip inserted] (Write student's inserted word.)
NONQUANTIFIABLE RESPONSES	
Pausing	Sally conducted the concert. (Indicate location of student's pause with double line.)
Calling of parts of words	The concert was extraordinary. [con, extra written above] (Write part where used.)
Insertions of parts of words	The concert was extraordinarily. [s, ily inserted] (Insert addition as called.)
Dialect difference	He goes to school. [goed written above] (Write differences in place.)
Inappropriate intonation	The concert" was outstanding. (Mark syllable that was emphasized inappropriately.)
Made-up words	The concert was extraordinary. [extrapatory written above] (Write make-up where used.)
Words provided by examiner	(Write word provided in appropriate space.)

Examiner should mark oral reading responses as the student reads.

Scoring Recognition of Words in Context

Determining numerical values in order to secure a "level" of word recognition in oral reading requires the following:

1. Count the total number of words in the passage that the student read.
2. Count the number of quantifiable errors called by the student; remember, these are the ones that change meaning.
3. Find the percent of words correct in context using the formula:

Total number of words in passage minus errors equals X divided by the number of words in the passage. For example:

$$250 - 7 = \frac{243}{250} = 97\%$$

Use the following criteria to determine reading levels as they correspond to percentages. These criteria are suggested for narrative or story-type materials.

Criteria for Oral Reading Levels: Words in Context

Independent level—95% or higher
Instructional level—85% to 94%

Figure 6–4 Elements of a Reliable Performance on IRI Assessment Activities

Code: PKC = Prior knowledge about content; PKL = Prior knowledge about language; P = Perceptions about content, reading process format for recall, etc.; H = Hypotheses; I = Inference.

QUESTIONS	COMMENTS/EVIDENCE
Information interests student. (PK,P)	
Student shares information that relates to prior knowledge. (PKL,PKC,P)	
Oral responses demonstrate a sense of cohesiveness:	
Information is related clearly. (PKL)	
Pronouns are defined easily. (PKL)	
Words substituted, one for the other, related passage meaning clearly. (PKL)	

Figure 6–4 Continued

        Student is aware of the audience for whom he/she is writing. Demonstrates this by repeating words important to the meaning of the written passage. (PKL,PKC,P,I) _____

Student responds correctly 80% or more. _____

Student uses own language when sharing information. (PKC,PKL,P) _____

Student uses synonyms for words or phrases that demonstrate knowledge of word meanings. (PKL,PKC,P) _____

Student shares information in logical order. (PK,P,I,H) _____

Student demonstrates ability to observe cause-effect relationships. (Uses connectives appropriately.) (PKC,PKL,I,H) _____

Student uses adjectives and other "colorful" words and phrases to share information from descriptive passages. (PKL,PKC,I,H) _____

Student recalls facts as described in passages. _____

Student makes predictions and/or infers events/situations that might happen as a result of text information. (PKC,PKL,P,H,I) _____

Student retells, without prompting, the information (story) from the passages using details. (P) _____

Student demonstrates abilities with at least three assessment tools. (P,PKL,PKC,H) _____

Student's name _____ Date _____

Examiner _____ Setting _____

_____

_____

Interactors _____

Content _____

classrooms. A major prerequisite for using any diagnostic procedure requires questions as a framework for observing behavior. Before entering into any sort of assessment, therefore, questions for observation, both formal and informal, ought to be developed and implanted in the examiner's mind in order for meaningful diagnosis to begin.

Formal procedures have already been described and can be applied to the formal (group-taking) and individual settings. Questions usually answered using formal procedures include:

1. Is the student able to read the text materials used for instructional purposes?
2. How much information does the student recall immediately after reading?
3. Is oral reading behavior "smooth"?
4. What sort of oral reading "miscues" (errors) occur? (A miscue is often defined as an unexpected response, i. e., "cop" for "policeman.")
5. How often do these miscues occur, and with what type of content materials are these most often observed?

C–A–L–M procedures for assessment permit teachers and diagnosticians to observe students' responses in informal and formal settings and in all environments—instructional, recreational, interactive, formal, and individual. Traditional diagnoses do not. Traditional or medical-type diagnostic procedures usually demand that the natural activities of the classroom cease and that a test-taking environment begin. This unnatural environment demands that teachers, as well as students, develop an unnatural posture for the activity. Our model insists that, as often as possible, diagnostic procedures become part of the natural classroom environment. This implies that diagnosis of strengths and needs occurs in all environments and settings, and during natural activities. Data is collected (with questions in mind) during reading instructional periods, as well as play periods, in the lunchroom when children read for relaxation, and in conversations. C–A–L–M suggests that examiners continue regular activities for data collections, not stop them in order to attend to one response to one test item.

C–A–L–M requires that the examiner:

- continuously watches behavior during reading and language arts activities
- notices spontaneous actions and responses of students
- creates instant questions about student behaviors, resulting from student's voluntary sharing of information
- attends to time and type of information in which the student uses prior knowledge with new data
- internalizes questions and information on observation checklists in order to permit continuous assessment to occur during the entire time students are in school settings.

We acknowledge and suggest the use of formal, standardized tests, since reality of testing in most situations demands such activities. We recommend, however, that all scores and evaluations resulting from standardized tests and tests developed to assess specific skills taught in school (often referred to as criterion reference tests) be confirmed with data collected using C–A–L–M.

We have attempted to create guidelines and procedures for C–A–L–M settings. We present these in the graphic organizer in Figure 6–5.

Assessment Procedures in Instructional Settings

Instructional environments require that diagnosticians present to students strategies that guide responses. We provide two goals for instructional settings: (1) to collect data for determining reading comprehension; (2) to collect evidence that indicates that a particular strategy helps a student retain data appropriately. Although all students possess a sense of order, specific expectations for ordering and structuring ideas from texts exist in school environments. Our suggestions provide frameworks so that students may respond as expected. Responses generated using these strategies allow us to analyze comprehension

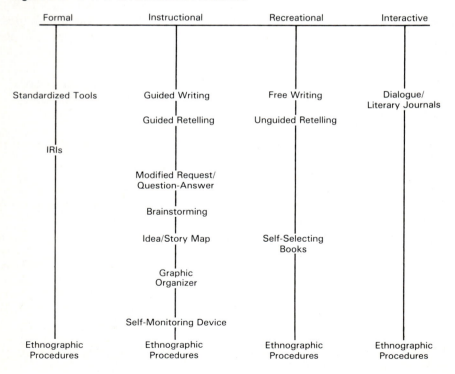

Figure 6–5 C–A–L–M Assessment Procedures

and retention. Since ethnographic procedures are recommended in all settings, it seems appropriate to begin with this approach to data collection.

Ethnographic Procedures

Since ethnographic procedures, described in depth in Chapter 3, focus on the study of "cultures," we are going to consider each ethnographic interview, formal or informal, and each piece of recorded data as information about a culture at a particular place and at particular times. Unlike medical model data which provides information culled usually from a single source, ethnographic data is continuous. It is somewhat like the videotaping of a group of students—a culture—and it displays the behaviors and emotions expressed by each over time (Smith, 1986). Ethnographic notetaking and interviews permit diagnosticians to draw conclusions about students based on accumulations of data.

Procedures

1. Define the setting for observations and interviews. Become a "participant" in the setting in which data collection occurs, since functioning as participant-observer permits your perceptions of student behavior to synthesize more clearly.

2. Be sure that you, the observer, have spent enough time in the setting in order to understand the interactions, realities, controls, and power structure that exist. Know, for example, who leads the students into and out of activities during lessons, lunch time, recess, or auditorium periods.

3. Prepare everyone who functions regularly in the environment for your forthcoming observations. Explain reasons for the procedures. You might say, for example: "I want to learn as much as I can about you, so that I can find just the right procedures to help you become a better reader (writer). In order to do this, I have to study your behavior as you read (or write). I need to see how you read during lessons, sometimes during free periods, sometimes with books that include assigned readings. In order to find out as much as I can I am going to write down everything I see that helps me learn about you. This will help us to make decisions about the kinds of materials and lessons that you need to use in order to help you become a more effective reader. Sometimes I may ask you questions about your feelings concerning the reading. And sometimes we may just talk about what you've read."

4. Collect data through observations and interviews. Be sure that notes are clear and made during the same time periods under the same conditions. The consistency is important for providing information from which to draw conclusions about behaviors. For example, if we are interested in a student's

oral reading behavior, we observe and record behavior during oral reading periods.

5. Use the following questions for conducting formal interviews. It is important, when interviewing, to provide the student with the opportunity to respond to these. In addition, the examiner *must* ask parallel questions of people important and prominent in the lives of the student.

Questions to students:

    a. Describe the place in which you interact with the teacher.
    b. Describe the person (people) you interact with.
    c. Describe all of the activities that you do with that person (name him/her).
    d. Describe all of the objects you use when you work with (name the person).
    e. Describe what usually happens when you work with (person).
    f. Tell me how you feel about (name the person).

Parallel questions to those in student's life:

    a. Describe the place where you work with (student's name).
    b. Describe what (student's name) looks like.
    c. Describe all of the activities you do with (student's name).
    d. Describe all of the things you use with (student's name).
    e. Describe what usually happens when you work with (student's name).
    f. Tell me how you feel about (student's name).
    g. Be sure also to ask informal questions, spontaneously.

Demonstration. The following example, developed by Gloria Smith (1986), should provide information that guides you to begin collecting and evaluating data about students' reading and writing behaviors in the instructional setting.

Conclusions/interpretations. Our notes are too brief to form adequate conclusions. We will, however, present conclusions for demonstration purposes. Many more observations and several interviews would be necessary to develop recommendations to guide Edith's growth. We can assume that Edith is reluctant to read. Her reluctance was exhibited by her procrastination when coming to the reading group. Insecurity, demonstrated by anxiety, seems to describe her feelings about herself in the reading group. She subvocalized (said to herself), and described her performance as "not so good." She seems to rely upon the opinion of others when discussing her reading ability. Edith seems embarrassed about her ability, as indicated by lowering her head and twisting her hair when asked how she felt about reading. These conclusions lead the diagnostician to suggest that building self-confidence is essential. When Edith feels better about herself as a reader she will probably improve her skills. *Hypothesis:* With strong support systems during reading activities, Edith should raise her self-concept during reading activities.

Case: Edith (Information from school and medical records as they would be reported in a traditional medical-type model report.)

Age: 8   *School:* Semirural school, Central New Jersey
Grade: First   *Sibling(s):* 1 brother, age 9—repeated first grade.
Parents: Father—Professor, university; *Mother*—Librarian, large corporation.
Family history related to learning: Several immediate family members with early learning problems. These seem to disappear with age (maturation).
Health: Pre- and neonatal—normal; normal birthweight; motor development—normal; speech, somewhat delayed; history of ear infection with accompanying high fevers; normal vision.
Behavior: Short attention span, impulsive and exhibits immature behaviors (i.e., sucks thumb, whines, etc.).
Reason for referral: Hits other children; calls out inappropriately; refuses to respond to requests made by teachers.
WISC = R scores: Verbal 115; Performance 113; IQ 114.
   Subtest: Vocabulary 17 (99th percentile)
   Picture completion 15 (95th percentile)
   Digit span 4 (very low—could not repeat numbers in reverse order)
Bender Gestalt results: Very poor performance
Standardized School Achievement Test: Above average in all areas except letter–sound relationships (total score placed her in the 6th stanine).

WORKING ETHNOGRAPHIC NOTES

Date: March 14   9:30–9:50 A.M.
Setting: Teacher has called children to reading group and conducts reading group activities.

9:30 Sat at desk looking at table top. Got up. Walked to front of room, turned around, went back to desk. Almost sat down, went back to front of room, got back. Came to reading group. Sat in place.
9:33 Opened book. Said, "I can't find the place." Accepted help from boy next to her. Handed the book to him. Took book back after place was located.
9:35 Held book on lap as others read. Subvocalized as each read out loud. Stayed on task, pointed to words, moved mouth as pointing occurred.
9:45 Twisted legs together tightly upon teacher's request to read. Read with false starts, regressions, repeated words, added words, repeated three words four times each. Looked from text to teacher, from teacher to text. Face flushed. Closed book after reaching end of reading.
9:47 Pointed and subvocalized following text as next student read.
9:48 Put fingers in mouth. Bent body over the book. Twisted hair with left hand. Began to swing legs. Rocked back and forth. Bent over book leaning head on knees.

INTERVIEW

Teacher: Tell me about your reading group.
Edith: Well, the desks don't move in my classroom. I am the farthest from the front. I sit near my friend Michele.
Teacher: Tell me about your reading group.
Edith: Well, I go to another room to read. It is a special teacher who helps kids who can't read good, like me. I like my real teacher better.
Teacher: Tell me about your friends in your reading group.
Edith: Well, they all read better than me. And my teacher knows that too, cause she always tells everyone else how good they read.
Teacher: Edith, tell me what you do in your reading group.

> *Edith:* I sit in the group and I take out my book, and I raise my hand to read the page that I want to read. I pay attention and my friend Michele doesn't. Sometimes the teacher yells because she puts her head in her lap and twists her hair.
> *Teacher:* Tell me about your reading, Edith.
> *Edith:* Well, it's not so good. The teacher tells me.
> *Teacher:* How do you feel, Edith, in your reading group?
> *Edith:* (Drops head, and twiddles her hair) I don't know. I feel dumb sometimes cause everyone reads better then me.

Guided Writing Procedures

Several guided writing procedures exist in the literature (Calkins, 1986; Graves, 1983; Smith & Bean, 1980). These have been developed in order to shift the paradigm from product to process orientation when students compose. This shift implies that when students write they begin with a purpose rather than just for the sake of writing (Calkins, 1986, p. 14). We know that students must write in order to become "writers." We also know that to effectively guide growth in writing, students must feel free to converse in written formats. They must speak for themselves and evaluate their efforts as they strive to form a collaborative relationship between themselves and the audience. Guided writing, therefore, becomes an essential strategy for evaluating growth in writing and for guiding students to become writers as well.

The purposes of guided writing are:

- To collect written data for evaluating students' growth in written responses to content and literature
- To infer, from observations and written materials, the processes most effectively used by students to compose written (and oral) texts
- To provide a vehicle for students to improve written language in response to reading
- To facilitate recall and retention.

Guided writing is appropriate for students at any age. It may be used with content materials, literature, or basal readers.

Guided writing procedures often begin with "brainstorming" in small groups of students or with individuals. Brainstorming begins by asking students to "storm their brains" and think about what to write. You might set an example by talking about something that occurred in your life. This usually provides a model for behavior. A less directed form of idea generation is referred to by Calkins (1986) as the "writing workshop." This one-half hour to one hour of writing at the beginning of each guided writing session is for creating ideas. It occurs in environments that are filled with several kinds of paper, writing materials, and several types of surfaces—desks, easels, chalkboards—for composing text. In a sense, the environment provides a "brainstorming" atmosphere, for the surroundings "expect" that one writes.

Teachers must be sure that students understand the activities that exist during the guided writing session. Activities, in the order in which they usually occur include: (1) rehearsal or brainstorming; (2) conferencing; (3) composing and recomposing; (4) editing; and (5) continuous self-evaluation.

Rehearsal. This is the "writing workshop" segment of a guided writing session. Set aside one-half hour to one hour of each session for rehearsal writing. Ask, "What are you thinking about writing?" Be relaxed and model behavior by generating a sincere interest in their responses and in creating text yourself. For elementary grade students, remember that writing and drawing go together. Children need to know that their text will *not* be edited, evaluated, or judged by the teacher in this phase. Remember, children at early ages are vulnerable. They sometimes feel awkward and self-conscious. We must encourage them to relax and trust. This means consistency in expectations and teacher behavior during the rehearsal/workshop writing period. Rehearsal for older children may include journal writing in response to reading, but also composing, editing, and self-evaluation.

Conferencing. As explained by Graves (1983), conferencing is a form of demonstration lesson to illustrate what students ordinarily don't see. The teacher writes in order to illustrate ways to create readable text. Work with one child or a small group. Use a chalkboard, easel, or overhead projector. Begin by saying something like the following:

> This morning on my way to school, I wondered what to write about. I remembered two thoughts that I had after reading two books, thoughts that might be interesting to you. These were:
>
> How I Felt Like Margaret in Judy Blume's Book
> The Time I Read *Leo the Late Bloomer* to a First Grade

The first happened to me when I was in the sixth grade. All the other girls had gotten their period. At least that is what my friends told me. Even my very best friend had gotten it. I told them I had it too, but I really didn't. I was really worried. I was so worried, that I almost spoke to my mom about it. But then it happened.
 The second topic happened when I was in the third grade. My teacher and the first-grade teacher decided that the older kids should read stories to the first-grade class once a week. We picked our own stories. I picked *Leo the Late Bloomer*. The book was about a baby tiger who couldn't read. It really got to me, because when I was in first grade my mother was called to school because I couldn't read either, and the teacher put me with the dummies.
 I like all of the topics because I can remember them really well from my childhood, but after telling you about them, I think that I want to write about the second topic, "The Time I Read *Leo the Late Bloomer* to a First Grade."

> Kids, talking about topics really helps me decide which is the best one to write about. The one I feel most excited about is usually the one that I like to write about because it is usually the best story.

This idea *must* be said clearly so that it is understood by children. Your purpose is to inform them that the relationship of their personal interest to books helps them create effective writing. You are directing the students to talk about topics related to prior knowledge (experiences) by *modeling* the behavior, not with direct intervention. This is a powerful approach to instruction since it is peer-oriented rather than authoritarian. It also implicitly demonstrates to the students feelings which say, "Gee, if the teacher can do it, so can I!" To illustrate the next phase of the process, you would then say: "I am going to brainstorm and write some words and phrases that I think of quickly. I intend to use them later when I write my story." You might write a title on the easel just to clarify topic selection. Next, you would say to the students: "When I write these words down, I can remember what really happened."

HOW I FELT WHEN I READ *LEO THE LATE BLOOMER*

Miss Maybe
She was weird because she did funny things.
Reading to the kids
Raining outside
The front of the room
Sweat on my forehead
Felt like the dummy
What I did to feel better so I could read.

Self-evaluation. Graves (1983, p. 46) suggests a form of self-analysis for guiding students to understand how to construct text. The guide displays two types of tasks: "thinking aloud" about the topic and the actual writing of the story itself. In other words, have the students write down what comes to mind as they think about their story—and have them write down what they remember of the story as well. The following demonstration should serve as a guide for carrying out this activity.

THINK ALOUD ABOUT WHAT I AM WRITING	WRITING
I need to start with where the story happened.	It all happened in my school when I was in the third grade. Miss Maybe was my teacher.
I think it would help to make the story better if I told about Miss Maybe.	Miss Maybe was really different. She always changed her nylon stockings in the classroom. She never ate with the other teachers either. She just stayed in the class and read alot.
Now I'd better tell what happened first in my story, or I won't stay on the topic.	Well, all of us had to read to the first graders. I was a terrible reader, and I always put my head down when Miss Maybe picked people to read, hoping that she wouldn't pick me. Well, looking down didn't work. One day she picked me.
Now I think it would be good to tell about how I felt when Miss Maybe called my name.	Well, when I heard my name, I got butterflies in my stomach, and I felt sweat on my forehead and my hands.

Although incomplete, this should give you some idea about how to proceed. When you have completed the demonstration, children might ask questions about additional things that happened in your story. Encourage the questioning. They might ask, for example, "Did you feel like Leo felt in the story?" Your response could be, "Oh that's a good thought. I think I'll write that I did feel like a dummy like Leo." Once children have finished asking questions, say, "Gee your questions helped me to see how I could make my story better. When you have completed your stories, I will meet with you and see if I have questions about them. That should help you make your stories better."

Composing. At this point, composing should begin. Say:

> Now it's your turn to compose. Take some paper, and think about some things in a book you are reading that you have strong feelings about. Try to think why you feel strongly about them. Ask yourself, did something in that story once happen to me? Is the main character like someone I really like or hate? Then I want you to work with your friend (specify a name), or me, and tell about the topics. Decide, after telling, which makes you feel the most excited, or angry, or anxious. Select the topic that makes you have the strongest feelings. Then "brainstorm" words or phrases on your paper. Once you have your list, begin writing. Remember, write down, or think to your self or out loud, what you will do before you write.

Direct student to write, and *you must write, too!* When the story has been written, meet with each student, and ask questions about each story as demonstrated in the self-evaluation section. This should help the student "fill in" where ideas need clarification, where more detail would make the story more effective.

Recomposing. This is the time to help students realize that *recomposing* is composing—we change or alter the text to make the piece more exciting. Say: "Now that you know what questions I need answered, add text in the appropriate places to answer the questions."

Editing. This is a last step in the writing process. Children should edit when possible. But teachers may have to correct errors. Remember, *all professional writers have editors who do these tasks.* Begin by guiding your student to look

Figure 6–6   About My Writing

THE IDEAS	CHECK
I have written all my ideas into my story.	_____
I got these from my own head and from brainstorming.	_____
My story has a beginning.	_____
My story has a middle.	_____
My story has an ending.	_____
When I read my story, I can close my eyes and have a picture in my head about the story. The picture tells me:	
what happened	_____
about people in the story	_____
what the people look like	_____
what the people do	
I think that when someone reads my story, they will be able to retell my story because they can see pictures of my story in their minds.	_____
THE WRITING	
I use one word to tell about an idea.	_____
I write short sentences.	_____
I write long sentences.	_____
I write "and" lots of times in one sentence.	_____
I use periods at the end of sentences.	_____
I use capital letters at the beginning of sentences.	_____
I think that people can read my handwriting.	_____
I need to use a typewriter or a computer because my handwriting is difficult to read.	_____
I reread my story for misspelled words.	_____
I reread my story and when my voice stopped I put a period at the end of that word.	_____

My signature _____

Date _____

The name of my piece of writing _____

_____

through the story, to notice, for example, all places where capital letters have been left out. Then, move to another—spelling or punctuation. Deal with *only* one type of error/correction at a time.

Continuing self-evaluation. After each step in the guided writing process, self-evaluation should be guided by the teacher. Students should also have available to them self-checking devices to help them notice characteristics of their writing. These will guide students to note how their writing has changed. (Figure 6-6).

Procedure with content materials. The guided writing procedure developed by Smith and Bean (1980) offers some helpful strategies for guiding students to recall information after reading content materials. Brainstorming can be used to generate lists of words and phrases resulting from reading. Once ideas are generated and written, the student might use the following guided writing worksheet to outline ideas. The topic, "Circus" is used to demonstrate the outline process. The second worksheet can be used to guide students to use each cluster to create paragraphs for their story.

Guided Writing Worksheet 1

Write a title on the first line. Put words and phrases in clusters because they belong together.

Place title here: _____

Cluster 1   Cluster 2   Cluster 3

_____   _____   _____

_____   _____   _____

_____   _____   _____

_____   _____   _____

Guided Writing Worksheet 2

Place cluster name here: _____

_____

_____

_____

_____

Direct students to use one cluster worksheet for each cluster of ideas generated in words or phrases on worksheet number 1. The checklist in Figure 6–7 may be used to observe students' growth in reporting information retained from reading following guided retelling in written formats.

Guided Retelling Procedures

Several researchers have found that when questions from stories focus on important ideas, students' listening and reading comprehension grows (Bridge & Sawyer, 1984). Training students to focus by guiding retellings appears to

Figure 6–7 Guided Writing Procedure Checksheet

Student _____ Setting _____
Date _____ Grade _____ Age _____

	YES	NO	NEED MORE DATA
Directed writing activities help the student generate personal ideas for composing.			
The student responds best to brainstorming: with a group of peers when working one-on-one			
Student is able to brainstorm alone using guide sheets to generate ideas for composing text.			
The "think-aloud" strategy is effective for the student for producing written text.			
The student is able to use "think-alouds" independently, effectively.			
The student is able to use "think-alouds" effectively when guided by teacher.			
The student seems to understand the difference between composing and editing.			
The student is able to use the guided writing worksheet 1 to gather information necessary to compose text based on content materials.			

Comments _____

be effective with elementary as well as secondary school students (Palinscar & Brown, 1983). Guided retellings using questions guide students to recognize text organizational patterns used by authors. This seems to improve reading comprehension (Allington & Strange, 1980; Readence, Bean, & Baldwin, 1981; Vacca, 1981). It seems appropriate, therefore, to direct students' retellings with specific questions. This guided strategy is effective for assessing students' recall from text, but it has been supported as a strategy for improving comprehension as well (Morrow, 1985; Beck & McKeown, 1981). We agree that a well-ordered set of directions and questions must be presented to students who have difficulty directing themselves to focus.

Guided retellings occur for several purposes:

- To provide a vehicle for determining recall of text or story
- To determine what a student recalls about the text or story
- To determine if the student uses prior knowledge in order to make meaning from text
- To determine how the student feels about the story or topic
- To determine the student's ability to infer and predict
- To determine if this instructional strategy guides the student to recall specific ideas, events, sequences, etc.

The guided retelling strategy for assessing and instructing students to comprehend text functions best in a one-on-one setting. The student and diagnostician-teacher should schedule a regular time for meeting and discussing text and/or literature materials.

Procedures.

    1. Call student to your conference table.

    2. Ask questions orally, deciding what focus the student needs. If, for example, the student must work on story setting, focus on that aspect of story.

    3. After retellings occur, give the student the worksheet in Figure 6–8. Ask the student to retell the story, as he or she did orally, but this time, to write it down. If the student has problems with this concept, use a tape recorder. Provide a recorder with questions for retelling. On tape, have the student retell (after hearing the teacher's voice asking the questions) the story as he or she did in the conference.

    4. We recommend that you reproduce the worksheet and have it available for students. Eventually, they will use it and retell their story without direct teacher guidance.

    5. Note that the questions in the worksheet are specific. Since students with problems may have trouble responding to direct questions, focusing may be difficult. The questions in some cases require a specific response. This may

Self-selection builds motivation.

stifle the troubled student's interaction and creative thought. For students whose attention to specific tasks is difficult, open-ended type questions may be more appropriate. These permit several responses and permit teachers to observe students' direction of thought in response to text.

After youngsters have read books that have been personally selected, the retelling guide in Figure 6–8 should help diagnosticians and classroom teachers to determine students' recall of story plot or theme, main characters, time and setting of the story, and important details. Teacher should notice, too, the vocabulary used. Using appropriate vocabulary when retelling helps us know about a student's text comprehension.

The conversation on pages 50–51 might occur once students make their library selections and have begun to read on their own. The annotations explain the teacher's direction and purpose when considering the student's book choice—in this case Edward Packard's *The Circus*. The dialogue illustrates the student's ability to understand the text structure. It discloses the child's interests, as well.

Figure 6–8 Guided Retelling Worksheet

(Appropriate for upper-elementary, middle, and secondary students)

Retell the story by answering the questions.

STORY'S SETTING

Where does the story take place? _____

_____

When does the story happen? (time) _____

_____

Tell everything that you can remember that helps me to get an idea of what things are like at the beginning of the story. _____

_____

_____

STORY'S GOAL

Why do you think the story ends as it did? _____

_____

Why does the main character do what he does? _____

_____

What else can you tell me about the goal of the main character? _____

_____

STORY'S PLOT

How does the main character try to reach his/her goal? _____

_____

What happens? _____

_____

What did the main character do to make something happen? _____

_____

How did it turn out? _____

_____

What happened next? _____

_____

STORY'S ENDING

Tell how the main character achieved his/her goal? _____

_____

If the goal was not achieved, how did the story end? _____

_____

What other information do you want to share about the story? _____

_____

JAMIE:	I picked my book, Mrs. Fantauzzo. It's about circuses.
TEACHER:	Great, come tell me about it. Tell me why you selected a book about a circus. (student's interest and purpose are questioned)
JAMIE:	Well, it's not the circus I really care about. You see this is a mystery story. And the mystery is you find out about it.
TEACHER:	Oh, you like to read mystery stories? (further explanation concerning choice still being sought)
JAMIE:	Yeah, but no.
TEACHER:	Whoops, you've got me confused. Now, tell me why you like a book about a circus that is a mystery.
JAMIE:	Well, when you read it, you find out how it ends.
TEACHER:	How do you feel when you wait to find out the ending? (trying to determine what the student means)
JAMIE:	Well, I'm not sure of what is going to happen, and I like that part. It is a mystery. (demonstrates understanding of the suspense aspect of a mystery)
TEACHER:	Then you like to take a guess about the end? (exploring the concept of inference/prediction)
JAMIE:	Yeah, that's what I like. I like to try to figure out what the end is going to be.

TEACHER: How can you do that? (probing for protocols—concept of what the student thinks he is doing when he is in fact anticipating or inferring the ending)
JAMIE: Well, when I read the book I will decide what the end might be because of what is in the story. But you see, this book helps you do it.
TEACHER: What do you mean?
JAMIE: Well, look. (Brings book to teacher, and points to specific section) You see, you read up to a page, and then there are some things—
TEACHER: What things? (probing for appropriate literary description)
JAMIE: Well, these. (Points to single directional sentences)
TEACHER: You mean sentences that tell you what to do?
JAMIE: Yeah, you see, if you want it to end one way you turn to the page it says.
TEACHER: Read the part to me.
JAMIE: See here. (Points and begins to read)
TEACHER: Tell me what the author does.
JAMIE: Well he tells you to read and go to a page you want for the ending.
TEACHER: So when he tells you to go to the end he is giving directions.
JAMIE: Yeah, he tells you what to do.
TEACHER: Then he "directs" you to decide how *you* want to end the mystery.
JAMIE: Right!
TEACHER: Right, what?
JAMIE: He tells you *how* he makes the story end.
TEACHER: Ah, then the author writes the story so that you can "predict" your own ending.
JAMIE: Yeah, but you decide too, how it will go.
(Direction has been given concerning the text structure and the author's purposes for writing as he did).
TEACHER: Jamie, tell me what is the most important idea, the main one, of the story. (directing retelling of main idea)
JAMIE: It's about a boy who is in a circus.

Jamie has demonstrated that he is able to tell about the story's main idea with teacher guidance. He has exhibited the ability to read a piece of literature, retain the main idea, and retell it using language conveying descriptive details. His recalls are sequential and in his own words. He recalls facts and infers from the information what he thinks will happen.

The retelling profile (see Figure 6–9) developed by Irwin and Mitchell (1986) provides a means for summarizing in a consistant format. The profile sheet, if used regularly, should permit teachers to note trends and changes over time.

Figure 6–9 The Qualitative Retelling Profile
(Reprinted with permission of P. A. Irwin and J. N. Mitchell, *The reader retelling profile: Using retellings to make instructional decisions.* Manuscript in preparation.)

Directions: Indicate with a checkmark the degree to which the reader's retelling includes the reader's comprehension in terms of the following criteria:

	NONE	LOW DEGREE	MOD. DEGREE	HIGH DEGREE
1. Retelling includes information directly stated in text.	____	____	____	____
2. Retelling includes information inferred directly or indirectly from text.	____	____	____	____
3. Retelling includes what is important to remember from the text.	____	____	____	____
4. Retelling provides relevant content and concepts.	____	____	____	____
5. Retelling indicates reader's attempt to connect background knowledge to text information.	____	____	____	____
6. Retelling indicates reader's attempt to make summary statements or generalizations based on the text which can be applied to the real world.	____	____	____	____
7. Retelling indicates highly individualistic and creative impressions of or reactions to the text.	____	____	____	____
8. Retelling indicates the reader's affective involvement with the text.	____	____	____	____
9. Retelling demonstrates appropriate reader's language fluency (vocabulary, sentence structure, language conventions, etc.).	____	____	____	____
10. Retelling indicates reader's ability to organize or compose the retelling.	____	____	____	____
11. Retelling demonstrates the reader's sense of audience or purpose.	____	____	____	____
12. Retelling indicates the reader's control of the mechanics of speaking or writing.	____	____	____	____

Interpretation: Items 1–4 indicate the reader's comprehension of textual information; items 5–8 indicate reader's response, and involvement with text; items 9–12 indicate facility with language.

Procedure for conducting and evaluating retellings. Morrow (in press) has developed a quantitative system for determining growth in comprehension. This system provides a numerical value when teachers and diagnosticians are interested in scores as a means to demonstrate growth. Morrow's procedure for assessing a student's retelling for its sense of story structure or inclusion of structural elements requires that the story first be parsed into five scoreable units: setting, theme, plot episode, and resolution. The units are defined as follows:

- **story setting**   the introduction of characters, the time and place of the story;
- **story theme**   the initial event that causes the main character to react, to form a goal or face a problem;
- **story plot**   episodes in which the main character attempts to solve the problem or reach the goal;
- **story resolution**   the outcome, which is usually the main character's solution to the problem or attainment of the goal, and the end of the story;
- **story sequence**   provides the opportunity to assess the student's ability to retell the story in appropriate sequential order.

Say to the student, "I am going to ask you to retell your story after you read it. Please retell it as if you were telling the story to a friend who has never heard it before." If the student is reluctant, Morrow suggests using prompts, but only if necessary. Suggest, for example, that he or she begin with "Once upon a time," or "Once there was . . .". If retelling stops before completion of the story, encourage continuation with language such as, "What comes next?" or "Then what happened?"

To assess the retelling, note the number of idea units the student includes within the first four categories, regardless of order. Use Figure 6–10 to record the idea units included. Credit is received for partial recall of the general idea. Once element inclusions are checked, observe the sequence of the retelling by comparing the order of the elements in the student's retelling with the proper order of the setting, theme, plot/episodes, and resolution. Analysis of the elements included in several retellings over time provides information for determining instructional needs. Simply checking element inclusion provides sufficient data to make appropriate instructional changes.

When numerical values are important for charting growth, record points for each element in appropriate section of Figure 6–10. In all sections of the figure, record the points earned for each element. Add the points for each section. In the section which assesses plot/episodes, however, use the following formula to adjust the number of events named by the student for that section to equal the percentage of the 10-point maximum. Use the following formula to calculate this sub-score.

Figure 6–10 Quantification of Retellings

Diagnostician _____ Student _____

Date _____ Setting _____

Directions for Assessing Story Structure

Check each element included by the student in retelling presentation. Record the number of points scored for each element.

SETTING (10 Points)
Introduction of characters (2 points for main character, 1 point for additional characters to a total of 5 points) _____
General statement of setting (5 points) _____
                                              Sub-total _____

THEME (10 points)
  Indicate event that set the goal for the story.
  or
  A goal becomes evident for the main character to achieve, or a problem to solve becomes evident.
                                              Sub-total _____

PLOT/EPISODE (10 points)
  Events leading toward accomplishing goal _____
  Events leading toward solving the problem _____
  (Adjust the number of events named by the student to equal the percentage of the 10-point maximum)   Sub-total _____

RESOLUTION (10 Points)
The problem is solved or goal reached (8 points) _____
The story is ended (2 points)   Sub-total _____

SEQUENCE (10 Points)
  The story is told using all four story structure elements as follows:
  Setting, theme, plot/epidoses, and resolution
(10 points—all four elements included) _____
(6.6 points—three elements included) _____
(3.3 points—two elements are in order) _____
(1 point—one element in order) _____
(0 points—none are in order)   Sub-total _____
  Do not score omitted elements.
  Total possible points = 50
                                              Total score _____

Quantification of retellings transcription and parsed story guideline. Morrow, L. M. "Retelling stories as a diagnostic toll." In Glazer, S., Searfoss, L. and Gentile, L. (In press). *Reexamining diagnosis in reading: New trends and procedures for classrooms and clinics*. Reprinted with permition of the International Reading Association.

Plot/Episode Equation

$$\frac{\text{Total score received for plot/episode}}{\text{Total plot/episode score for story used}} \times 10$$

Figure 6–11 provides an example of a retelling analysis using this formula. The equation, applied to this story follows:

$$\frac{12}{20} = .6$$

$$.6 \times 10 = 6.$$

The total score for the retelling in Figure 6–11 is 31.6. This score, compared to other retelling scores, over time, should demonstrate growth and change in student's ability to reconstruct stories after reading and listening to them.

Figure 6–11 Sample Quantification of Guided Retelling

Student: Girl, age 5
Story: Jenny Learns a Lesson

SAMPLE VERBATIM TRANSCRIPTION:

Once upon a time there's a girl named Jenny and she called her friends over and they played queen and went to the palace. They had to they had to do what she said and then they went home and said that was boring. It's not fun playing queen and doing what they say, she says. So they didn't play with her for seven days and she had she had a idea that she was being selfish, so she went to find her friends. And said, I have, let's play pirate, and they played pirate and they went onto the ropes. They just stayed on the shore and she called Help, help. They wouldn't come to help her. And then they played that she was a lady playing house. And they have tea. The end.

PARSED STORY GUIDESHEET:

SETTING (10 points)
   a. Once upon a time there was a girl who liked to play pretend.   5
   b. Characters: Jenny (main character), Nicholas, Sam, Mei Su, Shags the dog. (Total of 5. Give 2 points for "friends," and one for "friend."   4
                                                                       Sub-total   9

THEME (10 points)
   Every time Jenny played with her friends, she bossed them.   Sub-total   10

PLOT/EPISODES (10 points)
   First episode
      Jenny decided to pretend to be a queen.   1
      She called her friends and they came to play.   1
      Jenny told them all what to do and was bossy.   1
      The friends became angry and left.   1

Figure 6–11 Continued

```
Second episode
    Jenny decided to play dancer.                                          _____
    She called her friends and they came to play.                          _____
    Jenny told them all what to do and was bossy.                          _____
    The friends became angry and left.                                     _____
Third episode
    Jenny decided to play pirate.                                            1
    She called her friends and they came to play.                            1
    Jenny told them all what to do and was bossy.                            1
    The friends became angry and left.                                     _____
Fourth episode
    Jenny decided to play she was a duchess.                                 1
    She called her friends and they came to play.                          _____
    Jenny told them all what to do and was bossy.                          _____
    The friends became angry and left.                                     _____
Fifth episode
    Jenny's friends decided not to play with her again because she was so bossy.   1
    They did not play with her for many days.                                1
    Jenny became lonely.                                                     1
    Jenny went to her friends and apologized to them for being bossy.        1
        (Adjusted total for plot episodes)
                                                          Sub-total         6.0

RESOLUTION (10 points)
    a. The friends all played together and each person did what he or she wanted to do.   _____
    b. They all had a wonderful day and were so tired that they fell asleep.              _____
                                                          Sub-total         _____
SEQUENCE (10 points)
    Story told with elements in order (setting, theme,
    plot/episodes, resolution)                            Sub-total         6.6

TOTAL SCORE                                                                31.6
```

Modified Request/Question-Answer Procedure

This procedure combines two approaches for assessing comprehension ability: the question-answer relationship approach (Raphael, 1982) and the request procedure (Manzo, 1968). Both may be used for diagnosing comprehension. This combined procedure permits diagnosticians to focus on several abilities at once. The procedure should be used several times to acquaint students with its format, thus providing a comfort factor. The comfort relieves anxiety and tension often experienced in formal testing environments. The redundant use provides the diagnostician with several opportunities to observe students' behaviors under similar conditions while observing abilities and needs of each.

The purposes of the request/question-answer procedure are:

- To observe students' interests and content focus
- To assess students' abilities to comprehend text materials
- To assess students' abilities to understand the relationship between questions and answers
- To provide students with a means for becoming aware of the type of information sought by questioning, thus facilitating test wiseness.

Procedures.

1. Select a story for student(s) to read. If individually administered, the student and teacher should each have a copy of the story. When used in groups, multiple copies—one for each student—must be provided.

2. Prepare student for the session by saying the following:

> The purpose of this session is to find out how well you understand information that you read. In order to do that I am going to ask you to read this short passage (hand text to student) silently. When you are finished, you will ask me two questions about the passage. I will also read the passage and will ask you two questions, also.

3. The student and teacher read the passage silently, at the same time. This builds a sense of association while providing a model for behavior. When the teacher has completed the passage, he or she should put it away immediately, to demonstrate appropriate behavior.

4. Explain that the format of this session demands that all questions asked by either student or teacher must be answered, and without rereading.

5. Say, "I am ready to ask you a question. Are you ready?" Students may tell questions orally or write them before asking the teacher to respond. The examiner would then have several pieces of data in addition to student comprehension ability, including (a) short-term memory recall from reading and (b) short-term memory recall and the ability to recode the information.

6. Immediately after asking your question, say one of the following after the student responds: (a) "The question I asked made you think about information that is *right there* in the passage. You can go to the story and find the answer and read it right from the page." (b) "The question I asked made you *think and then search* for an answer. You knew that the answer was in the text, but it was hard to find. It was hard because the words that tell you the answer are not all in one place or may not be the same as those used in the question. So you had to think about what I asked for and then search for the answer." (c) "The question I asked made you decide that the answer could only be found *on your own*. The questions asked about something in the story, but the story won't help."

Here is a sample paragraph for you, followed by sample questions. An evaluation form is provided in Figure 6–12.

DEMONSTRATION PASSAGE

John came to visit Joan. Both had been away on a business trip and were anxious to see each other again. The separation had been difficult. The weather didn't help and neither did the reasons for the trip.

EXAMPLES OF QUESTION TYPES	
Right There	Who came to visit Joan? (John came to visit Joan.)
Think and Then Search	Why did John and Joan have difficulty getting together? (Both had been away. The weather didn't help.)
On Your Own	Why were John and Joan anxious to see each other? (They were in love.) (Each was interested in finding out what happened on the trips.) (They lived in the Caribbean where there was great weather, and the trips were to New York and Canada in January.)

7. Encourage the student to ask you a question. Respond to the question. Ask the student to identify the question type. If response is, "I don't know," accept it, at first. Plan for future instruction concerning the type of question asked.

8. Use the evaluation form recommended to record and interpret student's comprehension and recall (see Figure 6–12).

Figure 6–12 Request/Question-Answer Evaluation Form

STUDENT QUESTIONS

1. _____

_____

Comments: _____

_____

2. _____
   _____

   Comments: _____
   _____

3. How many questions required information that was "right there"? (factual) _____
4. How many were "think and then search" questions? _____
5. How many "on your own" questions were asked? (inference or prediction) _____
6. Were the student's questions like the teacher's? _____

   Comments: _____
   _____
   _____
   _____

7. Was the student able to identify the question types? _____
8. Was question-type identification immediate? ____ hesitant? ____ modeled after teacher? ____ improved after several tries? ____ (Skilled reading indicated when immediate, automatic responses are offered.)

   Comments: _____
   _____

Recommendations for further assessment: _____
_____

Recommendations for instruction: _____

Modified Request/Question–Answer Instructional Strategy Lessons

Question-answer strategies should begin by bombarding students with questions of the same type for one week, or five regularly scheduled instructional sessions. Four sample lessons are provided. Lesson one bombards students with a model. The second lesson encourages students to use the new information. The third lesson permits diagnosticians to observe students' understanding of the procedure. The fourth lesson helps students maintain the information.

Lesson one. Read a story to the student. After reading, encourage retelling. Write "right there" questions on the chalkboard or easel. Read a question. Say: "Tell me how you will find the answer to the question." Responses from students indicate their comprehension of the required materials. Probable responses to each type of question include:

Right There	"It is in the story."
	"Here it is. I'll read it."
	"The story tells you the answer."
	"I can read the answer to that question from the passage."
Think and Then Search	"I can find the answer by thinking about it."
	"The answer is in the story, but not in the same words as the question." Or, "The answer is in the story, but it is in more than one place."
On My Own	"I have to get the answer from my memory."
	"The answer is not in the story, but the story helps me to think about things related to the story that I already know."

Lesson two. Have each student select a passage. After reading, ask each to develop questions like the ones they just worked with. Display students' questions and have the author or peer identify the question type. If students can do this move on to Lesson 3. If not, then further instruction similar to that described in Lesson 1 should continue.

Lesson three. The third step in this instructional process is the test. Students are offered a passage to read and they are expected to create questions related to the passage. The student is asked to identify the question types learned.

Lesson four. Reviews are recommended weekly in classroom settings and every third meeting in tutorial or special school programs.

Brainstorming Procedures

This technique, highly recommended by Moffett (1983), promotes interaction, stimulates ideas, and uses ideas stored in long-term memory. Brainstorming is especially useful for guiding students into writing activities. Students make decisions about topics related to reading as ideas are generated in the session without evaluation. Judgments are withheld thus encouraging students to "speak out" by "storming their brains" for ideas related to the topic. The activities help students organize thoughts into categories. They realize how one topic is related to another. The procedure is appropriately used at all levels. The purposes of brainstorming, as a diagnostic technique, are:

- To assess prior knowledge about content
- To assess whether brainstorming is an effective technique for the student.

Procedure.

1. Begin by providing an example. Place the topic name at the top of a chalkboard or easel.
2. Say: "When I see this topic I think of _____." Write the word you think of on the board. Say: "Then I think of _____." Write more words. Say: "O.K., who thinks of something when you see _(topic name)_ ?" As students call out ideas, write them on the board.
3. For diagnostic purposes, focus on one student at a time. Note responses and behaviors. Record them in memory or on a tape. Transfer information from memory or tape onto evaluation form, as provided in Figure 6–13.
4. Brainstorm with students several times a week. Record responses and reactions.

Figure 6–13 Brainstorming Observation/Evaluation Form

Student's Name _____ Date _____

Purpose for Observation _____

_____

Setting _____

Topic _____

BEHAVIORAL OBSERVATIONS	Yes	Sometimes	No
Confirms idea with explanations.	___	___	___
Seems to perceive topic appropriately.	___	___	___
In conversations following brainstorming session, demonstrates knowledge of information in conversation.	___	___	___
Seems interested in topic.	___	___	___

Interest is demonstrated by the following behaviors: _____

_____

Comments: _____

TOPIC CONSIDERATIONS	Yes	Sometimes	No
Is the student able to identify an issue for study?	____	____	____
Does the student present solutions to problems?	____	____	____
Is the student able to move from one step to another in the learning process with some independence?	____	____	____

Interpretations and recommendations: _____

Story Maps

Often students know the information from narrative-type reading materials, but lack an intuitive sense for organizing that information. We know that story recall is better for students who are able to use an author's structure as a retrieval cue than for those who can't. Poor readers seem to benefit from instruction in story structure (McGee & Richgels, 1986; Pearson & Camperell, 1985). Story maps, therefore, can serve as guides for helping teachers and diagnosticians assess and teach students to improve comprehension (Fitzgerald & Spiegel, 1983). Guiding students' senses of story with maps that include questions helps them to learn to use questions for better story understanding (Beck & McKeown, 1981). Although some students have found story maps limiting, others find them helpful for collecting and organizing information for comprehension purposes (Moore & Readence, 1983; Alverman, Boothby, & Wolfe, 1984). The "sense of story" in readers' comprehension may develop, for some, just by reading. Others need direct instruction and, therefore, diagnosis to determine if this sense exists as a result of the instruction. Stories have predictable grammars. The readers who possess a sense of how stories progress, possess story grammars and can "predict" their organizations. Those who need guidance for recalling stories can gain this by learning to use story maps to guide themselves through narrative reading.

Procedure.

1. Give the students a story to read. Say: "I am going to give you a story map that should help you to remember what you read."
2. Show the students a story map. Three variations are illustrated in Figure

6–14. Say: "You will be expected to fill in the blanks after reading the story. Think about the story setting, where it takes place, who it is about, the problem, and the solution to the problem."

3. Then, have the students read the story.

Figure 6–14 Sample Story Maps

DIAGNOSTIC STORY MAP 1

Character(s): _____

_____

_____

Setting: _____

The problem: _____

The goal: _____

Events: _____

_____

_____

The resolution: _____

_____

DIAGNOSTIC STORY MAP 2

_____
(Name of Story)

WHERE	WHO	WHEN	PROBLEM	GOAL
_____	_____	_____	_____	_____
_____	_____	_____	_____	_____
_____	_____	_____	_____	_____

RESOLUTION

_____

_____

_____

INSTRUCTIONAL STORY MAP 3

SETTING AND CHARACTERS:

Question 1. Where does the story take place? _____

Question 2. When does the story happen? _____

Question 3. Who is the story about? _____

PROBLEM:

Question 4. What problem does Fred have to solve? _____

GOAL:

Question 5. What does Fred need to solve the problem? _____

Question 6. What does Fred need to do? _____

Question 7. What did Fred do first to solve his problem? _____

RESOLUTION:

Question 8. How did Fred finally solve his problem? _____

Question 9. What do you suppose he learned from the problem? _____

The following story is included to demonstrate the use of story maps for guiding students to generate questions for themselves in order to direct their reading.

THE BORROWED CAR

"You'd better be sure that you take care of the car," called Fred's father. "That means no accidents and no mess inside." "O.K., Dad," yelled Fred. "I'll be careful." As Fred drove along, he came upon two of his friends. Jim was eating an ice cream cone, and Connie cotton candy. These were their last treats from the carnival down the street, and they wanted their good time to last as long as possible. Fred saw the ice cream and candy, and his heart began to leap. "What if they mess the seats?" he thought. "Dad will have a fit and probably tell me that I can't use the car again." As the two friends approached the car, Fred decided that something had to be done to save his friendships and the car, too. Fred drove the car around the block before his friends saw him. "How can I give them a ride and keep the car clean?" he thought. As he approached the end of the street, Fred saw a dry cleaning shop. "Ah," he thought. "The plastic covers put over clean clothing might solve the problem." Fred stopped his Dad's car and parked. He approached the woman behind the dry cleaning counter. "May I purchase some of your plastic covering?" "It's not for sale, sir," she said. "Well you see, I have a problem," Fred said. As Fred described the situation, he spotted some plastic covering on the floor behind the counter. "Is that to be thrown away?" he asked. "Yes, it's in pieces," replied the woman. "May I have those pieces?" asked Fred. "Of course," the woman replied. Fred eagerly picked up the plastic. He ran to his car and draped the pieces over the seat covers. Then he drove quickly to meet his friends. As they opened the car door, Connie said, "What in the world is all of this plastic stuff for?" "Ah, well, you see, my Dad warned me about keeping the car clean, or else!" Fred replied. Before Jim and Connie got into the car, they dropped the napkins in their hands into a trash can. They didn't need them anymore; they had finished eating their snacks.

STORY MAP

Character(s): Fred, his father, the proprietor of the dry cleaning shop, and Fred's friends.
Setting: Inside the car and the dry cleaning shop.
The problem: Fred was "ordered" to keep the car clean, or else!
The goal: Keeping the car clean and keeping his friends.
    Event 1. Fred saw danger in keeping the car clean when he saw that his friends were eating sticky foods.
    Event 2. Fred gave himself some thinking time to try to find a solution to the problem.
    Event 3. Fred found a dry cleaning establishment that used plastic packaging materials.
The resolution: Fred put plastic over the car interior. The friends had already finished eating their sticky food.

Simplified Story Map. Since visual images of story structure seem to provide equipment necessary for creating text, it is important to provide simple as well as more complex maps for students. The following directions for creating a visual story map provide students with beginning steps to construct their own text. Creating visual imagery story maps permits students to focus on a main idea when writing. Or, visual story maps may also be used after reading to aid students' comprehension. Following are two different ways to use a visual story map:

1. Write the main idea of your writing topic (or the passage you have read) in the middle of the page, inside a circle. Next, draw spokes coming out from the circle. Write story details on the spokes.
2. Place the name of the main character in the middle of the wheel. Then place details about his or her appearance (adventures, etc.) on the spokes.

Figure 6–15 shows a sample map developed by an eight-year-old girl. The child developed the story map after reading a text about bees. The map was used as a guide for composing his own text.

166 Reading Comprehension and Retention

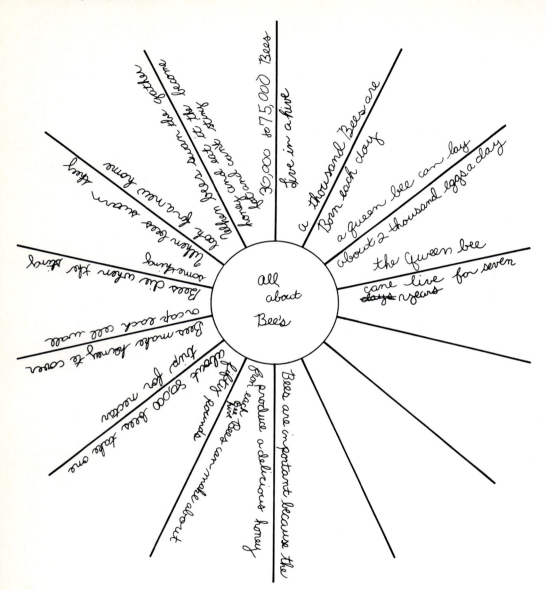

Figure 6-15 Sample Visual Story Map (Reprinted with the permission of Carolyn Lumia, parent of Margaret)

Graphic Organizers

Developed originally as a device to aid vocabulary learning (Barron, 1969; Earle, 1970), graphic organizers serve as diagnostic and instructional tools for defining hierarchical relationships among concepts. In other words, graphic organizers are visual displays of hierarchical sturctures of ideas in texts.

The graphic organizer may be used to serve the following purposes in diagnosis:

- To assess students' ability to skim the general format of a chapter in a text and determine purposes for reading
- To assess students' recall of information after reading a chapter of text material
- To assess students' ability to define related concepts
- To serve as an instructional tool to guide students to determine the important information in text materials
- To help students summarize information read in text materials.

Since graphic organizers are intended to be used for assessing content, it seems expedient here to list the most common text patterns students encounter in schoolbooks. These six expository text structures, as described by Readence, Bean, and Baldwin (1985), represent the macrostructures writers and readers use to recall text easily:

1. Cause/effect: Pattern links reason with results. Interaction between two or more ideas or events characterize this pattern. Social studies texts use this pattern often. (For example: Lack of money prevented the vacation.)
2. Comparison/contrast: Likenesses and differences between two or more objects are illustrated. (For example: Money and happiness are synonymous for some people.)
3. Time/order: Relationships between ideas and events are presented in sequential order. (For example: When he completes his medical degree he will seek an internship abroad.)
4. Simple listing: A nonorder listing of events are presented. (For example: She needs to shop for many things.)
5. Problem/solution: These are the interactions between two or more factors. A problem is stated and solutions provided. (For example: Forgetting to take medicines is a problem solved with a plastic device that has a built-in reminding mechanism.)
6. Argument: Pro and con arguments concerning a topic are the focus. (For example: Over the counter drugs should not be sold. Although they serve a purpose for some, they promote more than relief from pain.)

Procedures.

1. Provide students with a blank graphic organizer.
2. Instruct students to skim a text chapter.

3. Tell them to put the main concept at the top of the organizer.
4. Say: "Complete the organizer by filling in information as you see appropriate."

Sample graphic organizers are shown in the next three figures. (Note: the information about environments for living for different species was selected *only* to demonstrate the use of the instrument. The organizer in Figure 6–16 would appear in an outline as follows:

PLACES TO LIVE

    I. Humans
       a. Brick Dwellings
       b. Wooden Dwellings
   II. Birds
       a. Mud
       b. Sticks
  III. Fish
       a. Water
  IV. Insects
       a. Plants
       b. Humans

Students' knowledge can be assessed by presenting them with a listing of relevant vocabulary and requesting that they use a graphic organizer to demonstrate knowledge of the content. The following word list and instructions is an example of what might be given to students. "Arrange the following

Figure 6-16 Graphic Organizer for Places to Live

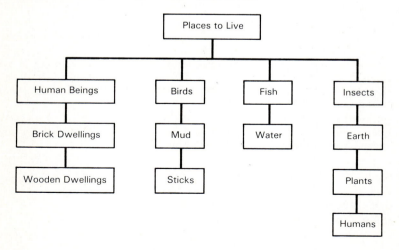

words by creating a graphic organizer. Be ready to justify your arrangement in writing or by telling it to me."

milk	cream	pork	mold
veal	curdling	cheese	lamb
marbling	eggs	egg nog	butter
dairy	meat	bacon	beef

A blank form may also be used to guide students to respond. An organizer might look like the chart in Figure 6–17. Figure 6–18 shows how the sample terms from the word list might be arranged.

Self-Monitoring Devices

Understanding what is known about a book before reading it is important for the reader. When the student is aware of what he or she knows about the book's topic, we can assume that the student will be able to predict his or her ability to comprehend the text. One's prior knowledge and the reader's ability to consciously determine how to use that prior knowledge to appropriately interact with text is essential for comprehension. We are interested in students understanding what they know about text. We want to help them to determine what information is stored in their memory. We want them to determine if that information is appropriate to comprehending the text. We want them to decide if they know enough about the content and vocabulary to understand the text. There are several kinds of information necessary for students' text comprehension. These include the book's (1) content, (2) vocabulary, (3) story structure, and (4) elements associated with organization of stories and texts.

Figure 6-17 Blank Organizer Format

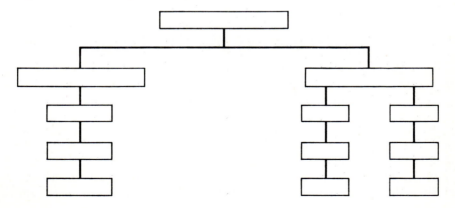

170 Reading Comprehension and Retention

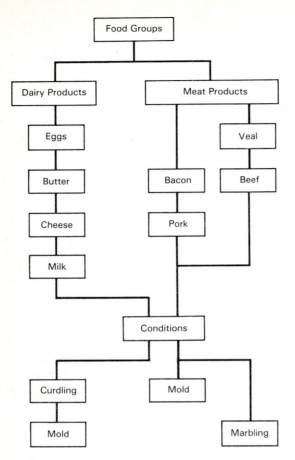

Figure 6-18 Graphic organizer for Food Group.

The self-monitoring device helps students search their memories to determine how much they already know about a book before they read it. Continuous use should help each student to know if a book can easily be read based on the possession of appropriate prior knowledge.

Directions. A self-monitoring chart (Figure 6–19) should be available for students to complete on their own before and after reading stories, content materials, and library books. It should help the student monitor his or her knowledge and determine success or failure with materials. When the student says, "I think I'll take another book. I don't think that I have enough prior knowledge about the subject in order to understand it," the student understands the concept of prior knowledge and it's relationship to comprehension of text materials. "Before" and "after" reading information should be compared in order for students to learn about themselves concerning their prior knowledge from experiences, reading, and school.

Self-Selecting Books

Becoming a reader means being independent. Students who feel confident will select their own materials in order to meet their recreational as well as their academic needs. Guiding students to become independent readers requires that each is provided with strategy for such behavior. Students will select their own reading materials when they are sure that they can read them. The following "fist-full-of-words" rule, well used by children for many years, works for building independence. We give our friend, Jeannette Veatch credit for this rule.

Figure 6–19 Self-Monitoring Chart

Title _____

Author's name _____

Reader's name _____

BEFORE READING	AFTER READING
What do you already know about this book without having read it? Make a list below:	Why did you like this book? What did you like about it?
	What did you not like about it?

Read your list again. Now, because you know these things, what do you think this book will be about? What will you find out about when you read this book?

_____
_____
_____
_____
_____
_____
_____
_____
_____

Tell what the book is about.

_____
_____
_____

Was your prediction right?
_____ yes _____ no

What is your kid's rating for this book?

1   2   3   4   5   6   7

terrible ⟵⟶ terrific

Look at your list again. What was in the book and what was not?

_____ _____
_____ _____
_____ _____

Figure 6–19 Continued

Directions. Say to the student: "Hold up your hand with all of your fingers straight up. Now you may select any book. Begin with one page. Read it to yourself. Each time you do not know a word, put a finger down. If all of your fingers go down on that page, you have a fist. Try to read three more pages. If you make a fist for all of the pages, the book is too difficult. Try another."

It is important to praise the student for discovering that a book is too difficult. Say, "I like the way you used the *fist-full-of-words* rule to find out that the book was too difficult. That really indicates that you know about your reading. Try another book."

Assessment Procedures In Recreational Settings

Recreational settings include those where reading happens by student choice. A student might, for example, choose to read a novel, complete a crossword puzzle, or read the funny papers during a study period or lunch break. A young

The "fist-full-of-words" rule permits youngsters to select their own reading materials confidently.

child might choose to read road signs, labels, or cans. Young and old may decide to relax out of doors, in bed, or on the beach by reading.

Recreational reading provides relaxation and diversion from the assigned or mandatory tasks of the day. We know of no previous discussions in the professional literature concerning diagnosis of students reading in naturalistic, recreational settings. It seems to us that recreational reading represents important aspects of reading ability. If students read well during these times, then instructional and related school reading activities ought to be altered to resemble recreational settings, when appropriate. Children who fail in reading might benefit from learning in environments that represent rest and relaxation. If professionals observe problem readers in successful recreational reading behaviors, these settings must be captured and transformed for instructional settings. Assessment techniques and instructional strategies suggested in this section can *only* be used in classrooms and clinics that promote "natural environments" for sharing text materials. These environments support the students' freedom to select literature of interest. Learning environments in schools that promote recreational reading and writing look at these processes as means to ends—not ends in themselves. The end result of literacy learning in school should be the development of interests for students. Figure 6–20 offers a summary guide for determining when the student reads for recreation. This is followed by strategies for observing responses resulting from recreational reading periods. Information should be collected over a one-month time period. At least three observations are recommended.

Students' Self-Perceptions

The checklist presented in Figure 6–20 should provide some information about students' views of themselves as readers and writers. Since the end result of literacy learning in school ought to be the development of readers who are interested in reading, additional information about interest seems important. Interest in reading depends a great deal on students' perceptions of themselves as readers. The questionnaire on page 176 should provide additional data about students' interests and perceptions of themselves in reading and related activities.

Figure 6–20 Summary Observation Guide for Recreational Reading Settings

WHEN DOES THE STUDENT READ FOR RECREATION?

_____ During free periods
_____ During snack or lunch period
_____ During an instructional period (e.g., holds selected reading material inside instructional text)
_____ After a successful learning experience
_____ While waiting for a school bus, a special teacher, etc.
_____ Other recreational reading times: _____

WHAT DOES THE STUDENT CHOOSE TO READ DURING RECREATIONAL READING PERIODS? (specify)

Text materials (specify) _____

Fiction (include authors and types of stories) _____

_____

Nonfiction materials (specify) _____

Comic strips or books _____

Crossword puzzles/word games _____

Jokes and joke books _____

Cookbooks _____

Books that explain "how to do it" _____

Riddle books _____

Trivia (facts) _____

Newspapers _____

News magazines _____

Other magazines _____

Summary and Observations: _____

_____

_____

_____

_____

How I Feel About Reading in School

Answer these questions as honestly as you can:

Do you think that your friends believe that you read for enjoyment? _____

What would your friend think if he/she saw you reading in the school lunchroom? _____

_____

What would your teacher think if he/she saw you reading a novel during study period? _____

_____

If you wrote a story (novel, article, comic strip) how would your teacher respond to it? _____

_____

Observational responses. Students who do not view themselves as readers *may* respond as follows:

> "If my friends saw me reading, they'd think I'd gone crazy."
> "I wouldn't be caught dead with a book in my hands around friends."
> "Reading is sissy stuff. My friends would think I was queer."
> "My teacher would scream if she saw me reading a novel. I never pay attention, and that would kill her."
> "She wouldn't believe it if she saw me reading anything."
> "I wouldn't give my teacher anything that I wrote. I'd flunk."
> "I don't know what my friends would think."
> "My mom and dad wouldn't care."
> "My teacher wouldn't pay any attention to me."

Look for consistent trends in responses. Ask yourself, Do responses project positive attitudes? Are responses negative, projecting feelings of inadequacies? Do these negative responses rely on the opinions of others? Do these responses seem valid? Has the child failed so often that the negative feelings override the student's ability to read and write?

Research studies suggest that students with reading difficulties seem to exhibit stress (Gentile, McMillan, & Swain, 1985). Studies indicate that when students experience emotional trauma during reading, the emotional drain may limit their willingness or ability to concentrate (Allington, 1980; Gates, 1941). Because many students with reading deficits experience stress, and because this stress provokes discomfort and negative feelings toward reading, poor self-concepts and perceptions about self as readers endure.

Recreational settings where pressure to report after reading is eliminated should help to relieve tension in order to make reading part of the student's life.

Unguided Retelling Procedures

Unguided retellings are vehicles that provide opportunities to assess students' comprehension of text through unaided recall in written or oral formats. Oral retellings are time consuming and require the attention of the diagnostician in spontaneous, unplanned settings. This procedure works with reluctant readers, who feel most comfortable retelling about reading during unplanned times. Playgrounds, lunchrooms, school corridors, and school bus stops are some of the places where informal, spontaneous oral retellings often occur.

The purpose of unguided retellings is to decide if students comprehend text as demonstrated through free, unaided, or unguided recall in oral or written forms in recreational, informal settings.

Procedures for unguided oral retellings.

1. Develop a posture that tells students that you are "eager" to listen to their retellings when they need to retell. Smiles, direct eye contact, and open acceptance of oral contributions of any sort contribute to the feelings that encourage freedom to share.
2. Encourage conversations about books. Begin, for example, by saying, "Gee, (student name), I just read something funny. When I see you tomorrow, remind me to tell you about it."
3. When students come to tell about their reading, intent *listening* is most important. Look at the student as if he or she is the *only* person in the world at that moment.

Procedures for unguided written retellings.

1. Provide a very personal vehicle for spontaneous responses to reading. This might be a notebook, diary, or individual sheets kept in a special folder referred to as a literary journal. The vehicle should be available for student use whenever any student wants to use it. It should be kept in student stations in self-contained classrooms or with the students' themselves in departmentalized programs.
2. Instructions should be shared initially. Say: "Use your literary journal to record everything you remember from your reading." These instructions ought to occur at the beginning of a group session, school year, or course. Offer them *only* to encourage reluctant students to write story recalls. Make written recall an expected activity that occurs at the same time each day. This builds routine.
3. Responses should be shared, regularly, in small groups or individually with the teacher. The summary sheet provided in Figure 6–21 might be used after each literary review.

The chart in Figure 6–22 can be used to note characteristics of students' written retellings. Written and oral retellings furnish diagnosticians with qualitative information about students' recall from reading. The checklist used

Figure 6–21 Evaluation Summary Form: Student's Free Recall from Reading in Recreational Settings

---

Student's name: _____

Responding to the following book (article, poem, etc.): _____
_____

Student recalled information in sequential order: _____

Student was able to capture the idea of the materials: _____
_____

Student retold part of the story: _____

Student retold the entire passage: _____

Student supported major ideas by including details. _____
_____

Student demonstrated knowledge of relationships. _____
_____

Comments/Recommendations: _____
_____

---

in oral language assessment, Figure 4–2, Chapter 4, may be used to determine the growth of retellings in both oral and written formats. Information noted from analyzing syntactic element distributions (described in Chapter 4, Figure 4–3) may be used to notice changes in syntactic structures including additions, deletions, substitutions, and rearrangements of words, phrases, and sentences. These analyses provide information concerning growth in language production during retellings. The modified version of Morrow's (in press) quantification procedure for assessing retellings in instructional and formal settings, may also be used (see Figure 6–10). All results provide information that indicates growth over time.

Figure 6–22 Monitoring Sheet for Writing

Child's Name _____ Examiner _____

1. Child writes in sentences. _____
2. Child uses sentences but each one is an independent thought. _____
   _____
3. Child wrote a story. _____
4. The story had a beginning _____ middle, _____ and end _____
5. The story had a main character. _____
6. There was a plot that was evident throughout. _____
7. The child seems to use vocabulary to enhance text. Adjectives _____
   _____ Adverbs _____
8. The child included the setting in the story. _____
9. The child wrote with a problem to be solved. _____
10. The child included a solution to the problem in the story. _____
    _____
11. The child was able to invent spelling. _____
12. The child found it difficult to invent spelling and asked for spellings. (You can only answer this if you were with the child, or know who did the testing) _____
    _____
13. The child seems to be able to write so that the print or manuscript is legible. _____
    _____
14. The child uses punctuation
    Capitalizations _____ Punctuation Marks: Periods, _____ commas, _____ exclamation points, _____ and question marks _____.
15. The invented spellings used by the child seem to tell us that he/she has some indication of the phonemic spelling system of language. _____

> 16. When asked to write the story, the child seemed to understand what to do. _____
> _____
>
> 17. When asked to write the story, the child seemed confused. (Describe behavior) _____
> _____
>
> 18. The child used several sentences, and different syntactic patterns.
>
>   (SV, SVO, SV Adj, SV Adv, etc.) _____

Figure 6–22 Continued

ASSESSMENT PROCEDURES IN INTERACTIVE SETTINGS

Another type of setting important to the C–A–L–M system is the interactive setting. We are concerned with assessing students' abilities to demonstrate comprehension from reading as they interact to share and receive ideas "naturally." Natural language interactions happen when at least two humans have the need to share or receive information. These interactive settings usually result from informal activities that promote communication. These informal situations must occur in order for children to develop a language system that functions appropriately. Halliday's (1978) functional interaction model for emergent oral language emphasizes that children learn language and meanings in contexts related to situations and through interaction with other people within social settings. Halliday states that:

> Language comes to life only when functioning in some environment. We do not experience language in isolation . . . but always in relation to a scenario, some background of persons and actions and events from which the things are said to derive their meaning. (1978, p. 28)

Children produce and respond to language based on initial interactions and perceptions of these interactions with important people. These people—parents, teachers, and peers—exchange meanings. Meanings develop from the perceived intent of both the sender and receiver.

Some interactive environments resemble the natural learning environment of the early learning periods. Others are created to facilitate interactive language in contrived ways. Childrens' initial understandings of what print means and how they can control their lives using this coding system relies on how each learns to perceive the notions imparted by people important to each during the early years (Bissex, 1980; Clay, 1975; Ferriero, 1982, Harste, Burke, & Woodward, 1981). Literature has clearly demonstrated that when children are surrounded by print, they use print and oral language and can make sense of it (Goodman, 1982). Several have noted that learning to speak and learning to write in natural ways occur in environments that interactively support and accept the student's early efforts to communicate in written and oral form, even when messages are offered in forms that are far from standard (Hoffman, 1982; King, 1982). We are interested in facilitating environments similar to that in the home that create the "naturalness" of language learning that occurs when children learn to talk. Although we respect the home environment, we must deal with school settings and recognize that differences between the contexts of home and school environments must exist (Cook-Gumperz & Gumperz, 1982; Heath, 1983). The following interaction between two children and their "onlooking" teacher may help to demonstrate the supportive school environment we recommend. The situation involved two boys, Oliver, age eleven, and Benjy, age seven. For several weeks, both had been writing their own book, after interviewing and spending time with a published author of children's books. They were in the editing stages of their sections of the manuscript. The teacher was sitting nearby, writing her own story, when the following conversation occurred:

BENJY: How are you doing, Oliver?
OLIVER: Not so great. I'm still writing this draft, and it doesn't sound right.
BENJY: Well, Oliver, what draft is this?
OLIVER: I think it's the fourth.
BENJY: Let me see it.
TEACHER: Gosh, fellas, I'm working on my sixth draft, and it's tough. I'm angry at myself.
OLIVER: You are, Mrs. Stellitano?
TEACHER: Yeah. I get so frustrated that I want to bang the table, just like I saw you do, Oliver.
OLIVER: Yeah, that's what I want to do when I hate my composition.
BENJY: Gosh, Oliver, this is good stuff. Your story makes me want to read the rest, but you need to finish it.
OLIVER: I know, but it's tough.
TEACHER: Your right!!! It is tough.
BENJY: Well, Oliver, you've got the hard stuff done, that's the story part. Now you just have the editing. I'll do that with you when I'm done with my writing today.
TEACHER: Me too, Oliver. Just come over when you need editing help.

The encouragement from Benjy coupled with the appropriate remarks from the teacher demonstrate interest and concern for Oliver's feelings. The teacher and peer support his efforts and emphathize with his frustrations. These kinds of interactions encourage students to continue to produce language. The naturally developed group (three persons) created a "work-along-side-of" environment that fostered a buddy system, which in itself, supplies support.

What Do We observe?

We want to observe students' reading comprehension in interactive settings. We want to look at the environment, the language interactions—both verbal and nonverbal—that affect language productions. We want to decide how these interactions help to encourage or discourage the production of language in response to reading. The observation guide in Figure 6–23 should provide structure for observations that demonstrate students' abilities to interact and share ideas from reading.

Creating an Interactive Setting for Diagnosis

The obvious way to study natural language seems to be in environments that simulate the language as students respond naturally to reading and listening in formal and informal classroom settings. We must, therefore, create settings

Discussing stories builds text comprehension.

Figure 6–23 Observation Summary Sheet for Interactions

When Do Students Demonstrate Text Comprehension With Others?

Diagnostician: _____ Date: _____

Student observed: _____

Interactions and setting: _____

_____

Describe setting in which comprehension is best demonstrated. Use more than one category, below, if necessary.

Small group _____ Large group _____

   Role play _____

   Writing alongside of peers and/or mentors _____

   Talking to a peer _____

   Talking to a teacher (adult) _____

   In the classroom _____

   In the school halls (playground, lunchroom, etc.) _____

What sort of information does student recall?

   Main ideas _____ Details _____ Plot _____

   Problems _____ Solutions _____

What patterns of organization does the student use?

   Logical sequential ordering _____

   Lists without obvious order _____

   Groups of unrelated ideas _____

   Groups of related ideas but in no logical order _____

Summary: _____

_____

that provide students with opportunities to respond to language in books as freely as possible with peers and adults in interactive ways.

Little research and practice exists considering reading and evaluation of behaviors in an interactive setting. The literature that does exist concerning evaluation of students' language behaviors in interactive settings has been conducted with preschool and kindergarten children (Genishi & Dyson, 1984; Baghban, 1984; Clay, 1982; Milz, 1985; Doake, 1985). The focus of most of these studies has been oral language behaviors, beginning writing, and reading-like behaviors. Clay's work (1968, 1982), particularly, strongly suggests that creating interactive settings and then "looking and seeing" children in classrooms in systematic ways provides valuable information about students' reading comprehension abilities. We have culled from the work of Clay (1982), King (1985), Lindfors (1985), and others in suggesting the following guidelines for creating interactive settings.

Guidelines and settings. Create an environment that encourages free oral language production. Provide chairs for lounge-type sitting, tables and chairs for writing and conversation, and book display areas that hold books, magazines, newspapers, and other reading materials for all to see. Place children in groups of two to four using the following criteria:

- Children should be approximately the same age.
- Sex preferences should be considered. Boys and girls at certain ages, usually nine to eleven, prefer to work with children of their own sex.
- Respect children's choices of books, friends, and materials by placing together children who seem to encourage each other to talk and write, and by providing materials based on students' interests.
- Schedule eight to ten two-hour sessions for diagnostic purposes.
- Provide games and other recreational activities that encourage interactive activities and be sure that at least one half-hour of the two-hour diagnostic session is spent observing children in interaction with informal literary materials.

Procedures. Procedures for collecting language samples in interactive settings include video and audio recording devices and teacher notes. Notes may be anecdotal. They may also be ethnographic in nature (see Chapter 3). The following strategies can be used to describe students' language productions in interactive situations:

1. Individual oral language assessment, Figures 4–2, 4–3, Chapter 4.
2. Assessing languages in interactive settings, Chapter 4, Figures 4–6, 4–7.
3. Unguided retellings, Chapter 6, Figures 6–9, 6–10.
4. Free writing (journals), Chapter 6, Figure 6–25.

Dialogue journals. Dialogue journals provide students with an opportunity to share, privately and in writing, their reactions and concerns about school and personal experiences with the teacher (Staton, 1980). The sharing provides supportive responses by the teacher without threat or evaluation as demonstrated in Figure 6-24, which presents Kai's journal entry and her teacher's response. Dialogue journals are used to encourage diarylike responses to things that take place in students' lives, in and out of school. Students' English teachers, particularly, have used this vehicle for determining students' progress in "talking" things in writing.

Dialogue journals can also be used to encourage students to respond to what they are *reading* as an aid to comprehension. Although unclear, it is generally accepted among educators that there is a relationship between reading and writing (Jaggar, Carrara, & Weiss, 1986). Reading seems to play an important role in learning to write (Tierney & Leys, 1984). The following example illustrates how one youngster used the language of text to produce her own.

The child was Marie. She was an eleven-year-old who had had difficulty reading since second grade. She was directed toward a picture book, *Rosie's Walk* by Pat Hutchins. Marie's purpose for learning to read the book developed from her desire to read stories to younger children. The book, a series of adverbial phrases, three to four words each, was rehearsed by Marie. After successfully reading the story to a group of six-year-olds, Marie wrote her own story, which read as follows:

MARIE

Marie the girl went for a walk, Over the hill, through a puddle, in the mud, past a bunch of guys through stones in a dump, under a tunnel, between a fence, and got home in time to watch TV.

The text reflects, almost exactly, the syntactic structure of *Rosie's Walk*, which reads:

Rosie the hen went for a walk, across the yard, around the pond, over the haystack, past the mill, through the fence, under the beehives, and got back in time for dinner.[1]

Thus, the book's syntactic system has helped to guide the student to composing text.

Writing practice is necessary for mastery of different modes of discourse. Good writers spend more time on their writing—planning, rereading, and revising—than poor writers (Stallard, 1974; Perl, 1979; Bridwell, 1980).

[1]Reprinted with permission of Macmillan Company from *Rosie's Walk* by Pat Hutchins. Copyright © 1968 by Patricia Hutchins.

3/9/85

I'm having a problem with shyness, and it's getting harder to meet other people and boys and get older. My mother knows that I'm shy, but she has never really talked to me about it. She gave me some tips, but they never work. It's even harder to meet boys because I'm never around them, and that no one I know that go to an all girls school. I also feel bad to say I don't have a boy friend. All of my girl friends have boy friends, even my very best friend in the whole world! I know I know how I know I'm left out!

please HELP!

Bye!

Figure 6-24

Dear Kai,
    I think you are very brave and very smart to be able to recognize your problem of shyness. It is painful, isn't it? Maybe you and I could talk about it sometime — that might give you some ideas.
    About boy friends, well, sometimes it takes a while to have a relationship with a boy. And if you are having fun when you are with boys and girls, that makes you very attractive to boys as well as girls.
    I'm sorry you feel left out — I'll give you a hug so you'll know you're not left out with me.
                Love,
                  Gloria

Figure 6–24 Student Entry and Teacher Response from a Dialogue Journal (Reprinted with permission of Paul A. Lee, father of Kai, and Gloria B. Smith. Taken from a dialogue journal, 1985).

Figure 6–25 Guide for Noting Changes In Composition/Comprehension as Illustrated in Journals

Text to which student is responding _____

Student's Name _____ Date _____

	YES	NO	NEED MORE DATA
1. Responses to reading are in order as author presents them.	____	____	____
2. Responses are sparce—just one idea, and not necessarily the main one.	____	____	____
3. Responses include only details, with little mention of main idea of story.	____	____	____
4. The structure of the text the student has read is helpful to his/her comprehension.	____	____	____
5. The text structure seems to hinder text comprehension as demonstrated in the journal entry.	____	____	____
6. Teacher dialogue seems to help student respond again (next time).	____	____	____
7. Student writes in journal without prompts.	____	____	____
8. Student entries seem to get longer and more detailed over time.	____	____	____
9. Entries are descriptive responses to reading.	____	____	____
10. Entries are narrative responses to reading.	____	____	____
11. Entries are explanatory responses to reading.	____	____	____
12. Reasoning seems to be part of the student's text production.	____	____	____

Comments/Interpretation: _____

_____

_____

_____

In order for students to become skilled writers demonstrating reading comprehension in written formats, they must have a vehicle for practicing writing. The dialogue journal provides that vehicle. For both types of entries—students' responses to their environment and their responses to reading— it serves as evidence for cataloguing students' growth over time. The adult—teacher or clinician,—plays a critical role in creating the optimal context for each student's literary development. The teacher must convince students that it is O.K. to express ideas sincerely, that ideas are important, and—in this vehicle—editing concerns (punctuation, spelling, etc.) are not.

Use the following steps to assess comprehension of text.

1. Collect samples of student's dialogues in response to reading. If entries are made daily, collect two for each week; if weekly, collect all entries.
2. Use the instruments on page 106, for determining growth and change in text comprehension as demonstrated through writing; the retelling profile, page 152; and the Morrow quantification retelling scale, pages 153–55.
3. Be sure to let students know if you are unable to respond to all entries they've made in response to reading. Ask that they mark those entries which must have your responses.

Figures 6–22 and 6–23 are convenient ways to summarize data over time.

SUMMARY

We have attempted, in this chapter, to recognize those aspects of comprehension that might be assessed—prior knowledge, students' text perception, and students' organizational abilities. We understand and have shared the notion that comprehension involves processes by which the reader "maps" the segments of text into preexisting units of knowledge. We have tried to help you understand that although a student may be able to understand the structure of a text, the student may not be able to relate the information from the text to knowledge already existing in his or her mind.

We have been cautious, yet adventurous in our presentation. We ask that you try the techniques presented in this chapter and use them in both empirical and ethnographic research studies to guide future teachers and diagnosticians to understand how students process information in order to comprehend.

QUESTIONS TO PONDER

1. Based on the explanation in this chapter, how would you differentiate between literal text comprehension and inferential text comprehension?
2. If a student seems to be having difficulties with comprehension, which of the following would demand priority in the assessment processes? Provide reasons:

    Text variables
    Prior knowledge
    Content perception
    Student emotional attitude
    Vocabulary related to content
    Self-concept
    Personal, out-of-school problems
    Other

3. How would you design a "process approach to assessing comprehension" that would satisfy parents, administrations, Boards of Education, and students?

REFERENCES

Allen, P. D., & Watson, P. J. (1976). *Findings of research in miscue analysis in classroom implications.* Urbana, IL: National Council of Teachers of English.

Allington, R. L., & Strange, M. (1980). *Learning through reading in content areas.* Lexington, MA: Heath.

Allington, R. L. (1980). Poor reader's don't get to read much in reading group. *Language Arts, 57*(8), 872–876.

Alvermann, D. E., Boothby, P. R., & Wolfe, J. (1984). The effect of graphic organizer instruction on fourth graders' comprehension of social studies texts. *Journal of Social Studies Research, 8,* 13–21.

Baghban, M. (1984). *Our Daughter learns to read and write.* Newark, DE: International Reading Association.

Barron, R. F. (1969). The use of vocabulary as an advance organizer. In H. L. Herber & P. L. Sanders (Eds.), *Research in reading in the content areas: First year report.* Syracuse, NY: Syracuse University, Reading and Language Arts Center.

Beck, J., & McKeown, M. G. (1981). Developing questions that promote comprehension: The story map. *Language Arts, 58,* 913–18.

Betts, E. A. (1957). *Foundations of reading instruction.* New York: American Book.

Bissex, G. (1980) *Genus at wrk: A child learns to write and read.* Boston, MA: Harvard University Press.

Bormuth, J. R. (1963). Cloze as a measure of readability. In J. A. Figurel (Ed.), *Reading as an intellectual activity.* Newark, DE: International Reading Association.

Bormuth, J. R. (1966). Readability: A new approach. *Reading Research Quarterly, 1,* 79–132.

Bormuth, J. R.(1968). Cloze test reliability: Criterion reference scores. *Journal of Educational Measurement, 5,* 189–196.

Bridge, C. A., & Sawyer, C. (1984, October). *Documenting the relationship between changes in student reading behaviors and instructional interventions in clinic.* Paper presented at the College Reading Association, Washington, DC.

Bridwell, L. S. (1980). Revising strategies in twelfth grade students' transactional writing. *Research in the Teaching of English, 14,* 197–222.

Brown, A. L. (1980). Metacognitive development and reading. In R. J. Spiro, B. Bruce, & W. Brewer (Eds.), *Theoretical issues in reading comprehension* (pp. 453–481). Hillsdale, NJ: Erlbaum.

Calkins, L. M. (1986). *The art of teaching writing.* Portsmouth, NH: Heinemann.

Carey, R. (1978). *A psycholinguistic analysis of the effect of semantic acceptability of oral reading miscues on reading comprehension.* Unpublished doctoral dissertation, University of Connecticut.

Clay, M. (1968). A syntactic analysis of reading errors. *Journal of Verbal Learning and Verbal Behavior, 7,* 434–438.

Clay, M. (1975) *What did I write?* Auckland, NZ: Heinemann Educational Books, Ltd.

Clay, M. (1982). *Observing young readers.* Portsmouth, NH: Heinemann.

Collins, A., Brown, J. S., & Larkin, K. M. (1980). Inference in text understanding. In R. J. Spiro, B. Bruce, & W. Brewer (Eds), *Theoretical issues in reading comprehension* (pp. 385–407). Hillsdale, NJ: Erlbaum.

Cook-Gumperz, J., & Gumperz, J. J. (1982) Communicative competence in educational perspective. In L. C. Wilkinson (Ed.), *Communicating in the classroom.* New York: Academic Press.

Czira, G. A. (1983). Commentary: Another response to Shanahan, Kamil, and Tobin: Further reasons to keep the doze case open. *Reading Research Quarterly. 18,* 361–365.

Doake, David B. (1985). Readinglike behavior: Its role in learning to read. In A. Jagger & M. T. Smith-Burke (Eds.), *Observing the language learner* (pp. 82–98). Newark, DE: International Reading Association.

Dreher, M. J., & H. Singer. (1980). Story grammar instruction is unnecessary for intermediate grade students. *The Reading Teacher, 34,* 261–268.

Earle, R. A. (1970). *The use of vocabulary as a structured overview in seventh grade mathematics.* Unpublished doctoral dissertation, Syracuse University.

Farr, R., & Carey, R. F. (1986). *Reading: What can be measured?* (2nd ed.). Newark, DE: International Reading Association.

Ferriero, E. (1982). *Literacy before schooling.* London: Heinemann.

Fields, P. (1960). *Comparisons and relationships of oral and silent reading performances of good and poor college freshman readers.* Master's thesis, Atlantic University.

Fitzgerald, J., & Spiegel D. L. (1983). Enhancing children's reading comprehension through instruction in narrative structure. *Journal of Reading Behavior, 15,* 1–17.

Ganier, A. S. (1976). The post oral reading cloze test: Does it really work? *Reading World, 16,* 21–27.

Gates, A. J. (1941). The role of personality maladjustment in reading difficulty. *Journal of Genetic Psychology, 69,* 77–83.

Gentile, L. M., McMillan, M. M., & Swain, C. (1985). Parents' identification of children's life crisis: Stress factors in reading difficulties in reading research in 1984. In G. H. McNinch (Ed.), *Fifth yearbook of the american reading forum* (pp. 68–71). Carrollton, GA: Thomasson Printing and Office Equipment.

Genishi, C., Dyson, & Haas, A. (1984). *Language assessment in the early years.* Norwood, NJ: Ablex.

Glazer, S. M. (1982). Current theory and classroom practice: Are their schemata related? *Reading Instruction Journal, 25*(2 & 3), 38–42.

Goodman, K. S. (1971). The search called reading. In Helen M. Robinson (Ed.), *Coordinating reading instruction* (pp. 10–14). Glenview, IL: Scott Foresman.

Goodman, K. S. (1982). *Language and literacy: The selected writings of Kenneth S. Goodman* (Vol. 2). Boston: Routledge & Kegan-Paul.

Goodman, K. S. (1985). Unity in reading. In H. Singer & R. Ruddell (Eds.), *Theoretical models and processes of reading* (3rd ed.) (pp. 813–840). Newark, DE: International Reading Association.

Graves, D. H. (1983). *Writing: Teachers & children at work*. Exeter, NH: Heinemann.

Halliday, M. A. K. (1978). *Language as social semiotic: The social interpretation of language and meaning*. Baltimore, MD: University Park Press.

Harste, J. C., Burke, C., & Woodward, V. (1981). *Children, their language and world: Initial encounters with print*. (Final Report, NIE research grant NIE-G-790132.)

Heath, S. B. (1983). *Ways with words: Language life and work in communities and classrooms*. Cambridge: Cambridge University Press.

Hoffman, S. (1982). *Parent's influence on children's learning to use print*. Association for Childhood Education, International Conference, Atlanta, April 1982; and World Congress on Reading, Dublin, July 1982.

Irwin, P. A., & Mitchell, J. M. (1986). *The reader retelling profile: Using retelling to make instructional decisions*. Manuscript in preparation: to be submitted for publication.

Jagger, A. M., Carrara, D. H., & Weiss, S. E. (1986). Research current: The influence of reading on children's narrative writing (and vice versa). *Language Arts, 63,* 292–300.

Johns, J. L. (1978). Basic reading inventory: Pre-primer-grade eight. Dubuque, IA: Kendall/Hunt.

Johnson, P. H. (1985). Understanding reading disability. *Harvard Educational Review, 55,* 153–177.

King, D. (1982). *Interrelationships and transactions: The education of a language user*. Paper presented at the International Reading Association Special Seminar, Impact of Child Language Development Research in Currirulum and Instruction, Columbia, MD.

King, M. L. (1985). Language and language learning for child watchers. In A. Jagger & M. T. Smith-Burke (Eds.), *Observing the language learner* (pp. 19–38). Newark, DE: International Reading Association.

Lindfors, J. W. (1985). Understanding the development of language structure. In A. Jagger & M. T. Smith-Burke (Eds.), *Observing the language learner* (pp. 42–56). Newark, DE: International Reading Association.

Manzo, A. V. (1968). *Improving reading comprehension through reciprocal questioning*. Unpublished doctoral dissertation, Syracuse University.

McGee, L. M., & Richgels, D. J. (1986). Attending to text structure: A comprehension strategy. In E. K. Dishner, T. W. Bean, J. E. Readence, & D. W. Mouse (Eds.) *Reading in content areas: Improving classroom instruction* (2nd ed.). Dubuque, IA: Kendall/Hunt.

Milz, V. (1985). First graders' uses for writing. In A. Jagger & M. T. Smith-Burke (Eds.), *Observing the language learner* (pp. 173–189). Newark, DE: International Reading Association.

Moffett, J., & Wagner, B. J. (1983). *Student-centered language arts and reading, K–13: A handbook for teachers*. Boston, MA: Houghton-Mifflin Company.

Moore, D. W., & Readence, J. E. (1983, April). *A quantitative and qualitative review of graphic organizer research*. Paper presented at the annual meeting of the American Educational Research Association, Montreal.

Morrow, L. M. (1985). Retelling stories: A strategy for improving young children's comprehension, concept of story structure and oral language complexity. *Elementary School Journal, 75,* 647–661.

Morrow, L. M. (In Press). Retelling stories as a diagnostic tool. In S. M. Glazer, L. W. Searfoss, & L. Gentile (Eds.), *Re-examining reading diagnosis: New trends and procedures in classrooms and clinics.* Newark, DE: International Reading Association.

Page, W. (1976). Pseudoscores, supercues, and comprehension. *Reading World, 15,* 232–238.

Palincsar, A., & Brown, A. (1983, January). *Reciprocal teaching of comprehension monitoring activities* (report no. 269). Urbana-Champaign, IL: Center for the study of reading.

Pearson, P. D. (1984). A context for instructional research on reading comprehension. In J. Flood (Ed.), *Promoting reading comprehension* (pp. 1–15). Newark, DE: International Reading Association.

Pearson, P. S., & Camperell, K. (1985). Comprehension of text structure. In H. Singer & R. B. Ruddell (Eds.), *Theoretical models and processes of reading* (3rd. ed.) (pp. 323–342). Newark, DE: International Reading Association.

Pearson, P. D., & Johnson, D. D. (1978). *Teaching reading comprehension.* New York: Holt, Reinhart & Winston.

Perl, S. (1979). The composing process of unskilled college writers. *Research in the Teaching of English, 13,* 317–339.

Powell, W. R. (1970). Reappraising the criteria for interpreting informal reading inventories. In D. Doboer (Ed.), *Reading diagnosis and evaluation.* Newark, DE: International Reading Association.

Powell, W. R. & Dunkeld, C. B. (1971). Validity of the JR & reading levels. *Elementary English, 48*(6), 637–642.

Rankin, E. F., & Culhane, J. W. (1969). Comparable cloze and multiple choice comprehension test scores. *Journal of Reading, 13*(3), 193–198.

Raphael, T. E. (1982). Question-answering strategies of children. *The Reading Teacher, 36,* 1816–1890.

Readence, J. E., Bean, T. W., & Baldwin, R. S. (1985). *Content area reading: An integrated approach.* Dubuque, IA: Kendall/Hunt.

Rumelhart, D. (1977). Understanding and summarizing brief stories. In D. LaBerge & S. J. Samuels (Eds.), *Basic processes in reading*: *Perception and comprehension.* Hillsdale, NJ: Erlbaum.

Rumelhart, D. (1980). Schemata: The building blocks of cognition. In R. Spiro, B. Bruce, & W. Brewer (Eds.), *Theoretical issues in reading comprehension* (pp. 33–58). Hillsdale, NJ: Erlbaum.

Rumelhart, D. (1984). Understanding understanding. In J. Flood (Ed.), *Understanding reading comprehension* (pp. 1–20). Newark, DE: International Reading Association.

Rumelhart, D., & Ortony, A. (1977). The representation of knowledge in memory. In R. D. Anderson, R. J. Spirs, and W. E. Montague (Eds.), *School and the acquisition of knowledge.* Hillsdale, NJ: Erlbaum.

Schatell, B. (1982). *Farmer Goff and turkey Sam.* New York: Harper & Row.

Shanahan, T., Kamil, M. C., & Tobin, A. W. (1982). Cloze as a measure of intersential comprehension: *Reading Research Quarterly, 17,* 229–255.

Shiffrin, R. M. (1977). Controlled and automatic human information processing: 1. Detection search, and attention. *Psychology Review, 84,* 1–66.

Smith, C., & Bean, T. W. (1980). The guided writing procedure: Integrating content reading and writing involvement. *Reading World, 19,* 290–98.

Smith, F. (1983). *Essays into literacy*. Exeter, NH: Heinemann.
Smith, F. (1985). *Reading without Nonsense*. New York: Teachers College Press.
Smith, G. B. (In press). Arrangements and grouping in ethnographic notetaking: Alternative approaches for diagnosis. In S. M. Glazer, L. W. Searfoss, & L. M. Gentile (Eds.), *Re-examining reading diagnosis: New trends and procedures for classrooms and clinics*. Newark, DE: International Reading Association.
Smith, G. B. (1986). *Ethnography as a tool for data collection in classroom and clinic*. Paper presented at the Eleventh World Congress on Reading, London, England.
Spache, G. D. (1976). *Diagnosing and correcting reading disabilities*. (p. 21). Boston: Allyn & Bacon.
Spiro, R. J. (1984) Consciousness and reading comprehension. In J. Flood (Ed.), *Understanding reading comprehension* (pp. 75–81). Newark, DE: International Reading Association.
Stallard, C. (1974). An analysis of the writing behaviors in good student writers. *Research in the Teaching of English, 8,* 206–218.
Stanovich, K. D. (1980). Toward an interactive–compensatory model of individual differences in development of reading fluency. *Reading Research Quarterly, 16,* 32–71.
Staton, J. (1980). Writing and counseling: Using a dialogue journal. *Language Arts, 57,* 514–518.
Tierney, R., & Leys, M. (1984). *What is the value of connecting reading and writing?* (Reading Education Report no. 55). Champaign, IL: Center for the Study of Reading.
Tierney, R., & Pearson, P. D. (1983, May). Toward a composing model of reading. *Language Arts, 60,* (5).
Vacca, R. (1981). *Content area reading*. Boston, MA: Little, Brown.
Wells, C. A. (1950). The value of an oral reading test for diagnosis of the reading difficulties of college freshman of low academic performance. *Psychological Monographs, 64,* 1–35.

SUGGESTED READING

Flood, J. (Ed.). (1983). *Understanding reading comprehension: cognition, language, and the structure of prose*. Newark, DE: International Reading Association. The twelve articles in this volume examine reading comprehension considering cognitive phenomena, language development and its relationship to reading, and the effects of text organization and structure on the reader.
Genishi, C., & Dyson, A. H. (1984). *Language assessment in early years*. Norwood, NJ: Ablex. The authors present a theoretical perspective on language development from a developmental point of view. Examples of oral language of children from birth to eight will encourage readers to observe and assess how children demonstrate language competence.
Glazer, S. M., Searfoss, L. W., & Gentile, L. W. (Eds.) (In press). *Re-examining reading diagnosis: New trends and procedures for classrooms and clinics*. Newark, DE: International Reading Association. A series of articles describing innovative approaches to diagnosing comprehension are included. Theoretical and practical issues are presented.
Heimlich, J. E., & Pittelman, S. D. (1986). *Semantic mapping: Classroom applications*. Newark, DE: International Reading Association. This monograph contains several practical suggestions for using semantic mapping for expanding organizational skills. Maps may be used as assessment tools, when teacher/clinics request that students tap their prior knowledge and vocabulary about topics.

Johnston, P. H. (1983). *Reading comprehension assessment: A cognitive basis.* Newark, DE: International Reading Association. This monograph draws together current theoretical and experimental information relevant to problems of assessing reading comprehension.

Mandl, H., Stein, N. L., & Trabasso, T. (1984). *Learning and comprehension of text.* Hillsdale, NJ: Erlbaum. Aspects of text structure, learning from text, and strategies that affect comprehension are studies by many leading professionals in this edited volume.

Spiro, R. J. (1980). *Theoretical issues in reading comprehension.* Hillsdale, NJ: Erlbaum. This basic text brings recent developments in several disciplines to the study of comprehension. The major focus is on understanding the processes involved in comprehension.

7

COMPREHENSION OF THE WRITTEN CODING SYSTEM

Awareness and Comprehension of Print

Activities for Developing Concepts About Print

Vocabulary Development

Word Recognition Strategies in Classroom and Clinic Settings

Strategies for Teaching Use of Context

Spelling Development

Decoding or Word-Identification Skills

Teaching Strategies for Decoding Development

Summary

Questions to Ponder

References

Suggested Reading

Children want and need to communicate with the world from birth. That communication begins naturally through listening, speaking, and nonverbal means. Learning to read and write, unlike listening and speaking, often requires more encouragement, guidance, and modeling from the environments in which children live. In this chapter we explore how young readers and writers gain control over the system of written language. Answers to these questions will guide our discussion:

1. How do young readers and writers acquire an awareness and an understanding of the mechanics of written language and its functions?
2. Why is vocabulary development a basic building block for reading and writing fluency?
3. How is spelling proficiency related to fluent writing and reading?
4. What decoding or word identification skills and strategies do readers need for fluent reading?
5. How do we diagnose and then assist readers and writers who may not have developed an understanding of the mechanics of our written language, a large vocabulary, or spelling skills?

AWARENESS AND COMPREHENSION OF PRINT[1]

Much of the recent research in early reading has focused on tracing what Yetta Goodman calls the "roots of literacy" which lie in the preschool language experiences of children. The importance of this foundation for later literacy development cannot be underestimated (Mason, 1984). The stronger and richer children's understanding of the nature and use of language before they come to school, the greater chance for success in formal instruction. The hundreds of hours of informal, functional, and recreational encounters preschool children have with print is of interest not only to researchers but to teachers and clinicians who work with children who have developed reading and writing problems.

Assessing children's comprehension of how language works and how they use language provides valuable insights and guidance for instruction. We can assist those children who have not had extensive early language experiences by providing for their needs as part of remedial programs, in both classroom and clinic settings. Two areas of assessment are important for our discussion: *print awareness* and children's comprehension of *concepts about reading and writing print*.

[1]This discussion is based on extensive quotes from *Helping Children Learn to Read*, Chapter 3, by Searfoss and Readence (Englewood Cliffs, NJ: Prentice Hall, 1985).

Print Awareness

K. Goodman (1980) described four kinds of early encounters preschool children have which shape their awareness and understanding of the uses of print.[2] These are:

Environmental reading. Reading one must do in the course of interacting with the world of print all around us. For young children, this world includes such diverse items as cereal boxes, toothpaste tubes, candy wrappers, traffic signs, and logos of favorite eating places, to name just a few. Children, through observing adults, through personally encountering environmental print, and also by watching television, develop an awareness of the functional nature of print.

Informational reading. Reading done by people as they seak information. Children see others read the newspaper for sports scores, cookbooks for recipes, road maps for directions (often too late, though!), and the refrigerator door for the daily school lunch menu. This type of reading helps children identify additional uses for print.

[2]Reprinted with permission of the National Council of Teachers of English, Urbana, Illinois.

Occupational reading. Job-related reading that children see other people do. At one time or another, all children observe schoolteachers, lawyers, mechanics, and bank clerks referring to print as part of their jobs.

Leisure reading. Reading people do for pleasure and relaxation. Children become aware of this function of print when they observe adults sharing funny cartoons, jokes, and signs. Also, sometimes adults choose to read to children, making reading a leisure activity both for adult and child.

Children learn a great deal from these encounters and acquire complex concepts about print and its uses. Such concepts include:

1. Print always means something, whether we can understand it or not.
2. Print tells us something, because it shows us how to find things we like, such as favorite foods or television programs.
3. Print helps us gain control over our world because it's dependable. A sign or a label should be written and displayed in the same way, day after day.
4. Print and talk seem to go together. Adults seem to spend lots of time talking about print.
5. Print, adults, talk, and kids go together, too. We have plenty of talks every day about print, with adults and with each other.

Procedures for Assessing Print Awareness

Print awareness can be assessed in classrooms by watching children as they are engaged in environmental, informational, occupational, and leisure reading activities. The activities below are examples of behaviors which can be observed:

1. Discussing uses or purposes of environmental signs and labels.
2. Pointing to environmental print and verbally labeling it.
3. Drawing signs or labels for objects, animals, or classroom events.
4. Asking questions and showing interest in the reading and writing activities of others, including the teacher.
5. Choosing reading and writing activities during free time.

On an individual or small-group basis, in either a classroom or clinic setting, print awareness also can be assessed by using a simple informal inventory (see Figure 7–1). Items should be selected carefully from the children's environment and presented one at a time for identification. A tape recorder may be used to allow a more relaxed atmosphere, since it will free the teacher from attending too much to the mechanics of administering the inventory. To personalize the list, food and other household items used by children should be selected, as well as local street and business signs. Empty cartons may be used for perishable items. On page 200 is a list of questions to ask:

Figure 7–1 Print-Awareness Inventory

ITEM	IDENTIFY YES/NO	NOTES
1. Milk carton	_____	
2. Picture of STOP sign	_____	
3. Toothpaste carton	_____	
4. Cereal box	_____	
5. Fast-food restaurant items	_____	
6. Soap carton	_____	
7. Soup can	_____	
8. Soda or pop bottle or can	_____	
9. Public phone sign	_____	
10. Picture of highway signs of local interest	_____	
11. Other?	_____	

Note: Although specific brand names were not used in this sample inventory, teachers should use those brands available in their locale. For example, fast-food restaurant items will vary from one location to another. Additional items may be added, such as school signs and other places of interest locally.

> What is this?
> What does it say?
> Where does it say that?
> What do you do with this?
> Have you ever seen this before?

Activities for Developing Print Awareness

Activities which can be used to develop print awareness include:

1. Include an environmental print area as part of classroom units. Displays—including bulletin boards with various nutrition and consumer-education themes—might serve as the focus of a unit on the four basic food groups; they

can be portrayed with actual objects, pictures, or empty containers used to illustrate each group. Ingredients from the four basic groups may be used to plan nutritious meals and to depict them on a display table. Magazine and newspaper ads are a readily available, inexpensive source of pictures to be clipped and turned into collages; central themes can be safety signs, words related to specific occupations, and directional indicators.

2. Personalize children's desks, cubbyholes, and lockers by labeling them with children's names.
3. Label familiar objects and places in the classroom.
4. Develop familiarity with signs and their functions by taking small groups of children for walks around the school building (Mason & Au, 1986, pp. 47–48). By discussing a sign you help establish its function. Mason and Au suggest this procedure: Stop in front of a sign and ask the following questions:
   a. *What does that sign say?* Usually someone will know and read it aloud. If not, ask, "What do you think it says?," then help them to figure out the words. An exit sign is ideal for beginning this activity because it is common, uncomplicated, and likely to be prominently located.
   b. *Can you read that word or those words?* Put your hand under the word you want them to name and move your hand from left to right. Then give each child an opportunity to read.
   c. *Why is that word there? What does it mean?* Elicit answers about its use or function.

d. *Are there any other signs like this around here?* Encourage children to explain why there is only one "Principal's Office" but several "Exit" signs. See if anyone can lead the group to another Exit sign.
e. *Copy sign words onto tagboard.* Say the words and then name each letter as you form it to help the children remember the word. At first use the same upper-case letters as that in the real sign, but later transcribe the words in lower case.
f. *Put copies of the signs at a word-learning table for review by the chidlren.* When a child forgets what one of the words says, a quick trip down the hall will usually be enough to spur recall. Later children can print the words themselves or copy them to label their drawings.
g. *Keep track of the signs noticed by the children and added to the collection.* Eventually, there will be enough for a classroom book called "Signs in My School."

Concepts about Print

The roots of literacy include not only an awareness of the uses of print but a specific understanding of the mechanical aspects of reading and writing. A high level of print awareness, surprisingly, does not also insure that children acquire these mechanical concepts about print (Y. Goodman & Altwerger, 1981). These print mechanics include:

Form concepts. These concepts are the "building blocks" of books: title, pages, lines, letters, words, sentences, punctuation marks, and paragraphs. Teachers routinely ask questions that assume these concepts in beginning readers. For example, "Look at the first page of our new story and find the title" or "Is there a word you know in the title?"

Orientation and directionality concepts. These concepts relate to "how print goes," or how it is arranged in books: Books have a beginning, middle, and end, pages go from top to bottom, lines move left to right, and illustrations and text work together. Also included in this category are the order or sequential nature of words, sentences, and paragraphs (first word, second sentence, last paragraph). Questions teachers ask that relate to these concepts include, "What does the picture on the second page tell us about what might happen next?" or "Who can find and read the first sentence and tell us the name of the dog?"

Uses of book-print concepts. Book-print concepts are established as children realize that books are useful and that different kinds of books have different uses. Some books give pleasure, while others are more serious and give information, directions, or facts. Pleasure books begin on the first page and have a middle and an end; many other kinds of books can be entered anywhere, depending on what the reader wants from the book.

We must keep in mind that concepts about print do not develop in isolation. They develop naturally and must be assessed naturally, in the context of meaningful communication. The rewards to children who have developed those concepts are many, as Jewell and Zintz state so eloquently in the text *Learning to Read Naturally*.

> These, then are some of the rewards, the rich dividends that accrue to those children whose parents provide them with many opportunities to experience books and other print in the everyday world. Through the early years, children are exposed to written language in its total context via stories or words and phrases in a meaningful environment. The sense, the whole, comes first; otherwise, there is no basis for meaning. From repeated experiences through listening to and following along in story reading, children gradually move toward the parts that make up text—the words and the letters that have little or no meaning outside a total context. They move along the same path and in much the same natural way that they come to know and to speak their language. (1986, p. 14)

Procedures for Assessing Concepts about Print

Concepts about print may be assessed by observing how children handle and use the most common form of print found in the classroom, the tradebook. Children can be informally observed in these activities using tradebooks:

1. Recreational and independent reading time.
2. Independent browsing in the classroom book corner or school library.
3. Sharing and talking about books with other children.
4. Reading to others.
5. Writing stories, letters, messages to others, especially after listening to a story.

In individual or small-group settings, teachers can use an informal inventory that involves book handling (see Figure 7–2). A series of short questions asked in an informal, relaxed manner will enable you to assess specific concepts about book print. Ask each child to bring a favorite book—and also have available several books that you consider appropriate but unfamiliar to the child. Begin the session by talking about the book the child brought. Then use the questions in Figure 7–2, first with the favorite book and then with an unfamiliar one. Modify the questions as you need to, rewording them as necessary.

Agnew (1982) devised a method for informal diagnosis of young children's concepts about print using dictated stories. The teacher first works with the children to develop an experience story and records it on a large chart. Then the teacher prepares several sentence strips and individual noun and verb word cards taken from the story. We have selected just one of Agnew's many tasks which we feel assesses some important basic concepts about print.

Figure 7–2 Book-Print Inventory

Child _____ Date _____

BOOK TITLE _____

_____

Responses Using
Favorite Book

√ = Correct or
    appropriate response
0 = Incorrect or inappropriate
    response
? = Can't tell

BOOK TITLE _____

_____

Responses Using
Unfamiliar Book

1. What is the title of the story?

2. Find the title and point to it.

3. Where does the story begin?

4. Show me the end of the story.

5. Show me a picture you like.

6. Can you read, or pretend to read, for me?

7. Show me how you read by using your finger.

8. (Turn to a page) Where do we start to read?

9. Where do we go next?

10. Find a page you want me to read to you.

11. (Read page to child) What happened on this page?

12. (Open question)

Ask the child to point to the place in the chart story or on the sentence strips to answer such questions as:

1. "Where is the *beginning?*"
2. "Where is the *end* of the story?"
3. "This word is ———." (Point to the word in story and name it.) "Where is the beginning of the word?" "Where is the end of the word?"
4. "This word is ———." (Point to the word in the story and name it.) "Now look at this sentence strip. Point to the same word on the sentence strip."
5. "This word is ———." (Point to the word in the story and name it.) "Here are two word cards from the story. One of them is *different* from ———." (Repeat the word that was just identified in the story). "Point to the word that is different from ———." (Repeat the word just identified).
6. Here is the *first* word in the story." (Point to the word in the chart story.) "You point to the *last* word in the story."
7. "Here is the first letter in the word ———." (Point to the word in the story as it is named.)
8. "Point to the *last* letter in the word ———." (Repeat the word just identified.)
9. "Run your finger under a *line* in the story. Show me another line."
10. "Point to the *top* of the page. Point to the *bottom* of the page."

Assessment of concepts about print is intimately linked to instruction. Some sample activities to develop concepts about book print are presented next in this chapter.

ACTIVITIES FOR DEVELOPING CONCEPTS ABOUT PRINT

Introduce nursery rhymes. Nursery rhymes that are read and reread aloud to children help them become aware of the relationship of print to speech and other mechanical and orientation concepts.

Use journals with beginning readers. Techniques discussed in Chapter 6 work well with students of all ages. (See pages 184 to 189.) It is important, however, to respect the individuality of journals. Emphasis must focus on using written text much like oral communication. Freedom to write just to share ideas or release personal feelings encourages children to use the coding system often.

Have the children make their own books. *The Shape Book* and *The Me Book* (Clavio, 1980) are two simple types of books for children to make.

The Shape Book is an exercise in creative thinking. It allows each student to make at least two pages quickly, and it can usually be completed in one period. Each student is given an abstract shape cut from tagboard. Be sure all the shapes are the same. The students are to make as many drawings of real things as possible. They are to begin with the abstract outlined shape given to them, and make it part of the drawing. The shape must be visible in the drawing and should be traced from the tagboard cutout for uniformity. It can be turned in any direction. The words are simple and repetitive, with only the name of the object changing. For example, given a simple circle, some first graders made a circle book: "At first it was a sun, and then it was a clock, and then it was a wheel, and then it was a ball." In virtually no time, this large-group project can show a whole class all the steps in the bookmaking process.

The Me Book is a longer project that gives students a chance to learn more about the process by writing about themselves. Since students know about their own lives, material for writing is plentiful. Even the youngest students can make this kind of book with the help of dictation. By the time the students have written about and illustrated the many facets of their lives, they will have learned the bookmaking process page by page. These books build self-concept and give the teacher a chance to learn about the students. Some titles include *The Book About Me, My Book,* and *There Is Nobody Just Like Me.*

Writing without a pencil. Tompkins (1981) described some activities involving a wide variety of materials that stimulate children to communicate. Some of Tompkins' alternatives included:

Brush and water on chalkboard	Pudding fingerpaint	Letter blocks
Flannelboard	Glue with beans and popcorn	Foam letters
Letters cut from newspapers	Typewriter	Blocks
Magic slates	Letter cookies	Magnetic letters

VOCABULARY DEVELOPMENT

The importance of a large vocabulary in fluent reading has been established for many years. The exact nature of how words are learned, the defining of "knowing" words, and the effects of vocabulary instruction on reading comprehension are the controversial areas of current research and writing. (See Beck, McKeown, & McCaslin, 1983; Cockrum, 1986; McKeown, Beck, Omanson, & Pople, 1985; Mezynski, 1983; Nagy, Nerman, & Anderson, 1985; Stahl & Fairbanks, 1986). Classroom teachers and clinicians, however, accept the importance of students' abilities to recognize quickly—or "at sight"—a large number of words. As Gough (1984) wrote: "Word recognition is the foundation of the reading process" (p. 225).

Word recognition skill is like recognizing objects we know (trees, automobiles) or familiar people (bank clerks, relatives). We recognize thousands of objects, people, and words "on sight" because we are familiar with them and their function and relationships to us. Learning to recognize words is a lifelong process. We are always learning that some new, different arrangements of marks on pages—letters—represent different sounds and meanings. Part of vocabulary development, therefore, is sight word-recognition, or the ability to quickly "know" what a word means. In some amazing way, the human mind is able to organize a set of characteristics or features of letters and words, and respond automatically, having predicted meaning accurately. (For extensive discussions of word recognition theories, see Gough, 1984; and Henderson, 1982).

In this chapter, we will discuss how to assess and how to teach vocabulary. We begin with a discussion of assessing sight words through word lists and proceed to assessment of words by context and category methods.

Procedures for Assessing Vocabulary Using Word Lists

Commercial or published "word lists" or lists of "basic sight words" have been used for many years to assess vocabulary in readers, in either list format, word cards, or as part of an informal reading inventory.

Selected word lists include:

Basic Elementary Reading Vocabularies (Harris & Jacobson, 1973)
Dolch Basic Sight Vocabulary Cards (Dolch, 1981)
American Heritage Word Frequency Book Carroll, Davies, & Richmond, 1971)
The Living Word Vocabulary (Dale & O'Rourke, 1976)
Kucera–Francis List (Kucera & Francis, 1967)
A Teacher's Wordbook of 30,000 Words (Thorndike & Lorge, 1944).
The Reading Teacher's Book of Lists (Fry, Polk, Fountoukidis, 1984)
Ginn Word Book for Teachers (Johnson, Moe, & Baumann, 1983)

It is interesting to note that in our observations over the years in classrooms and clinics, it is mainly children with reading problems who are administered word lists. Children who appear to be learning to read are rarely administered these lists. Therefore, word lists have been viewed as instruments of specialists or clinicians, beyond the use of classroom teachers. They have attained, because of their use in remedial and diagnostic settings, an importance and aura of validity far beyond their ability to help us assess children's reading ability.

Word lists are typically based on frequency of word use in instructional materials and in some cases the world of print outside of schools. Most are for the early grades, with a few designed for middle grades, upper grades, and adult use. They are administered to assess word recognition in isolation, with quickness and accuracy of response being considered. A grade-level indicator of performance is often assigned to the results of a word recognition test.

There are probably more disadvantages to isolated word lists. Advantages include:

1. Quick and easy to administer, requiring minimum time for administration.
2. Words are usually chosen from standard vocabulary lists in common use to develop basal reader materials and other supplementary, instructional reading materials.

Disadvantages include:

1. Word lists do not assess reading ability; they assess only instant recognition by pronunciation of words in isolation. The syntactic, semantic, and pragmatic language systems are not present and must be created by the child. Generalizing how a child would recognize the same words in context with a variety of reasons for reading is a leap we are not willing to make from administration of isolated word lists. Commercial or published word lists also deny the values, beliefs, and experiences the reader brings to the test.
2. Word lists may not include a representative sample of the words children will encounter later in all instructional materials, especially content area subjects.
3. Instruction cannot be based on the results of a word-list test of word recognition.

Considering all the disadvantages we state above, we frankly advocate very limited use of word lists in the diagnostic process. We suggest they can be useful as *part* of a commercial informal reading inventory (for example, Silvaroli, 1986; Johns, 1985) to assist in determining at which levels to begin testing reading comprehension. Used as a means to determine at which level to begin comprehension testing, word lists are probably a time-saver for the clinician since they are quick and easy to administer.

A second use of word lists—overcoming some of the disadvantages we cite—are personal word lists developed jointly by the teacher and student. These personal lists can be administered with a commercial list and performances compared and contrasted.

Teacher–Student Word Lists

Word lists developed by students and teachers more closely resemble meaningful language and consider interests, cultural differences, values, morals, and beliefs. Personal word lists can be developed with students, using words from their experiences and from content-area textbooks and units of study. Words drawn from students' experiences can be collected using the Modified Key Word Method (later in this chapter).

Words used in content-area textbooks and classroom units can be added to student word lists and also stored. These words can be useful for both assessment and instruction in vocabulary. Words requested for compositions are another source of vocabulary.

Performance on personal word lists cannot be assigned a grade-level score, and results must be described annotatively. Responses can be expressed numerically, though, in a baseline percentage. Comparing results over time of words called correctly will demonstrate growth in vocabulary. The traditional word lists described earlier should be used in conjunction with personal word lists. Administration of word lists should be individual for testing purposes and take place in a quiet place free of distractions. The commercial word list and personal word list should be written on individual word cards, with lists interspersed in any order.

Procedures for Testing

Use the following procedure for testing with word lists. Say: "I think that you will be able to read some of the words written on these cards. I am going to show them to you one at a time. You say the words as soon as you see them." Flash each card at eye level for five seconds. Place words called correctly and incorrectly on two separate piles. At the completion of the testing session, show the student how many words were correctly recognized and record the number and/or percentage on a graph or chart. Periodic appraisals are important for assessment purposes and to create motivation for learning.

During and after the administration of the word lists, ask yourself the following questions. Record answers to these questions immediately after the test session.

Writing words daily helps children build vocabulary for reading as well as for writing.

1. Which word list served to be more successful for the students?

   ____Commercial ____Personal
2. What kinds of words were most easily recognized by the student?

   ____Describing ____Naming ____Action

   ____Connecting ____Pronouns ____Denoting time and manner
3. Did the student *elaborate* or *explain* the word after recognizing it?
4. Did the student try to "sound out" the word? If so, note which ones and student's pronunciation.
5. Other behaviors you think important? (List)

The results of administering word lists can be summarized as follows.

COMMERCIAL/PUBLISHED LISTS PERFORMANCE	PERSONAL WORD LIST PERFORMANCES
1. Report results as directed in publisher's manual. Give grade level or other indicator of performance as recommended.	1. Report the sources of words in personal word lists, for example, field trip, science unit.
2. Analyze errors in words incorrectly called. Note any obvious trends or important student comments.	2. Analyze errors in words incorrectly called. Note any obvious trends or important student comments.
3. Develop a summary statement of student performance. For example: "From responses made by _____ on word recognition tests, he/she is performing at _____ grade level. This grade level does not mean _____ can read materials at that level. Words on these lists are presented in isolation. Words in books and other kinds of print are presented with other words, in context. These require different skills. We can say that _____ is reading words at sight at _____ grade level, as estimated by the test publisher. "It is important to compare the performance on word recognition tests using word lists with comprehension in story materials and other types of school reading. No grade placement or other instructional decisions should be made using only word list grade-level scores."	3. Develop a summary statement of student performance. For example: "Words were taken from _____'s personal experiences and school work. Of the _____ words presented in isolation, _____ percent were called correctly. This is a change of _____ from the last testing."

Compare and contrast performance on commercial and personal words. It is sometimes valuable to compare and contrast a student's personal list with the commercial list, noting any similarity and difference in actual words and in categories of words. The less relationship between the two lists, the easier it is to see why the student has been classified as a remedial reader, especially if commercial list performance is lower than personal list performance. Commercial word lists are very often part of a battery of testing completed in a short period of time, since they are quick and easy to administer.

WORD RECOGNITION STRATEGIES IN CLASSROOM AND CLINIC SETTINGS

The number of times students need to be exposed to words before recognizing them instantly or "at sight" continues to be the subject of much discussion in the literature. Factors such as word frequency in print, word length, prior knowledge of the students—combined with sociolinguistic factors such as interest, intent, and features of the learning environment—all complicate the issue for researchers and practitioners. Betts made an educated guess in 1946 that approximately twenty-five exposures is average. Many have abused this suggestion, expecting youngsters to learn words after twenty-five flashes of a word card. The issue is not only the number of exposures but also the nature and quality of those exposures. Merely flashing word cards does not involve students in active learning, in which they are asked to use linguistic and cognitive skills and abilities to learn to recognize a word. Whether Betts was close or not in his estimate is unimportant. Learning, retention, and instant recall of words is based on planned instruction, supervised practice, and extensive independent reading. The strategies suggested in this chapter for developing word recognition are based on this principle.

Pattern Method

The English language has many characteristics that may cause confusion for the reader. There are inconsistencies in the way words are spelled; many have the same sounds but are spelled with different letters. Others are spelled the same but sound differently. In order to solve these linguistic problems, we propose encouraging students to observe patterns in the language. Students are guided to look for visual elements of words that are the same. Looking for the same elements helps categorize and organize print into consistent visual patterns. There are many regular visual patterns in English that can be taught as part of a word recognition instruction and which will aid students in recalling words "at sight." The Pattern Method follows a three-step teaching and learning procedure designed to teach patterns. The example below teaches the *at* pattern.

Step 1: Introducing the Pattern

Sample: Begin the lesson at a chalkboard or chart by reading the following printed poem:

> I have a *cat*. (Point to cat)
> Whose name is *Pat*
> Who wears a *hat*.
> (Motion to students to say "hat" as you do)
> He has a *bat*
> (Motion again, for them to say bat)
> Who is very *fat*.
> One day the bat *sat*.
> On a great big *mat*.
> Good-by *cat*.
> Good-by *cat*.

Repeat the poem, holding your hand, as if it was a ruler, under the *at* word at the end of each line.

Say: "What is the same about these words?" (Responses might include—"They end with at," "They rhyme," "They are three-letter words," "They have different beginnings.")

When the discussion seems completed, have the students complete a worksheet similar to Worksheet 1.

Worksheet 1

c at ⟶	cat
b at ⟶	bat
f at ⟶	_____
s at ⟶	_____
h at ⟶	_____
m at ⟶	_____

Step 2: Practicing the Pattern

Use Worksheet 2 at another session. Say: "Cut out each letter box. Paste it next to an *at*, to make a word."

This step provides visual blending words. Students should recognize that putting letters next to others makes one unit, a word.

Worksheet 2

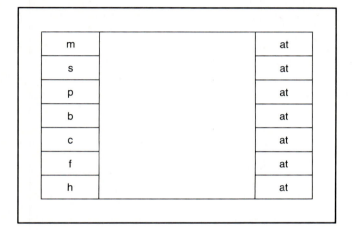

Step 3: Assessing the Pattern

Ask children to write as many *at* pattern words as they can remember on a sheet of paper. Help the students notice that by putting a different letter in front of the pattern *at*, they create another word. Step 3 can be an individual activity followed by sharing of responses in small groups with teacher guidance.

It is also important that students observe patterns in books. A few examples of published pattern books are listed below. Of course, children can produce their own pattern books and illustrate them. A variety of different kinds of paper, writing tools, and other craft materials should be available to encourage bookmaking.

Many commercial books are also excellent for encouraging word pattern recognition. For example:

Hop on Pop (Dr. Seuss, 1963)
Are You My Mother? (Eastman, 1960)
Jen the Hen (Hawkins, 1985)
Jamberry (Degen, 1983)

Hand, Hand, Fingers, Thumb (Perkins, 1969)
"I Can't," Said the Ant (Cameron, 1961)
Did You Ever See? (Einsel, 1972)

Modified Key Word Method

The Modified Key Word Method is adapted from Ashton-Warner (1963) and adds a tracing step based on Fernald's work (1971). Words come from discussions of student's experiences. The method can be used one-to-one or in small groups not larger than six or eight students.

Each student must have a mailing envelope, legal size if possible, with "Word Bank" written on the front. The student's name should precede the phrase to personalize the envelope. Begin eliciting key words in an informal, personal way. Veatch and colleagues (1979) describe the first step in key words.

ELICIT A KEY WORD FROM EACH CHILD

The word a child gives must have an emotional impact for her; otherwise, it will probably not be retained. The teacher tells the class that he wants them to tell him their favorite word, one that makes them feel happy, sad, or angry, or one that is funny or scary. The children should be asked questions like, "What are the best words you can think of" or the "scariest word" or "the nicest thing." All words should be accepted. If the teacher doubts that the child is giving a word of real power, he can ask, "Why do you like the word?" He should then let his conscience be his guide. The more powerful the word is, the better. (p. 28)

Students are then asked to trace their words, as recommended by Fernald (1971): The word is written for the student individually, either in script or in manuscript depending on the student's mode of writing. A strip of paper four inches by ten inches or index cards may be used for each word. The student is asked to trace the word using the index finger of the "writing hand." Tracing occurs using that finger and saying each syllable aloud as it is traced. The student matches vocal output with tracing and is encouraged to "hold" the vowel sound until the next consonant is traced. The student says and traces the word several times. Then the student is asked to write and say the word on a new sheet of paper or on a wall chart or chalkboard. Words learned are placed in the word bank envelopes with the students' name on it. Searfoss and Readence (1985) and Veatch (1986) recommend a "ring of words." This is made simply with a shower curtain ring. A punch can be used to make a hole in each word card. Word banks may be stored in individual file folders, cubbies, or in a central location. Student word rings can be stored on a pegboard—a peg labeled for each child.

Several important aspects of this procedure should be noted: (1) touching and saying the word at the same time is important; (2) the words learned

Word identification games help children increase word-recognition skills.

should be written from memory, *never* copied; (3) words should always be written as a unit, not in syllable form; (4) saying and tracing must occur together; and (5) rehearsal for retention must continue daily.

Once the student is confident that the word is known, the word is written by the student in a space designed and labeled just for each student on a chalkboard or easel. Placing the student's name on a space away from the desk area permits youngsters to move from tables to other areas. This helps test the student's memory of word images. The word card is left at the desk. A peer partner is assigned, and a daily time period is set for working together; the partners flash word cards for each other one at a time. This daily activity should become a routine procedure. It builds independence and responsibility as well as at-sight vocabulary.

If the student does not know a word, the option to discard it ought to be given. Value in learning a special word is built when students make decisions to keep or discard word bank entries. Additional reinforcement activities with individual pairs or small groups include making a picture booklet of words for which each child draws a picture; sharing categories of words with classmate—such as the funniest, scariest, longest, shortest words; constructing an alphabet book; or creating sentences or stories using personal vocabulary.

These books might be read by students onto a tape and reinforced again when each listens to their reading.

Assessing Vocabulary in Context

All human experience is context dependent. Indeed, human behavior can hardly be interpreted without context (Readence, Bean, & Baldwin, 1985, p. 92).

Recognition of words, as with other human behaviors, can be quite different in context than isolation. When words are presented in context, their meanings are chameleonlike, shaped by the meanings of other words. Readers receive syntactic and semantic cues from print—pragmatic cues from the reading environment—which determine purpose, intent, and authenticity. The skilled or fluent reader predicts meaning based on all of these contextual clues. We can assess the ability to recognize words "at sight" and to identify unknown words through context by asking these questions:

1. What happens when the reader encounters an unknown word necessasry for meaning?
2. Does the reader use meaning-seeking strategies that use all the context clues available?
3. Does the reader use inappropriate or irrelevant skills or avoidance techniques which prevent him or her from identifying a word?

There are a few commercial published tests which have the capacity to assess the student's ability to use context clues. Those that do are listed here:

Decoding Inventory (Kendall/Hunt, 1986)
Diagnostic Reading Scales (McGraw-Hill, 1981)
Woodcock Reading Mastery Tests (American Guidance Service, 1973)

If these tests are used, our preference is to combine them with estimates of ability to use context clues derived from teacher–student-constructed tests.

Teacher–Student Tests of Words in Context

Creating a teacher–student test of word recognition in context has several important advantages over commercial tests of the same skill:

1. The results of the testing can be used immediately to plan teaching and learning.
2. The test builds confidence since the student leaves the test setting with the ability to use context clues reinforced.

3. The student sees using context clues as a useful tool for reading, not simply responses to an artificial test format.
4. Teacher–student tests of words in context use the word banks created from students' experiences and context-area textbooks and units of study (see earlier in this chapter).

Constructing a teacher–student word-context test begins by selecting words from the student's word bank. Each word is first presented in isolation with the student guessing word meanings. Next, the student is given a context to verify and modify the initial prediction of word meaning. (We want to find out if the student does use context to determine word meaning.) The test can be administered orally, in writing, or in a combination of both to assess the ability to use context during oral and silent reading. Regardless of which format is used, discussion of how and why the meaning of a word was predicted is essential to observe the student's use of context clues. The number of words tested will vary, depending on age and reading ability. A few sample test formats are listed below:

ISOLATION	CONTEXT
poltergeist	Does your house have a *poltergeist* living in it? Do you hear strange noises at night? List some words which describe what a poltergeist might do or look like.
brash	Alex was *brash* when he answered his teacher. His teacher sent him from the room. Have you ever been brash in school or at home? Want to tell how and what happened to you?

The sentences which surround the words above should help the reader predict, verify, and modify—if necessary—initial guesses at word meanings. The following checklist can be adapted and used to record and interpret test performance. Checklists can be compared over time and used as a guide for instruction and to record evidence of progress in using context clues.

Checklist Assessing Words in Context

Form of Test: ____ oral ____ written ____ both
Number of Words: ____ Words from Experiences: ____
                                Words from Content Areas: ____

Number correct/Number attempted   Percent
    Isolation: ____/____   ____
    Context: ____/____   ____

The student exhibited these consistent behaviors during testing which appeared to indicate difficulty using context clues:
_____ Reread several times and arrived at incorrect response.

_____ Made false starts when reading and responding.
_____ Took too long to read and respond.
_____ Asked for approval or feedback repeatedly.
_____ Appeared to guess randomly.
_____ Uses other skills ineffectively, for example, phonics, structural analysis.

Students who fail to recognize words in context may rely too much on other skills, believe that simply rereading a number of times will result in meaning, or refuse to respond and risk failure again. A short summary statement in addition to the checklist above will assist in planning instruction and in informing parents and others who work with or see the student in reading settings:

> Alex was able to assign appropriate word meanings to 65 percent of the test words in isolation. When tested in context, Alex read orally in a low voice and in a monotone fashion. For each sentence read orally, he read it silently first. For those sentences read only silently, he appeared to be rereading each one several times before responding. Alex was able to complete 30 percent of the responses in context orally and about 20 percent silently. His first responses were usually correct; when reread his second attempts were incorrect and he rarely self-corrected. Alex appears to have difficulty understanding how context clues can be useful. Instruction in how to use context clues should be accompanied by oral talk-through sessions to model successful use of context for Alex.

Next we present several teaching strategies for encouraging the use of context clues. Each one of these strategies can be used to teach and encourage independence in using context clues.

STRATEGIES FOR TEACHING USE OF CONTEXT

Preview in context and *writing in context* are two teaching strategies for showing students how to use context to predict meaning. We recommend consulting the Suggested Readings section of this chapter for additional resources, especially Thelen (1984); Johnson and Pearson (1984); and Readence, Bean, and Baldwin (1985).

Preview in Context[3]

The preview in context is an informal discovery procedure for teaching new vocabulary. It draws its strength from students' prior knowledge and the analysis of the immediate context in which words occur. The method is simple, it requires minimal teacher preparation, deals with words that are relevant to

---

[3]Readence, Bean, & Baldwin, *Content-Area Reading,* 2nd ed. (Dubuque, IA: Kendall/Hunt Publishing, 1985), pp. 102–103.

current reading assignments, and is helpful in teaching students to resolve and remember the meanings of new words. The present procedure is similar to the context strategy presented earlier, except that this new strategy utilizes a question-and-answer sequence. The procedure is designed for older elementary, junior and senior high school students. Preview in context is a four-step procedure.

1. Preparation. Select vocabulary from a passage or chapter that students will soon read. Choose words that are both important and likely to engender confusion as students read. Present only a few words at one time to prevent the lesson from becoming tedious.

2. Establishing context. Direct students to each word and its surrounding context. Read the passage aloud to the students as they follow along in their own texts. Then, have students read the passage silently.

3. Specifying word meaning. Use the questioning procedure to help students identify the probable meaning of the word in its existing context, as in the following example sentence:

The culpable actions of the driver resulted in a short jail term and the loss of his license.

TEACHER:	What does the sentence tell you about the word "culpable?"
STUDENT A:	I guess the driver did something bad.
TEACHER:	What do you suppose he did?
STUDENT B:	He probably got drunk and ran over someone.
TEACHER:	How should he be treated?
STUDENT C:	He should be punished.
TEACHER:	Then what might a culpable action be?
STUDENT D:	Something you should get punished for.

4. Expanding word meanings. After students understand the meaning of the word in its given context, extend their understanding by briefly discussing antonyms, synonyms, or alternative contexts for the word. Such discussions will develop schemata for words and insure the students will recognize their meanings when they appear in other contexts. For example:

TEACHER:	Can you name other actions which we would consider culpable?
STUDENTS:	Hitting a teacher, robbing a bank, not doing your homework, cheating on your income tax, smoking in school.
TEACHER:	Look at how "culpable" is used in your book. Are there any words we could substitute that would make the sentence mean about the same thing?
STUDENTS:	Criminal, punishable, illegal.

Writing in Context[4]

The teacher-directed procedure of writing in context should help children with difficult content-area vocabulary that they encounter. Writing in context can be used with vocabulary that carries a heavy meaning load and is identified as such by the author of the text. For example, the words *photosynthesis* and *chlorophyll* might be key meaning words in a unit on plants. The steps to writing in context are:

1. *Copy*. Children copy from the chalkboard a content-vocabulary word that the teacher knows they will encounter as they read.
2. *Guess meaning*. Children read the text silently until they encounter the copied word. At this point they stop and try to write down a synonym or short definition. Guessing is encouraged, as is quick response time.
3. *Reread*. The teacher rereads aloud to the children the paragraph containing the word, carefully noting context clues, margin notes, or any graphic aids to meaning that can be used to figure out the word.
4. *Revise*. Children are then asked to use the new information to revise the original meaning they wrote.

Writing in context is appropriate to help children decode vocabulary as it appears in context. The words will typically appear again and again throughout the chapter or unit. Keeping the silent reading to a few pages is recommended, in order to avoid the problem of too many children finishing earlier or lagging behind the others in the class. Either the glossary that may accompany the text or a dictionary should also be available to help refine the meaning provided by the text. In a content textbook, however, the most important words—those that carry considerable meaning to the topic under study—are usually specifically defined in context for children.

Both preview in context and writing in context furnish ongoing diagnostic information, in addition to being instructional strategies.

SPELLING DEVELOPMENT

Spelling, spelling, spelling. Can it be taught? Are good spellers born, or are they made that way by drill, drill, drill? Will my students who can't spell really grow up and get jobs where secretaries will do their spelling for them? All of these questions really hint at the same basic issues in spelling development. We are concerned in this text primarily with assessing and assisting students who encounter difficulty in reading and writing. Spelling is a *supportive* language skill crucial to communicating thoughts, wishes, and information through

---

[4]Searfoss & Readence, *Helping Children Learn to Read* (Englewood Cliffs, NJ: Prentice-Hall, 1985), pp. 161–162.

writing. Furthermore, good spellers seem to also be good readers, for the most part (Harris & Sipay, 1980). In this section we want to present some ways to assess spelling ability and some teaching strategies to assist students whose ability to communicate through writing is impaired because of spelling problems. We based our selection of assessment and teaching strategies on these conclusions from the literature.

1. Good spellers seem to be able to use their knowledge of phoneme/grapheme correspondences (sound to letter regularity) *and* their visual memory for words as they spell. There is enough consistency in phoneme/grapheme correspondences in English to justify using word analysis techniques which focus on phonic elements and regular patterns or phonograms as part of spelling instruction.

2. Visual memory is an important part of being able to spell but has not been widely accepted as part of spelling instruction, in spite of the long history of the relationship (Durrell, 1956; Groff, 1977). As Groff noted: "It is clear that attention must be given to the visual imagery of words in spelling instruction. After children have utilized phonic cues to the spelling of a word, they must then decide if the word 'looks right'" (p. 18).

3. Successful, confident spellers develop the combined ability to reproduce consistent phoneme/grapheme correspondences and to hold irregular spellings in visual memory. We feel there is an intuitive sense of "how language works for writing." The student might ask, "What letters stand for that sound? What combinations or patterns of letters make that word?"

4. The source of words for spelling instruction and practice should be words students need for written communication. As Veatch observed about weekly, predetermined spelling lists: "The traditional Friday spelling test is a list of words. A list of words, regardless of whatever fascinating and dramatic sentences might be dreamed up by those teachers pronouncing the words, does not SAY anything. A list is not the way in which communication takes place" (1986, p. 442).

5. Spelling instruction *must* be related to written composition. Spelling ought to be considered a tool for producing language that communicates ideas. Generating these ideas, in most cases, is simple for most students; but some are still overconcerned with "correct" spelling, thus inhibiting production. It seems important to assess a student's spelling by considering its effect on composing.

Procedures for Assessing Spelling Ability

Spelling ability can be assessed by a number of informal procedures. These include observation, phonemic scoring, and analysis for spelling trends in personal words and composition.

Observation

Durrell's (1956) pioneering work in spelling ranks him as one of the few researchers whose work has "stood the test of time." We have selected and adapted some questions from his 1956 text which seem relevant to the assessment of spelling ability today and consistent with recent conclusions from the literature. These questions should guide our observations of students in a variety of settings where spelling is important or required:

Are the meanings of the words to be spelled known to the students? If the meanings of words are unknown to students, they are simply spelling nonsense words that will never appear in their compositions. They will not learn to spell these words or, if they do, the words will be forgotten quickly.

Does the student hear sounds in spoken words? The ability to spell correctly elements of words—regular patterns or phonograms—indicates that the student can hear sounds and represent them in print.

Does the spelling difficulty rest upon inaccurate pronunciation of words? Mispronounced words will appear as misspelled words. We would like to add that mispronunciation leading to misspelling is more likely to occur in longer words because of missing letters or other elements.

Is the student's visual memory of words adequate for spelling? Visual memory can be tested by showing the student unfamiliar words—one at a time for two or three second exposures—and then having the student attempt to write the words. Longer-term memory can be tested by asking the student to write the same word at progressively later times without reexposure (thirty seconds, several minutes, an hour, next day). This "test" is really informal, and certainly a student could not be expected to learn a word and accurately spell it after a two- or three-second exposure. What should be noted are differing performances and consistency—that is, the longer the time since exposure, the worse the recall of an unfamiliar word.

Are there any systematic errors in the student's spelling? It is probably less important to classify and attribute some linguistic reason or label to a systematic error than it is to point it out to the student and show him or her ways to compensate. For example, some students simply "forget" the final *e* on words or spell *-tion* as *-shun*.

Phonemic Scoring System

Assessment of spelling ability is possible using a system developed by Temple, Nathan, and Burris (1982).[5] The system yields a score indicating phonemic awareness of the language system. Keep in mind that learning to recognize and spell consistent phoneme/grapheme correspondences and patterns in our language is *one* sign of a good speller, but only one. The phonemic scoring system is useful for placing a student on a continuum of development in phonemic awareness. When combined with analysis of spelling errors in compositions and in relation to Durrell's questions, scores add much for explaining students' spellings based on developmental spelling trends. We will present the scoring system in this section and demonstrate its applications later. The categories or stages in the system of Temple, Nathan, and Burris are as follows:

Prephonemic spelling—Score value 0. This stage of spelling development is demonstrated when the student writes letters. A student may represent words by a single letter or two. If a few words are written, they are not usually within the student's reading vocabulary.

Early phonemic spelling—Score value 1. Words begin to reflect phoneme knowledge at this stage. Students seem to be aware of how words work. They are in the process of discovering how letters represent sounds. Noticeable in this stage is the fact that often one phoneme is represented correctly but the rest of the word in which the phoneme appears is randomly spelled.

Letter name spelling—Score value 2. During this stage, the student breaks words into phonemes which are represented with letters of the alphabet. The student who begins to read will pass through this stage quickly.

Transitional spelling stage—Score value 3. During this stage, the student uses many traditional spelling rules, but they are often employed incorrectly. These spellers will use silent letters for markers, for example, as well as conventional spelling which has been learned. Often students in this stage will use rules employed in earlier stages, particularly the letter-naming stage of spelling development. During this stage, even if words are misspelled they often look correct. Composition will usually reflect knowledge that includes:

>Marking rules (periods, question marks, etc.)
>Phonological rules
>Morphological rules

[5]Adapted from, C. Temple, R. Nathan, and N. Burris. *The Beginnings of Writing.* Boston: Allyn & Bacon, Inc. 1982.

Correct spelling stage—Scores value 4. This score is given when spelling is correct.

Personal Spelling Words

A traditional approach to assessing spelling through word lists can be acceptable *if*—and that is a big *if*—the words are taken from the student's personal word bank. Spelling lists can be developed to assess visual memory of words, patterns, and common spelling rules. The words in the bank determine what element is the focus of assessment. Words can be chosen with common patterns—for example, *-at*, *-op*, *-ing* words—or they can reflect common spelling rules as described by Flood and Salus (1984):

1. Proper nouns and most adjectives formed from proper nouns begin with capital letters:
   Puerto Rico
   Puerto Rican
   Chinese pastry
2. Words ending in a silent *e* usually drop before adding a suffix beginning with a vowel; however, they keep the *e* before a suffix beginning with a consonant:
   take—taking
   pile—piling
   time—timely
3. Words that end in a *y* preceded by a consonant change the *y* to *i* before adding a suffix, unless the suffix begins with *i*:
   lobby—lobbies—lobbying
4. Words of one syllable—or words accented on the last syllable—which end in a single consonant preceded by a single vowel, double the final consonant when adding a suffix beginning with a vowel:
   get—getting
   drip—dripped—dripping
   commit—committed—committing—commitment
5. Rules for using possession:
   a. The possessive of a singular noun (including those ending in *s*, *z*, *ss*, or *x*) is formed by adding '*s*.
      Tina's car
      James's desk
      Sox's stadium
   b. The possessive of a plural noun ending in *s* is formed by adding an apostrophe.
      girls' dog
   c. The possessive of a plural noun not ending in *s* is formed by adding an '*s*.
      children's books
6. Words ending in *y* preceded by a vowel do not change the *y* to *i* when adding a suffix:
   stay—stayed—staying

Personal satisfaction result from counting the number of words each learns to write.

The following directions can be used to administer a personal spelling list test. Our sample administration contains fewer words than you would normally administer; total number should probably be eight to ten words for grades 1 and 2, and gradually increase at upper-grade levels.

1. I am going to ask you to write words, one at a time. My purpose is to find out how you think the words are spelled.
2. If you do not think you know how to spell a word, just try to figure it out.
3. I am going to read a word. Then I will use the word in a sentence. After reading the sentence, I will say the words again. (Try to personalize the sentences as much as possible by relating the word to the student's experiences.)
4. You will *not* be graded on the test. I will look at the spellings of words to describe where you need help. So, do your very best.

The following words were taken from a test of a student's personal words (we call her "Caroline"). We sampled a few words and then included a

thares   pan aBls
Hat fath   Sr bres
Wap crM   BlBrs

brief analysis. Administration of isolated words *must* be accompanied by an analysis of misspelled words from compositions. In fact, if you must choose between testing in isolation and analysis of errors from a composition, pick the latter.

1. pen   Caroline uses a *pen* to write letters to her friends.
2. sled   Caroline has a new *sled* for the snow this winter.
3. mice   We have two small, gray *mice* in our classroom.
4. train   We took the *train* to the city to go to the zoo.

A few of Caroline's spellings are shown below and scored based on the Temple, Nathan, Burris (1982) system.

Student: *Caroline*   Grade: *2*   Age: *7*

WORD	SCORE	
1. *pn*	2	
2. *sld*	2	
3. *mis*	3	
4. *traen*	3	
Total Score	10	Average = 2.5

Caroline's total score was found by adding the score for each word. An average score was also computed (10/4 = 2.5). Her score indicates that spelling development tested from personal words in isolation is probably between the letter-naming stage and the transitional stage to standard spelling.

Spelling in Compositions

Along with a score from a test of personal words in isolation, a score in context with some analysis of spelling errors is necessary. A sample of misspelled words was taken from Caroline's compositions and is presented in Figure 7–3. We adapted this presentation format from Ganschow (1984).
      The samples of Caroline's writing were taken from compositions completed during free-writing periods, during which students were expected to write about anything they desired. A daily, free, or unassigned writing period where students can write without concern for time, spelling, or topic choice is one source of writing samples. Other assigned compositions should also be analyzed and compared with performance on personal word list tests and free or unassigned writing samples.

Figure 7–3 In-Context Spelling Analysis

Student: *Caroline*   Age: _____   Grade: _____

Personal Word List Score/Average   In-Context Score/Average
           10/2.5   15/1.5

STUDENT'S SPELLING	SCORE	CORRECT SPELLING	TREND ANALYSIS
thares	1	cherries	sh = th
hat fath	2	hot fudge	th = dge: Knows initial consonants; understands word concepts (2).
wap crm	2	whip cream	Vowel confusions and omission; knows initial consonants and blends.
pan a Bls	1	pineapple	Vowel confusion; sees word as three; knows initial consonant; uses *bl* in place of *pl*; syllables represent word units.
Srbres	2	strawberries	Blend omission: sees initial and final consonants.
BlBrs	1	blueberries	Vowel omission; knows blends.
Thatrda	2	Saturday	TH = S: Vowel omission; hears three-syllable construction.
krdth	1	carriage	K = C; th = dge
ias krm	2	ice cream	Vowel omission; has acquired intonational concepts, beginning and ending phonemes.
rat	1	raisin	Responds to initial consonants; nonphonetic.

Analysis of Caroline's Spelling Trends

Observations of Caroline's spellings indicate that no word was conventionally spelled throughout. There is indication, however, that she has a sense of the phonemic system. Words begin, in most cases, with correct initial consonants or ones that sound like the correct letters (*k* for *c* in *carriage*). The exception—

th for *ch*—is noted in two places indicating a learned (intentional or unintentional) response to the phonemic system. There are consistent omissions of vowels in several places (*crm* for *cream* and *BlBrs* for blueberries). There seems to be, too, an interchangeable use of *c* and *k* (*crm* and *krm* for *cream*). In only one instance was Caroline's spelling nonphonetic. She seems to be aware of blends with two letters but not three (*bl* is used for *blue,* but *srbres* is used for *strawberries*). A glance at the list—and analysis of errors—demonstrate that Caroline is writing, in most cases, what she hears. In all but one word the spellings make sense linguistically. Caroline's performance in context is lower when scored phonemically. With other linguistic cues (syntax and semantics) present, she may not focus or attend to phoneme/grapheme relationships as closely. Her spelling test scores may reflect that she is a better speller than her written compositions indicate.

Some recommendations for instruction would include encouraging daily writing, editing activities, and directing Caroline's attention to the similarities and differences between her spellings and standard spellings. These and other instructional strategies are discussed next in this chapter.

Instructional Strategies for Spelling Development

1. Encourage daily writing activity. Daily writing seems to offer students the practice they need to feel more confident about spelling. Diaries, letters, journals, poems, and both assigned and unassigned writing are vital parts of the spelling program

2. Allow time for editing. Show students how to be their own editors and also include peer-editing time. For example, occasionally direct the students to notice similarities and differences in words. Keep a variety of dictionaries and other reference tools easily available. If word processing is available for students, be certain spelling software is included. One caution: Avoid presenting a list of "spelling demons" for students to use. Nothing can be more discouraging to a poor speller than seeing a list of demons he or she will probably never learn to spell. "Demons" presented one at a time as they arise in class writings will seem less threatening.

3. Base spelling activities on words from personal word banks and student's written compositions.

4. Practice visual memory skills by holding up flash cards of individual words or projecting them onto a screen using an overhead transparency. Expose a word for five seconds, remove it, and have the student write the word from memory. If production is a problem, have the students choose the word from word cards displayed on a bulletin board or written on the chalkboard. Be certain to include some words that will not be flashed. After matching the flashed word with one on a card or from the board, the student can then copy the word on paper or build the word from letter cards provided for them.

5. Teach a few spelling rules (see Personal Spelling Words, this chapter)

by illustration and example, using personal words or words from students' compositions.

6. Review phonics and structural analysis skills, especially common patterns or phonograms, affixes, and root words.

7. Use oral and written rhyming activities to develop language sense.

8. Phonics can be taught using games and other activities—such as those Veatch (1986) calls "phonics on the hoof": Discovering which words are alike provides an informal—that is, "on the hoof"—means of teaching those phonetic elements that happen to be in the given set of words. Maybe there are words that rhyme or contain the same number of vowel sounds. Maybe there are words that begin like someone's name.

9. Use visual discrimination and memory exercises constructed in the format, presented in Figures 7–4 and 7–5 (Greene, n.d.). The guides are somewhat time consuming to construct and should be used for words important to content-area units of study or words students really want to learn to write. One adaptation is to have the students construct them for each other, too. Blank pages with the boxes drawn can be given to students to use to create worksheets.

10. Try a contract system to help students who might respond to a systematic way of learning to spell. Each week the students contract to learn to spell words they select. The teacher can give a pretest and record the results and discuss with the students how they intend to study their words each day until they are ready for a posttest. Students should be encouraged to try a variety of ways of studying their words until they determine what works best for them. These include tracing the word—as mentioned above—practicing visual memory of the words with a friend, asking for someone at home to help by reviewing words, constructing a personal word bank or visual discrimination exercise, to name a few. Teacher or students can record the week's spelling activities and discuss which forms of study the students found most effective.

A sample weekly activity card or sheet might include the following information:

Name _____ Date _____
Words to be learned: Pretest: Correct/Possible

_____   _____/_____

_____

_____   Study Methods:

Posttest: Correct/Possible   1. _____

      _____/_____   2. _____

                                      3. _____

Construction Guide—Visual Memory for Spelling Worksheet.

Box 1: Print a simple sentence using a second word or foil, which is clearly incorrect, in the sentence. The foil may look like or unlike the target word to be learned (*open* in our example) depending upon your sentence.

Box 2: Print the target word clearly as a model in this box.

Box 3: Construct a matrix of 15 real words, 5 of which are the target word. Make sure that the first foil words are quite unlike the target word. Do not use reversals or letter reorganization of the target word in this box, that is at least one letter in each foil needs to be different.

Box 4: Make the target word with letters removed one at a time. There should be as many items as there are letters (or phonemes) in the word.

Box 5: Make one or two rows of random letters. Embed the letters of the target word in correct sequence in each line.

Box 6: Construct a matrix of 15 words, 5 of which are the target word. Construct the foil words by reversing or reorganizing the letters of the target word this time or by changing single letters of the target word. (Note that Boxes 7 and 8 test learning of the target word.)

Box 7: Draw a box with short lines for each letter of the target word.

Box 8: Draw a box with only a solid line in it. The last direction on the worksheet tests the student's ability to spell the word without any clues by turning over the sheet and writing the target word from memory.

A Final Note on Spelling

Spelling is a mechanical part of writing. Observing students' spelling reveals information for teaching. Assessment and instruction in spelling must be based on what we learn from our observations of students as they try to communicate through writing. A computer or a secretary can correct spelling errors, but not the ideas that words represent.

DECODING OR WORD-IDENTIFICATION SKILLS

The terms decoding, word identification, word analysis, and phonics have become interchangeable at the level of practice to describe how readers pronounce and recognize words already stored in their memories. At the level of research and theory, however, these terms have been assigned precise and often conflicting definitions by a variety of writers. For our discussion of decoding—or word identification—in this chapter, we will stay at the level of practice. We refer you to extensive discussions of research and theory on decoding in the work of Johnson and Baumann (1984), and especially in Calfee and Drum (1986).

Our discussion will assume that the purpose of decoding instruction is to help students use the graphic and sound systems found in written language

Figure 7–4 Constructing a Visual Discrimination and Memory Worksheet with Directions for Its Use

Box 1
Look at the top box. Choose the word which best completes the sentence. Circle it.

1

Box 2
Look at the word in the second box.

(Model)
2

Box 3
In the top part of the center block, find the word 5 times. Circle it each time.

3

Box 4
In the next part of the center block, make each word look like the model word by adding the missing parts.

4

Box 5
In the third part of the center block, find the letters of the model word in order. Circle each letter.

5

Box 6
In the bottom part of the center block, find the word 5 times. Circle it each time.

6

Box 7
In the bottom box with the spaces for the letters, try to write the model word without looking at the model. Then check your word with the model.

7

Box 8
In the empty bottom box, try to write the word without looking at the model. Then check your word with the model.

8

Turn the page over and try to write the word. Check it with the model. Then turn the paper over and again try to write the word without looking. If you can write the word, go to the next word.

Figure 7–5 Visual Memory for Spelling Worksheet

together to make meaning of print. Specifically, the justification or rationale for *any* decoding instruction must meet the conditions Spache and Spache outline for phonics instruction:

> The rationale for teaching decoding (phonics) varies from one author to the next. Some think of it as the most essential tool for learning to read, and that skill in this area should be manifest at all ages up to and including the college level. In truth, its justification lies in the fact that it helps *beginning readers only* to pronounce and thus recognize words for which auditory memories are already stored. In other words, decoding functions with simple, known words but not with harder or technical terms that are unfamiliar. It is a distinct aid in early reading stages but deteriorates as the normal reading vocabulary expands beyond the individual's auditory vocabulary. Decoding produces a pronunciation of a word that is helpful in its recognition—*if* the pronunciation is similar to the spoken version of the word and *if* some meaningful associations to that word have already been stored in the reader's memory. Without previous knowledge of the word, decoding produces only a meaningless group of sounds. (1986, pp. 489–490)

Decoding lessons designed to help students master the graphophonic cue system are included as part of holistic reading instruction, which pays attention to the interaction of graphophonic, syntactic, and semantic cue systems within the pragmatic contexts in which they are used (Eeds, in press). Assessment of decoding ability must also consider the same interaction and the affect of pragmatic contexts. We agree with Eeds when she concludes that it is important for students to understand how the cue system works and its role in fluent reading, and when she cautions us that simply mastering the graphophonic cue system will not solve all our reading problems—a warning too often forgotten in the diagnosis of reading problems, especially for beginners who encounter difficulty in learning to read.

Assessing Decoding Ability

To guide our assessment of decoding ability, we offer the following questions for teachers and clinicians as each assesses decoding in a variety of settings: When reading, does the student use

- letter sounds?
- regular patterns; cluster or common phonograms?
- knowledge of affixes and root words?
- context in combination with other deciding skills?

Formats for assessing decoding skills should be varied, ranging from formal test settings through analysis of spelling in writing samples. In this chapter, we suggest the following formats and urge you to add information from others as they arise.

1. Checklist Assessing Words in Context (see page 217)
2. Informal reading inventories (see page 128).
3. Phonemic Scoring System (see page 223).
4. In-Context Spelling Analysis (see Figure 7–3)

Keep in mind that the model of diagnosis we advocate requires assessment in a variety of formats so that questions can be raised, tentative answers formed, and questions revised, based on those tentative answers.

Lists of constructed words are generally developed to assess the student's ability to respond specifically to individual letter sounds and structural elements of words. Such lists usually lacking written context and should never be used as the sole basis for assessing decoding skills. When combined with measures of decoding ability which consider context, they give us a broader picture of a student's ability to decode words and where to begin instruction. Searfoss and Jacobs (1979) developed a list of constructed words which can be used to assess phonics and structural analysis knowledge in isolation. Responses to individual words should be analyzed. It is important that several practices of sample constructed words be given so that students are familiar with the task and respond to the words exactly as presented (see Figures 7–6 and 7–7).

The following are procedures for using constructed word lists:

Directions. Say: "The purpose of this test is to find out if you can say some words you have never seen before. Pronounce each one the best way you can as I point to them. Let's try a few practice words first." (Point to practice words and be certain the student understands the test procedure before administering the entire list.)

Record. Mark a plus sign on the blank when the student's response is correct. Record *NR* for no response. Record an error with the most accurate spelling possible. For example:

Informal reading inventories, such as those developed by Silvaroli (1986) and Johns (1985), can be used to analyze a student's responses to words in isolation and in context by modifying traditional error-pattern analysis procedures. As we examine oral-reading errors resulting from the administration of an informal reading inventory, the *quality* of errors should be assessed along with the *quantity* of errors. The quality of an error can be determined by asking the question, "Did the error result in inaccurate comprehension?" Errors which limit comprehension are far more serious and deserve close attention. Those which do not appear to affect comprehension are probably not worth counting.

Johns has developed some qualitative analysis procedures for use with his *Basic Reading Inventory* (1985) which may be used as an alternative to

Figure 7–6 Initial Screening. (*Source:* L. W. Searfoss & H. D. Jacobs, *Decoding Inventory*. Dubuque, IO: Kendall-Hunt 1979. First Edition, page 13.)

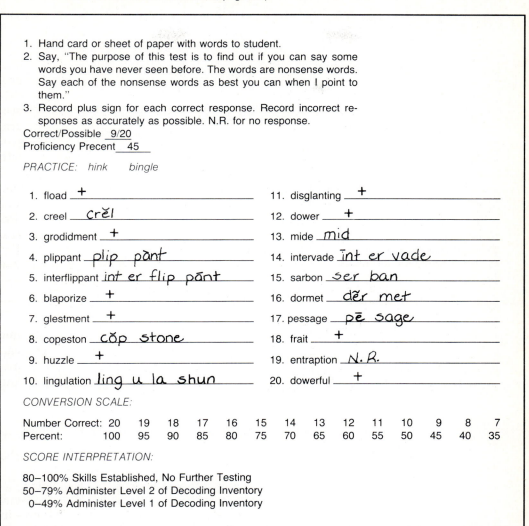

his suggested error analysis. His modified approach is used after administration of the inventory and considers each error as a *miscue* and evaluates its graphic similarity with the actual word and its context acceptability. While this optional qualitative procedure requires more time than the standard analysis, it can yield valuable information about how the reader uses the three cue systems interactively in a test setting.

Figure 7–7 Decoding Inventory Subtests

LEVEL R—READINESS
1. Auditorily discriminating phonemes within words
2. Visually discriminating graphemes
3. Naming letters

LEVEL 1—BASIC DECODING SKILLS
4. Hearing & labeling initial single-consonant phonemes
5. Hearing & labeling final single-consonant phonemes
6. Hearing & labeling initial consonant-cluster phonemes
7. Hearing & labeling final consonant-cluster phonemes
8. Pronouncing vowel-consonant phoneme clusters
9. Hearing syllables within words
10. Dividing words into syllables
11. Estimating words from affixes
12. Using context clues

LEVEL 2—ADVANCED DECODING SKILLS
13. Hearing & labeling initial consonant-cluster phonemes
14. Hearing & labeling final consonant-cluster phonemes
15. Pronouncing vowel-consonant phoneme clusters
16. Hearing syllables within words
17. Dividing words into syllables
18. Estimating words from affixes
19. Using context clues

Henk (1985) suggests a procedure which not only includes a qualitative analysis of oral-reading errors after the administration of an informal inventory, but recommends some modifications in the administration procedures when it is difficult to determine if an error is or is not negatively affecting comprehension.

1. After the passage has been completed, direct the child back to the text and ask that the entire sentence be reread aloud.
2. Write the word on the board or a separate piece of paper and ask the child to identify it.
3. Pose a question that requires understanding of the term, such as, "What do you mean by a couple hundred yards?" More often than not, this procedure will help the teacher determine if the reader's comprehension has in some way been limited. These probes are particularly necessary when none of the accompanying comprehension questions tap the child's understanding of the term or of the concept it conveys.

One specialized informal reading inventory which assesses only decoding skills is the *Decoding Inventory* (Jacobs & Searfoss, 1986). The inventory assesses phonics, structural analysis, and context clues. The subtests are organized to include readiness for decoding skills, as well as basic and advanced skills. Unique to the tests are devices for assessing the ability to decode words using context clues. Students are asked to respond to key words in isolation prior to reading a short passage and then to respond to those same words after encountering them in context. This feature makes it possible to determine if students are able to adjust or determine meaning based on context clues. Figure 7–7 illustrates the various subtests of the Decoding Inventory.

Analysis of writing samples is a format for assessing decoding skills that can "piggyback" onto the analysis of spelling in compositions. Return to Figure 7–3 and reread the analysis of Caroline's spelling ability presented there. Included there is information of use in determining how spelling ability and decoding ability are interrelated. Information from the analysis of written compositions can be combined with other information about decoding ability from constructed work lists and informal inventories, too.

TEACHING STRATEGIES FOR DECODING DEVELOPMENT

1. When selecting materials to reteach and review decoding skills, select those which follow these guidelines:

   a. Involve students in active learning, not passive worksheets or computer programs (which are little more than "dittos on a screen"). Computer software should be interactive.
   b. Be certain phonics and structural analysis lessons proceed analytically, that is, begin with whole words which include an element to be learned. Preferably these words should come from the students' personal experiences. This "whole to part" learning is much more interesting for both teacher and learner.
   c. Teach students to use an analogy strategy for decoding (Markle, 1986). For example, when teaching the new word *which,* review all known words beginning with *wh*—such as *white, why, when*—and help students note the similarities among the words. If the known words you select are personal ones, all the better.
   d. Plan for oral instruction *and* practice, especially for phonics lessons. Hearing students responses as they practice decoding skills allows for immediate, timely feedback at the moment of instruction.
   e. Include phonics or structural analysis generalizations which are useful to students. Obscure or seldom used rules are of little use to students who are already having difficulty learning to read.

2. Reinforce structural analysis skills by helping students develop confidence in attacking longer words. Present a word to the students that you know is within their meaning vocabulary. If you are not certain the word is already "in the students' heads," pronounce it and determine if the meaning is known. Next, isolate some common clusters or phonograms and question the student as follows (questioning procedure somewhat related to earlier work by Glass, 1973):

Point to the *cluster* and ask:

"What letters make the ____ sound?"

Then ask:

"What sound does the letter ____ make?"

Repeat with other words containing the same *clusters*. For example: *longest* (*est* cluster)

"What letters make the *est* sound?
"What sound does *est* make?"

(Other words: *tightest, highest*)
For example: *unthinkable* (*un, think, able* are possibilities)

"What letters make the *un* sound?"
"What letters make the *ink* sound?"
"What letters make the *able* sound?"
"What sound does *un* make?"
"What sound does *ink* make?"
"What sound does *able* make?"

(Other words: *undrinkable, unworkable*)

SUMMARY

Helping students understand the written coding system assists them in gaining control over the system of written language. Assessment of print awareness, concepts about print, vocabulary development, spelling ability, and decoding ability help teachers learn about a student's level of control over the written language system. Assessment, of course, must be followed by instruction which treats language holistically and includes strategies designed to give students the confidence they need to use language.

QUESTIONS TO PONDER

1. How is gaining control over the written coding system similar to learning to drive a car?
2. Do games designed to reinforce phonics and structural analysis skills build language confidence and control?

3. Is it fair to say there really is a fourth cue system—the pragmatic cue system of language?
4. How does reading to preschool children affect their print awareness and their concepts about print?

REFERENCES

Agnew, A. T. (1982). Using children's dictated stories to assess code consciousness. *The Reading Teacher, 35*(4), 450–454.
Ashton-Warner, S. (1963). *Teacher* New York: Simon & Schuster.
Beck, I. L., McKeown, M. G., & McCaslin, F. S. (1983). Vocabulary development: All contexts are not created equal. *Elementary School Journal, 83,* 177–181.
Betts, E. (1946). *Foundations of reading instruction.* New York: American Book Company.
Calfee, R. & Drum, P. (1986). Research on teaching reading. In M. C. Wittrock (Ed.), *Handbook of research on teaching* (3rd ed.) (pp. 804–849). New York: Macmillan.
Cameron, P. (1961). *"I can't," said the ant.* New York: Coward-McCann.
Carroll, J. B., Davies, P., & Richmond, B. (1971). *American heritage word frequency book.* Boston: Houghton-Mifflin.
Clavio, D. (1980). A student author project: Integrating language arts. *Proceedings of the Annual Reading Conference of Arizona State University, 3,* 11–18.
Cockrum, W. (1986). *Effect of vocabulary instruction on reading comprehension.* Unpublished doctoral dissertation, Arizona State University, Tempe, AZ.
Cohn, M. & D'Allesandro, C. (1978). When is a decoding error not a decoding error? *The Reading Teacher, 32,* 341–344.
Dale, E. & O'Rourke, J. (1976). *The living word vocabulary.* Elgin, IL: Dome.
Degen, B. (1983). *Jamberry.* New York: Harper & Row Junior Books.
Dolch, E. W. (1981). *Dolch basic sight vocabulary cards.* Champaign, IL: Garrard Publishing Company.
Durrell, D. D. (1956). *Improving reading instruction.* New York: Harcourt, Brace, World.
Eastman, P. D. (1960). *Are you my mother?* New York: Random House.
Eeds, M. (In press). Holistic assessment of decoding ability. In S. M. Glazer, L. W. Searfoss, & L. M. Gentile (Eds.), *Reexamining reading diagnosis: New trends and procedures in classrooms and clinics.* Newark, DE: International Reading Association.
Einsel, W. (1972). *Did you ever see?* New York: Scholastic.
Elliott, S., Nowosad, J., & Samuels, P. (1981). "Me at school, me at home": Using journals with preschoolers. *Language Arts, 58,* 688–691.
Fernald, G. M. (1971). *Remedial techniques in basic school subjects.* New York: McGraw-Hill.
Flood, J. & Salus, P. H. (1984). *Language and the language arts.* Englewood Cliffs, NJ: Prentice-Hall.
Fry, E. B., Polk, J. K., & Fountoukidis, D. (1984). *The reading teacher's book of lists.* Englewood Cliffs, NJ: Prentice-Hall.
Ganschow, L. (1983). Teaching strategies for spelling success. *Academic Therapy, 19*(2), 185–193.
Glass, G. G. (1973). *Glass-analysis for decoding only.* Garden City, NY: Easier to Learn Materials.
Goodman, K. (1980). Viewpoints . . . from a researcher. *Language Arts, 57,* 846–847.

Goodman, Y. M. & Altwerger, B. (1981). *Print awareness in pre-school children* (Research Paper no. 4). Tucson: University of Arizona, Program in Language and Literacy.

Gough, P. B. (1984). Word recognition. In P. D. Pearson (Ed.), *Handbook of reading research* (pp. 225–253). New York: Longman.

Greene, F. P. (no date). Clinic materials. N. Syracuse, NY: Syracuse University Reading Clinc.

Groff, P. (1977). *Phonics: Why and how.* New York: Silver Burdett Company.

Harris, A. J. & Jacobson, M. D. (1973). Basic vocabulary for beginning reading. *The Reading Teacher, 26*(4), 392–395.

Harris, A. J. & Sipay, E. R. (1980). *How to increase reading ability* (7th ed.). New York: Longman.

Hawkins, C. & J. (1985). *Jen the Hen*, New York: G. P. Putnam's Sons.

Henderson, L. (1982). *Orthography and word recognition in reading.* New York: Academic Press.

Henk, W. (1985). Assessing children's reading abilities. In L. W. Searfoss & J. E. Readence (Eds.), *Helping children learn to read* (pp. 280–320). Englewood Cliffs, NJ: Prentice-Hall.

Jacobs, H. D. & Searfoss, L. W. (1986). *Decoding inventory* (2nd ed.). Dubuque, IA: Kendall-Hunt.

Jewell, M. G. & Zintz, M. V. (1986). *Learning to read naturally.* Dubuque, IA: Kendall/Hunt.

Johns, J. (1985). *Basic reading inventory* (2nd ed.). Dubuque, IA: Kendall/Hunt.

Johnson, D. D. & Baumann, J. F. (1984). Word identification. In P. D. Pearson (Ed.). *Handbook of reading research* (pp. 583–608). New York: Longman.

Johnson, D. D., Moe, A. J., & Baumann, J. F. (1983). *The Ginn word book for teachers.* Lexington, MA.: Ginn.

Johnson, D. D. & Pearson, P. D. (1984). *Teaching reading vocabulary.* New York: Holt, Rinehart & Winston.

Kucera, H. & Francis, W. N. (1967). *Comparative analysis of present day American English.* Providence, RI: Brown University Press.

Kuhns, C. O., Moore, D. W., & Moore, S. A. (1986). The stability of modified miscue analysis profiles. *Reading research and instruction, 25,* 149–159.

Markle, A. (1986). *Decoding ability of good and poor readers.* Unpublished doctoral dissertation, Arizona State University.

Mason, J. M. (1984). Early reading from a developmental perspective. In P. D. Pearson (Ed.), *Handbook of reading research* (pp. 505–544). New York: Longman.

Mason, J. M. & Au, K. H. (1986). *Reading instruction for today.* Glenview, IL: Scott, Foresman.

McKeown, M. G., Beck, I. L., Omanson, R. C., & Pople, M. T. (1985). Some effects of the nature and frequency of vocabulary instruction on the knowledge and use of words. *Reading Research Quarterly, 20*(5), 522–535.

Mezynski, K. (1983). Issues concerning the acquisition of knowledge: Effects of vocabulary training on reading comprehension. *Review of Educational Research, 53,* 253–279.

Nagy, W. E., Herman, P. A., & Anderson, R. C. (1985). Learning words from context. *Reading Research Quarterly, 20*(2), 233–253.

Nicholson, T. & Hill, D. (1985). Good readers don't guess—taking another look at the issue of whether children read words better in context or in isolation. *Reading Psychology, 6,* 181–198.

Perkins, E. (1969). *Hand, hand, fingers, thumb.* New York: Random House.

Readence, J. E., Bean, T. W., & Baldwin, R. S. (1985). *Content area reading* (2nd ed.). Dubuque, IA: Kendall/Hunt.

Searfoss, L. W. & Jacobs, H. D. (1979). *Decoding inventory.* Dubuque, IA: Kendall/Hunt.

Searfoss, L. W. & Readence, J. E. (1985). *Helping children learn to read.* Englewood Cliffs, NJ: Prentice-Hall.

Silvaroli, N. J. (1986). *Classroom reading inventory* (5th ed.). Dubuque, IA: William C. Brown.

Spache, G. D. (1981). *Diagnostic reading scales.* Monterey, CA: CTB/McGraw-Hill.

Spache, G. D. & Spache, E. B. (1986). *Reading in the elementary school* (5th ed.). Boston: Allyn & Bacon.

Suess, Dr. (1963). *Hop on pop.* New York: Random House.

Temple, C., Nathan, R., & Burris, N. (1982). *The beginnings of writing.* Boston: Allyn & Bacon.

Thelen, J. N. (1984). *Improving reading in science.* Newark, DE: International Reading Association.

Thorndike, E. L. & Lorge, I. (1944). *A teacher's wordbook of 30,000 words.* New York: Teachers College, Columbia University.

Tompkins, G. E. (1981). Writing without a pencil. *Language Arts, 58,* 823–833.

Veatch, J. (1986). *Reading in the elementary school* (3rd ed.). New York: Richard C. Owen.

Veatch, J., Sawicki, F., Elliott, G., Flake, E., & Blakey, J. (1979). *Key words to reading: The language experience approach begins* (2nd ed.). Columbus, OH: Charles E. Merrill.

Woodcock, R. W. (1973). *Woodcock reading mastery tests.* Circle Pines, MN: American Guidance Service.

SUGGESTED READINGS

Calfee, R. & Drum, P. (1986). Research on teaching reading. In M. C. Wittrock (Ed.), *Handbook of research on teaching* (3rd ed.) (pp. 804–849). New York: Macmillan. Discusses in detail instructional research on decoding, word meaning, and various forms of comprehension.

Cohn, M. & D'Alessandro, C. (1978). When is a decoding error not a decoding error? *The Reading Teacher, 32,* 341–344. Includes practical ways for teachers and diagnosticians to respond to students' decoding errors.

Henderson, E. H. & Beers, J. W. (1980). *Developmental and cognitive aspects of learning to spell.* Newark, DE: International Reading Association. With a focus on spelling theory and research, the authors emphasize teaching principles and generalizations to guide spelling instruction.

Johnson, D. D. & Baumann, J. F. (1984). Word ientification. In P. D. Pearson (Ed.), *Handbook of reading research* (pp. 583–608). New York: Longman. Extensive chapter which presents research on instructional practices in word identification, or how children are taught to read words.

Johnson, D. D. & Pearson, P. D. (1984). *Teaching reading vocabulary.* New York: Holt, Rinehart & Winston. Gives activities for the development of a meaning vocabulary, including basal reader and content-area vocabulary.

Kuhns, C. O., Moore, D. W., & Moore, S. A. (1986). The stability of modified miscue analysis profiles. *Reading Research and Instruction, 25,* 149–159. Findings of the study are interpreted as evidence that reading researchers and diagnosticians should be cautious when inferring reader's strategies on the basis of a subset of miscues obtained from the oral reading of a passage.

Nicholson, T. & Hill D. (1985). Good readers don't guess—Taking another look at the issue of whether children read words better in context or in isolation. *Reading Psychology, 6,* 181–198. The results of this series of experiments suggest that what separates good readers from poor readers is the ability to decode words independent of context.

Readence, J. E., Bean, T. W., & Baldwin, R. S. (1985). *Content area reading* (2nd ed.). Dubuque, IA: Kendall-Hunt. Chapter 5, Vocabulary Strategies, gives several pre- and postreading strategies for introducing, reinforcing, and extending the meanings of content-area terminology.

Sorenson, N. L. (1985). Basal reading vocabulary instruction: A critique and suggestions. *The Reading Teacher, 39*(1), 80–85. Lists six misconceptions about words and vocabulary instruction, and suggests more flexibility and teacher monitoring in teaching vocabulary.

Spache, G. D. & Spache, E. B. (1986). Reading in the elementary school (5th ed.). Boston: Allyn & Bacon. Chapter 12, Word Recognition Techniques and Skills, discusses recent research and practice in phonics, structural analysis, and context clues. Specific teaching strategies are included for each skill area.

Stahl, S. & Fairbanks, M. M. (1986). The effects of vocabulary instruction: A model based meta-analysis. *Review of Educational Research, 56*(1), 72–110. Results of vocabulary research indicate a significant effect of direct vocabulary instruction on children's comprehension of text. The most effective vocabulary teaching methods included both definitional and contextual information, involved students in deeper processing, and gave a number of exposures to the words.

Thelen, J. N. (1984). *Improving reading in science*. Newark, DE: International Reading Association. A good mix of the practical and the theoretical in science reading with examples and suggestions for teaching both content and reasoning processes.

Tovey, D. R. & Kerber, J. E. (1986). *Roles in literacy learning*. Newark, DE: International Reading Association. *Part 1* (pp. 1–32), Role of the Parent, emphasizes the crucial role of reading to and with children before formal schooling by relating book events to real life, by expanding the child's word, by imparting book sense, and by helping the child get meaning from text and pictures. *Part 2* (pp. 33–64), Role of the Teacher, focuses on function, meaningful contexts, communication, sensitive observation, and noninvasive assistance with extensive literature and writing experiences.

8

PHYSICAL FACTORS AFFECTING LANGUAGE LEARNING

Physical Factors

Visual Factors

Auditory Factors: Hearing or Acuity

Allergies

Nutrition

Alcohol and Drug Abuse

Perceptual and Neurological Factors

Summary

Questions to Ponder

References

Suggested Reading

Seeing, hearing, and attending are a few of the important physically related factors which affect language learning. This chapter will provide answers related to the following questions about the relationship between physical factors and language learning:

- What physical factors are related to language learning?
- Why and how does each factor affect language learning?
- How can educators identify and assess the ways in which language performance is inhibited by physical problems?
- How can instructional settings be modified to accommodate students when a physical factor is responsible for hindering language learning?

PHYSICAL FACTORS

A variety of physical factors have been correlated with the development of reading and other language skills in students for many years. The nature of that relationship, both quantitatively and qualitatively, has been the subject of debate and research. (See Bond, Tinker, Wasson, & Wasson, 1984; Gillet & Temple, 1982; Harris & Smith, 1980; Morris, 1966; Robinson, 1946; Spache, 1976a, 1976b). Rather than enter into further debate, we acknowledge that for *some* students, physical factors—alone or in combination with other factors—can play a role in the difficulties children encounter when learning to read and write.

As we suggested in earlier chapters, a diagnosis should have as its goal the improvement of instructional conditions rather than simply the investigating and listing of suspected causes. A diagnostician, like a detective, must not be satisfied with a narrow approach to diagnosis. For some students the initial modifications in classroom instruction based on diagnosis may not yield results. As students' responses to instruction continue to be observed and they are interviewed as part of the learning process, the diagnostician may begin to suspect other inhibiting factors. However, as Brown stated so well:

> Often, the only way to find out whether there are other elements in a student's situation that adversely affect his learning is by beginning a good instructional program and watching his response. It is usually possible within two or three weeks to determine whether the student appears to be making the expected progress. If progress is good, the teacher has saved the time that otherwise would have been expended on diagnosis of inhibiting factors; if progress is poor, the teacher should begin to investigate possible influences affecting the student's learning. (1982, p. 154)

Rather than make diagnosis of physical factors part of a routine "battery of tests" administered to every student being diagnosed, we advocate that diagnosticians observe and assess physical factors only when initial modifications of the instructional program appear ineffectual. The following graph should help you to better understand our position.

WHEN TO ASSESS PHYSICAL FACTORS

STEP 1: OBSERVE LEARNING PROGRESS IN MODIFIED INSTRUCTIONAL
PROGRAM AFTER INITIAL DIAGNOSIS

Progress Observed ↓ Continue Instruction

Little or No Progress ↓ Extended Diagnosis to Consider Physical Factors ↓ Referral to Appropriate Specialists and/or Modify Instructional Setting

Classroom teachers and clinicians must be able to use information about the relationship of physical factors to language learning in order to guide instruction. It is crucial, therefore, that they recognize when physical factors may inhibit language learning. We are not trying to suggest that classroom teachers and clinicians become amateur optometrists, audiologists, or neurologists—that is, practice medicine without a license. Yet, armed with some basic information from the research literature and familiar with suggestions for adjusting instruction, both classroom teachers and clinicians can assist students with physical problems to become more successful language learners.

In this chapter we will consider these factors as they relate to learning: visual acuity; auditory acuity; visual and auditory perception; allergies; drugs, and alcohol; and neurological symptoms. For each of these factors, we will discuss how it influences language learning, explore background information related to it, examine ways to assess each factor and adjust instruction and, finally, consider the option of referral to specialists.

Before beginning we need to make some general comments about the role of physical factors as causes of reading and other language-learning problems. With the mounds of conflicting data in this area, we believe it is too simplistic to attribute the cause of something as complex as a reading problem to a single factor. This naive line of reasoning belies and contradicts the underlying nature of the reading process as we have come to understand it in the past twenty-five years. People are highly individualized in their responses to variations in each of the factors we discuss in this chapter. The complex nature of the reading process dictates that diagnosis be as broad in practice as the reading act itself and not focus on a single factor. With these cautionary comments, we proceed to our discussion.

VISUAL FACTORS

Seeing clearly is crucial to learning in school. The number and variety of visual tasks presented to students each day is staggering. When a student's eyes function well, visual demands are handled with ease. Students are asked to read books, magazines, computer screens, chalkboards, and wall charts. Eyes help students copy from chalkboards and charts (and even from other students' papers at times). They are essential in writing journals, taking notes, viewing films and filmstrips, and many other school tasks.

The relationship of vision to learning to read is one of the most researched and discussed topics in the literature. It is beyond the purpose of this text to review all of the often conflicting literature in detail. Spache listed some reasons for contradictions in research studies: (1) tests used to measure the same visual function may yield different results across tests; (2) current school vision tests are unreliable because of their brevity; (3) the developmental nature of vision is ignored; (4) the ability of individuals to adapt and live with visual problems is not considered; and (5) some researchers treat each visual function (fusion, acuity, clarity) separately and ignore combined effects of vision problems (1976b, pp. 46–47).

From our reading of this literature, we have selected some conclusions which are supported by research relating visual problems to reading ability:

1. Visual problems may interfere with learning to read. The more severe the visual problem, the greater the interference.
2. Visual problems are not usually a major, single cause of reading difficulty. When problems are corrected, students usually begin to progress in learning to read and write.
3. Students with visual problems tend to have slightly more reading problems as a group than students without visual problems. However, some students appear to overcome visual problems with extra effort in school. Other students, often with similar problems, are unable to compensate for their visual problems. Thus, generalizing about the effects of a type of visual problem (for example, nearsightedness) is difficult because students cope differently with similar problems.
4. Farsightedness (difficulty seeing clearly at near point), fusion (blending individual images from each eye), and oculomotor coordination (moving the eyes together) are problems associated with reading difficulties.
5. Students with vision problems may not realize they see print "incorrectly"—or not as others do—since their problems may have been present from birth.
6. Reading only *begins* with the eye. Reading, as Kolers (1969) pointed out some years ago, is "only incidentally visual." It is a meaning-seeking, cognitive process, dependent far more on the reader's background of experiences, language functioning, attention and motivation, and social context than on vision. These nonvisual factors play critical roles in reading. As Frank Smith wrote:

   Insufficiency of nonvisual information can make reading impossible, because there is a limit to how much visual information the brain can handle at any one time. There is a bottleneck in the visual system between the eye and brain.... It is possible to look but not be able to see, no matter how good the physical conditions. (1982, p. 11)

7. Classroom teachers are in the best position to recognize vision problems which inhibit language learning in school.
8. Nearsightedness, although usually not listed as a major cause of reading problems, does contribute to difficulty in reading when instruction in school requires students to attend closely and copy information printed on chalkboards or wall charts. Some children who are nearsighted may also have astigmatism, which causes minor physical discomfort. Headaches may result affecting student's attention to instruction.

Vocabulary Related to Vision

VISUAL PROBLEM	SYMPTOMS
Farsightedness or *hyperopia*	Difficulty seeing at near point (distance at which print is normally held). Farsighted students have difficulty focusing on near objects for periods of time. This sustained attention may result in eye strain.
Nearsightedness or *myopia*	Difficulty seeing at far point (distances at a few feet or more). Nearsighted students have difficulty focusing on distant objects for extended periods of time. When associated with another eye problem such as astigmatism, nearsightedness can cause discomfort including headaches.
Astigmatism	Blurring of vision at near or far point; lack of clear vision. When astigmatism is combined with farsightedness, it is especially related to reading problems; it is only slightly related when combined with nearsightedness.

Reading and writing require eyes that work together (*binocular coordination*). Eyes must move together across a line of print, left to right, and up and down pages of print. If they do no work together efficiently or if they do no focus together in a single image (*fusion*), vision will obviously be affected. Some problems of binocular coordination and fusion are constant and occur all the time as students read or write. Other times, these problems seem to come and go. As students' eyes tire from reading and writing tasks, they may begin to have difficulty in keeping the print in focus. We will not discuss the many technical terms associated with binocular coordination and fusion because they are less frequent causes of visual problems than farsightedness or nearsightedness. This does not mean we do no take these problems seriously, but rather their accurate diagnosis in school settings is difficult to accomplish and should be reserved for specialists. The classroom teacher and clinician can best serve to assist in identifying students with potential binocular or fusion problems and referring them as quickly as possible. Our emphasis in this chapter is on recognizing that these problems may exist and when their existence is confirmed, adjusting classroom instruction accordingly.

Identifying and Assessing Vision in the Classroom

In this section we will briefly mention students who have been *identified previously* as having visual problems. Then we will consider ways to identify those students with *no prior history* of visual problems.

At the beginning of the school year, teachers should review the cumulative record files of students to note histories of vision problems. This task minimizes repetitive referrals, resulting in quicker modifications of instruction.

Identifying students with no prior history of vision problems begins with daily observations of students' responses to reading and writing instruction. It is in these informal settings that teachers may discover the first signs of a potential visual problem affecting language learning. What do you look for? And when you find it, what does it mean? What do you do next? These questions and others guide your continuous observations of students. Structured observations, using vision checklists, can bring a systematic approach to identifying visual problems.

A review of such published checklists led us to conclude that there are some significant problems that must be overcome if these checklists are to be valid and useful to teachers. First, they often contain too many items. The lists we examined varied from nine to over fifty items in length. Second, some of the symptoms described on the lists were easily observed (squinting) while others appeared vague (fatigue in one eye). Third, some items seemed to rely on students reporting their symptoms to the teacher (headaches or blurry vision). Fourth, a few checklists attempted to relate certain symptoms to specific visual difficulties, which is far beyond the ability and training of most teachers we know. Fifth, many of the symptoms listed as visual difficulties disappear spontaneously when students are given less frustrating materials (Gillet & Temple, 1982). *Thus, poor vision may be erroneously blamed for a reading problem.* Finally, regardless of how valid and reliable a checklist, none of them specify the number of symptoms that indicate the need for referral to a specialist, an adjustment in classroom instruction, or both.

Given all the problems associated with vision checklists, we still believe they can be valuable guides to identifying students with vision problems affecting language learning. The checklist we present in Figure 8–1 draws upon the work of many writers on this topic. We acknowledge their work and hope they view ours as a continuing refinement to help teachers become more reliable observers of students' visual performances. To use our checklist effectively, students should be observed under the following conditions:

1. Continuously, over time, at least for several weeks
2. During direct instruction in reading and writing
3. During independent practice in reading and writing
4. In small-group, large-group, and individual settings
5. In a variety of environments such as during recess, in gym class, and the lunchroom.

250 Physical Factors Affecting Language Learning

Figure 8–1 Vision Checklist (Classroom)

Student _____   Date(s) Observed _____

Settings Observed _____

Frequent, unusual, or daily appearance of:
- ___ Redness around eyes, eyelids
- ___ Rapid, uncontrolled blinking
- ___ Squinting
- ___ Crusts around eyelids
- ___ Turning of one or both eyes in or out
- ___ Tearing
- ___ Bloodshot eye or eyes
- ___ Frequent sties

Behaviors which occur consistently and are inappropriate for age and/or grade level while reading and writing:
- ___ Holds print too close
- ___ Holds print too far
- ___ Loses place
- ___ Needs marker, finger to keep place
- ___ Writing is laborious
- ___ Error rate increases with time on tasks
  - ___ reading   ___ writing
- ___ Holds book/paper at odd angle

Makes errors while copying from:
- ___ Chalkboard
- ___ Wall chart
- ___ Book, reference
- ___ Workbook page

While oral reading:
- ___ Rereads, skips lines
- ___ Confuses left-right
- ___ Misreads known or familiar words

Student reports:
- ___ Headaches
- ___ Burning or itchy eyes
- ___ Print blurry
- ___ Double vision, letters or words float
- ___ Nausea while doing close work
- ___ "Can't see"
- ___ "Can't do this right"

Record results of informal tests below with plus sign:
INFORMAL TEST 1   Tracking seems Smooth (S), Difficult (D) for student.
  ___ Circular motion   ___ Vertical   ___ Horizontal
INFORMAL TEST 2   Convergence seems Smooth (S), Difficult (D) for student.
  ___ double image appears at 3–5 inches on inward motion toward eyes
  ___ single image reappears at 5–6 inches on outward motion from eyes

---

Not included on the checklist above are some general classroom behaviors which may be associated with potential vision problems. Since most of these behaviors can be associated with other factors related to unsuccessful school achievement, we simply list them here for your reference. If a potential vision problem is identified in a student, these behaviors will further add to the reliability of the checklist. These general behaviors are:

    Consistent posture deviations
    Inattentive to board or chart work
    Disinterest or resistance to close work
    Easily fatigued
    Daydreaming
    Misaligning numbers in math problems
    General difficulty with small-motor, eye-hand coordination tasks

As the teacher observes—and before any conclusions are reached—a number of additional steps should occur. Parents should be contacted and asked to complete a brief checklist developed for home use. This checklist is presented in Figure 8-2.

The most important finding from observation is a student's success in learning to read and write. Symptoms should help to explain failures rather than be used solely for identifying visual problems. Also, counting the number of symptoms and concluding that the more symptoms present the greater the likelihood a visual problem exists is *one* way to increase reliability. However, given the extraordinary power of students to compensate for visual difficulties, one symptom may be just as powerful a clue that a visual problem exists for some students as five or ten symptoms for other children.

Finally, looking for a common pattern across children with visual problems is not necessarily reliable. While a vision specialist may be able to identify and predict vision problems based on hundreds of clients, classroom teachers and diagnosticians generally do not have sufficient experience. So we suggest doing a number of observations, say three to five, to be spaced over two or three weeks and to occur in a variety of settings, as we mentioned earlier. Confirmation of similar behaviors from parents or other adults at home will also increase the reliability of classroom observations.

Now that teacher observations have been collected over time, parents have been involved, and a few behaviors which are indicators of a potential vision problem have been identified, what next? Classroom teachers have only a few more steps to follow before referring the student for vision testing by specialists. First, and especially with children in K–3, several informal classroom tests can be administered. Then, all of the data collected so far can be discussed with the school nurse and/or school reading specialist to determine the next step.

The informal tests explained below do not take the place of testing by a vision specialist; rather, they provide additional information to determine if a referral is necessary and to assist the specialist in completing their diagnosis more efficiently.

Figure 8–2 Vision Checklist (Parent)

Student _____ Date(s) Observed _____

Do you notice any of the following symptoms when looking at the student's eyes?
____ Redness around eyes, eyelids   ____ Tearing
____ Rapid, uncontrolled blinking   ____ Squinting
____ Blood-shot eyes   ____ Frequent sties
____ Crusts around eyelids
____ Turning of one or both eyes in or out

When you observe the student reading, writing, or doing other close work do you notice any of these behaviors?
____ Holds print too close
____ Holds print too far
____ Holds book/page at odd angle
____ Needs marker or finger to keep place
____ Sits too close to TV
____ Writes slowly and with difficulty
____ Loses place easily
____ Confuses directions on games, puzzles
____ Struggles with fine-motor tasks
____ Misaligns numbers in math problems
____ Makes errors while copying from books, other references, or workbook pages

Does the student ever report any of the following symptoms?
____ Headaches or eyes hurt   ____ "Can't see"
____ Burning or itchy eyes   ____ "Can't do this right"
____ Print is blurry   ____ Double vision
____ Letters or words float   ____ Nausea while doing close work

Comments/Other Observations:
_____
_____
_____

Informal test 1. Use the point of a pen or small, shiny object held about twenty inches away from the student's eyes. Rotate the pen or object in a large circle (360 degrees). Observe first one eye and then the other eye. Next, slowly move the pen or object vertically above and below the student's eyes and horizontally to the left and right of the student's eyes. Watch carefully for difficulty in following the pen or other object and for smooth movements of the eyes. If the student has any difficulty, repeat the test, and be certain the directions were understood by the student sufficiently. Ask the student to retell the directions to you.

Informal test 2. Hold the pen point or shiny object in a horizontal line and about twenty inches from the bridge of the student's nose. Ask the student to tell you how many points or objects he or she sees at that distance. Tell the student to follow the pen or object—as you *slowly* move it toward the nose-bridge—and to tell you when two objects are seen. This should occur at about three to five inches from the bridge of the nose. *Slowly* withdraw the pen or object and ask the student to tell you when one object is seen again (about five to six inches). Watch the student's eyes carefully for smooth, regular converging movements until the single image is lost. As with Test 1, if the student has difficulty, repeat the test and make certain directions were understood.

These tests assess *tracking and convergence ability* at distances necessary for reading and writing. Some vision experts (Spache, 1976b) suggest automatically repeating each informal test several times, since it is often difficult for teachers to judge student performance. Repeating the tests at intervals during the day or on the next day increases the reliability of results. With very young children it is very important to be certain they understand the directions. This can be confirmed by asking each child to repeat them before being tested.

Finally, teachers must practice on willing adults and children who have no vision problems to be comfortable with these procedures. Keep in mind that we suggest using these informal tests as supplements to teacher observation, parent observation, examination of medical records, and interviews with parents or other adults in the home. Together, all of these will help form the picture of a potential vision problem in a student worth pursuing through referral to specialists.

So, where are we with classroom identification of potential vision problems? Before any referral is made, the teacher should discuss the results of observations, informal tests, parental interviews, and review of medical history from school records with the school nurse, the reading specialist, or both. School policies should be checked to be certain proper referral procedures are being followed. If there are indicators that a vision problem is the cause of a student's lack of achievement, a referral is in order. In some schools this referral is to a reading specialist or school nurse for further testing. In other schools, it may mean a parent conference and the recommendation that the student's eyes be examined by a professional, either privately or through some other agency.

Informal test 3. One more type of testing is often done before final referral to a vision specialist (optometrist or opthalmologist) is recommended. Testing involves using an instrument which tests a wide range of visual functions. Most commonly used are the Keystone Visual Survey Tests with the Keystone

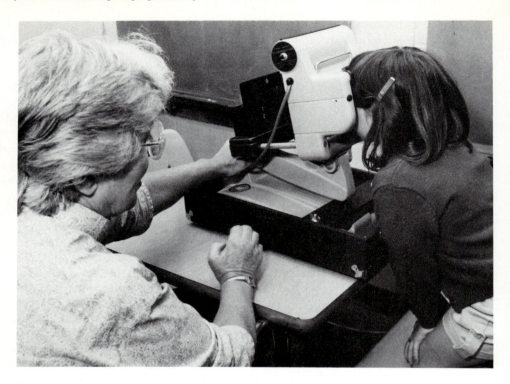

This telebinocular vision-screening device tests a wide range of visual functions.

telebinocular machine. These tests screen for nearsightedness, farsightedness, fusion problems, depth perception, and color blindness. Recently, modifications of the original Keystone procedures have helped overcome some of the criticism of the tests. Frankly, the testing of vision by reading clinicians bothers us a bit. We realize that referring students to a specialist based only on the classroom teacher's observations may result in parents spending money to discover no problem exists. However, using the teacher and parent vision checklists we presented earlier, involving the school nurse, and conducting a conference—including all concerned with the student's vision—does provide, in our opinion, a reliable means of referring students for examination by a vision specialist.

    At this point we recommend two procedures for clinical use with the caveat that clinicians must be properly trained to perform them. Results obtained from these procedures should be considered preliminary to later referral to a vision specialist. The two procedures we suggest clinicians consider are the Walton Modified Telebinocular Technique (MIT) (Schubert & Walton, 1980) and the New York State Optometric Association (NYSOA) Screening Battery (Cohen, Lieberman, Stolzberg, & Ritty, 1983).

The Walton MIT procedure uses the telebinocular and additional lenses to screen for amblyopia (dimness of vision), nearsightedness, astigmatism, farsightedness, and eye muscle imbalances. The procedure must be administered by a trained clinician. The NYSOA was developed for the New York Optometric Association to screen for visual skills necessary for academic tasks and success in classroom learning settings. The tests can be administered without a vision specialist.

Adjusting for Students with Visual Problems

Some suggestions we make concerning adjusting classroom conditions to accommodate students with visual problems apply to all students. These help create a healthy vision climate in classrooms. We will list these suggestions first and then move to adjustments for specific vision problems. We acknowledge as we go along the work of G. Spache (1976), one of the few reading experts to pay close attention to the general vision conditions in classrooms. For younger children in primary grades—who are usually farsighted and see more clearly at a distance—Spache suggests great use of chalkboards, wall charts, books with large-sized type, and sight-saver typewriters with type larger in size than pica or elite characters. Also, beginning writers should have writing paper of good quality, wide lines, and a choice of writing tools to fit a variety of writing tasks. General classroom conditions for a healthy vision climate at all grades should include:

> Textbooks and writing paper of good quality and with appropriate type size and line spacing
> Nonreflecting, light-colored walls and work surfaces which minimize glare
> Work surfaces for students that are not flat (twenty degrees or so off horizontal) so students do not tilt heads down at an angle
> Working areas placed away from major light sources (especially windows to avoid glare)
> Adjustable desks and chairs for ease in writing, reading, and other close work
> Adequate and even lighting throughout the room. (Adapted from Spache, 1976b)

Adjustments in the classroom to accommodate students with the most common types of vision problems are listed in the following. We begin by considering improving the instructional environment for students with visual problems that are very severe—the visually impaired or handicapped.

Visually impaired or handicapped students' needs can be met by:

> Reducing visual learning tasks in the classroom such as copying from the chalkboard or wall charts
> Selecting a peer buddy with better vision to work with the visually impaired student

Supplementing reading instruction with direct instruction in listening comprehension

Including direct instruction in study skills so students can learn from content-area textbooks and other reference materials.

Using a poor-vision aid, such as the Visolett (Lackey, Efron, & Rowls, 1982), a page-size lens which produces a 1.7 magnification of print with edge-to-edge clarity. Poor-vision aids offer some obvious advantages over large-print materials: lower cost; increase in kinds of print available to partially sighted students; and, more natural reading setting for students who do not like to use large-print materials. In addition the Visolett is small enough to be carried in pocket or purse. Lackey, Efron, and Rowls concluded after a research study with elementary and junior high school students that Visolett was "as effective or more effective than large print materials in fostering an increase in the amount of reading" (p. 92).

Nearsightedness in students can be accommodated by:

Moving them to the front of the class when seating arrangements are fixed
Allowing them to move about more freely in a room with movable seats
Reminding students to use corrective lenses if they have been prescribed.

Farsightedness in students can be accommodated by:

Allowing them to move about more freely in the classroom when they need to read wall charts or other posted materials
Monitoring chalkboard or wall-chart copying tasks to see if they are causing discomfort
Reminding students to use corrective lenses if they have been prescribed.

Astigmatism in students can be accommodated by:

Allowing them to move about more freely in the classroom or moving to a front desk if seating is fixed
Monitoring and reducing close reading or writing tasks if discomfort occurs
Reminding students to use corrective lenses if they have been prescribed.

The suggestions given in the following for students with eye-tracking (oculomotor) problems, eye-focusing (accommodative) problems, and eye-teaming (binocular) problems are taken directly from Rouse and Ryan (1984).

Eye-tracking problems of students can be accommodated by:

Allowing student to use a finger or marker when reading
Minimizing chalkboard-to-desk copying
Indicating the target the student should attend to by pointing to it

Eye-focusing problems can be accommodated by:

Minimizing chalkboard-to-desk copying
Shortening visual work periods
Allowing breaks during longer reading sessions

Eye-teaming problems can be accommodated by:

Allowing them to use finger or marker while reading
Minimizing chalkboard-to-desk copying
Shortening visual work periods especially on near tasks

AUDITORY FACTORS: HEARING OR ACUITY

Auditory factors, especially acuity (hearing ability), have been related to language learning for many years. Developing an oral language system in the preschool years depends on children's ability to hear. And the oral language concepts and vocabulary children acquire before formal schooling are critical factors in successfully learning to read and write in school.

While most of the reading we adult readers do is silent and would appear to depend very little on our hearing ability, it is not so for learning to read and to write. Instruction in both reading and writing relies heavily on oral activities, oral directions, and phonics lessons. As Gillet and Temple note:

> Across the entire spectrum of approaches, some features of every beginning reading program are standard: learning of letter names and sounds, use of simple phonic analysis strategies to decode words, and frequent oral reading. These activities put a premium on clarity of hearing, and the youngster with auditory problems is at a distinct disadvantage. (1982, p. 309–310)

There are two major categories of auditory problems: (1) deafness from birth and (2) deafness which develops because of illness or accident. As we searched through the literature concerning auditory problems and reading, we found that these two categories share many of the same effects on learning to read. However, deafness from birth (prelingual hearing impairment) results in the greatest disadvantage since the development of oral language is so dependent on normal hearing. Those who become deaf or hearing-impaired after years of normal hearing have many advantages over those children deaf from birth. There is no opportunity to develop an oral language system without the ability to hear. As we present some conclusions from the literature, we will try to differentiate between these two kinds of hearing impairments.

1. Auditory problems, especially loss of hearing, interfere with learning to read. The more severe the hearing impairment, the greater the interference.
2. Just as with vision, hearing is only part of learning to read. Reading is a meaning-seeking cognitive process, dependent more on the reader's back-

ground of experiences, language functioning, attention and motivation, and on the nature of instruction than on hearing. Instruction for hearing-impaired students must look beyond the impairment and toward building cognitive and language skills (King & Quigley, 1985).
3. Full linguistic competence in reading is seldom attained by most deaf students (Andrew, 1984; King & Quigley, 1985).
4. Deaf or severely hearing-impaired students do not always have cognitive or perceptual problems as well.
5. Among the auditory-acuity problems related to learning to read and write are those involving *pitch* (tone, high to low) and *volume* (loudness) or both.
6. Some children do overcome a hearing impairment while others may not. The level of impairment, type, duration, time elapsed from detection to treatment, parental cooperation, and the desire of the child to read are among the factors working together which determine how children compensate for hearing losses (Bond, Tinker, Wassen, & Wassen, 1984).
7. When a hearing impairment can be minimized or corrected, students will begin to make progress in oral language development and in learning to read.
8. As with vision, teachers are the first line of defense for identifying children with hearing impairments.

Vocabulary Related to Auditory Acuity[1]

Hearing losses in decibels are often categorized as: mild—up to 40 db; moderate—up to 55 db; moderately severe—up to 70 db; and, profound—above 90 db.)

Deafness: Degree of hearing loss that causes communication problems even with amplification
Decibel (db): Standard unit for measuring sound loudness or intensity (standard classroom conversations are about 60 db).
Pitch: Tone of a sound from high to low; measured in frequency or Hertz (Hz)

Identifying and Assessing Auditory Acuity

In this section we will discuss (1) students who have been identified previously as having a hearing loss, and (2) those without prior histories of hearing problems.

As with vision problems, teachers should review the cumulative record files of students to identify those with histories of auditory problems. When no prior history exists, identifying students with auditory problems begins with daily observations of students' responses to reading and writing instruc-

[1]The following reference was consulted in developing these definitions: T. L. Harris and R. E. Hodge (Eds.), *A Dictionary of Reading and Related Terms* (International Reading Association; 1981).

tion. It is in these informal settings—the same settings in which visual behaviors can be observed—that teachers may discover the first signs of a potential auditory problem affecting language learning. What do you look for? And, when you find it, what does it mean? What do you do next? To guide your observations, we present a classroom checklist of auditory symptoms in Figure 8–3.

Figure 8–3 Hearing Checklist (Classroom)

Student _____   Date(s) Observed _____

Settings Observed _____

Frequent, unusual, or daily appearance of:
____ Discharge from ear(s)   ____ Redness around ears(s)

Behaviors which occur consistently and are inappropriate for age and/or grade level while reading and writing:
____ Requests to have directions repeated
____ Misunderstands oral directions
____ Seems confused during conversations
____ Turns or places one side of body or head near speaker
____ Cups ear(s) to hear
____ Adjusts volume on listening-center activities too high

Speech is:
____ Unusually loud
____ Distorted or indistinct
____ Monotone
____ Combination of above

Student reports:
____ Earaches
____ Dizziness
____ Ringing in ears
____ "Can't hear"
____ Difficulty with listening to tapes or records

Comments/Observations: _____
_____
_____
_____

Not listed among the symptoms on our checklist are some general classroom behaviors which may be associated with auditory problems. These general behaviors can be indicators of other factors related to unsuccessful school achievement, and we simply list them here for your reference. If a potential auditory problem is identified in a student, these behaviors may add to the reliability of the checklist:

> Frequent colds, sore throats, allergylike symptoms
> Inattentiveness and/or daydreaming
> Avoidance or diversion behaviors during listening tasks

As with vision problems, parents should be asked to use a brief checklist at home to focus their attention on the student's hearing ability. A checklist for home use is presented in Figure 8–4.

When interpreting any checklist, it is important to remember the suggestions we made for the vision checklist, earlier in this chapter.

Now, what do you do next? At this point, all of the data collected so far can be discussed with the school nurse and/or school reading specialist. When a hearing loss is suspected, further screening using an audiometer is often done in the school or clinic setting before final referral to an auditory specialist (audiologist). Special training is required to use an audiometer properly. Spache, while recommending its use in school settings, offered these cautions:

> At the hands of the teacher this screening procedure is, of course, not perfectly reliable, for testing conditions are seldom well controlled. Moreover, temporary conditions such as any type of upper respiratory infection may well detract from the accuracy of the instrument. Group testing is even more fallible, as the present author once discovered in testing a small school population. Because of the incidence of winter colds and the intrusion of extraneous noises in the environment, follow-up testing some months later indicated, to his embarrassment, that most of the original diagnoses of hearing losses were false. In our experience, teachers have learned to give the testing efficiently and properly, but they need to be reminded that the screening is a dichotomous way of identifying those who may not have a significant loss in auditory acuity, not a diagnosis as a basis for classroom treatment of the hearing difficulty. (1976a, pp. 47–48)

Adusting for Auditory Acuity Problems

Our suggestions for accommodating in the classroom the needs of students identified as having auditory acuity or hearing loss problems are taken from a diverse body of literature. We offer some general suggestions specifically for

Figure 8–4 Hearing Checklist (Parent)

Student _____ Date(s) Observed _____

Do you notice any of the following symptoms when watching the student in listening situations?
____ Discharge from ear(s)
____ Redness around ear(s)
____ Asks to have directions repeated
____ Misunderstands oral directions
____ Seems confused during conversations
____ Turns or places one side of body or head near you while you talk
____ Cups ear(s) to hear

When you listen to the student talk, do you notice any of the following speech behaviors?
____ Unusual loudness
____ Distorted or unclear speech
____ Monotone
____ Combination of above

Does the student ever report any of the following symptoms?
____ Earaches
____ Dizziness
____ Ringing in the ears
____ "Can't hear"
____ Television, radio, stereo not loud enough

Comments/Observations: _____
_____
_____
_____

---

use with students who are completely or profoundly deaf. We do not pretend to be experts in deaf education; our interpretations of the literature in that field were influenced by the work of Ewold (1981) and Andrews (1984). These writers stress the importance of manual communication, either a sign system or fingerspelling, during the preschool years. We believe that preschool deaf children must be involved in a program emphasizing a total communication approach. A total communication approach enables deaf children to acquire language skills using a manual system in addition to oral English (lip reading).

Carlsen (1985) offered suggestions for accommodating the needs of deaf students:

> Use a sight-word method which stresses whole words for beginning reading instruction. Deaf students do not have the auditory feedback hearing students do in order to benefit from phonic methods often used in beginning reading programs.
> Explore special materials available for use with deaf students. Write to: Dormac, Inc., P.O. Box 752, Beaveton, OR 97075; Newby Visualanguage, Inc., Box 121A EN, Eagleville, PA 19408.
> Make things visual. Use chalkboards, overhead projectors, pictures, and charts.
> Write storybooks of stories students dictate. Have students illustrate them.

Accommodating Hearing-Impaired Students

Some of our suggestions below are applicable to deaf students as well since categories of hearing loss are not distinct, ranging from profoundly deaf to severely impaired to mildly impaired.

1. Move students to the front of the room if seating is more traditional; allow them to move more freely in a room with movable seats.

2. Remind students to wear hearing aids or amplification devices if they have been prescribed. Be familiar with the particular device a student is using. Teachers should ask parents or an auditory specialist for information on the features of particular devices students are prescribed. There have been some recent advances in amplification procedures which are considerable improvements over standard hearing aids. One of the most promising for school or group listening settings is the Phonic Ear Personal FM hearing system which uses wireless radio transmission between the speaker and listener. The speaker's voice is transmitted to each listener's hearing aid clearly with no interference through a device attached to the ear and linked to small transmitters carried on the speaker and listener. More information can be obtained by contacting: Phonic Ear, Inc., 250 Camino Real, Mill Valley, CA 94941.

3. Select a peer buddy with better hearing to work with the hearing impaired student.

4. Encourage the student to watch your face carefully when you are speaking.

5. Adjust phonics instruction to accommodate student's ability to hear high and low tones. Spache (1976a) offers these comments about phonics instruction:

> Hearing losses in the upper pitch range, the high tones, affect the ability of students to deal with some consonant sounds and blends (for example, *s, l, t*).

Hearing losses in the lower range, the low tones, do not affect acquiring phonic skills as much as losses in high tones. Vowel sounds and some consonants (*m, g, b, h*) occur in the lower pitch range. While inaccuracies in the pronunciation of these sounds may occur, usually the message can be understood.

Enunciation and articulation are often affected in students with severe hearing impairments. Speech therapy should be explored for these students.

Misarticulation or mispronunciation of a sound/symbol correspondence does not really matter *if* the association is constant each time the symbol is presented, especially in students with severe speech impairment accompanying a hearing loss. Consistency of sound–symbol association is more important than exact pronunciation as the student tries to use phonic clues to trigger meaning.

6. Consider using some alternative or supplementary instruction to phonics, especially in students with severe hearing losses. Modified cloze procedures and extra emphasis on context strategies are potentially useful methods (Readence, Bean, & Baldwin, 1985; Searfoss & Readence, 1985).

7. Be aware of the advantages and disadvantages of using a strictly basal-reader approach, especially with severely hearing-impaired students. Hasenstab and McKenzie (1981) found basal readers in wide use in reading instruction for hearing-impaired students. Strengths and weaknesses of leading basal series are listed below:

STRENGTHS	WEAKNESSES
High-interest stories	Uncontrolled vocabulary (too many new words for a story; rapid "jump" in difficulty between levels)
Helpful supplementary materials	Inappropriate language level
Attractive format	Phonetic emphasis
Low or controlled vocabulary	Low interest at higher levels
Sequential skill development	Acceleration rate too rapid
Appropriate language level	Insufficient repetition of words and/or skills

8. Use the language-experience method to teach reading. Teachers might wish to review the basic assumptions underlying this method before using it with hearing-impaired students. Both Hall (1981) and Searfoss and Readence (1985) present concise summaries of how to use the language-experience method.

9. Include intensive instruction in vocabulary, developing not only specific word meanings but strategies for learning to cope with unfamiliar words and word learning. Special attention should be given to words with multiple meanings and figurative language. (See Johnson & Pearson, 1984; Readence, Bean, & Baldwin, 1985; Searfoss & Readence, 1985)

ALLERGIES

It is hard to find someone today who isn't "allergic" to something! For many of us, "being allergic" may mean simple hay fever, rose fever, or a mild rash. Today, however, we are learning of chemical and food allergies, and even of "natural pollutants" causing "environmental illnesses." How seriously should we consider this explosion of interest in allergies? Remember the hypoglycemia craze of a few years ago? While some people did suffer from the illness, many of us developed the symptoms after reading an article in the popular press or a sensational newspaper we found at the supermarket checkout stand. Are allergies also a fad—rather than the real cause of a myriad of human ailments and even learning problems in our schools? It is clear to us that allergies do affect learning, and an awareness of the role of allergies in learning problems is important to understand.

First, all symptoms associated with allergies can also be symptoms associated with other physical factors. Fatique, hyperactivity, sneezing, redness around the eyes, ear discharges, and headaches are a few of these. Note, however, that several of these symptoms were associated in our earlier discussion with vision and hearing problems and will later be related to nutritional problems. This situation causes confusion and long delays in identifying allergies as the primary cause of a learning problem.

Second, recent discussions of the relationship of various kinds of allergies to learning problems go far beyond the traditional definition of allergies, even among some allergists, the experts in the field. The systemic effects—impairments to nerve, motor, and psychological functioning—are far more serious threats to language learning than symptoms which usually send people to an allergist (sneezing, sinus problems, wheezing, rashes).

Finally, allergic reactions to the same substance may vary greatly across individuals. Some people rarely sneeze or wheez as symptoms of allergic reactions to common irritants such as pollens. Instead such people may react by becoming extremely fatigued, moody, or lethargic.

These are a few of the issues which make relating allergies to learning problems, identifying students with allergies, and then developing instructional adjustments in the classroom very complex and often difficult.

Listed below are some conclusions and comments from the literature on the relationship of allergies and learning problems.

1. Most medical doctors find it difficult to understand the complexity of the relationship between allergies and learning problems. Educators lag even further behind, with the relationship barely at an awareness level and with few opportunities to learn about allergies and learning problems in teachers' preparations of course work.
2. Allergies are clever. They mask themselves as many symptoms in a variety of combinations—even for two individuals allergic to the same substance(s).

3. There is sufficient evidence to relate food allergies to learning performance. Crook (1980), Rapp (1985), Stronck (1980), and Vass and Rasmussen (1984) present convincing evidence of this relationship. Crook bluntly states that what a child eats can make him or her "dull, stupid, or hyperactive" (p. 281).
4. Vass and Rasmussen argue just as forcefully that educators charged with counseling and guiding students who have learning problems must look at whole human beings. They write:

> The challenge is to broaden our perspective and look at children as whole human beings without separating mind and body. If we do not try to meet this challenge we can hurt those children we are attempting to help. Counselors need to be aware that an assessment of a child's problem that does not include the possibility of allergy, when, in fact, allergy does exist, will create a situation in which no amount of counseling or other therapeutic measures will succeed and the child may be irreparably harmed. (1984, p. 247)

5. The range of allergies that can affect language learning is quite broad. Glines and McGovern (1983) called this situation "hidden allergies" and include adverse reactions to *chemical pollutants* (food additives and preservatives, paints, insecticide sprays, hair sprays, cleaning solutions, perfumes, and deodorants, to name a few) and *natural pollutants* (wood smoke, grasses, weeds, trees with strong scents, animal danders, to name a few).
6. Nutritionists consider some foods to be causes of behavior and learning problems. Often called "junk foods," these include candy and soft drinks, which contain excessive sugar and artificial colorings or preservatives that seem to affect behavior. However, for some allergic students, replacing these foods with those of greater nutritive value—such as milk, cheese, nuts, or even certain fruits—may not be desirable. Some students are very allergic to these foods and have severe reactions to them. We are not arguing that "junk foods" are nutritive and healthful; rather, that when allergies are being considered as a possible cause of a student's language-learning problems, the complexities of allergies prevent hard-and-fast rules about what is "good" or "not good" for students to eat.
7. *Clinical ecology* has emerged as a field of study. A clinical ecologist is concerned with allergic reactions in humans after they have been exposed to foods, chemicals, and common irritants. Educators should pay special attention to the work of clinical ecologists in the professional literature as they attempt to clarify the role of allergies in language-learning problems in the future.

Vocabulary Related to Allergies

Allergy: Extreme sensitivity to a specific substance such as pollens, dust, foods, chemicals.

Allegen: Medical term for a substance which causes an allergic reaction.

Allergic reaction: Physical, mental, or emotional symptoms as a result of being exposed to a substance. These range from mild (sneezes) to severe (difficulty breathing).

Systemic allergic reaction: Allergic reaction which affects the entire body—tissues, nerves, muscles.

Allergy tests: Extensive laboratory testing performed by a medical doctor to identify substances which may be causing allergic reactions or symptoms.

Desensitization treatment: Known also as "allergy shots," this long-term treatment for certain kinds of allergies consists of the patient being injected on a regular basis with small doses of specially prepared extract. The goal is to help the patient build some resistance to the allergic substance(s) so symptoms are lessened when the patient is exposed in the outside world to these same substances. Must be preceded by allergy tests and supervised by a medical doctor, generally an allergist.

Elimination data: Controlled diet in which substances, especially foods, suspected of causing allergic reactions are removed from the diet and then slowly reintroduced over time to assess sensitivity to each substance.

Identifying and Assessing Allergies in the Classroom

As they look for signs of other physical factors that might affect learning, teachers should review cumulative records at the beginning of the school year to identify students with a history of allergy problems. Observation of students' responses to reading and other language instruction may also reveal signs of allergy problems which affect language learning. To guide your observations when allergies are suspected, we next present two checklists, one for classroom use (Figure 8–5) and one for use by parents (Figure 8–6).

Figure 8–5 Allergy Checklist (Classroom)

Student _____   Date(s) Observed _____

Settings Observed _____

Frequent or chronic:
____ Colds
____ Sore throats
____ Wheezing
____ Earaches or infections
____ Coughing
____ Runny nose

Eyes are:
____ Puffy   ____ Watery   ____ Have dark circles
____ Rubbed frequently

Does the student frequently report any of the following?
- ___ Stuffy nose
- ___ Ears hurting
- ___ Muscle or joint aches and pains
- ___ Chronic fatigue
- ___ Headaches
- ___ Abdominal pains

Does the student exhibit any of the following during learning activities?
- ___ Short attention span
- ___ Wide swings of moods or emotions
- ___ Wide variations in activity level
- ___ Irritability
- ___ Overactiveness

Has the student been referred for any other physical problems such as poor vision or hearing? List below.

Comments/Observations: _____

_____

_____

_____

Figure 8–6 Allergy Checklist (Parent)

Student _____   Dates(s) Observed _____

Does the student have any allergies you know of? (For example: bee stings, foods, dust). List them below:

_____

_____

_____

Do you know anyone in your family who has allergies? If so, list the person, how they are related to the student and the allergy. For example: Lydia Jones, grandmother, bee stings.

_____

_____

_____

Does the student complain of any of the following? (Use a check mark beside those which apply.)
Frequent:
___ Colds   ___ Sore throats
___ Coughing   ___ Ear infections
___ Stuffy nose   ___ Headaches
___ Tiredness   ___ Muscle or joint aches and pains
___ Dark circles under eyes

Do you notice mood swings or frequent changes in physical activity from energetic to listless?

_____

_____

_____

Comments/Observations: _____

_____

_____

_____

As with identifying other physical factors, parents should be involved and asked to use a home allergy checklist. When interpreting both the classroom and parent checklists, the same suggestions we made for interpreting auditory and vision checklists apply (see the pertinent sections, this chapter).

Now, what do you do next? If an analysis of classroom and parent checklists and cumulative records reveals a behavior pattern that could be allergy related, the classroom teacher should consult with the school nurse or other school medical consultants and with parents about possible referral to an allergist. This step should not be taken until other physical factors with similar symptoms have also been assessed and eliminated as the causes of language-learning difficulties.

Adjusting for Students with Allergy Problems

Suggestions based on the work of Glines and McGovern (1983) and our own experience follow. If used, they should make the classroom and school healthier environments for all—for teachers and students, and especially for those with allergy problems.

1. Urge students and staff to be cautious about wearing heavily scented perfumes or colognes around allergic persons. Smoking should be avoided, for a number of reasons, but especially for the effect on allergy sufferers.

2. Modify the school's health, home-economics, and science facilities to reflect medical and safety regulations related to exposure to common chemicals both on the skin and by inhalation.

3. Ensure that school lunch programs offer options which allow students to avoid common food allergy reactions. Work with parents so that special meals can be prepared at school or brought to school and properly stored without students feeling that they are inconveniencing anyone.

4. Offer students more healthful choices in snacks and avoid processed foods. Support the elimination of snack foods—which are almost pure sugar—and provide a wide variety of nonprocessed foods.

5. Consider carefully the timing of school remodeling projects such as painting and installation of new carpeting. Debris from renovations are sources of irritants and can move through an entire building via the ventilation system, even when only one area is being remodeled.

6. Use toxic cleaning agents very carefully—the stronger the odor, the more potent the agent.

7. Keep a list posted of all students with severe allergic reactions to specific substances and what measures are to be taken in case of reactions.

8. Be alert to the possible affects of allergies on hearing, attention span, and general alertness of students. A student whose hearing is impaired or who feels tired and uncomfortable finds it difficult to concentrate on language instruction.

9. Special attention should be given to allergic students participating in phonics lessons which require a high level of auditory acuity and perception. Some students in the early primary grades miss much phonics instruction because of allergy-related difficulties. Be considerate of first- or second-graders who have severe ear problems requiring surgery (usually to insert drainage tubes in their ears) due to allergies. Instruction in phonics can be very difficult for these students. The Suggested Readings section at the end of this chapter contains sources of information offering additional recommendations for working with allergic students in school settings.

NUTRITION

We often hear the truism, "You are what you eat." Those who eat lots of candy, often feel sluggish, almost as heavy as a pound of chocolates. The more we eat the candy, the heavier we become. Our minds feel as heavily weighted with excess "fat" as our bodies. If, on the other hand, we eat fresh vegetables and salads, we can feel the "crispness" of these earth grown nutritious foods, and gain energy from their nutrients as well as their good taste. "Good food for thought" means good food for physical as well as mental growth. The research literature indicates a critical role for proper nutrition in both physical and mental development particularly for reading and writing activities. The earlier attention is given to good nutrition, the better for the child. Although researchers have been unable to identify the unique contributions of various nutrients to intelligence, learning, and behavior, adequate nutrition is clearly linked to language learning, reading, and writing development. How one feels, thinks, and perceives the world is influenced by dietary intakes (Martin & Martin, 1982).

Although classroom teachers have little control over the nutrition of children, there is much teachers can do to educate children in proper nutrition and also to become knowledgeable themselves about symptoms in children's behavior which indicate nutritional deficiencies. General conclusions from the research indicate:

1. Malnutrition is not limited to low-income families.
2. Biochemical conditions can be a cause of some abnormal physical, socioemotional, language, and learning states.
3. Improved behavior can be affected by reducing certain dietary substances such as sugar, food dyes, and junk foods, or by adding certain substances such as iron.

Malnutrition. Seven out of every ten children in the United States suffer from some effects of malnutrition (Clark, 1980). There is some evidence that both severe and moderate malnutrition are associated with poor development, intersensory organization, visual discrimination ability, and language development (Stevens & Baxter, 1981).

Two types of malnutrition have been identified. The first type results from starvation and calorie deficiency; it is called *maramus* (Norwood, 1984). Although maramus is a severe problem in developing countries, it is less common in the United States. Characteristics of the maramus child, according to Hamilton and Whitney (1982), follow:

1. Appears to be physically "skin and bones" only, much resembling a wizened little old person
2. Often sick because resistance to disease is low
3. Wasted muscles, including vital muscles such as heart muscles
4. Slow body metabolism resulting in low body temperature
5. Little fat to insulate against cold
6. Usually lacking in love and emotional security.

The tragedy of maramus is that it occurs most commonly in very young children when the child's brain is growing at a rapid pace, thus depriving the body of the energy required for adequate brain development. Some researchers feel the damage done is irreversible and permanently effects learning ability (Hamilton & Whitney, 1982).

A second type of malnutrition is a protein deficiency known as *hypoproteinosis*. This form of malnutrition, although less obvious, is more insidious since the individual's nervous system and brain are irreversibly impaired

(Clark, 1980). In protein deficiency, some body fat is retained but there exists a metabolic imbalance of protein. It occurs not only in lower-socioeconomic children but also in affluent families, due to poor food choices.

Children with protein deficiency are less able to learn, have lower intelligence quotients, and exhibit poorer language development (Pertz & Putnam, 1982). Conversely, too much protein results in an inadequate intake of other nutrients (Norwood, 1984) creating a nutritional imbalance.

Iron deficiency. Researchers also find a connection between an iron-deficient diet and learning. Iron is necessary so oxygen can be carried throughout the body, including the brain. Iron-deficient children may appear lazy, easily tired, and sometimes dizzy (Hamilton & Whitney, 1982). Iron deficiency was reported to be associated with significantly lower scores on intelligence and vocabulary tests and with slower reaction time (Stevens & Baxter, 1981). We caution that much more evidence is needed to determine the exact effects of iron deficiency on intelligence and learning.

Sugar excess. The amount of sugar in the American diet has been under attack for several years, to the point where the sugar industry is presently in a slump. Obesity and its resulting negative psychological effects is one likely consequence of excessive sugar intake. There may be others.

Hyperactivity in children has been linked to sugar as well as to refined foods, food additives, and artificial colorings (Norwood, 1984; Charleton-Seifert, Stratton, & Williams, 1980). One or two children in a classroom of twenty *may be* hyperactive. Symptoms of hyperactivity may include motor restlessness, short attention span, poor impulse control, learning difficulties, and emotional instability.

It seems sugar in the diet becomes a problem only if taken excessively or in place of other essential nutrients. Most nutritional experts agree that moderate amounts of sugar in a well-balanced diet are not harmful except for diabetics (Norwood, 1984; Pertz & Putnam, 1982).

It is difficult to separate the effects of improper nutrition from the effects of other environmental and genetic factors. However, evidence is accumulating that the nourishment of children plays an important role in mental development and learning capacities. Thus, teachers must be alert to the role nutritional deficiencies play in children's learning and development and alleviate problems wherever possible.

Identifying Nutritional Deficiencies in the Classroom

Again, the first step for teachers in identifying nutritional deficiencies is to review the cumulative record files of students to identify those with histories of such problems. Following this step are the daily observations of students' general appearances and their responses to school activities throughout the day. Writing observations on individuals' file cards over time is necessary for finding trends or changes. What do you look for? And, what do you do next? Unfortunately, unlike some other variables, *there is no single checklist which can be used, given the conflicting symptoms associated with various types of nutritional deficiencies.* For example, iron-deficient children are often lethargic and appear "lazy"; children who consume excess sugar can appear hyperactive. Rather than relying on a checklist, teachers should familiarize themselves with the various types of nutritional deficiencies and be aware that these deficiencies are not stereotypically related or confined to any particular socioeconomic or ethnic class (Glazer, 1983).

Becoming a Nutritional Activist

Because a proper diet is critical to learning, teachers should become activists in nutrition education. One need not be a physician to facilitate better nutrition among children, even though children with severe nutritional problems should be referred for medical help. Some suggestions for teachers to improve nutrition among children are:

1. Teachers should read about and become well informed on nutrition and the symptoms of malnutrition.
2. Teachers should be alert to food allergy reactions in children, and they should discuss symptoms (for example, rashes, wide swings in mood) with parents.
3. Nutrition education should be a comprehensive component of the school curriculum from kindergarten through high school. The objective of this program includes developing optimum lifelong nutritional habits. Social studies and science curricula might include lessons in consumer education, food habits, and cooking styles. State and county health departments often provide assistance in planning instruction.
4. Teachers should help maintain a nutritionally balanced menu in school. Allow students some choices, such as a salad bar.
5. Teachers should communicate regularly with parents, school nurses, dieticians, nutritionists, and pediatricians about nutrition problems and solutions.

ALCOHOL AND DRUG ABUSE

The use and abuse of alcohol and drugs by larger and larger numbers of teenagers and at earlier and earlier ages is a growing problem in our society. The National Institute on Drug Abuse reported that chemical abuse has become the leading problem of growing up today in our country. Alcoholism among youth has risen over 300 percent during the last decade (Svobodny, 1982); 35 percent of twelve to eighteen year olds are current users of marijuana (Sherman, Lojkutz, & Steckiewicz, 1984); some teenagers begin drinking as early as thirteen and begin smoking between ages nine and eleven (Bloom & Greenwald, 1984). Schools have been disappointingly ineffectual in the prevention of this growing problem. What do we know about causes of drug abuse? What can we do in the way of education and prevention?

Research points to the family as the primary influence on whether or not children use alcohol and drugs. Nine family factors related in the research literature to drug use are parental absence, autocratic or laissez-faire discipline, scapegoating, hypocritical morality, parent–child communication gap, parental divorce, mother–father conflicts, and the use of psychological crutches to cope with stress (Jurich, Polson, Jurich, & Bates, 1985). Drug users reported lack of support and communication from their parents, double messages, and inconsistency in discipline as related to drug use. Parents of drug users often seem to exhibit a lack of ability to cope with stress, and a propensity for using psychological crutches—such as drugs or denial—to win immediate gratification or comfort. The absence of the father from the home significantly affects the behavior of adolescents, resulting in greater use of alcohol, marijuana, and higher rates of sexual activity according to some researchers (Stern, Northman, & Van Slyck, 1984); this is especially so for male adolescents. The data from the last study points to the importance of the father as a key figure in value formation and as a role model for adolescents.

In addition, psychological factors have been reported as being correlated to chemical use. These include low self-concept, inadequacy in relating to others, inability to cope with problems, and a noncaring attitude about school (Svobodny, 1982). Students who abuse their bodies with drugs cannot think clearly and therefore, may find reading difficult.

Symptoms of chemical abuse. Behavior resulting from alcohol and drug abuse cannot be identified definitely since many possible sources for abnormal behaviors exist. However, some indications of alcohol and drug abuse could be:

1. Child showing evidence of erratic attention (that is, active participation followed by inattentiveness within a few minutes of time)
2. Drastic behavior changes (that is, hyperactivity, paranoia, excessive anger, or explosive temper)
3. Wearing sunglasses
4. Physical symptoms such as weight loss, bloodshot eyes, puffy look to the face, or fatigue.

Suggestions for schools. Schools cannot solve family problems, but schools must share a responsibility for drug education beginning at the elementary level. It seems obvious we need to start preventive programs at younger ages than adolescence. What can we do?

1. Help counteract the media's commercial exploitation of drugs by educating students about how they are being manipulated. Start an early (kindergarten)

and realistic education program on the effects of drugs. Contact local and state drug enforcement agencies for assistance. State departments of education frequently provide resources, too.
2. Maintain a continuing in-service education program for teachers about drug abuse, strategies for teaching prevention programs, and techniques for recognizing symptoms of alcohol and drug use in students. The best possible help for children who are chemical abusers are informed and caring teachers.
3. Help children relate to others in a positive, responsible manner. Develop new strategies for students who are in trouble.

PERCEPTUAL AND NEUROLOGICAL FACTORS

Perceptual and neurological influences on language and reading are classified with other physical factors because the types of tests used to measure them often rely on physical responses from students. As we mentioned in Chapter 2, we believe this classification is probably incorrect, but perceptual and neurological issues will be considered in this chapter on physical factors for convenience. We are not experts in perception or neurology and do not have the knowledge necessary to create a separate, in-depth discussion. In fact, we hope to confine our discussion to what we know, rather than venture into areas of psychological and neurological functioning beyond our expertise. Unfortunately, other educators in reading and special education do not always respect their limitations. The writers and researchers we have used as resources in preparing comments on perceptual and neurological factors were carefully chosen. We refer you to the Suggested Readings section of this chapter and urge you to explore these issues in greater depth on your own.

Perceptual Factors

Even though the research literature for nearly twenty years has provided little evidence that children who fail to learn to read and write do so because of visual or auditory perceptual deficits, the myth persists. Why, in the face of almost overwhelming evidence, do we still cling to these notions? For many reasons: We shall explore a few of them here and try to place the issue in proper perspective.

What Is Perception?

Perception is the way we organize our ideas about the world, predict what may happen, or anticipate what is coming next in life, in speech, or in print. As we stated in Chapter 2, our visual and auditory perceptions result more from our stored memories about the world than they do from the immediate or visual stimulations our senses encounter. We learn to predict, hypothesize, and take educated guesses about the present based on the past. Each of us has stored memories of how language works for us, how others use language, and what uses to make of language. Reading comprehension depends on sensing, finding, demanding, building, and creating meaning as a simultaneous learning–teaching process. We are the learner on one hand, yet, on the other hand, we teach ourselves as we make sense of print (reading). We use print (writing) to help others know how, and if, we have made sense as we attempt to communicate. This is perception! And, a major reason we can reject a narrow perceptual-deficit explanation (visual–auditory) for why some children have difficulty learning to read and write is precisely because it *is* too narrow to express and explain the complexity of human perception.

Another major weakness of the perceptual-deficit viewpoint is its built-in normative standards of what is acceptable and what is deviant visual or auditory performance. Deviations from norms result in labels, especially if that deviation is below the average performance. Naour has written about this assumption of normative perceptual performance based on the erroneous idea that all students receive identical information from the environment:

> Nothing could be farther from reality. Although we share similar features in receiving the stimuli, each individual is unique in interpreting information and in the manner in which such information is used to construct reality. Since individuals bring to the world different genetic variables, experience different environments, and have unique developmental histories, they construct reality in subtly different ways. The mechanisms of sensory perception vary dramatically among individuals due to differences in the functional organization of the brain during development. These differences are caused by the interaction of genetic, environmental, and developmental variables. . . . The final result of such differences in perception is performance variability. (1985, p. 101)

Variability, then, is normal in perceptual performance, not abnormal. Arbitrary limits of normal performance set by test assessing auditory and visual "perception" are just that, arbitrary. The resulting labels for performance often used to identify these limits are also arbitrary.

It is important to note that while students' perceptual performances vary, so does the instructional setting in which some students are supposed to acquire reading and writing. Some students whose families move several times during their elementary school years, or whose reading programs change from year to year within the same school, may adapt to this variability in instruction quite easily. Other students, however, may be unable to adjust to changes in home or school settings and reflect this inability on tests of perceptual performance. This variability in test scores has been a classic symptom of reading or learning disability.

Allington (1982), among others, has investigated reasons for the continued belief in the "perceptual deficit hypothesis." Although professionally embarrassing, his reasoning seems powerful. He believes that some researchers—through conviction rather than evidence—perpetuate the hypothesis and that practitioners continue to test and teach as if the hypothesis were valid because that is what they were taught to do. If current research in this area were included in programs designed to prepare teachers and diagnosticians, perhaps the hypothesis would be better understood.

Finally, the reason we believe that educators continue to cling to the auditory and visual perceptual-deficit hypothesis may be the tests themselves. The tests yield quantifiable data which lead to easily followed instructional interventions. The tests, however, do not really measure the complex perceptual processes necessary to read and write, and the instructional materials can do little to alter perceptual processes. Both the test scores and instructional materials provide masks for educators of the very real language-processing problems some children have as they read and write. (See Richardson, Di-Benedetto, Christ, & Press, 1980; Kavale, 1982; Kampwirth & Bates, 1980.)

The foregoing helps convince us that it is largely a waste of time to search for and administer tests which are "supposed" to assess visual and auditory perception and to relate test scores to problems in learning reading and writing. Our time can be better spent observing and interviewing students as they interact and use reading and writing as a means of communication—*then* we can influence the quality of that communication.

Neurological Factors

Relating language-learning problems to neurological deficits or organic brain defects has been a controversial issue for many years. We again refer to the work of George Spache. In his chapter on neurological defects and dyslexia, Spache comments with feeling when he states:

> If an author may be permitted a personal note, we must say that this is one chapter that we were loath to write. The looseness with which descriptive terms are applied to what we have called reading disability for some thirty years; the rapidity with which even newer terms are being coined; and the multiplicity of symptoms that are supposed to characterize this new disease "dyslexia" make an author feel that he does not want to touch the subject. (1976b, p. 178)

Spache's statement summarizes as well the dilemma of the present authors, even today. We shall attempt to clarify the issues, when possible, and indicate the contradictions and confusions caused when neurological factors become linked to language-learning problems.

Organizing the research and literature into three broad categories may remove some of the confusion. These categories include (1) gross and severe injury or damage to the central nervous system, (2) distinct clinical syndromes, and (3) nonspecific labels.

Gross and severe injury or damage to central nervous system. Serious damage to the central nervous system—especially those sections of the brain which control language learning—has been studied by neurologists. Reading and writing become difficult or impossible skills to acquire in the presence of organic malfunctions of the brain (Mosse, 1982). The damage may be the result of genetic factors, birth injury, or related to head injuries. Children with neurological involvement initially exhibit medical problems. Once symptoms of neurological damage are analyzed they may be referred for special instruction, sometimes in institutional settings.

Distinct clinical syndromes. These syndromes involve patterns of behavior, some of which are labeled neurological in nature. Descriptions of these syndromes usually include reference to possible damage to the central nervous system, including the brain. Obvious brain damage usually affects language tasks. While these clinical syndromes appear to be a medically based problem, the etiology is "most difficult to establish and must remain tentative in most cases" (Mosse, 1982, p. 42). Thus, the relationship between neurological factors and language-learning problems becomes clouded and confusing. When there are no medically verifiable gross or severe indicators of extensive brain damage, relating language-learning problems to a malfunctioning central nervous system becomes difficult. Much of the research in clinical syndromes occurs in medical settings or has a medical bias.

Nonspecific labels. A third category found in the literature relies heavily on the use of a variety of nonspecific labels. Much of this literature deals with reading problems and their probable neurologically based causes. Studies are usually conducted by psychologists, special educators, and reading educators. These studies have produced a long list of nonspecific labels including "minimal cerebally impaired," minimal brain damage," and "nonspecific learning disability."

The labels assigned to children with language-learning problems often match the names of subtests on assessment batteries. Many of the subtest questions are concerned with recall of information. One such subtest requires that the student listen to a series of numbers (refered to as digits) and then repeat them in reverse order. This exercise is asking the student to recall and reverse information out of context. The digit recall is sometimes thought to resemble the recalling activities that children use right after hearing or reading a passage in a text or storybook. If the student has a problem with recall, often that student is said to have a perceptual or auditory processing deficit. When we review the activity, we agree that there is little resemblance between recalling digits in reverse order out of context to recalling a story or information from a book. Analyses of those subtests indicate that there appears to be only a slight relationship between test data and reading and writing. The vague terms, questionable tests, and pseudomedical relationships discussed in this literature lead us to conclude that the diagnostician's time and energy might be better spent observing and interviewing children in a variety of language tasks. We do not deny that the descriptive cluster of behaviors—observed when students take these tests—are exhibited by those who are having difficulty learning to read and write. But guilt by association (or causality by the same) is simply not good enough for us. It is too simplistic to explain anything. It creates the impression that children bring language problems to learning situations rather than considering the broader issues which involve the complexity of language acquisition and the resulting effects of language instruction.

We believe that damage to the central nervous system probably plays a significant role in some children's language and learning problems. But we also believe that the numbers of children in whom language deficits result from problems in the central nervous system are fewer than some people claim. Overestimation has lead to confusing, unfair, and inappropriate labeling.

We now turn our attention to two other areas related to the neurological factors: (1) *reversal tendencies* and how they affect reading and writing ability, and (2) *dyslexia*, which as a term is often used interchangeably with central-nervous system malfunctioning.

Reversal tendencies. Are reversal tendencies signs of neurological damage? Are such behaviors developmentally part of learning to read and write? Will they disappear as language fluency increases? The phenomenon of reversal errors in the beginning reading and writing behaviors of children has been studied for many years. Attempts to relate reversal tendencies to neurological defects have received far more attention in the literature than they probably deserve. Somehow, we are fascinated with reversals and continue to ponder their causes. Kauffmann's (1980) exhaustive review of literature on the topic led him to conclude that it is possible to *predict* future reading failure in some children based on their early tendency to reverse letters. But his evidence ends there, and he does not find support suggesting that reversals are, in fact, symptoms of neurological malfunctioning.

We agree with Deno and Chian's findings supporting the view that the problem of reversals can be better explained educationally than neurologically. They state:

> Apparently, the problem [of reversals] persists because the responsible educators assume that its origins are neurological and that direct intervention, therefore, is unwarranted. The net effect is that the errors continue and eventually become a criterion for labeling the child as learning disabled and explaining reading and writing failure. (1979, p. 45)

Cohn and Stricker (1979) concluded that their data on first-graders provided evidence that letter-reversal errors are not necessarily indicators of a basic perceptual or cognitive deficit. So, if we subtract neurological, perceptual, and cognitive deficits as causes, we are still left with the fact that some children do reverse letters and words as they learn to read and write. Their reversals, however, while inappropriate in context are usually meaningful in isolation (Harman, 1982). Reversal errors are symptoms, but probably not of some neurological deficit. Neither do they appear to be predictors of neurological problems. For beginning readers they seem to be a natural part of learning to read. In older students with reading and writing problems, they are fascinating to observe and will probably continue to hold a level of importance in diagnosis far beyond their power to explain anything, in spite of the efforts of many educators, including ourselves, to place them in perspective as by-products of reading.

Dyslexia. Finding definitions for dyslexia is easy; understanding the authors' perceptions of those definitions is not so easy. It seems to us that if the term disappeared tomorrow, no serious harm would come to the diagnostic world. We do feel an obligation to present our views and to try to help you understand why clarity and consensus are not found by simply reading more and more of the literature on dyslexia, since definitions and explanations are indeed "fuzzy."

The following are some definitions of *dyslexia* that helped us in approaching this subject. Abrams (1981) in the *Dictionary of Reading* is probably the most direct in his defintiion of legitimate dyslexia. His years of experience cross both medical and educational settings, thus providing him with a unique perspective:

> Dyslexia is a rare but yet definable and diagnosable form of primary reading retardation with some form of central nervous system dysfunction. It is not attributable to environmental causes or other handicapping conditions. (Harris & Hodges, 1981, p. 95)

Hynd and Hynd (1984) cite three conditions which must be met for the term dyslexia to be appropriate:

1. The failure to learn to read—despite adequate sensory processes, intelligence, and opportunity—must be documented.
2. The reading disability must be severe, with a substantial discrepancy between expected levels of performance and actual levels.
3. The deficit in reading achievement must be attributable to central nervous system dysfunction, with concrete evidence of the deficit supplied by a neurologist or neuropsychologist.

By these definitions, dyslexia involves malfunctioning of the central nervous system that can be medically verified. Even Hynd and Hynd's first and second conditions can be misinterpreted and vague, in spite of their intent to clarify. What constitutes evidence of "adequate sensory processes," "intelligence," or "expected levels of performance"? It is these conditions which led Harris and Hodges (1981) to state:

Due to all the differing assumptions about the process and nature of possible reading problems, dyslexia has come to have so many incompatible connotations that it has lost any real value for educators, except as a fancy word for a reading problem. (1981, p. 95)

Gentile (1985), after a thorough study of the issue, estimates that only 1 or 2 percent of all problem learners might be classified as truly dyslexic. The vast majority of individuals with reading problems, Gentile writes, can be helped by educational means and, moreover, that continuing to perpetuate the myth that dyslexia is widespread among problem learners is actually injurious, since it delays or prevents instruction and other forms of intervention which can help overcome reading difficulties.

We regret that, for us, dyslexia has become a term useful only as an imprecise and vague label which should be abandoned by educators.

Suggestions for Classroom Teachers and Clinicians

1. Read the professional literature on the relationship of neurological factors and language learning. Pay special attention to the work of experts in the relatively new field of *neuropsychology*.

2. Avoid using the term *dyslexia*. Instead, describe observed behavior in settings where reading occurs.

3. When you encounter a label for a language-learning problem which suggests or connotes a neurological deficit, request evidence. Begin by asking to see the tests. Ask also for samples of reading and writing behaviors under a variety of conditions and environments (see C–A–L–M model in Chapter 2).

4. If special instruction has been carried out, determine what kind, how long, and what were the effects of the instruction on language performance. Ask for progress reports which were prepared as part of the special instruction.

5. If diagnostic procedures indicate damage to the central nervous system, seek confirming medical evidence.

6. Even when damage to the central nervous system has been confirmed, be aware that recent studies, as Mosse stresses, "have shown that the brain has powers of compensation, realignment, and self-restoration. Organic does not mean the child's fate is sealed and that he is doomed, as far too many parents, teachers and clinicians think" (1982, p. 51).

7. In kindergarten and first grade, accept reversals routinely and without fuss as signs of development. Reversals should show a tendency to decrease as reading fluency and confidence increase.

8. When reversal tendencies appear to occur beyond the beginning reading stages, use Harman's (1982) suggested teaching strategies. Two adaptations of Harman's strategies follow:

a. For beginning readers only, assume they do not know the word; give it to them without comment. This strategy is not appropriate for older readers in the second grade and above.
b. For older readers, let them read to the end of the sentence to add context after the reversed word. Most readers will notice something odd and self-correct. If readers do not self-correct and meaning is affected, then the teacher should reread the sentence as the student did. Discuss the appropriate, expected response and the observed one. Only if the reader consistently fails to see the difference should any further diagnosis be attempted.

We might add that the focus of further diagnosis should be on comprehension, during silent and oral reading.

SUMMARY

We have presented a variety of physically related factors that often affect language learning. Research and writing relevant to these factors has been summarized. We have described assessment techniques as well and offered suggestions for adjusting the instructional setting. Throughout the chapter we stressed the interrelatedness of the factors discussed and placed them in a realistic perspective in terms of their effects on language learning.

QUESTIONS TO PONDER

1. Select one of the factors discussed in the chapter for further study. Use the Suggested Readings section to track down additional information sources. Consider adding to what was presented in the chapter in the form of a short paper.
2. Has the chapter helped you to understand the role of physically related factors in language learning? Did any of the information we presented contradict your view before reading the chapter? If so, which ones? How?
3. Apply one of the classroom checklists found in this chapter (for vision or hearing) to several students in a variety of settings. Compare and contrast the results. Include the use of the parent checklist if you can.
4. What local resources are available to provide additional information about each factor discussed in the chapter, especially on nutrition, drugs and alcohol, and allergies?
5. Summarize the role of each factor in language learning as it was presented in the chapter. How could you explain this information to parents?

REFERENCES

Abrams, J. (1981). Personal communication to the editors. In T. L. Harris & R. E. Hodges (Eds.), *A dictionary of reading and related terms* (p. 95). Newark, DE: International Reading Association.

Adler, S. (1982). Nutrition and language-learning development in preschool programs for children with learning disabilities. *Journal of Learning Disabilities, 15,* 323–325.

Allington, R. (1982). The persistence of teacher beliefs in facets of the visual perceptual deficit hypothesis. *The Elementary School Journal, 82,* 351–360.

Andrews, J. F. (1984). *How do young deaf children learn to read? Children's emergent reading behavior* (Tech. Rep. no. 329). Champaign, IL: University of Illinois, Center for the Study of Reading.

Bloom, M. D. & Greenwald, M. S. (1984). Alcohol and cigarette use among early adolescents. *Journal of Drug Education, 14*(3), 195–205.

Bond, G. L., Tinker, M. A., Wasson, B. B., & Wasson, J. B. (1984). *Reading difficulties: Their diagnosis and correction* (5th ed.). Englewood Cliffs, NJ: Prentice-Hall.

Brown, D. A. (1982). *Reading diagnosis and remediation.* Englewood Cliffs, NJ: Prentice-Hall.

Carlsen, J. M. (1985). Between the deaf child and reading: The language connection. *The Reading Teacher, 38*(4)1, 424–426.

Charlton-Seifert, J., Stratton, B. C., & Williams, M. C. (1980). Sweet and slow: Diet can affect learning. *Academic Therapy, 16*(2), 211–216.

Clark, R. M. (1980). Nutrition and learning. *The Clearing House, 55,* 300–304.

Cohen, A. H., Liberman, S., Stolzberg, M., & Ritty, J. M. (1983). The NYSOA vision screening battery—A total approach. *Journal of the American Optometric Association, 54*(11), 979–984.

Cohn, M. & Stricker, G. (1979). Reversal errors in strong, average, and weak letter namers. *Journal of Learning Disabilities, 13*(5), 533–537.

Crook, W. G. (1980). Can what a child eats make him dull, stupid, or hyperactive? *Journal of Learning Disabilities, 13*(5), 53–58.

Deno, S. L. & Chiang, B. (1979). An experimental analysis of the nature of reversal errors in children with severe learning abilities. *Learning Disability Quarterly, 2,* 40–45.

Ewoldt, C. (1981). A psycholinguistic description of selected deaf children reading in sign language. *Reading Research Quarterly, 17,* 58–59.

Gentile, L. M. (1985). Remedial reading: A question of will as much as skill. In L. W. Searfoss & J. E. Readence (Eds.), *Helping children learn to read* (pp. 408–427). Englewood Cliffs, NJ: Prentice-Hall.

Gillet, J. W. & Temple, C. (1982). *Understanding reading problems: Assessment and instruction.* Boston: Little, Brown.

Glazer, S. M. (1983). Good food for good thoughts . . . A healthy partnership. *Early Years, 14*(4), 28–36.

Glines, D. & McGovern, J. (1983). Hidden allergies hamper students and staff. *Educational Leadership, 40*(6), 59–63.

Gormley, K. A. & Geoffrion, L. (1981). Another view of using language experiences to teach reading to deaf and hearing impaired children. *The Reading Teacher, 34*(5), 519–524.

Hall, M. (1981). *Teaching reading as a language experience* (3rd ed.). Columbus, OH: Charles E. Merrill.

Hamilton, E. & Whitney, E. (1982). *Nutrition: Concepts and controversies.* St. Paul, MN: West Publishing Company.

Harman, S. (1982). Are reversals a symptom of dyslexia? *The Reading Teacher, 35*(4), 424–428.

Harris, L. A. & Smith, C. B. (1980). *Reading instruction: Diagnostic teaching in the classroom* (3rd ed.). New York: Richard C. Owen.

Harris, T. L. & Hodges, R. E. (Eds.). (1981). *A dictionary of reading and related terms*. Newark, DE: International Reading Association.

Hasenstab, M. & McKenzie, C. (1981). A survey of reading programs used with hearing-impaired students. *Volta Review, 83*, 383–388.

Hirsh-Pasek, K. & Freyd, P. (1985). Reading styles for deaf and hearing individuals: The importance of morphological analysis. *Literacy Research Center, 1*(1), 3.

Hynd, G. W. & Hynd, C. R. (1984). Dyslexia: Neuroanatomical/neurolingustic perspectives. *Reading Research Quarterly, 19*(4), 482–498.

Johnson, D. D. & Pearson, P. D. (1984). *Teaching reading vocabulary* (2nd ed.). New York: Holt, Rinehart & Winston.

Jurich, A. P., Polson, C. J., Jurich, J. A., & Bates, R. A. (1985). Family factors in the lives of drug users and abusers. *Adolescence, 20*(77), 143–155.

Kampwirth, T. J. & Bates, M. (1980). Modality preference and teaching method: A review of the research. *Academic Therapy, 15*(5), 597–605.

Kaufman, N. L. (1980). Review of research on reversal errors. *Perceptual and Motor Skills, 51*, 55–79.

Kavale, K. (1982). Meta-analysis of the relationship between visual perceptual skills and reading achievement. *Journal of Learning Disabilities, 15*(1), 42–51.

Kellam, S. G., Brown, C. H., & Fleming, J. P. (1982). Social adaptation to first grade and teenage drug, alcohol and cigarette use. *The Journal of School Health, 52*(5), 301–305.

King, C. M. & Quigley, S. P. (1985). *Reading and deafness*. San Diego, CA: College Hill Press.

Kolers, P. A. (1969). Reading is only incidentally visual. In K. S. Goodman & J. T. Fleming (Eds.), *Psycholinguistics and the teaching of reading* (pp. 8–16). Newark, DE: International Reading Association.

Lackey, G. H., Efron, M., & Rowls, M. D. (1982). For more reading: Large print books or the Visolett? *Educating the Visually Handicapped, 14*, 87–94.

Martin, D. & Martin, M. (1982). Nutritional counseling: A humanist approach to psychological and physical health. *The Personnel and Guidance Journal, 61*, 21–24.

Morris, J. E. (1966). *Relative efficiency of reading and listening for braille and large type readers* (Conference Reports, pp. 65–70.) Washington, DC: American Association of Instructors of the Blind.

Mosse, H. L. (1982). *The complete handbook of children's reading disorders*. New York: Human Sciences Press, Inc.

National Institute on Drug Abuse. *It starts with people: Experiences in drug abuse prevention*. U.S. Department of Health, Education and Welfare: Alcohol, Drug Abuse, and Mental Health Administration. Rockville, MD: DHEW Publication No. (ADM).

Naour, P. (1985). Brain/behavior relationships, gender differences, and the learning disabled. *Theory into Practice, 24*(2), 100–105.

Norwood, G. R. (1985). A society that promotes drug abuse. *Childhood Education, 61*, 267–271.

Norwood, G. R. (1984). *The relationship of health and nutrition to the learning process*. Paper presented at the Annual Meeting of the Association for Childhood Education International, Vancouver, British Columbia, Canada. (ERIC Document Reproduction Service No. ED 248 955.)

Pertz, D. L. & Putnam, L. R. (1982). An examination of the relationship between nutrition and learning. *The Reading Teacher, 35*(6), 702–705.

Pipher, J. R., & Rivers, C. (1982). The differential effects of alcohol education on junior high school students. *Journal of Alcohol and Drug Education, 27*(3), 73–83.

Rabin, A. T. (1982). Does vision screening tell the whole story? *The Reading Teacher, 35*(5), 524–527.

Rapp, D. J. (1980). *Allergies and your family*. New York: Sterling Publishing Co.

Readence, J. E., Bean, T. W., & Baldwin, R. S. (1985). *Content area reading: An integrated approach*. Dubuque, IA: Kendall-Hunt.

Richardson, E., Di Benedetto, B., Christ, A., & Press, M. (1980). Relationship of auditory and visual skills to reading retardation. *Journal of Learning Disabilities, 13*(2), 77–82.

Robinson, H. M. (1946). *Why pupils fail in reading*. Chicago: University of Chicago Press.

Rouse, M. W. & Ryan, J. B. (1984). Teacher's guide to vision problems. *The Reading Teacher, 38,* 306–317.

Schubert, D. G. & Walton, H. N. (1980). Visual screening—A new breakthrough. *The Reading Teacher, 34,* 175–177.

Searfoss, L. W. & Readence, J. E. (1985). *Helping children learn to read*. Englewood Cliffs, NJ: Prentice-Hall.

Sherman, R. E., Lojkutz, S., & Steckiewicz, N. (1984). The ADE program: An approach to the realities of alcohol and drug education. *Journal of Alcohol and Drug Education, 29*(2), 23–33.

Smith, F. (1982). *Understanding reading* (3rd ed.). New York: Holt, Rinehart & Winston.

Spache, G. D. (1976a). *Diagnosing and correcting reading disabilities*. Boston: Allyn & Bacon.

Spache, G. D. (1976b). *Investigating the issues of reading disabilities*. Boston: Allyn & Bacon.

Stern, M., Northman, J. E., & Van Slyck, M. R. (1984). Father absence and adolescent "problem behaviors": Alcohol consumption, drug use and sexual activity. *Adolescence, 19,* 301–312.

Stevens, J. J., Jr. & Baxter, D. H. (1981). Malnutrition and children's development. *Young Children, 36*(4), 60–71.

Svobodny, L. A. (1982). Biolgraphical, self-concept and educational factors among chemically dependent adolescents. *Adolescence, 17,* 847–853.

Vass, M. & Rasmussen, B. (1984). Allergies: The key to many childhood behavior abnormalities. *Elementary School Guidance and Counseling, 18*(4), 242–247.

SUGGESTED READING

Allington, R. L. (1982). The persistence of teacher beliefs in facets of the visual perceptual deficit hypothesis. *The Elementary School Journal, 82*(4), 351–360. Reports that teachers still accept the perceptual-deficit hypothesis, regardless of the lack of support in research for these beliefs.

Bloom, M. D. & Greenwald, M.S. (1984). Alcohol and cigarette use among early adolescents. *Journal of Drug Education, 14*(3), 195–205. A study reporting cigarette smoking to be a more peer-oriented and drinking a more family-oriented behavior.

Bradley, B. (1983). I learned to read, again. *Learning, 11*(9), 50–52. Describes a reading specialist's experiences of relearning to read following a stroke.

Dequin, H. C. & Johns, J. L. (1985). Literacy resources in the United States and Canada for visually impaired students. *Journal of Reading,* 29, 148–154. Lists and describes materials and support services with addresses available for visually disabled persons.

Glazer, S. M. (1983). Good food for good thoughts . . . A healthy partnership. *Early Years, 14*(4), 28–31. Proper foods and a booklist for children are geared to parents.

Gentile, L. M., Lamb, P., & Rivers, C. O. (1985). A neurologist's views of reading difficulty: Implications for remedial instruction. *The Reading Teacher, 39,* 174–182. Gives a neurologist's five major views on reading difficulties and identifies implications for instruction.

Hynd, G. W. & Hynd, C. R. (1984). Dyslexia: Neuroanatomical/neurolinguistic perspectives. *Reading Research Quarterly, 19,* 482–498. Argues that there is concrete evidence dyslexia exists and is neurological in nature.

Kavale, K. (1982). Meta-analysis of the relationship between visual perceptual skills and reading achievement. *Journal of Learning Disabilities, 15,* 42–51. Reviews research among visual–perceptual skills and reading achievement.

Keyes, S. & Block, J. (1984). Prevalence and patterns of substance use among early adolescents. *Journal of Youth and Adolescence, 13,* 1–13. A study reports the prevalence and patterns of substance use among fourteen year olds.

King, C. M. & Quigley, S. P. (1985). *Reading and deafness.* San Diego, CA: College Hill Press. Extensive appendices on materials, techniques, and references for teaching reading to deaf children.

Marlowe, M. & Errera, J. (1982). Low lead levels and behavior problems in children. *Behavioral Disorders, 7,* 163–172. A study reporting lead levels correlate with distractibility, aggression, disturbed peer relations, and immaturity.

Moss, H. L. (1982). *The complete handbook of children's reading disorders* (chap. 2). New York: Human Sciences Press. A thorough discussion of the organic bases of reading disorders.

Musatti, T., Mecacci, L., & Pietro, P. (1981). Effects of age and reading ability on visual discrimination. *Perceptual and Motor Skills, 52,* 537–538. A study suggesting that the development of some visual skills is a by-product of learning to read.

Norwood, G. R. (1985). A society that promotes drug abuse. *Childhood Education, 61,* 267–271. Lists the forces in society that manipulate children into inappropriate behaviors related to drug use.

Rabin, A. T. (1982). Does vision screening tell the whole story? *The Reading Teacher, 35,* 524–527. Describes two improved visual screening tests and cautions about their limitations.

Rapp, D. J. (1985). *Allergies and your family.* New York: Sterling Publishing. Chapter 7 describes unsuspected allergic diseases and Chapter 17 lists allergies related specifically to school.

Rouse, M. W. & Ryan, J. B. (1984). Teacher's guide to vision problems. *The Reading Teacher, 38,* 306–317. Looks at vision problems in visual acuity, visual skills efficiency, and visual perceptual–motor development, pointing out symptoms and suggesting what teachers can do to help.

Sherman, R. E., Lojkutz, S., & Steckiewicz, N. (1984). The ADE program: An approach to the realities of alcohol and drug education. *Journal of Alcohol and Drug Education, 29*(2), 23–33. Describes implementation and concerns of an alcohol and drug education program for teachers.

Smith, W. (1984). Intermittent eye malfunctions and their effect on reading. *The Reading Teacher, 37,* 570–576. Describes the complexities of vision malfunctions, their relation to learning disabilities, and possible corrective training.

Spache, G. D. (1976). *Investigating the issues of reading disabilities* (chapter 7). Boston: Allyn & Bacon. A thorough review of dyslexia to 1976. Good for background and for understanding the historical roots of the term *dyslexia.*

Svobodny, L. A. (1982). Biographical self-concept and educational factors among chemically dependent adolescents. *Adolescence, 17,* 847–853. Results of a survey indicate low self-concept, inadequacy of relating to others, inability to cope with problems, and a noncaring attitude about school among drug dependent adolescents.

Swallow, R. (1981). Fifty assessment instruments commonly used with blind and partially seeing individuals. *Journal of Visual Impairment and Blindness, 75*(2), 65–72. Gives the age/grade for which fifty instruments were designed, time required, a brief description, and name and address of publishers.

Thatcher, R. W., McAlaster, R., Lester, M. L., & Cantor, D. S. (1984). Comparisons among EEG, hair minerals and diet predictions of reading performance in children. (pp. 87–96). New York: *Annals New York Academy of Sciences.* Discusses the predictive value of measures of hair mineral concentration and refined carbohydrate intake to reading performance.

Theory Into Practice (1985), vol. 24, issue no 2. The entire issue is on learning and the brain.

Vogel, J. M. (1980). Getting letters straight. In U. Frith and J. M. Vogel (Eds.), *Some perceptual prerequisites for reading* (pp. 20–42). Newark, DE: International Reading Association. Discusses evidence that young children's orientation errors with letters and numbers are a direct consequence of children's orientation concepts and processing strategies.

Wood, T. A. (1981). Patterns of listening and reading skills in visually handicapped students. *Journal of Visual Impairment and Blindness, 75,* 215–218. Study results indicate that listening was the superior learning mode across grade levels for visually impaired students.

Wunderlich, R. C. Jr. (1981). Nutrition and learning. *Academic Therapy, 16,* 303–306. Food allergies and toxins are related to learning disorders.

9

PROCEDURES FOR CLASSROOM DIAGNOSIS

Linking Diagnostic Questions, Variables, and Procedures

Organizing and Reporting Diagnostic Information

Sample Classroom Diagnosis Report

In Chapter 9 we present sample classroom diagnostic procedures and address the following questions:

- How are diagnostic procedures applied to the classroom setting?
- How can classroom diagnostic information be organized and reported?

The purpose of this chapter is to demonstrate how some of the procedures we have discussed in Chapters 3 through 8 can be used to "open up" reading diagnosis in the classroom.

Figure 9–1 graphically outlines classroom-diagnosis procedures to be used by the teacher throughout the school year. Reading diagnosis relies on procedures that help to observe the behaviors of students in their learning environments. These procedures are also appropriate for use in clinical diagnosis. While the classroom teacher may not use all of the procedures, it is important that we offer them as potential aids in the classroom. Most are used

in their original formats; others are simplified for use by the classroom teacher, who cannot devote as much time to diagnosis as a clinician would in a clinic setting.

The sample Classroom Diagnosis Report that comprises the bulk of this chapter is one way to organize such a report— and only one way. It makes considerable use of checklists. These checklists display a variety of information about student behaviors. They are designed to serve as a model or exemplar for you. We urge you to develop a format which fits your own needs and makes efficient use of your own time and energy as a classroom teacher.

Figure 9–1 provides a schematic representation of the classroom diagnosis process. Five questions guide classroom diagnosis based on the Continuous Assessment of Language Model (C–A–L–M). These are:

1. Is the student making progress in language growth?
2. Are modifications in instruction effective?
3. What growth is evident and what needs are still apparent after modifications are made?
4. Is additional diagnosis necessary?
5. Which resource persons can add additional information or assistance?

Classroom diagnostic procedures used to answer the five classroom-diagnostic questions depend heavily on consistent daily observations for extended periods of time, on interviews, and on informal assessment procedures. These procedures, described in Chapters 3 through 8, should be referred to when necessary in reading this chapter. Procedures for classroom diagnosis were selected with the variables—controls, elements, and forms—first discussed in Chapter 2. We suggest you review Chapter 2 before proceeding. You will probably notice only some of these variables and procedures in our sample Classroom Diagnostic Report at the end of this chapter. The age, grade, and kinds of students you teach each year will determine which procedures you select from the array of traditional and nontraditional ones presented in this text.

To help you as you read this chapter, we restate here the diagnostic variables from Chapter 2. Next, in our sample Classroom Diagnosis Report, we will link the five initial questions posed in this chapter with diagnostic variables and procedures selected from Chapters 3 to 8.

DIAGNOSTIC VARIABLES (Chapter 2)

1. Effective learning environments
2. Oral language fluency
3. Written language fluency
4. Comprehension and retention
5. Understanding of the written coding system
6. Physical factors
7. Self-esteem

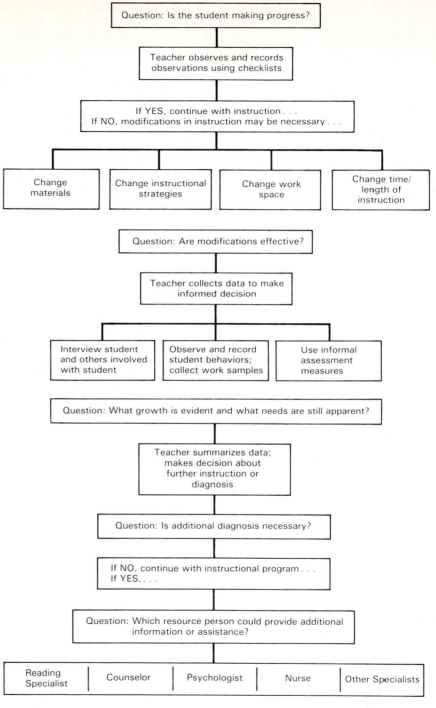

Figure 9–1 Schematic Representation of the Classroom Diagnosis Process.

In Chapter 2 we explained how we believed that assessing self-esteem was directly linked to assessing the other six diagnostic variables we proposed. Chapter 9 presents a checklist for recording observations of a student's learning behavior associated with self-esteem. As students are observed in a variety of settings, behaviors which give clues to their levels of self-esteem can be found. We observe and make notes about their peer interactions, interest in learning, self-direction, and other task-related behavior. Patterns emerge as we note frequency of behaviors. Equally important are comments on the appropriateness of specific behaviors. For example, under peer interaction behaviors, being influenced by peer responses can be a positive behavior if the student responds to the suggestion of a peer to correct an error; or it can be detrimental, if the student is too easily influenced and constantly responds to peer suggestions, lacking confidence in his or her own ability.

LINKING DIAGNOSTIC QUESTIONS, VARIABLES, AND PROCEDURES

This next section focuses on our selection of variables and procedures used in the sample Classroom Diagnosis Report, pages 293 to 306. We will state each initial diagnostic question and then explain how we used a variety of assessment tools chosen from the first eight chapters to construct our diagnostic report for a student whom we will call "Jennifer." As you read this section, you will also be asked to refer to the sample Classroom Diagnosis Report which follows it. Each diagnostic question we ask about Jennifer is linked to appropriate variables and diagnostic procedures. Initially, we pose five questions about Jennifer, based on a review of her cumulative record folder and classroom performance. These questions are:

1. When and how successful is Jennifer in instructional settings and with instructional materials?
2. How does Jennifer express ideas orally?
3. How does Jennifer express ideas in writing?
4. Would Jennifer's history of allergies affect learning?
5. What clues do we have about Jennifer's level of self-esteem, specifically her attitude toward reading?

1. When and how successful is Jennifer in instructional settings and with instructional materials? Instructional settings and materials strongly influence a student's success as a learner. Both the instructional setting and materials must be assessed as part of any classroom diagnosis. Jennifer's diagnosis begins with an assessment of her classroom learning environment. Figure 9–2 is a checklist constructed from a more comprehensive one found in Chapter 3. We simplified it for use in our sample Classroom Diagnosis Report.

In addition to assessing the physical classroom environment, we also decided to use the observational guide—in its original format—for recreational reading settings found in Chapter 6. See Figure 9–3 in the sample report.

Finally, to determine how successful Jennifer is in learning from instructional materials, we used story-retelling (Figure 9–4) and modified "request" procedures (Figure 9–5) from Chapter 6. These procedures will provide us with information about how well Jennifer comprehends and retains information.

2. How does Jennifer express ideas orally? Jennifer's oral language fluency was assessed by observing and noting over time how she used oral language controls (see Chapter 4). Figure 9–6 in the sample report is a checklist for guiding observations of how effectively Jennifer used these controls. It has been modified for classroom use.

3. How does Jennifer express ideas in writing? Figure 9–7 of our report presents procedures for assessing Jennifer's narrative writing ability (Chapter 5), and Figure 9–8 assesses her ability in composition related to reading comprehension, as illustrated in journals (Chapter 6).

Procedures for Classroom Diagnosis   293

4. Does Jennifer have any physical factors which might affect learning?
After reviewing Jennifer's cumulative record folder, we decided to use the classroom and parent checklists for collecting information about allergies (Chapter 8). These checklists are presented in Figures 9–9 and 9–10 and are used in their original formats.

5. What learning behaviors give clues to Jennifer's level of self-esteem? The checklist of learning behaviors in Figure 9–11 was designed specifically for use in classroom diagnosis, as we mentioned earlier in this chapter.

ORGANIZING AND REPORTING DIAGNOSTIC INFORMATION

Diagnostic information is useless unless it is related to instruction *and* reported effectively. The format we suggest here—used in the sample Classroom Diagnosis Report—is useful for classroom teachers when talking to parents. It can be helpful in selecting and explaining modifications in instructional settings and materials. Finally, it can be used to justify referrals to the school reading specialist, psychologist, social worker, and others if additional diagnostic procedures are recommended. The sample Classroom Diagnosis Report has six sections:

1. Background Information
2. Summary of Observations
3. Summary of Interviews
4. Assessment Checklists
5. Conclusions and Interpretations
6. Recommendations

Each section also contains questions raised by the information gathered or examined. These questions may be answered in another section of the report, or may remain unanswered and become a blueprint for additional diagnosis.

SAMPLE CLASSROOM DIAGNOSIS REPORT

Classroom Report: Jennifer

Grade __5__   Date of Diagnosis Began <u>Sept. 5</u>
Age __11__   Date of Report <u>Oct. 15</u>

1. BACKGROUND INFORMATION

(Brief family, medical history; notes from school; talks with parents).
1. Oldest of 3 children

2. No vision/hearing problems reported
3. Normal childhood
4. No record of referral or special help
5. History of colds and allergies
6. Firstborn American in family
7. Mother reports: "nervous child; loves to read; worries about school; plays with older kids."
8. K–2 teachers' comments:
    K: "nervous child, eager to do well"
    1: "small, shy; willing to please; friendly; well-mannered"
    2: "Average student; very nervous; fidgets, talks a lot"

QUESTIONS

1. What behaviors lead people to think Jenny is nervous?
2. Does she really love to read?
3. Why does she select older playmates?
4. How severe are the reported allergies?
5. How do Jenny's parents expect her to perform in school?

2. SUMMARY OF OBSERVATIONS

Number of observations 3 Settings: library period; reading story aloud to children; reading group. Jenny sniffled through all 3 observations, which were spaced over a two-week period. She asked for approval several times when selecting a library book. She responded incorrectly to questions during reading group while rubbing her chin. Leaned on other children during story time.

QUESTIONS

1. Do allergies really interfere with learning?
2. Are there any reading situations in which Jenny is relaxed and comfortable?
3. How can I find out if she does like to read?
4. Is she nervous in other settings?

3. SUMMARY OF INTERVIEWS

Interview with physical education teacher
Questions Used for Interview:
1. Does Jenny's attitude and negative feelings about gym carry over to other areas of school?
2. Do allergies interfere with reading and writing?
Notes: Jenny is eager to please; sniffling is annoying; leans on friends; doesn't volunteer.
Interview with Jenny
Notes: Asked her, "How do you feel about gym?" Answer: Gym is O.K. I get tired and hate to perspire. Sometimes I feel like I'm going to lose the games we play.

4. ASSESSMENT CHECKLISTS

Figure 9–2 Assessing The Classroom Environment

	YES	NO
PHYSICAL ENVIRONMENT		
Are bulletin boards visually attractive?	✓	
. . . used for instruction?		✓
. . . prepared by students?		✓
Is student work displayed in the classroom?	✓	
✓ frequently _____ somewhat _____ not much		
How are student desks arranged?		
_____ rows _____ circle ✓ clusters _____ other		
Are desks arranged so students can see chalkboards?	✓	
INTERACTIONAL ENVIRONMENT		
Are purpose(s) and importance of activities explained to students initially?	✓	
Are directions and explanations clearly stated?	✓	
Are student responses encouraged?	✓	
Is feedback given?		
_____ frequently _____ sometimes _____ rarely		
✓ positive and helpful _____ negative _____ both		
Are different-size groups used?		
_____ whole ✓ small ✓ triads/pairs		
Is peer tutoring organized and used for instruction?		✓
Are classroom rules defined?	✓	
. . . displayed?	✓	
. . . reviewed as needed?		
Are consequences for rule violations defined?	✓	
. . . clear to students?		
Do students monitor classroom behavior?		
Are student opinions and attitudes elicited?	✓	
How? _____ journal writing		
✓ whole class discussion		
_____ individual conferences		
Is decision making teacher-centered?		
. . . teacher and student centered?	✓	
MATERIALS, TEXTS, REFERENCES		
Are books available to meet the reading interest of students?		✓

	Yes	No
Are books available to meet the reading abilities of students?		✓

Are adopted texts appropriate for students considering (1) interests and (2) reading ability? _____ _____

Are dictionaries available of several reading abilities? _____ ✓

Are reference books (encyclopedias, cookbooks, arts and crafts books) available to meet the interests and reading levels of all? _____ _____

Is there a variety of literature for all levels and interests? _____ ✓

Are there game books to solve word problems available? _____ _____

Are there tapes and book sets for listening and reading together? _____ ✓

Are poetry and rhyming books available? ✓ _____

Are books available that include "predictable" language for the young and remedial reader? _____ _____

Are alternate texts available to further interest and encourage investigation of ideas? _____ _____

Are paper and hardback books available? _____ _____

Are there varieties of writing tools available? (X) ✓ _____
Pencils _____ Crayons _____ Ballpoint Pens _____
Ink Pens _____ Chalk _____ Colored Markers _____
Typewriters _____ Paints _____ Erasers _____

Is there a variety of paper available? ✓ _____

Are there materials for construction for response to reading available? _____ ✓

Are drama materials available for response to reading? _____ ✓
Costumes _____ Wigs _____ Crape Paper _____ Props _____
Performance Areas: Formal _____ Informal _____

Is hardware for response to reading and writing available? ✓ _____
Tape Recorders ✓ Video Equipment _____
Still Camera ✓ Transparencies _____
Typewriters ✓ Overhead Projector ✓
Computers ✓

QUESTIONS:

1. Is the environment appropriate for Jennifer's learning abilities and style?
2. How do we know that Jennifer feels comfortable in the environment?

Figure 9–3 Observation Guide for Recreational Reading Settings

When does the student read for recreation?
_____ During free periods
_____ During snack or lunch period
_____ During an instructional period (e.g., holds selected reading material inside instructional text)
_____ After a successful learning experience
_____ While waiting for a school bus, a special teacher, etc.

Other recreational reading times: Reads only during SSR

What does the student choose to read during recreational reading periods? (specify)

Text materials (specify) _____

Fiction (include authors and types of stories) Beverly Cleary books
_____

Non-Fiction materials _____

Comic strips or books _____

Crossword puzzles/word games _____

Jokes and Joke Books _____

Cookbooks _____

Books that explain "how to do it" _____

Riddle Books _____

Trivia (facts) _____

Newspapers _____

News Magazines _____

Other Magazines _____

Other _____

Summary and Observations: Jennifer does not appear to be a self-motivated reader who reads for fun.

QUESTION:
What type of activities and materials might help Jennifer to read more?

Figure 9–4 Assessing Story Structure and Retelling

Diagnostician _____ Student's Name __Jennifer__

Date: __Sept. 20__ Setting: __Oral re-telling of basal story__

Directions for Assessing Story Structure

Check each element included by the student in retelling presentation.

	YES	NO	NEED MORE DATA
Setting			
Introduction of characters		✓	
Inclusion of other characters	✓		
General statement of setting	✓		
Theme			
Indicates event that set the goal for the story		✓	
The problem to solve	✓		
Goal to be achieved by main character	✓		
Plot			
Events leading toward accomplishing goal			
Events leading toward solving the problem	✓		
Resolution			
The problem is solved or goal reached	✓		
The story is ended	✓		

Comments: __Jennifer gave a very accurate account of the story, no extra words; left out any emotional responses of characters.__

QUESTION:

What strategy will help Jennifer use emotional language to describe her feelings about stories?

Figure 9–5 Modified Request Procedure: Request/Question–Answer Evaluation Form

Student Questions

1. Very factual e.g. "Who is the boy in the story?"

Comments: Jennifer responded so little during the activity, the results gave little information

2. Her questions could be found "right-there" on the page in the text

Comments: She seems to be cautious and afraid to take risks.

3. How many questions required information that was "right there." (Factual) 3

4. How many were "Think and then search" questions? (Inference or prediction) 0

5. How many "On your own" questions were asked? (Inference or prediction) 0

6. Were the student's questions like the teachers? factually, yes

Comments:

7. Was the student able to identify the question types? No

8. Was question-type indentification immediate? _____ hesitant? _____? modeled after teacher _____? improved after several tries _____?
(Indicates skilled reading when immediate, automatic responses are offered.)

Comments:

Recommendations for further assessment:

None

Recommendations for instruction:

Needs more interactive oral discussions of what is being read

QUESTION:

When does Jennifer talk and discuss freely?

Figure 9–6 Oral Language Fluency Classroom Assessment Checklist

LANGUAGE CONTROL	SETTING IN WHICH ACTIVITIES OCCUR				
	FORMAL SETTING	CONVERSATION	FREE PLAY	SMALL GROUP	FREE REGULATED ACTIVITY (LUNCH)
FUN LANGUAGE					
Rhymes, copying language from story					
Makes up poems using language from several situations.					
Develops nonsense words and codes for communication.					
INVESTIGATIVE LANGUAGE					
Asks "why" about content or literature.					
Notices specific objects, points of view, events in stories or experiences and asks, "What's that?"					
Is curious to learn how things work—ideas, objects, events. Will ask questions that include, "How do you do it? Show Me."					
LANGUAGE FOR CONTROL					
Directs as leader or parent. Says for example, in several settings: 1. "Give me that—" 2. "Come here—" 3. "You do that!—" 4. "Stop doing that—"					
CONCRETE LANGUAGE					
Describes visual phenomena—objects, plants, changes in plants, animals (for example, describes with adjectives, and by comparisons).	√				

EMOTIONAL DESCRIPTIONS				
Says, things like— "My head hurts." "I feel like crying." "I'm lonesome."	✓		✓	
INTERDEPENDENT/INTERACTIVE LANGUAGE				
Encourages dialogue by using language such as— "Tell me about it—" "How are you?" "What would you like?" "Why do you want to do that?"				

COMMENTS:

Jennifer seems to use concrete language controls in both oral and written form. Describes situations, ideas, activities that involve self very concretely.

QUESTIONS:

1. In what setting can we encourage Jennifer to use emotional language to retell stories from reading?
2. Will the use of a tape recorder help the retelling process?

Figure 9-7 Assessing Narrative Writing

STUDENT: Jennifer	YES	NO	NEED MORE DATA
1. The student is writing to an audience. That audience is _Teacher_	✓		
2. The narrative has a main a. focus b. character	✓ 	 	
3. The narrative includes a series of related events about the focus or character.		✓	
4. The narrative includes a setting.	✓		
5. The topic is carried throughout the narrative.		✓	

6. If a story, events include:
   a. beginning ✓
   b. ending ✓
   c. middle series of events ✓
   d. supporting characters ✓

COMMENTS: Writing is very much a copy of something she is reading. Short sentences, little interaction; she keeps to the point, writes short stories (3–5 lines).

QUESTIONS:
1. How can we encourage Jennifer to want to write thoughts and experiences?
2. What writing strategies help Jennifer to take risks during writing?

Figure 9–8 Composition Related to Reading Comprehension as Illustrated in Journals

Text to Which Student Is Responding ___Cleary's—"The Cat Ate My Gymsuit"___

Student's Name: ___Jennifer___   Date: ___Sept. 20___

RESPONSES TO READING ARE:	YES	NO	NEED MORE DATA
1. In order as author presents them...	✓		
2. Sparce—just one idea, and not necessarily the main one...	✓		
3. Details with little mention of main idea of story...		✓	
4. The structure of text which the student reads is helpful to his/her comprehension...	✓		
5. The text structure seems to hinder text comprehension as demonstrated in the journal entry...		✓	
6. Teacher dialogue seems to help student respond again (next time)...	✓		
7. Student writes in journal without promps.	✓		
8. Student entries seem to get longer and more detailed over time.		✓	
9. Entries are descriptive responses to reading...		✓	
10. Entries are narrative responses to reading...	✓		
11. Entries are explanatory responses to reading...		✓	
12. Reasoning seems to be part of the student's text production...		✓	

COMMENTS/INTERPRETATION: Very "cut and dry" re-statement of what she read.

QUESTIONS:
1. What strategy encourages Jennifer to use details for describing information in text materials?
2. In what setting will Jennifer use details?

Figure 9–9 Allergy Checklist (Classroom)

Student _____Jennifer_____ Observation Dates ___Sept. 5, 15, Oct. 7___

Settings Observed Reading class; playground

Frequent or chronic:
- ____ Colds
- ____ Sore throats
- ____ Wheezing
- ____ Ear aches or infections
- ____ Coughing
- __✓__ Runny nose

Eyes are:
- ____ Puffy
- ____ Rubbed frequently
- ____ Watery
- ____ Have dark circles

Does the student frequently report any of the following?
- __✓__ Stuffy nose
- ____ Ears hurting
- ____ Muscle or joint aches and pains
- __✓__ Chronic fatigue
- ____ Headaches
- ____ Abdominal pains

Does the student exhibit any of the following during learning activities:
- ____ Short attention span
- ____ Wide swings of moods or emotions
- ____ Wide variations in activity level
- ____ Irritability
- ____ Overactiveness

Has the student been referred for any other physical problems such as poor vision or hearing? List below.

Comments/Observations: Jennifer appears tired and sniffles a great deal.

QUESTION:

Does Jennifer need to be tested medically for allergy causes?

Figure 9–10 Allergy Checklist (Parent)

Student _____Jennifer_____ Date(s) Observed _____

Does the student have any allergies you know of? (For example: bee stings, foods, dust). List them below:

Yes, severe in spring and fall, grasses, dust. No food allergies.

Do you know anyone in your family who has allergies? If so, list the person, how they are related to the student and the allergy. For example: Lydia Jones, grandmother, bee stings.

No one under treatment; mother has lots of "hay fever."

Does the student complain of any of the following? (Use a check mark beside those which apply)

Frequent:
- __✓__ Colds
- _____ Coughing
- __✓__ Stuffy nose
- __✓__ Tiredness
- _____ Dark circles under eyes
- _____ Sore throats
- _____ Ear infections
- _____ Headaches
- _____ Muscle or joint aches and pains

Do you notice moods or frequent changes in physical activity from energetic to listless?

Sometimes Jennifer gets tired and does not want to do her homework

Comments/Observations: Jennifer takes a prescription antihistamine during the worst times of allergy season

Figure 9–11 Learning Behavior Checklist

Settings ____Classroom; gym class____   Dates ____Sept. 7; Oct. 1____

Observed ____After school games____

BEHAVIORS

FREQUENCY OF OCCURRENCE
5 = frequently 4 3 2 = occasionally
1 = rarely

PEER INTERACTION

Behavior	Frequency
Interacts with others	2
Initiates peer interaction	1
Assumes authority with peers	1
Helps others	1
Influenced by peer responses	5
Aggressive toward others	1

Comments on appropriateness of peer interaction behaviors

____Rarely chooses to interact; relies on teacher to initiate____

INTEREST IN LEARNING

Participates in class discussions	2
Asks questions related to work	2
Open to new ideas	1
Learns from mistakes	3
Asks for clarification	5

Comments on appropriateness of interest in learning behaviors

Interests seem buried; seeks teacher approval

SELF-DIRECTION

Goal-oriented	4
Uses a variety of language controls	1
Works independently	3
Monitors own work	5
Confident in language tasks	1
Takes risks in language tasks	2

Comments on appropriateness of self-direction behaviors

Will do something over and over, until she "gets it right"

TASK-RELATED BEHAVIORS

Organizes work and ideas	3
Makes decisions	1
Initiates trial-and-error methods	2
Expresses task satisfaction	1
Follows directions	4
Accepts criticism from others	4
Tolerates more than one task	1
Concerned about quality of work	5
Adheres to classroom procedures	5
Completes assignments	5

Comments on appropriateness of task-related behaviors

Overly concerned about being "right"

GENERAL COMMENTS

Not an active learner; generally pulls back from participating

QUESTIONS:

1. What strategy and in what setting is Jennifer most active as a learner?
2. Since Jennifer appears to ask questions easily, how can we use questions to help her use a variety of language controls, new ideas, with new words?

5. CONCLUSIONS AND INTERPRETATIONS

1. Continuously seeks approval from teacher and classmates.
2. Relies frequently on teacher to make decisions about quality of her work.
3. Avoids risks by responding only when asked.
4. Developed "nervous" behaviors to help get her through (e.g., chin scratching, leaning on others).
5. Reading ability—especially comprehension—needs further evaluation. Hard to estimate; has some problems in retaining information and discussing what has been read.
6. Writing was factual, right from text.
7. Understands orally very well.
8. Limited independence in completing tasks.
9. Not much interest in learning; goes through the motions of trying, but mainly to see if she is right.

6. RECOMMENDATIONS

1. A "boost Jenny's self-confidence campaign" to build self-esteem should be tried.
2. Give Jenny some read-along story tapes to complete on her own.
3. Place her in charge of organizing a language game during recreational reading or other free times.
4. More paperback books on her level need to be in the classroom.
5. Use reading activities which involve questioning, such as Modified ReQuest, DRTA (Directed Reading/Thinking Activity).
6. Work with librarian to assist Jenny in learning to pick books on her level, by herself. Try "Rule of Thumb," "Fist-Full," or "Words Rule" with her. [See page 171 of text for descriptions of rules.]
7. Focus comprehension instruction on prediction, opinion, evaluative questions.
8. Use stories which require more imagination and visualizing events, characters.
9. Involve Jenny in paired reading and writing activity conferences with someone in her class at or slightly below her reading level.
10. Follow-up services are recommended:
    a. Allergies—Consult with her medical doctor as to exact nature of allergies.
    b. Reading—Reading specialist to suggest comprehension-assessment classroom teacher can give.
    c. Self-concept—If the "boost Jenny's self-confidence campaign" appears not to work, involve counselor/psychologist, and parents.

10

PROCEDURES FOR CLINICAL READING DIAGNOSIS

Referral System

Cursory Screening

Clinical Diagnosis

Sample Case Report: Long Form

Special Note on the Long-Form Report

Sample Case Report: Short Form

Summary

Chapter 10 includes detailed procedures for clinical reading diagnosis. Clinical diagnosis has usually been conducted by trained professionals outside of classroom settings (for example, school-district, university, or private clinics). Although clinical reading diagnosis retains many of the procedures used in classroom diagnosis, it goes beyond them. Clinical diagnosis focuses on the same variables as classroom diagnosis. Students are observed, tested—formally and informally—and interviewed. Background data is collected and reviewed with those variables in mind—ones which should look familiar to you by now:

1. Effective learning environments
2. Oral language fluency
3. Written language fluency
4. Comprehension and retention
5. Comprehension of the written code system
6. Physical factors
7. Self-esteem and self-confidence.

Procedures for clinical diagnosis are outlined in Figure 10–1. It is important to learn as much about each student as possible. We, therefore, recommend eight to ten two-hour sessions for a complete reading diagnosis. The process, however, begins with a cursory screening, which helps determine to what extent further assessment is needed. Both the cursory and complete screening begin with a referral.

REFERRAL SYSTEM

Referrals for extensive reading diagnosis usually come from parents, physicians, and psychiatrists, reading specialists, child-study teams, or from screening committees—whoever has collected data that indicates further investigation seems needed. Initial screening includes (1) a telephone interview, (2) information from parents, and (3) information from school. Samples of forms used at the Rider College Reading/Language Arts Clinic in New Jersey are included in this chapter. Data collected using these initial referral procedures may prevent serious errors concerning the selection of further diagnostic and instructional procedures.

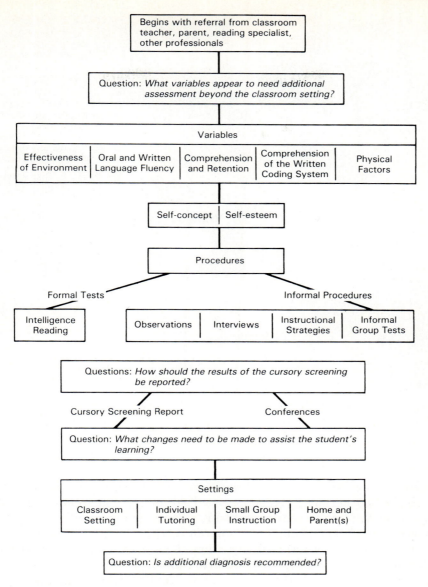

Figure 10–1 Cursory Screening

A well-trained paraprofessional can secure important information during telephone interviews.

Telephone interview. Trained paraprofessionals use careful questioning over the telephone to encourage responses from parents, grandparents, or guardians about their children's reading problems. (These adults usually phone for information about reading diagnosis programs.) The telephone interviewer plays a major role when collecting information about a student, since information is often difficult to obtain. Often adults are unable to answer questions, or are reluctant to do so. Such resistance usually demonstrates difficulty in facing problems. A skilled paraprofessional conducting the initial telephone interview is able to elicit information about such clients, by asking questions and carefully asking them again, and by listening patiently for answers. The paraprofessional's ability to determine relevant from irrelevant information determines the effectiveness of this initial screening. Figure 10–2, showing a form used to collect data by phone, provides some insight into the type of information sought.

Figure 10–2 Telephone Interview Form

```
DATE OF CALL _____ PROGRAM INTERESTED IN _____
REFERRAL _____
CLIENT'S NAME _____ HOME PHONE (_____) _____
HOME ADDRESS _____ CITY, STATE, ZIP _____
DATE OF BIRTH _____ AGE _____
SCHOOL ATTENDING _____
GRADE IN SCHOOL _____ RETAINED IN _____
REASONS FOR INTEREST IN CLINIC _____
_____
_____
_____

PREVIOUS TESTING _____
_____
_____
_____

FATHER'S NAME _____ OCCUPATION _____
PLACE OF EMPLOYMENT _____ PHONE (_____) _____
MOTHER'S NAME _____ OCCUPATION _____
PLACE OF EMPLOYMENT _____ PHONE (_____) _____
SIBLINGS AT HOME (NAMES & AGES) _____
EYE EXAM—YES _____ NO _____ WHEN _____ OPTOMETRIST _____
OPTHAMOLOGIST _____ RESULTS _____
HEARING EXAMINATION—YES _____ NO _____ WHEN _____ WHERE ____
RESULTS _____
```

HISTORY OF EAR INFECTION _____

_____

_____

MOTHER'S HEALTH BEFORE AND DURING PREGNANCY _____

_____

_____

COMPLICATIONS AT BIRTH _____

_____

SERIOUS ILLNESSES OF CHILD _____

_____

_____

_____

Parent information. Information requested of parents or guardians add data about students. Historical information about preschool years and home life confirms telephone information as well as observations and intuitions based on formal and informal assessment. The more data we have, the more we can learn about students. This data should be collected on a form similar to Figure 10–3.

Figure 10–3 General Information Form

The information which you provide on these pages will be used for clinic purposes only. It will help us to better determine the pupil's needs. Thank you for your cooperation.

GENERAL BACKGROUND

Student's Name _____

Student's Address _____
                                    (Street)

_____
   (City)   (State)   (Zip)

Telephone: (_____) _____

Student's Date of Birth: _____ Age: _____ Sex: _____

Student currently enrolled in grade _____

Student's School: _____

School Address: _____

If student is not in school, student's place of employment and business address:

_____

Name(s) of Parent(s) or Guardian(s) residing with student:

_____
    (Name)   (Relationship)

_____
    (Name)   (Relationship)

Name(s) of Parent(s) or Guardian(s) *not* residing with student:

_____
    (Name)   (Relationship)

_____
    (Name)   (Relationship)

Father's Occupation: _____ Mother's Occupation: _____

_____   _____
       (Business Address)   (Business Address)

_____   _____
        (Business Phone)   (Business Phone)

Reason for student attending the special program:

_____

_____

_____

Any additional information:

_____

_____

_____

FAMILY HISTORY

1. Number of children currently living at home with student: _____

2. Student's place in the family (oldest, youngest, etc.): _____

3. Languages spoken in the home: _____

4. Have you or any other members of your family ever experienced reading difficulties? If yes, please explain.

   _____
   _____

5. To what extent is reading a recreational activity in your home?

   _____
   _____

Any additional information:

_____
_____
_____

STUDENT'S HEALTH HISTORY

1. What is the general health status of the student? Please include the date of the most recent physical examination.

   _____
   _____
   _____

2. At approximately what age did the student say his/her first word?

   _____

3. At approximately what age did the student toilet train?

   _____

4. Did the student walk and speak first words at an earlier or later age than other children in the family?

   _____

5. Please check any of the following illnesses that the student has had.

	AGE		AGE
___ Measles	___	___ Scarlet Fever	___
___ Mumps	___	___ Rheumatic Fever	___
___ Chicken Pox	___	___ Whooping Cough	___
___ German Measles	___		

Other illnesses including accidents and surgery:

_____

_____

_____

6. Has the student ever worn glasses or contact lenses? _____

   Does he/she wear them now? _____

   Are the corrective lenses prescribed for reading? _____

7. When did the student have an eye examination?
   Please summarize the results of this examination:

   _____

   _____

8. Has the student ever been troubled with ear infections? If yes, describe the nature of these infections.

   _____

   _____

9. Have you ever been notified of any hearing problem based on school screening? If so, please explain.

   _____

   _____

10. Does the student have a history of allergies? If so, explain.

    _____

    _____

STUDENT'S EDUCATIONAL HISTORY

1. Please check if student has been enrolled in any of the following special school programs:

    ____ Program for the gifted or talented

    ____ Program for remedial reading

    ____ Speech program

    ____ Compensatory education program (math and/or reading)

    ____ Other _____

2. If student has ever skipped a grade, please indicate which one: _____

3. If student has ever repeated a grade, please indicate which one: _____

4. The student exhibits strengths in these: The student exhibits deficits in these:

School subjects: _____   School subjects: _____
_____   _____
_____   _____

Extracurricular activities: _____   Extracurricular activities: _____
_____   _____
_____   _____

5. How do you think the student would describe his/her reading and academic abilities?

    _____

    _____

    _____

6. Has the student had a reading diagnosis prior to coming to the clinic? If so, where and when was it done?

    _____

    _____

    (If possible, we would like a brief summary of the results of the diagnosis. You may submit this to our office.)

_____   _____
Signature   Date

School information. Information from schools provides valuable data for diagnostic and instruction purposes. This data should be sought *only* with permission from those contracting services. A cooperative relationship between schools, clinic, and client insures confidence that all are working in the best interest of the client. Since some information from schools is best shared *only* with professionals, it is suggested that school personnel mail forms directly to clients. Figure 10–4 shows a form used to gather initial screening information from knowledgeable people at the student's school.

Figure 10–4 School Information Form

The information gathered on this form will be used to determine diagnostic and instructional needs, *only.*

Teacher's name: _____ Day Phone: _____

School: _____

Student's Name: _____ Birth Date: _____

In what grade did you teach this student? _____

Dates in which student was in your classes: _____

If testing has occurred in your classroom, please list the name of the test, and the student's score:

_____

What materials are being used for reading instruction with this student? _____

If the class is organized into instructional reading groups, in what group is this student? _____

_____

If you teach spelling, what is your approach? _____

_____

Is the student successful with this approach (or materials)? _____

_____

Can the student retell information after hearing it in lectures? _____

_____

Can the student follow directions after hearing them? ____ Can the student follow directions after reading them from a book? ____ From the chalkboard? ____

Can the student recall information after reading silently? ____ Orally? _____

When student recalls information from reading, what is remembered? Facts: ____ Details: ____

If stories, the Plot: ____ Time and setting: ____ Specifics about characters: ____

How well does student express him/herself in writing? _____
_____

Does the student have any physical condition (i.e., glasses, hearing problems, allergies, etc.) that seems to interfere with learning in school (be specific)? _____
_____
_____

Is the student able to attend to assigned tasks? _____
_____

Are the student's behaviors appropriate for classroom activities (explain)? _____
_____

Is there other information that you feel would help us to work with this student? _____
_____

Teacher's Signature: _____ Date: _____

CURSORY SCREENING

A three-hour procedure, the cursory screening uses formal and informal tools to assess the need for further reading diagnosis and appropriate instruction. During this short session we gather some information about:

1. Abilities to manipulate ideas (mental abilities)
2. Reading comprehension
3. Listening comprehension (attention)
4. Oral language fluency
5. Written language fluency
6. Ability to interact with other students.

The cursory screening period should include (1) a formal testing period, (2) an informal writing period and discussion session, and (3) a structured-play period for children between the ages of six and fourteen. These multiple settings provide information about students' abilities to function with written and oral language in several settings. Because we are interested in ineffective interaction, cursory screening *must* be scheduled as small-group activities so interactions between students and teachers can be observed.

Formal Assessment

The cursory screening begins with a formal testing period. We suggest that group tests of reading and intelligence be used. Group assessment, using formal tools, resembles most school testing procedures. It is important for professionals to observe students' behaviors during these testing sessions. It is important, too, to look at students during sessions which are "unnatural" in order to determine if that environment is stressful. The test scores are not the important data for our purposes. Important data includes observations of the student's actions during the testing session. Actions, rather than scores, are important responses, since group tests have several limitations.

1. Group tests are less valid than individual tests.
2. Intelligence tests that require reading are more of a test of reading ability than of intelligence.
3. Individually administered intelligence tests that do not require reading will probably give a better estimate of performance than group or individual tests where reading is necessary.
4. Certain individual tests for assessing intelligence can *only* be administered by a trained professional.
5. Tests of intelligence to determine reading ability are more important for older than younger students. (Spache, 1976)

Our purposes for suggesting group tests of intelligence is to gather firsthand information about students as they interact with the act of taking formal reading and writing tests. They are also important to include since most communities value the results. Examiners can observe students' abilities to stay on a task for extended periods and their abilities to follow oral and written directions.

Several group intelligence tests and group reading tests are included in Appendix B. The intelligence tests yield scores which are thought to indicate academic potential, general intelligence based on knowledge learned in and out of school, and mental maturity. Group reading tests attempt to screen reading comprehension and vocabulary. These abilities are usually reported as grade equivalents. Some include a section for testing students' speed of reading. Almost all testing materials include a test booklet, instruction manuals for those administering the test, and subtests. Reading-ability tests include several forms of the same test, so that pretesting and posttesting can be conducted to determine the effects of instructional intervention.

Informal Assessment

The informal assessment portion of the cursory screening includes paper-and-pencil tests, checklists, observations, and interviews. We believe that informal assessments are more reliable as measures of abilities than standardized reading tests alone (Farr, 1969). This statement is justified by the fact that the more samples of behaviors we collect, the more likely is our assessment to be accurate (Harris & Sipay, 1980, p. 172).

Assessment tools for informal diagnostic procedures. We suggest that the informal portion of the cursory screening be conducted in groups to replicate, as closely as possible, the schoollike setting. Students about the same age who

Table 10-1 Observing Mental Abilities In Informal Group Settings

MENTAL ABILITY	PERFORMANCE	TASK
Does student understand the concepts of similarities and differences?	Categorized ideas, objects, experiences, pictures. Matches each appropriately.	Using a series of uncaptioned pictures, ask students to put pictures together that belong. Say, "Think why they belong together." (Use with readers and nonreaders.)
Oral language fluency; comparing and contrasting; hypothesizing.	Selects appropriate responses from a number of ideas, concepts, experiences, pictures.	Give students a series of phrases like the following: "A bird in the hand is worth two in the bush"; "It's raining cats and dogs"; "She has a green thumb"; "He has a hole in his head"; "I feel blue." Ask each to write or say how these are alike. (Appropriate for age 8 or older.)
Can student recall groups of ideas?	Can retell information immediately after hearing or reading it.	Read or tell a story to students. Ask each to retell the story onto a tape. Notice what the student recalls. Is the story plot, sequence, details, main idea (all, or some of these) recalled?
Has common sense reasoning. Understands social and cultural aspects of community. Can make judgments with these in mind.	Seems to respond to problems appropriately for age.	Say: "If you had only twenty cents and bus fare was twenty-five cents, what would you do to get on the bus?" "If there was a fire in your house, and you were alone, what would you do?"
Has accumulated a body of information that seems appropriate for his/her age.	Can discuss some cultural, social, human interests using facts learned in and out of school.	Play "Trivial Pursuit." Do crossword puzzles. Play other word games.
Has an oral vocabulary that permits him/her to share ideas, facts, and concepts.	Speaks and is understood by peers and adults.	Read a story. Have each student retell the story onto tape or to group (six is desired group size).

possess similar interests should be grouped together. All variables—language controls, elements, and forms—may be observed in most informal settings. It is efficient, however, for diagnosticians to focus attention on one variable each time the data is collected and reviewed. Once data about students' behaviors, in several settings, is collected, intelligent decisions concerning pedagogical changes can be made.

Observing mental abilities. Suggested activities for observing mental abilities important for reading activities are included in Table 10–1. The activities permit the observer—during the informal portion of cursory screening—to look at students' abilities to:

1. Notice differences and similarities
2. Recall information for short periods of time
3. Use "common sense"
4. Demonstrate their knowledge of information gained from interactions in school and from life outside of school.

Table 10–2 illustrates the relationship of skill performance on these tasks to reading ability. Mental skills—including attending to task, sense of independence and self-confidence, and the ability to make decisions—add to the student's general reading ability and are observable during activities. Table 10–3 offers additional informal measures for determining each student's ability to exercise these skills.

Reading comprehension. Testing comprehension during listening is important. Reading a story with a clear plot and clear supporting details that illustrate the interactions of well-defined characters will help you observe com-

Table 10–2 Relationship of Mental Skills to Reading Ability

MENTAL SKILLS	READING ABILITIES
Notices likenesses and differences.	Similar to letter discrimination and letter–sound discrimination. Notices differences between capital and small letters, manuscript and script forms.
Recalls information for short periods of time.	Immediately after hearing or reading text, can recall ideas in oral or written formats.
Demonstrates ability to use common sense.	Can solve problems while reading—makes decisions about what to read, can think like the author, can respond to text like others might.
Has a general fund of knowledge resulting from interactions in and out of school.	Can talk about information. Relates old information (prior knowledge) to materials currently used.
Can express ideas orally.	Has collected enough vocabulary to put the author's ideas into his/her own words. This demonstrates text comprehension.

Table 10–3 Activities to Assess Mental Skills

SKILLS	TASK	RELATED READING BEHAVIOR
Staying on task; attending to others; book selection; making decisions.	Ask student(s) to select a book. All, including the teacher, read silently. Teacher should share reading content, serving as model. Note which students follow.	Independence and self-confidence; decision making; feelings about books (how does student handle book—a "living" thing, carelessly, etc.).
Verbal fluency; willingness to share; ability to wait for his/her time to share; remarks seem appropriate; sits still and attends to others.	Prepare groups of 3 × 5 cards with a phrase or word written on each. These should be age-appropriate. Have group sit in a circle around a table or on a rug. Place cards, face down, in the middle of the circle. Clockwise, ask a student to pick a card and tell what he/she thinks of when he/she sees the word or phrase. After response is offered, card should be put at bottom of deck.	Prior knowledge; sense of story; self-concept; organizational skills; oral fluency.
Ability to attend to task; physical coordination of hands and eyes.	Play a physically energetic game e.g., Monkey in the Middle: A student stands between two children playing catch; the "monkey" in the middle tries to get the ball.	Small- and large-muscle control important for writing and keeping one's place in a text; spacial relationships—Can student write in appropriate space, etc.?

prehension as your students retell the story to you. Good books for students of all ages are included in Appendix A. Story-telling strategies can be found in Chapter 6:

1. Guided Retellings, page 146
2. Simplified Story Map, page 165
3. Unguided Retelling, page 177

Oral language fluency. Students' abilities to express themselves determine effective interactions. Record language samples during informal guided conversations, and determine the syntactic complexity by using the procedures in Chapter 4, Figure 4–3 (Checklist to Assess Oral Language Maturity).

Written language fluency. Designate approximately fifteen minutes for writing. Stimulate students to write by encouraging them to talk about a story, or by using brainstorming (Chapter 6) or unguided retelling activities (Chapter

6). Measure samples using the holistic scoring system described in Chapter 5, page 97.

Ability to interact with others. We recommend close observation of students as they work with one another. Figure 10–5, an observation checklist, should guide your observations and evaluations of students' successful interactions with others.

Figure 10–5 Observation Checklist

FORMAL SCHOOL SETTING

Student seems to have difficulty during formal testing situation. It is exhibited in the following ways:

PRETEST BEHAVIORS

Taps pencil _____

Annoys others _____

Continuously asks questions of teacher _____

Often asks to leave the room _____

Complains of feeling ill _____

Loses writing tool _____

Complains that directions are unclear _____

Says several times, "What should I do?" _____

DURING TEST TAKING

Looks around the room _____

Tries to gain information by looking at the work of others _____

Seems to have difficulty sitting still _____

Breaks pencil points over and over again _____

Scratches out responses again and again _____

Asks to leave the room several times _____

AFTER TEST TAKING

Hands in materials without reviewing responses _____

Asks questions about test answers of other students _____

INFORMAL TESTING SESSIONS

SMALL-GROUP TESTING

Oral responses are short (one word or phrase) _____

Raises hand, but when called has nothing to share _____

Criticizes responses of others _____

Remarks negatively about responses offered ("That's dumb"; "Why do we have to do this?," etc.)
_____

When asked to respond, does not _____

Does not look directly at teacher _____

Other _____

INFORMAL INTERACTIONS DURING TESTING SESSION

When walking about the room:

    shoves others intentionally _____

    pushes at furniture and other movables _____

    stalls, appearing to look at pictures, etc. _____

    waits for directions _____

    stands alone _____

    seems to be daydreaming _____

    cries, or says, "I can't do it" _____

    Other _____

Does the adult who delivers and picks up the student at testing site:

    remark about child's performance in negative way? _____

    request information from the teacher about the student's

    behavior? _____ performance on test? _____

    other? _____

Formal Tools Used in Assessment: _____

Informal Procedures Used for Assessment: _____

_____

Conclusions: _____

_____

_____

_____

Recommendation: _____

_____

_____

Figure 10–5 serves as a guide for observing student's interactions during the assessment activities. Record observed behaviors that seem important on the appropriate line. Indicate the behavior described in the checklists by writing "yes," or "no," or "sometimes."

Interviews During Cursory Screening

Interviews are informal. They "just happen" in the corridor, the classroom, in the office areas, or on the school grounds. They ought to be spontaneous. Keep the following questions in mind as you walk about and interact with students, staying ever-prepared for an off-the-cuff testing session:

1. Tell me about yourself.
2. How do you feel about school?
3. What is your favorite thing to do when you're not in school?
4. What do you like best about school?
5. Who is your favorite person to be with?

Parallel questions may be asked of parents, classroom teachers, and others who interact with the student. It is important to note consistencies in response. Inconsistency denotes probable difficulties.

Cursory screening should lead to recommendations for further assessment, or referral to other professionals when appropriate. The data collected during the screening can be summarized in prose format or on the summary sheet, Figure 10–6. The results of the cursory screening are used to determine the nature of further diagnosis and instructional change.

Figure 10–6 Summary of Cursory Screening

DATA INDICATES FURTHER TESTING IS NEEDED: YES   NO

Oral language fluency   ____   ____
Written language fluency   ____   ____
Comprehension and Understanding–Perceptions of Test   ____   ____
Written coding system   ____   ____
Physical factors
   vision   ____   ____
   hearing   ____   ____
   muscle control   ____   ____
   allergies   ____   ____
   neurological   ____   ____

Data indicates that further assessment is needed in areas of self-confidence and esteem.

_____

Data indicates that psychological assessment is needed.

_____

Formal tests administered: _____

_____

Informal assessment activities used (Describe activity and skill observed during these):

_____

_____

_____

Signature of Diagnostician: _____ Date: _____

CLINICAL DIAGNOSIS

Clinical reading diagnosis includes assessment in all areas covered in this text. Diagnosticians use formal and informal tools, and they expect that clients will simultaneously engage in self-assessment. The professional—responsible for supplying instruments and strategies for assessing growth and needs—works with the client for eight to ten two-hour sessions. During these sessions clients are tested and are guided in the use of learning strategies. Students also engage in activities promoting self-assessment and encouraging independence and self-confidence. Altogether, this clinical diagnosis permits observations of students in all of the settings mentioned below:

1. Instructional
2. Recreational
3. Interactive
4. Formal testing (individual and group)
5. Individual instruction and assessment

With the benefit of these multiple sessions and multiple activity settings, diagnosticians are able to develop a case report that allows teachers and parents—and students—to discover students' learning abilities and needs. The diagnostic report must be prepared so that all participants—students, parents, classroom and special teachers, and other professionals—are able to effectively use the information reported. It must include data from all sources of observation, reflecting an integrated approach to language. It must provide data that justifies suggested improvements in environments and instructional procedures. It should include recommended books for the student to read and self-monitoring devices. The case report we recommend should use the following format:

1. Ask questions about the student.
2. Collect data (over time, focusing on questions).
3. Answer those questions (ones that can be answered).
4. Develop new questions reflecting further student behaviors (based on intervention from the diagnostician/teacher).

To share the many types of case reports that the authors have seen employed in the past decade would take a book in itself. We have chosen, therefore, to present two basic case reports as models: a long form and a short form. The first represents a comprehensive report describing a student's interaction with assessment tools and instructional strategies. This *long form* should serve as a guide for developing your own; you may choose to report either more or less data, this determined by time, audience and experience with reporting. The *short form* provides the minimal information necessary for recommendations concerning effective strategies for student learning. Begin by using the following set of guidelines.

Conferences should be for the child. Discussions ought to focus on strengths and needs.

Guidelines for Writing Reports

1. Collect all data in a file folder before beginning. The data includes:
   a. Telephone Interview Form
   b. School Information Form
   c. General Information Form
   d. Previous diagnostic reports, if these are available
   e. Results of formal and standardized type assessment tools
   f. Data gathered from other resources (psychologists, psychiatrists, etc.)
   g. Informal data, including transcriptions of oral language (individual or interactive); writing samples from guided and unguided activities; responses to reading in several settings; data reflecting students' attitudes about themselves and learning (include ability to be independent and responsible for learning).
2. Begin writing the report by outlining sections, focusing on the specific language variables in each.
3. Begin each section with questions focusing on behaviors concerning the variable.
4. Report results using objective language.
5. Interpret results using subjective language that is tentative. Words and phrases reflecting tentative decisions include: "It seems that . . ." "It may be that . . .," "Data suggests that . . ." Tentative language reflects an awareness of the continuous changes in human behaviors.

6. Conclusions *must* be supported with data. This data should be included throughout the case report. A general summary statement may be written at the end of the report, or at the end of each section of the report which serve as conclusions based on the data.
7. Recommendations must be specific. Include intervention strategies that should help the student, and describe these in a step-by-step format so that those working with the student—and the student, too—can easily learn to use these as guides for growth.
8. Final reports are best utilized when they are submitted to the student in a conference setting.
9. The final report should be typed and error-free. A cover letter might share important uses of the report, including the fact that multiple audiences may read and understand its contents.

Sample Case Reports

We believe that diagnosticians must be comfortable with both collecting and analyzing data. The varied forms of data collecting techniques permit diagnosticians and students to interact with different forms of assessment, thus allowing professionals to note when comfort for students, as well as themselves exists. We believe that assessment results acquired in natural environments probably represent students' strengths. We know, however, that the testing notions set forth and carried out for nearly one hundred years cannot be abandoned. Too many people, students and professionals, would feel uncomfortable. Our sample case report respects the notions and research of many in the field and, therefore, attempts to fuse formal and informal data to help our readers learn how to describe a students' literacy behaviors. Descriptions of formal tests are included in this case report so that readers may understand what the tools are attempting to assess.

SAMPLE CASE REPORT: LONG FORM

READING/LANGUAGE ARTS CLINIC
Communico, New Jersey

August 14, 1988   Katherine Jo Read, M.A. Director

CLIENT: Margo M.
ADDRESS: 542 Writing Lane
                   Lingo, New Jersey 19880
DATE OF BIRTH: January 1, 1975
AGE: 13
GRADE: 8
SCHOOL: Cagney Middle School
                   Mesa, New Jersey
DIAGNOSTICIAN: F. Phillip, M.A.

BACKGROUND INFORMATION

Margo is a pleasant, sensitive, and cooperative thirteen year old enrolled in the eighth grade at the Cagney Middle School. Her mother contacted the Clinic by phone on recommendation of her teacher who felt that there was evidence to support a need for additional information concerning Margo's learning abilities, particularly in reading and related skills. Assessment, the teacher felt, seemed necessary since Margo's performance was erratic. The General Information Form filled out by Margo's mother stated that Margo was having difficulty with reading, language arts, social studies, and science. Her mother described Margo as "very creative. She enjoys art, chorus, and gym in school and attends art and dance classes after school." Medical records showed that Margo had recently undergone surgery to remove impacted wisdom teeth. According to her mother, the experience did not seem to impair her ability to take part in activities usually experienced by thirteen year olds. Her medical history also showed that Margo has many food allergies. This has, according to her mother, no effect on her social life. Margo's health, at the present time, is good.

The following describes the tools and strategies used to assess Margo's academic strengths, needs, and learning styles. The results of the assessment—what it seems to reveal and how the findings may affect Margo's performance in school—will be shared. Strategies for effective instruction will be described. These should help Margo improve her strengths in academic areas.

INFORMAL TOOLS AND STRATEGIES USED FOR ASSESSMENT

—Mental Abilities Activities
—Unguided Story-retelling
—Guided Story-retelling
—Writing Stage Checklist
—Story Maps
—Graphic Organizer
—Holistic Scoring

—Brainstorming
—Language Control Checklist
—Vision Checklist
—Hearing Checklist
—Allergies Checklist
—Informal Conversations

FORMAL TOOLS USED FOR ASSESSMENT

—Slosson Intelligence Test
—Peabody Picture Vocabulary Test
—Durrell Analysis of Reading Difficulty
—Botel Milestone Tests (level 4–12)
—Woodcock Reading Mastery Tests
—Test of Written Language (TOWL)
—Coopersmith Self-Esteem Inventory
—Keystone Telebinocular Test of Vision
—Audiometer (Hearing)

INTELLECTUAL ASSESSMENT

Question. How does Margo respond to activities designed to demonstrate intellectual abilities often associated with school achievement?

Activities were used to build rapport and to provide activities for observing Margo's ability to solve problems in informal settings [see Table 10–1]. Discussion concerning school was initiated to try and determine Margo's ability to use appropriate general information in conversation. Her ability to observe similarities and differences was assessed using selection of pictures, words, and phrases, and of stories with similar meanings but presented in different versions. Selecting appropriate responses and noting similarities and differences provided information related to Margo's ability to select appropriately in school. Margo's ability to recall information immediately after hearing it was assessed by repeating series of numbers, letters, and ideas in sequences and by retelling several stories. These activities sometimes resemble lecture activities, thus demonstrating Margo's ability to recall from lecture-type activities in school. Observations of Margo's problem-solving ability continued in all sessions. The Slosson Intelligence Test (SIT) added further problem-solving data. This standardized tool derives its items from the Revised Stanford-Binet Intelligence Scale. Results correlate highly with other widely used intelligence tests. It was believed that Margo had limited reading abilities, and limited readers score significantly lower than good readers on tests of intelligence that require reading. The SIT requires no reading and, therefore, seemed appropriate as a measuring tool. The following describes the eight different types of items in this test and what they presume to measure:

Information: General fund of knowledge, long-term memory for experiences, education, and general intelligence.
Comprehension: Practical knowledge of everyday experiences, logical solutions, common sense, and general intelligence.
Arithmetic: Attending to task or concentration, reasoning in arithmetic, ability to use abstract concepts numerically.
Similarities and Differences: Abstraction and concept information skills; relationships and associations of ideas and general intelligence.
Vocabulary: Expressive language, word knowledge, and verbal fluency.
Digit Span: Concentration, ability to attend to task, immediate auditory sequencing, rote memory.
Auditory Memory of Sequences: Concentration and auditory memory of meaningful materials.
Visual–Motor: Eye–hand coordination, motor control, visual–motor integration.

Margo's percentage scores on the eight test items of the SIT follow:

Information	56 percent
Comprehension	67 percent
Arithmetic	54 percent
Similarities and Differences	91 percent
Vocabulary	41 percent
Digit Span	40 percent
Auditory Memory of Sequences	0 percent
Visual–Motor	100 percent

Scores on this instrument indicate that Margo's ability to make judgments about "everyday" events surpasses most others her age. General knowledge and math skills seem slightly above average. Her ability to relate to information in school texts also seems adequate. Margo's ability to select appropriate information from an array of items seems outstanding (91-percent correct). Her knowledge of word meanings may be limited, this indicated by a less than average score on vocabulary items (41-percent correct). Her ability to repeat information in sequence also appears below that of others her age (40-percent correct). If her responses characterize school performance, oral lectures and directions might not be the best way for Margo to receive information. Concentration may be difficult. The inconsistency in performance concerns the examiner. Uneven behavior may result from lack of attention to task due to some emotional distractions.

Informal activities requiring similar behaviors described in the foregoing seem to confirm the SIT scores. Margo was asked to retell different stories from beginning to end after hearing or reading several during the sessions. She retold major portions of stories leaving out relevant descriptive details. Retelling also revealed misinterpretations, this probably due to a lack of understanding word meanings. Margo usually repeated information from texts in the same order as written by the author. The retellings seem to reveal lack of attention to detail and skeletal recalls. Margo paused when recalling information, using one word over and over again. She often used different words, after repeating one several times, but words selected were often inappropriate. Her need to use a variety of words seems to indicate an awareness of audience. Her limited vocabulary probably hindered her performance, and therefore her effectiveness with audience. Since word knowledge (vocabulary) plays a major role in comprehension, further formal testing, using the Peabody Picture Vocabulary Test (PPVT) seemed appropriate. The revised edition, Form M, resulted in a raw score of 115 indicating an age equivalent of eleven years and one month. A percentile rank of 24 placed Margo in the fourth stanine, thus below others of her age, further indicating that knowledge of vocabulary necessary to comprehend text seems limited. All measures, formal and informal, seem to confirm the examiner's intuitions concerning vocabulary knowledge and inability to attend to task.

Question for future observations: Are lack of attention to tasks, reporting details, and limited vocabulary consistent problems in other academic settings?

ORAL LANGUAGE FLUENCY

Questions.

When is Margo able to use oral language fluently in order to share information from text?
What types of situations encourage Margo's oral language fluency?

Oral language fluency was measured with several formal and informal tools. Oral responses to (1) the Peabody Picture Vocabulary Test, (2) the Coopersmith Self-Esteem Inventory, (3) informal conversations, and (4) interviews were recorded in writing and on tape and then transcribed. An analysis of (5) syntactic complexity and (6) vocabulary in context, and of (7) language controls in several settings, were observed. Conversations encouraged by the examiner using several different language controls occurred in order to discover the control to which Margo responded most fluently.

Analysis of the complexity of syntax indicates that Margo used relatively difficult elements of grammar in order to express herself. The oral language was composed of kernel sentences (subject-verb-adverbials, subject-verb-object) which were often transformed and included dependent clauses, adverbial additions at the beginnings and ends of sentences, many adjective additions, and several gerunds. All of the language additions mentioned are elements designated "less easy" and "moderately difficult" to process. Margo's oral language, although limited in vocabulary, demonstrates a level of sophistication seldom observed in oral language behavior of youngsters or adults. Complex syntactic structures seem to demonstrate the ability to manipulate ideas. The arrangements of words in sentences, not necessarily vocabulary, demonstrate problem-solving abilities. Margo's ability to manipulate syntax seems to indicate a level of performance more sophisticated then her vocabulary development demonstrates.

The examiner used investigative, concrete, interactive, and emotional controls periodically in oral texts, seeking to discover to which control Margo responded most fluently. No one control seemed to encourage oral language. A combination of investigative and emotional language used by the examiner, however, encouraged Margo to produce more oral responses than the use of other controls. These controls encouraged language in response to text when brainstorming accompanied by a story map was used. Margo used concrete language as a control in almost all oral language productions. Her oral texts were narrative and descriptive, referring to things that could be seen or heard. On several occasions she used tentative emotional descriptions ("I'm not sure I can do that," "I feel like I can't"). The emotional descriptions were used in response to items on the Coopersmith Self-Esteem Inventory and in informal conversations. Words placed in story maps in response to stories were often emotional. Data suggests that Margo shares ideas orally in a fluent way. The data further suggests that, with increased vocabulary knowledge, Margo's reading ability would probably increase.

Question for future observations: What strategies (interventions) encourage vocabulary growth and positive self-esteem?

Written language fluency questions:

Is Margo able to share ideas and experiences in written formats?
Does Margo use language demonstrating an awareness of audience?
Is written syntax as varied as oral syntax?
What strategies guide Margo to produce effective written language?

(1) The TOWL, (2) writing-stage checklist, (3) writing forms, as well as (4) a holistic scoring device were used to determine Margo's ability to share ideas in written form. In addition, the complexity of her written syntax was observed to determine how well she manipulates syntax. Strategies were used to guide Margo to generate ideas and construct text in response to reading. Each session required Margo and the examiner to write in a journal. This activity helped Margo gain control over communication in written form.

The TOWL resulted in a written story in response to three pictures. This standardized tool was used to measure thematic maturity and expressive vocabulary. The test authors define thematic maturity as the ability to write in a logical, sequenced manner basic to effective written communication. The subtest used to assess thematic maturity, therefore, measures a student's ability to write in a way that easily and efficiently conveys meaning. A sample of the student's spontaneous writing is evaluated according to a specific criteria relating to the quality of the piece. Vocabulary is measured by randomly selecting twenty-five words from the student's spontaneously written story. These words are assigned a value that was derived from their occurrence in basal reading series, school workbooks, and newspapers. Punctuation and capitalization were also observed. A ninth-grade equivalent is the highest that one can score on this test. Margo's scores appear in the following:

SUBTEST	GRADE EQUIVALENT
Thematic Maturity	8.9
Vocabulary	9.0
Spelling	5.4
Punctuation and Capitalization	7.5

Margo wrote the following in response to three sequential pictures.

SAMPLE 1

one day alot of animals were found in a hot place on a wierd planet called numbell and some people found them and brought them back to there Planet called Kenos so after they loaded up 7 flyers they all went back and all the kids loved the animals so they planted all kinds of trees and busses for them to eat from and they did. After a while even more flyers came with even more animals but the kids and Adults mad good homes for the animals. Mosst of the animals had little kids mates. and they were all very happy.

Margo's ability to write in a logical, "easy to understand" manner seems to coincide with her oral language retellings. She seems to be able to share ideas so that others can follow and comprehend them. She combines elements in a creative way, making the story one that an audience would find interesting. Her story includes emotional language as well as language demonstrating the use of concrete phenomona. There seems to be an innate ability to predict appropriate endings to passages. A second sample, written in her journal, demonstrates similar abilities:

SAMPLE 2

When i grow up I would like to first go to collage and after that I would like to be a teacher for little kids like in 2nd grade.
 after that I would like to get married and have about 2 or 3 kids.
 When my kids grow up I would like to be an Arcatec because I like to draw and design houses.

Margo's vocabulary score was higher on the TOWL than on the SIT or the Woodcock Reading Mastery Test. This is probably accounted for by the instrument (TOWL) which rates interesting language highly. Margo uses interesting language in novel syntactic structures. It seems that real experiences help Margo use creative syntactic arrangements—colorful words and phrases. Margo's spelling scores on the Woodcock Reading Mastery Test were low. The subtests used measure phonetic analysis, or word-attack skills. Spelling and word attack require similar abilities. Her scores on both subtests are comparable. Margo's ability to compose is more highly developed and more important than spelling or phonetic analysis. Her editing skills, too, seem to be less well developed. As noted in several of her passages, capitalization and punctuation are almost ignored. Oral language does not reflect this behavior. Lack of real audience may be responsible for lack of punctuation. When Margo retells stories orally, she uses interesting intonations, pitch, and juncture to demonstrate special parts of the story. Her voice drops, appropriately, at the end of a thought unit, as well. When she writes, she should probably read the story outloud so that she can hear when punctuation is needed. Each time Margo retold a story, in unguided or guided procedures, she would talk into a tape. She then would transcribe the tape onto paper. Once the transcription was produced, she would follow her text listening for voice drops and pauses. Margo punctuates appropriately when directed to write as described above. This technique worked when Margo retold stories from experiences or from hearing text read to her. Word lists resulting from brainstorming about text or experiences generated diverse vocabulary related to topics. As the sessions progressed, less repetition of words and more risk-taking in word use resulted in varied language.

Margo can be described as an "emergent writer." Her writing samples are informative, include a variety of syntactic elements, and focus on specific topics. Holistic scoring of her passages resulted in an average of 2.5 on ten pieces of written text collected during the sessions. This score characterizes the emergent writer who writes a skeletal account of an incident, with some elaboration and details. Margo's unguided writing was candid, honest, and more communicative than guided retellings, especially when content focused on sharing life's experiences.

Question for future observations: Will guided retellings, based on self-selected reading, encourage vocabulary growth?

COMPREHENSION AND RETENTION: ONE'S PERCEPTIONS OF TEXT

Questions: When does Margo recall information from reading? In what settings—and with what strategies—is information from reading recalled most successfully?

The ability to understand and recall information from oral and written text is the focus of this section of the report. Margo's inconsistent feelings about herself seem reflected in her performance on reading and listening skills (see section of report on self-esteem).

Margo's shaky self-esteem—coupled with her desire to be well liked, her many interests outside of school, and her creative abilities—seems to facilitate comprehension in recreational, interactive, and individual settings. Her performance declines in formal-test and group-instruction settings.

Text comprehension and recall ability were assessed in formal-test settings using the oral and silent reading section and the listening comprehension section of the Durrell Analysis of Reading Difficulty Test, The Botel Reading Milestone Test—Advanced Subtest (4–12), and the word- and passage-comprehension sections of the Woodcock Reading Mastery Test. As with most such tests, these tests were administered in a formal atmosphere. Informal procedures included unguided and guided retellings, story maps, graphic organizers, and brainstorming.

Durrell Analysis of Reading Difficulty Test. Using the Silent Reading Subtest, Margo was asked to read a passage silently and respond in an unaided recall situation under timed conditions. Comprehension scores are based on the number of "memories" recalled. This format resembles unguided retellings of stories. Listening comprehension required the diagnostician to read a story outloud to Margo, who was then expected to orally answer comprehension questions read by the examiner.

Oral reading was assessed under timed conditions as was silent reading. In these subtests, student recall is based on correct responses to specific questions. Various types of oral errors are documented during the oral reading. Although reading out loud probably demonstrates only oral performance skills, this section of the test was administered to observe consistencies in recall when reading silently, when listening, and in oral performance as well. Comparisons in performance are important in determining preferred learning modalities used by the student in different settings. Results of these subtests follow:

SILENT READING

GRADE LEVEL	TIME	NUMBER OF MEMORIES RECALLED
3	32 seconds	12 (passing)
4	40 seconds	16 (passing)
5	74 seconds	8 (failing)
6	79 seconds	8 (failing)

LISTENING COMPREHENSION

GRADE LEVEL	COMPREHENSION SCORE (PERCENTS)
4	100 (passing)
5	64 (failing)
6	25 (failing)

ORAL READING

GRADE LEVEL	TIME	ERRORS	COMPREHENSION (PERCENTS)
3	45 seconds	3	94 (passing)
4	49 seconds	2	100 (passing)
5	76 seconds	4	39 (failing)
6	92 seconds	13	55 (failing)

Margo's performance scores are consistent across modes. When she read silently her lips moved, sounding out the words. Observations of Margo in silent-reading activities illustrate her need to convert silent reading into oral language. She would also say aloud the stories as she wrote them in her journal. This "saying" was also observed during silent recreational reading in the lunch room, while waiting for the school bus, and in study hall when she engaged in reading activities for pleasure.

Although Margo's oral-reading performance was "choppy"—with many words called incorrectly—oral errors did not seem to be a factor hindering reading comprehension in this formal test-taking setting. A look at silent- and listening-comprehension scores indicate that her comprehension scores were similar. Margo probably converted silent- and listening-reading behaviors into oral language by subvocalizing and "saying" the story to herself. In all settings, Margo seems to need to hear herself read in order to recall text.

Botel Reading Milestone Test. The advanced subtest was administered in order to assess and compare performance in an alternate setting. This tool—in contrast to the Durrell test—proports to measure reading comprehension using single sentences, rather than longer passages. Margo was required to read each sentence and then to select the appropriate word that can be used in place of one that is underlined. This test uses both cloze and multiple-choice formats. Performance seems dependent upon knowledge of vocabulary and the ability to use context to derive meaning from text. Results of the testing for Margo reveal the following:

Fourth-grade level:	90-percent correct
Sixth-grade level:	70-percent correct
Eighth-grade level:	60-percent correct
Tenth-grade level:	80-percent correct
Twelfth-grade level:	60-percent correct

Inconsistency in performance was again demonstrated. Scores, unexpectedly, moved from high to low to high to low. (More typically, scores decline steadily.) Short-term memory seems, again, to be Margo's problem. She seems to recall best when reading orally or when subvocalizing in silent-reading activities.

Guided and unguided retelling and modified request procedures. These procedures were used to compare behavior and performance trends in formal testing with trends in instructional settings. Guided retelling helped Margo focus on selected information for recall whereas unguided retelling required recall of information which was selected by Margo. Results of unguided retelling might be compared to scores on the silent-reading section of the *Durrell,* which requires unguided retelling. The modified request procedure requires that the student construct questions after hearing, reading, or listening to text materials. The student might also be asked to review a photo, picture, or series of pictures and construct questions, thus checking visual comprehension. The procedure utilizes single questions rather than questions about a passage, much like the Botel Milestone. Unlike that tool, however, responses are based on student questions. By writing questions the student selects the focus, permitting the diagnostician to determine the student's perceptions of the text—that is, (1) Does she focus on main ideas?, (2) Is she close to the author's perceptions concerning importance of content?, (3) Is she able to predict appropriately what the expected focus ought to be? Story maps and graphic organizers as well as brainstorming techniques were tried to determine their effectiveness for story comprehension and retention.

Guided retellings. In each of the eight sessions guided retellings were employed. For the sake of brevity, guided retellings described in this report were based on Beverly Cleary's book *Fifteen* (New York: Dell Publishing Company, 1956), a book selected by Margo. Social studies information—a three-page summary of the development of Philadelphia taken from the textbook *America Is* by H. Drewry and T. O'Connor (Merrill Publishing Company, 1987)—was used for content retellings. This text is used by Margo in school. Guided literature retellings focused on the story's goal and plot, and content retellings dealt with facts and implications based on historical data.

Unguided retellings. In order to demonstrate text comprehension when content was of interest, unguided retellings were used. Margo's oral retellings—carried out in private conferences with the clinician—revealed empathy with the main characters of stories. As Margo retold the story about the fifteen-year-old "Jane" and her dreams of having a boyfriend, for example, Margo smiled and moved her hands to help illustrate ideas about waiting for phone calls from a boy. She spoke about similar feelings when she met a boy in her reading class in school. "You see," she stated, "he was having a birthday party. A lot of kids in my class were invited and I wasn't. Then one day, I got an invitation to the party in the mail." Margo related that incident when she talked about the time "Jane," the main character in the story, thought of ways to meet "Stan," the boy in the story; and then, Margo went on to tell, after all of the plans, he called, "just like that!" Receiving the mailed invitation in real life seemed, to Margo, to be "just like that" experience of "Jane's". Margo's prior knowledge about experiences concerning boys and dates seemed to be responsible for guiding her interest and story retention. She was asked to predict what she thought would happen with Stan's and Jane's relationship after reading the first chapter. Predicting story outcomes was requested during all sessions for most reading. The predictions for this story were written in list format. Margo wrote the following:

1. Jane would think of ways to see the delivery boy again.
2. The boy would call her when she did not expect him to.
3. The boy would be the nicest in the school.
4. The boy would also be the most popular.
5. Jane's classmates would be jealous.
6. After a few dates, friends might think they were a couple.
7. Jane and Stan will go steady.

Margo presented her predictions sequentially. This sequence of events was close to the author's. Margo's feelings, experiences, and expectations—as a preteen—seemed to help her to predict appropriately and successfully.

Guided retellings of literature. This procedure focused on the story's goal and main characters. Minor characters were discussed in conferences, and features, as they relate to the main characters, were illustrated, after discussions and use of story maps. Guided retellings helped the diagnostician to observe, and further confirm, that Margo responds best to information that has personal meaning in her life. The story map responses (see Chapter 6 for form) are demonstrated by one included here. Information was dictated by Margo onto tape and transcribed by her onto the story map.

> *Character(s):* Jane—a girl who feels about boys like I do. She's always afraid of not getting a date, and then, "just like that," the best one calls her for a date.
>
> *Setting:* This happened in school. That's where it [encounters with boys] always happens to me.
>
> *Problem:* Jane's problem is getting Stan to be her boyfriend.
>
> *Goal:* Jane wants to do everything with Stan; go to dances with him, walk in the halls in school with him, and talk to him on the phone all the time. She wants her parents to think that this is O.K. to do.
>
> *Events:*
> 1. Jane had a baby-sitting job.
> 2. This boy who was delivering food for the pets came while she was baby sitting.
> 3. Jane liked him. She liked him so much that she wanted him to call again.

4. She thought of lots of ways to get him to call.
5. She tried to get the baby sitting job at the same house thinking that he could deliver the food again.
6. She tried to find out who he was by asking people. That was tough because she didn't want anyone to know how she felt except, maybe, her best friend.
7. Then, he called.

Resolution: Jane and Stan were boyfriend and girlfriend. They could talk to each other alot. They even laughed about a date that turned out to be a mess—the one when they went to China Town for Chinese food, and Jane hated Chinese food. I guess it all worked out well, because they could talk and laugh about it.

Unguided retelling with content materials. This procedure revealed very different results. When asked to retell information dealing with the development of Philadelphia, Margo seemed to draw a "blank." She stared at the examiner with wide eyes and her face became pale. After waiting for several minutes, she said, "I don't remember." When retelling on this subject was requested in peer groups, Margo dropped her head and folded her hands. She offered no response and, when called upon to respond, said, "I don't remember." Guided retellings were tried to help Margo generate information specifically from content texts.

Graphic organizers. To help Margo recall information from content reading, graphic organizers were also employed. These visual organizers seemed to aid Margo's recall of information that seemed unavailable to her when unguided retellings were requested. She labeled the information and categorized it. One example is displayed here:

PROBLEMS	*PHILADELPHIA EDUCATION*
Fires	Some girls did not go to school
Keeping it clean	Some people paid for it.
	A good school opened for boys.

Graphic organizers worked as a strategy for text recall only after the diagnostician brainstormed with Margo about the content texts. Without that approach, Margo seemed unable to respond and share information.

Based on data in this report, it seems that Margo comprehends text best when she is interested in the materials. She comprehends material best when she hears herself read or when the materials are read to her. When guided—using brainstorming, story maps, and graphic organizers—Margo demonstrates retention of some content materials. Margo's personal experiences seem to help her to comprehend content. She was best able to share incidents and events from stories when similar events had happened to her. This information confirms data secured with the intelligence assessment cited earlier in this report. Information was recalled in skeletal form. In all of Margo's retellings vocabulary was limited. She used the same words over and over again to share information. Margo seems able to generalize content from reading, but has difficulty infering beyond the text.

Questions for future observations: Which strategies continue to help Margo demonstrate comprehension with both literature and content material? What strategies will improve her recall in formal as well as informal settings?

WRITTEN CODING SYSTEM

Questions.

> How does Margo's knowledge of vocabulary affect comprehension of text?
> How well does Margo perform on formal versus informal tools for assessing vocabulary knowledge?
> Are relevant words, placed in personalized settings, comprehended more easily than isolated words?

The Woodcock Reading Mastery Tests. The letter identification subtest of the Woodcock tests provided the formal assessment scores for Margo. The letter-identification subtest demonstrated high scores. However, word comprehension (which requires the student to complete an analogy) and passage comprehension (where the examinee selects the correct word to complete a short passage) demonstrated low vocabulary understanding. When words were presented out of context (in isolation), Margo failed. She found it difficult to provide analogies and was unable, on most items, to provide words to complete short passages. During formal testing she appeared nervous (head down, biting nails, swinging leg back and forth) and distracted. Her inability to stay on task demonstrated, once again, either lack of knowledge or little interest. When content seemed familiar, her responses were usually correct. Margo's low scores (fourth-grade equivalent and lower) reflect insufficient vocabulary knowledge, too. Knowledge of content and literature vocabulary were assessed with teacher-made materials. Words from *Fifteen,* from the summary about Philadelphia, and from other content and literature sources used during instructional periods were placed in the context of short passages. This type of assessment was carried out at each session. Margo was asked to supply meanings for words within the context of passages, but not passages from text materials. Examples of these follow:

promissory: The promissory note included monies owed to her mother to pay for her new dress. In what other situations would you write promissory notes? _____

_____

animated: When he spoke, his eyes were bright, he used lots of facial expressions, and waved his hands all around. Everyone said he was the most animated speaker they had ever seen. When have you been animated? _____

Margo identified word meanings when words came from her reading and were placed in context, as appears here. She said, for example, that *promissory notes* would be used when promising homework to teachers, when promising to complete chores around the house for Mom and Dad, and when promising to help a friend with his homework. She said that she appeared *animated* when she was angry—her face turned red and she made wrinkles in her forehead—and after she got a call from her boyfriend. Evidence reported above, and the other data gathered over time, demonstrates clearly that Margo understands words and their meaning when (1) they appear in the appropriate context and (2) there is personal meaning attached to the words. Isolated words which do not pertain to Margo's life and prior knowledge seem to mean nothing to her, thus resulting in poor text comprehension. Encouraging reading and writing where interest and experience in content prevail seems to be an effective way to increase knowledge of vocabulary, thus word comprehension. Activities demonstrating text comprehension should probably be set in recreational and one-on-one settings for greatest success.

Question for future observations: What strategies will "entice" Margo to continue to read?

PHYSICAL FACTORS

Questions:

Do any auditory or visual factors interfere with Margo's reading abilities?
Do allergies interfere with Margo's reading and writing behaviors?

In order to identify physical factors that might cause reading and writing problems, visual and auditory screenings were carried out. Most deficits detected in such screening examinations are easily corrected with glasses or hearing aids. The Keystone Telebinocular Test of Vision determined the status of Margo's vision since squinting was noticed. The examiner checked for far-point and near-point fusion, color perception, depth perception, hyperphoria, and usable near- and far-point vision. Margo passed all tests for all areas screened except that of usable near- and far-point vision in the left eye. If an eye examination by an opthalmologist was carried out within the last six months and no problems were revealed, the findings reported here may not be significant. If, however, Margo has not had a medical eye examination, it is recommended.

Auditory assessment was carried out with an *audiogram*. This test was given for both the right and left ears. Margo was asked to detect tones at different levels of loudness measured in decibels (dB) and at different frequencies measured in hertz (Hz). At 20 dB, Margo could detect all frequencies tested between 1000–8000 Hz in both ears. Her right ear was even more sensitive than her left. At 20 dB, Margo could also detect frequencies between 125–750 Hz. Her auditory acuity appears to be normal, with a slight right-ear superiority. Informal classroom and parent checklists for both vision and hearing confirm the formal results. Margo is able to see individual words and text passages—on chalkboards and on papers at her desk—easily. She is able to hear normally, both in large rooms and when someone speaks to her in close proximity. Her seeing and hearing abilities are more than adequate for successful reading, writing, and listening in school settings.

The allergy checklist (see Chapter 8) confirms information from parents. Margo is allergic to some foods. Symptoms upon exposure include hacking (a dry cough), tearing eyes, and tiredness. It is important to observe these symptoms if they occur and to determine if Margo has eaten foods which may cause them.

SELF-ESTEEM

Question: How do Margo's feelings about herself affect her academic performance in reading and language arts?

Since Margo's self-esteem seemed fragile in several settings, it seemed appropriate to collect much data—informally and formally—to substantiate the clinician's intuitions. The Coopersmith Self-Esteem Inventory and informal conversations were used to provide additional data about Margo's feelings toward herself in relation to parents, peers, teachers, and others in her life, in and out of school. Statements on the Coopersmith test—such as, "I often feel ashamed of myself"—were read by Margo, who was expected to respond to each statement by circling "Like me" or "Not like me."

Responses reveal that Margo's self-esteem seems positive much of the time. She appears comfortable with herself at home and in social environments. She seems less secure about school. She also appears to be puzzled by her inconsistent performance both on tests and in school subjects. Statements in informal conversations illustrated that Margo seemed a bit hesitant about school. When asked if she had a good time there, her comment was, "I have a better time after school." In a discussion concerning her teachers, she said, "They are always nice, but most of them like the other kids better then me." She added, "I get in trouble in school, sometimes." In the context, trouble seemed to mean less-than-average performance in academic tasks. Margo's strong social skills and her desire to be liked seem to compensate for her feelings about herself in school-related activities. She seems creative, with an ability to solve problems in many areas. We must work toward helping Margo use this creative ability to solve school problems as well. Praise that describes desired behaviors should encourage Margo to repeat such behaviors for further success.

SUMMARY AND IMPLICATIONS

Margo's school history and performance in the Clinic's program provided data for determining her strengths and needs in reading and related activities. She has demonstrated success as well as failure. This inconsistent pattern of performance is of great concern.

Formal and informal tools for assessing intelligence (the ability to solve problems) indicate that Margo has the ability to perform tasks much like others her age. The inconsistencies in behaviors, however, were observed in all situations. Her comprehension and ability to determine similarities and differences—on test items, in stories, and in writing—were usually adequate for her age. She demonstrated this ability when retelling correctly in most literature activities and in content activities when guidance was provided. Remembering things right after hearing them—general information, data from lectures, short spans of numbers or letters, vocabulary, items in sequence—seems, however, to present problems for Margo.

Oral language provides satisfactions for Margo most of the time. She is able to retell stories, relate incidents, and share experiences. The success of these activities relies heavily on prior experience. Limited vocabulary seems to be responsible for those times that Margo has difficulty sharing. Margo needs to learn appropriate strategies for recalling information delivered in a lecture that requires "staying on task listening behaviors." Individual and recreational situations seem to provide successes, whereas small- and large-group activities do not. Her struggle to reuse words, or to use alternate words effectively, as well as low scores on tests that determine vocabulary knowledge, help to confirm these conclusions. In spite of a limited vocabulary, Margo employs varied and creative syntax demonstrating an ability to manipulate ideas. Increasing vocabulary and word comprehension is a major goal for Margo.

Written language fluency sometimes coincides with her oral language behaviors. Margo's compositions are written in a logical order, in predictable sequences. She creates a storyline but omits the details and descriptive language that build vivid pictures for the reader. Punctuation is seldom used correctly. Margo possesses the ability to create story, as demonstrated in oral language and in guided written retellings. In addition to increased vocabulary, audience awareness skills must be developed (editing, sentence expansion, combining, and so forth) for more effective communication. High interest, prior experiences, and recreational or individual settings encourage Margo's written language production.

Text comprehension and retention varies with the materials and settings. Formal and informal test results indicate that Margo reads at a level lower than her grade and age expectations. She comprehends and retains information best when she hears herself read the text. Retention seems best when guided responses are requested. Margo responds well when single sentences are used to encourage single-sentence responses. When materials include interesting content—or content which Margo knows about—her comprehension seems to improve in oral and written forms. Again, Margo learns from text best when reading aloud to herself. She needs guidance in learning to listen to directions, in gaining information from lecture situations, and in listening required in auditorium settings. Data collected about Margo's comprehension of the written coding system was limited to vocabulary knowledge. The decision to focus on this variable seemed reasonable since this limitation was observed repeatedly.

Margo is physically in good health. Her hearing and sight are normal. Her allergies to foods could hinder her school performance if coughing and teary eyes are noticed. Asking what she ate is the first step for determining if these symptoms are allergic reactions to foods.

Self-esteem plays a major role in Margo's school activities. She seems to feel good about herself socially but probably feels inadequate academically. She says, repeatedly, "I'm sort of cute, but not smart. My friends believe that, and I know it's true." She also maintains, in informal remarks, that "my teachers don't think I'm too smart and I know that because they always give me extra help." The tentative language consistently offered suggests an unclear view of self. This seems reasonable since inconsistencies in academic performance appear over and over again. Margo seems aware of these "ups and downs." They seem to represent the confusion of her feelings about herself as a learner. It is essential that strategies for building up Margo's feelings about herself as a student be employed. Strategies for self-assessment must also be used. These will help Margo monitor her own behavior and note growth.

RECOMMENDATIONS FOR THE TEACHER

1. We have learned from this assessment over time that Margo seems to recall information best when she sees and hears it simultaneously. It is recommended, therefore, that she use a tape recorder in class lectures. It is important to supplement lectures, not only with taperecordings, but with charts, graphics, pictures, diagrams, and other concrete illustrations of topics covered in lecture settings. Margo must be encouraged to listen to these lectures and, try, if possible, to follow a transcription of the tape.

2. Comprehension strategies that guide recall and retention include story maps, graphic organizers, outlines, and flow charts. One way to use these follows:

Direct Margo to think about what the content of reading is before she reads it. Say: "What do you already know about the materials?" Have her make a list of these ideas. They may be written on a story map, in a graphic organizer, or in a list. Say: "Now that you've made your list, see if you can guess (predict) what the content is about." After she reads the pertinent written material, tell her to reread her predictions. Say: "Look at your original list. How many of these items did you know about? What other information did you need to know, that was in the reading, that would have helped you to predict more accurately? What do you recall?" These tools can also be used as retelling guides, when Margo is working on her own during recreational or free periods.

3. Prereading strategies for tapping prior knowledge are important for helping Margo comprehend text. Brainstorming, group discussions, and predicting activities that are similar to recommendation 2 are suggested.

4. Class projects requiring individual research help to develop vocabulary and independence, and help build self-esteem. Margo *must* select her own topic.

5. Create self-monitoring devices. Such a device for a research project might appear as follows:

Check Here

I have selected my topic _____

I am interested in this topic because _____

First I need to decide what I want to learn. So, I have asked at least three questions

about the topic. They are: _____
_____

I have gone to the library and selected books to help answer my questions. The

names of the books and their authors are: _____
_____

I have checked with my teacher for help when I need it. [Add additional points to fit the project, assignment, etc.]_____

6. Help Margo increase her knowledge of word meanings by listening to her tell

about her reading. Reading and retelling about content help to build vocabulary in the content area.

7. Assign a short passage to Margo and another student. Have each read it and then discuss the meaning. Be sure that interesting words are included in each passage. Inform Margo and her partner that there are interesting and unusual words in the passage. One of the major purposes for reading and sharing ideas is to see if Margo can determine with her partner what the words mean based on the passage's content. Be sure that the content of the passage reveals the meanings.

8. Teach Margo the meaning of prefixes, suffixes, and word roots. The following serves as a example lesson:

Say as you write the following words on a chalkboard, "I am writing a list of words on the board. See if you can tell me about the words." Write:

> *bicycle*   *biceps*
> *bifocals*   *bicentennial*
> *biannual*

Say: "Look at the list. What do you notice?" All responses should be accepted. But the one the teacher really wants is, "They all have *bi-* in the beginning." Then ask, "What is a *bi*cycle?" Wait for responses. "What are *bi*focals?" Permit students to answer after each. The conclusions should be that each of the words has something to do with two things, ideas, etc. Continue this sort of activity over time with many prefixes, suffixes, and word roots. Once students have built a working knowledge of word parts, play a game. Ask them to make up their own words, using a list of parts posted in a convenient place. The list should be familar to them. Examples of student-made words follow:

> *microdermazitz:* (noun) a small pimple on your skin.
> *bonohomo:* (noun) a good man.
> *trimicrohomos:* (noun) three small men.

9. Margo should keep a list of all of her assignments. When assignments are given orally by the teacher, Margo should tape record the assignment. She should also check with her teacher, by repeating the assignment orally, to be sure that she understands the information. Oral repetition—to confirm assignments, directions, instructions of any kind—should help Margo retain and comprehend the information.

10. A daily journal should be kept. Margo should be encouraged to write about events, feelings, likes, dislikes in this journal. Teacher responses should be delivered as if in a letter. Comments should parallel Margo's entry, and content should be empathetic. For example, if Margo writes, "I hated that math assignment," a teacher's response might be, "Sometimes I hate things that I am required to do also. It is difficult and I find that I really wish I could throw it away. But then I make a list of the things that I really hate, and check each one off as they are done. I really feel good when I see the list getting smaller. I am sorry that you feel so badly about math. Come to me, if I can help."

11. Praise Margo by stating the behavior which was appropriate. If, for example, she wrote a composition and began editing for punctuation on her own, you might say: "I am so pleased that you decided to begin to edit yourself. I like the way you turned on the tape recorder, read your composition, and followed along, making periods when you heard

your voice drop." Be sincere when you confirm the desired behavior by expressing it in a way similar to the above.

PARENT RECOMMENDATIONS

1. Talking to Margo—discussing trips, books read in the family, television programs, and other ideas—helps to build vocabulary. When she does not understand a word, be sure Margo asks for the meaning. Explain it within the context of a sentence. If, for example, the word *frigid* is used, say: "You feel frigid in the winter time when it is freezing. You would shake, have a red nose, and ears that feel numb from the cold."
2. Select a family television program. Read the description of that program in *TV Guide,* and have each member of Margo's family predict what the events, the main character, and the final solution might be. If content materials in school focus on a particular country, try to find a show or movie that focuses upon that content. If Russia were the focus, a film like *Dr. Zhivago* would be most helpful for developing concepts, vocabulary, and knowledge about Russian customs, history, and traditions.
3. Be sure to have Margo's eyes checked by a physician (opthalmologist) if this has not been done within the past six months.
4. When you are reading something yourself, point out the interesting points to Margo. This provides a model for her to do the same.
5. Encourage Margo to keep a diary. Do *not* read it, ask to read it, or infer that you will read it. Provide a model by keeping a diary, too.
6. Let Margo know that you have faith in her ability to do well in school. You must believe this, however, in order to help her believe it.
7. Share the "Recommendations for the Teacher" with Margo's teachers in school. Encourage them to use these ideas to help Margo grow in academic areas.
8. Counseling, to help Margo improve her self-esteem, would be helpful. Talking to an unbiased individual trained in handling preteens who need to feel better about themselves, often helps to increase feelings about self and, in turn, to increase school achievement.

SPECIAL NOTE ON THE LONG-FORM REPORT

This serves as a comprehensive model for learning how to use data and language effectively in the reporting process. All reports do not have to be this comprehensive. Elaboration is required when students demonstrate needs. It is important to share information, with both professionals and parents, that clearly explains observed data, confirms needs, and offers concrete examples and specific recommendations. The recommendations should be specific so that those guiding the student can be as successful as possible. Some of the recommendations in this report are specific, and some are not. Refer to descriptions of strategies in this text, and use these as recommendations when appropriate.

SAMPLE CASE REPORT: SHORT FORM

This report is based on assessment using instructional strategies. A brief summary of the student's interactions in the academic environment ought to accompany the report. Included in that summary should be (1) general information about past performance and background information relevant to learning, (2) information from screening sessions, (3) books read by the student during the instruction, (4) vocabulary learned for writing and reading, and (5) suggested books for the student to read at home and in school. Recommendations to parents may also be included. We have found that this form helps since it is specific and takes a relatively short period of time to complete. Teachers have a guide so they might continue to use successful strategies.

NAME: Joseph P.
ADDRESS: 30 E. Brown Road
Tempe, AZ.
AGE: 10
SCHOOL: Cagney Elementary
CLINICIAN: Cynthia, M.A.
DATE: July 6–31, 1987

Joseph is a pleasant ten-year-old boy who has attended the Reading/Language Arts Clinic on several previous occasions. He was enrolled in the clinic by his parents who were interested in encouraging him to develop his strengths in reading and language arts. Although Joseph does many things well, he often appears uncomfortable, his behaviors reflecting these feelings.

At this time, Joseph is sometimes willing to read but experiences difficulty staying on task in silent-reading activities for short periods. He is able to visit the Clinic library and can select books he can read. After selecting books, he often talks with other students instead of reading. When asked by the teacher to begin reading, Joseph sits down, begins to read, but is often unable to continue. During sessions, Joseph read all or part of the following books:

Your Choice Snoopy (Charles M. Schulz)
The Gorilla Joke Book (Phil Hirsch)
Freckle Juice (Judy Blume)
Henry and Ribsy (Beverly Cleary)

Joseph's teacher also read aloud each week. Joseph sometimes appeared to enjoy listening to literature read aloud. On some occasions he would sit quietly and listen to the story; at other times he talked to students.

Joseph demonstrated in several ways that he understood the literature he read and the stories he listened to when his teacher read to him. He was able to write questions about his reading and could answer questions asked by other members of his group. He could write factual questions ("What was Henry's dog's name?") and appeared most comfortable when he was asked to compose these questions and ask them of other students.

Joseph was also able to recall by retelling stories orally to the teacher. His retellings consisted of facts logically ordered as he reconstructed the story. He also included, in the retellings, impressions of feelings and thoughts of characters. He was able to remember information that related to story elements, including plot, setting, and character, and could identify and discuss these parts of a story. He would begin retelling when this activity was requested by his teacher. He often interjected additional story details when other students were retelling. Joseph appears to enjoy oral rather than written retellings. He prefers to talk about, rather than write about, what he has read.

Joseph usually wrote one or two sentences in his journal at each session. He wrote about school and playing soccer. Sometimes he wrote, "I hate to write in my journal." Joseph did not answer the teacher's questions when she responded to his journal entries. He wrote about events and activities in his life.

Joseph does not appear to enjoy writing when it is offered as one of the day's activities. Although he wrote an original and thoughtful story entitled "The Fast Rabbit," he insisted afterward that he "hated writing." This confirms Joseph's preference for oral composition. He composes interesting and original material in oral form but seems reluctant, and is sometimes distraught, when asked to write it down. Joseph often appeared hesitant to begin activities, requiring assistance and encouragement before getting started. He insisted activities were uninteresting to him. It is the responsibility of adults, teachers, and parents in Joseph's life to help him feel relaxed if success with reading activities is to be fulfilled.

A Suggested List of Books for Joseph

Babbit, Natalie	*The Search for Delicious*
Cleary, Beverly	*Ralph S. Mouse*
	Ramona and Her Father
dePaola, Tomie	*The Prince of the Dolomites*
Goble, Paul	*Buffalo Woman*
Grimm, Jakob and Wilhelm (Retold by Trina Schart Hyman)	*Little Red Riding Hood*
Lobel, Arnold	*The Book of Pigericks—Pig Limericks*
Mayer, Marianna	*Beauty and the Beast*
Mayer, Mercer	*East of the Sun and West of the Moon*
Rylant, Cynthia	*When I Was Young in the Mountains*
Spier, Peter	*Peter Spier's Rain*
Steig, William	*Dr. DeSoto*
Van Allsburg, Chris	*The Wreck of the Zephyr*
White, E. B.	*Charlotte's Web*

(Reprinted with permission of parents of Joseph P. and of Cynthia Hickman, teacher and report writer.)

SUMMARY REPORT
READING/LANGUAGE ARTS CLINIC

Student: Joseph P. **Date:** July 1987

Student's Age: 10 **Clinic Teacher:** Cynthia, M. A.

RECOMMENDED STRATEGIES FOR GUIDING GROWTH IN COMPREHENSION AND RETENTION	TEACHER'S COMMENTS/SUGGESTIONS
Unguided Story Retelling 1. Student reads assigned or unassigned reading. 2. Student *immediately* after reading, retells to the teacher or peer, everything that he/she recalls." Student can either tell *orally,* or in writing, in a journal type format.	Joe is able to retell orally what he has read. He begins retelling when asked by his teacher to do so. He can provide details about what he has read and sometimes is able to reconstruct the story he has read in logical order.

Guided Story Retelling
1. Student reads assigned or unassigned reading.
2. Student is asked to recall one of the following:
  a. everything he/she can recall about the main character;
  b. everything he/she can recall about the setting (time, place the story occurs);
  c. everything he/she can recall about the main character's appearance.
(Guided retelling directs student to recall specifics. Decide what is important for student's focus, and request this for at least four consecutive sessions. Then move to another focus, but come back to the original focus occasionally, to keep student in practice.)
3. Student may recall orally, or in written form, as in a journal or diary.
4. Retelling might occur in a small group, where each student shares selection. It may be done in an individual conference format.
5. Notice what student recalls. This helps to determine what focus is needed.
	Joe also participates successfully in guided retelling of what he has read. He is able to remember information that relates to story elements such as plot, character, and setting and can discuss these parts of a story with help from his teacher. Joe chooses to retell orally rather than in written form. He is sometimes reluctant to share what he has read but, with encouragement, will talk with his teacher and other students about what he has read.

ReQuest Procedure (A. Manzo, 1979) 1. Student(s) and teacher silently read selection, together. 2. Student and teacher close book, and both write questions about selection. 3. The teacher asks questions to student, and then the student exchanges roles and asks teacher questions. This may be done with peers as well.	Joe is able to compose questions orally about his reading and can answer questions asked by other members of his group. He asks factual questions such as "What was the dog's name?" When asked to write these questions, he chooses instead to ask them orally of his teacher or other students.

Brainstorming 1. In groups (no more than ten) brainstorm an idea. 2. Ask students to say what they think of when they are asked to think about *(topic)*. 3. Write, on a chalkboard or easel, key words or phrases, as student says them. This activity can be used after reading as a recall procedure. It can be used as a prereading activity to prepare students for reading.	Joe's clinic group used this procedure after reading to recall all they could remember about what they had read. As with retelling, Joe is able to remember details about what he had read and so had much to offer as students contributed ideas and thoughts for their teacher to write on the blackboard.
Directed Reading Activity This is an activity which requires the reader to focus when reading. It is direct intervention to guide recall by a teacher. 1. Ask student to read in order to answer a specific question about an item, idea, event in the passage. 2. Student is asked to identify the kind of information required (inference/fact). 3. Student is asked, after reading, to find information in text that is "right there." He/she is asked to reread that information. 4. Student is asked to "infer" from information in text, the answer.	Joe was asked to read and to answer questions about the plot, setting, or characters in the story he selected from the library. He answered these questions successfully and was able to identify the kind of information required with guidance from his teacher.
Uninterupted Sustained Silent Reading (USSR) 1. All in environment select a piece of reading material. 2. All should sit in a quiet place and read. Reading *must* be silent, uninterupted, and sustained for a designated amount of time. 3. Sharing time should follow. Teacher should begin, by voluntarily sharing "something special" from the reading. 4. Students, voluntarily, will begin to share. *Caution: The teacher must serve as a model in this activity and* READ.	Joe experiences difficulty in visiting the clinic to find a book he is able to read. He usually told his teacher he "didn't like to read" and would select a book only after additional encouragement from her. He experienced difficulty in sitting quietly while reading and sometimes returned his library book without reading it.
Main Idea Maps 1. Ask student to write "main idea" in center of map. 2. Have student write one idea, event on each spoke. 3. Have student convert "spoked" idea map into traditional format, on sheet below. 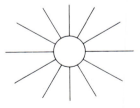	Joe was able to use these maps to chart the plot, setting, and characters in stories he read with encouragement from his teacher. He was told before reading began he would be asked to make one of these maps, and was able to do them orally, with his teacher writing on the blackboard, as well as in written form when he worked alone.

Story Structure Worksheet (Dreher & Singer, 1980) Provide student with following worksheet with each story. Fill in with parts of the story that fit the worksheet questions. 1. Setting Where does story take place? _____ Who is (are) main character(s)? _____ When does the story happen? _____ 2. Story Goal What is the goal of the main character? _____ 3. Story Plot How does the main character try to reach the goal? First try _____ What happens? _____ How did it turn out? _____ Second try _____ What happens? _____ How did it turn out? _____ Ending Did the main character reach the goal? _____	Joe was able to use a story structure worksheet successfully although he appeared most comfortable with this strategy when it was used in a group with his teacher participating.
Cloze Procedure (Taylor, 1953) 1. This activity occurs after reading a selected passage. 2. Teacher deletes every 5th word in passage with approximately 50 for the total passage. This is presented in worksheet format and presented as a postreading activity. 3. You may accept *only* exact words as correct. You may choose to select synonyms or other replacement words, when appropriate. *Caution: delete words beginning with second sentence and ending with next to last sentence.*	Joe was able to successfully complete activities using the Cloze procedure. He appeared to work best when sitting next to his teacher and when he could read aloud the sentences he was attempting to complete.
Reading To 1. Read a story to student. An older student should be listening to a novel, younger to a shorter story. 2. Discuss story, by retelling. 3. Use unique vocabulary when you retell to student. 4. Ask student to retell story. 5. If student comprehends unique vocabulary, he/she will use it.	Joe sometimes appeared to enjoy being read to. He would sometimes sit quietly and follow the text of the story as his teacher read. He sometimes volunteered to tell what he remembered about the story and was able to recall details about the plot, setting, and characters of the story.

RECOMMENDED STRATEGIES FOR WRITTEN LANGUAGE FLUENCY	TEACHER'S COMMENTS/SUGGESTIONS
Dialogue Journals 1. Time is provided for students to write entries in journal. These entries "may" be related to reading, or they may not. 2. Teacher responds, in writing, to student's entry. The teacher's responses should be reflections on student's entry. They should be an attempt to extend the student's idea. *Caution:* Teacher responses are *not* critical or evaluative. The major purpose for dialogue journals is to provide students with an opportunity to share, privately, reactions to reading and other events in their lives, in writing. Critical comments could stop the freedom to share honestly and freely.	Joe usually writes one or two sentences in his journal. He talks about what he does after school and about playing soccer. He answers the questions his teacher asks him in her entries and offers information that expands his answers. He cometimes chooses not to write in his journal and writes instead, "I hate to write in my journal."
Invented Spelling When student writes, encourage him/her to write without concern for spelling. Say, "Write the word like you think it is spelled. Remember, only you have to be able to read it now. After you finish composing, I will help you edit, and spell words correctly."	Joe uses invented spellings when he writes. He occasionally asks for help in spelling a word but appears comfortable creating his own spelling. These spellings should be permitted since they allow him to express his thoughts spontaneously and imaginatively when he writes. If his compositions are to be read by others, they should be edited by Joe and an adult so that the final draft is correct.

Written Story Analysis
1. Student reads assigned reading.
2. Student is asked to recall what s/he has read by writing sentences about:
  a. the plot
  b. the setting
  c. the characters
3. Student is asked to choose two words from the story that were new to her/him and to use them in a sentence.
4. Student is asked to write two questions about the story.
5. Student is asked to compose a new title for the story.
	Joe was able to use this strategy successfully to help him remember what he had read. He seemed to enjoy answering questions and offering information orally, but was willing to write this information when encouraged to do so by his teacher.

STRATEGIES FOR BUILDING INDEPENDENCE, SELF-CONFIDENCE, AND SELF-DIRECTION	TEACHER'S SUGGESTIONS/COMMENTS
Redirecting Questions (This strategy is used after students have had an explanation directed to them). 1. When student says, "How do I do it?" "What should I do next?" Say, "What do you think you do?"	Joe asked questions of his teacher infrequently. When questions were redirected to him, he often replied "I don't know." He would then pause and was frequently able to answer the question.

2. When student asks, "How do you like my work?" Say, "What do you think of it?" (Agree with student evaluation). 3. When student asks how to solve a problem, say, "What do you think you need to do?" "How would you begin?" 4. When student says, "Where does it belong?" or "Where should I put it?" Say, "Where do you think it belongs?" "Where do you think you should put it?"	
Directed Praise Praise must be specific and to the point. When a student does something that is appropriate respond as demonstrated below: "I like the way you wrote that paper. It is all about one topic." "I like the way you rejected that book. You discovered that it was too hard using the "fistful-of-words rule." "I like the way you are staying on task and completing your work."	When praise is given directly to Joe by his teacher, he makes few responses. He sometimes shrugs his shoulders or walks away from his teacher, and says nothing to his teacher in return.

Checklist References

Dreher, M. J., & H. Singer. (1980). Story grammar instruction is unnecessary for intermediate grade students. *The Reading Teacher* 34:261–268.
Manzo, A. V. (1979). The request procedure. *Journal of Reading* 2:123–126.
Taylor, W. L. (1953). Cloze procedure: A new tool for measuring readability. *Journalism Quarterly* 30: 632–636.

SUMMARY

The diagnostic reporting system—including the cursory screening—provides information for teachers and parents, and for specialists including psychologists, psychiatrists, and pediatricians. It is important that information be as reliable as human data can be. That means collecting information about the student in several settings several times. The data collection must span time, so that the teacher/researcher learns to know the students, their likes and dislikes, their strengths and needs.

    The strength of our reporting system is the focus on behavior based on initial questions. Interpretations of behavior gain credibility because multiple tools and multiple activities over time provide the hard data—behavioral evidence—for conclusions and implications. We recommend that reporting be as positive as possible. Use implicit and explicit negatives infrequently. Try to tell what the student *can* do rather than what she or he *cannot* do.

Clinical reports provide information that describes the student's abilities and needs at the time the observations are collected and analyzed. Human behaviors change as students grow and, therefore, conclusions are *never* definitive. Be flexible when describing students as well as yourself, and all will gain from educational experiences with language.

REFERENCES

Farr, R. (1969). *Reading: what can be measured?* Newark, DE: International Reading Association.

Harris, A. J., & Sipay, E. R. (1980). *How to increase reading ability.* (7th ed.). New York: Longman.

Spache, G. D. (1976). *Diagnosing and correcting reading disabilities.* Boston: Allyn and Bacon.

APPENDIX A Suggested literature for diagnosis and instruction

Cynthia Mershon Hickman, West Windsor-Plainsboro Regional School District, Princeton Junction, New Jersey

This bibliography has been prepared to assist classroom, special reading teachers and parents in using literature as an alternative means for observing, assessing, and diagnosing children's ability to comprehend and decode text. Literature can provide the opportunity to observe children's interactions with print, their reactions and responses to many facets of language and reading. It offers a framework for diagnosis based on how readers process language. Observing children's experience with literature provides data that may be useful in reaching conclusions about their successes or failures with reading.

Diagnostic procedures should be flexible enough to discover what reading is for each child and when each does it well. Literature, with its endless forms and variations, facilitates an open-ended approach to diagnosis: We can select a variety of books for a variety of purposes. We can observe continuously, over time, children's responses to literature in many situations. These observations can then be recorded and interpreted to discover children's strengths and needs. The resulting picture of the child's language behaviors enables us to make meaningful suggestions for improving student learning.

Literature can be useful to developing readers in several ways. It can guide children to develop oral and written language fluency by providing them with the opportunity to hear and to read enjoyable rhyming and repetitive language which becomes a "built-in" rehearsal system for learning vocabulary. Comprehension of text can also be enhanced as children read books whose inherent structure contributes to their sense of story and to their understanding of story grammar. In addition, guided interaction with literature may help children to find something of themselves in the lives of others and thus better understand their own problems and concerns.

Literature, at its best, possesses great power and mystery. Books have consequences. They alter children's attitudes and perceptions, and, as a result, change their lives. They stretch children's imaginations, extend their experiences, and offer them increased awareness of the people and world around them. Every book is essentially unfinished; the child completes it for himself, bringing to it his own thoughts and ideas and taking from it what he needs to know and understand. Giving children the chance to get lost in a book may enable teachers and parents to find ways to ensure those children become better readers.

HELPING CHILDREN DEVELOP ORAL AND WRITTEN LANGUAGE FLUENCY

We can learn much about children by listening to the language they bring with them to school. By observing their language behaviors in school in several settings and in their interactions with other children and adults, we may ask ourselves questions about the language they use to make themselves understood:

- Do they ask questions of others?
- Do they give commands to others?
- Do they describe the world around them using interesting language?
- Do they talk about their feelings and emotions?
- Do they use language to encourage interactions?

Observing children's reading selections over time may provide information about their dominant language control. Children may select books that use language similar to that which they do to control their own worlds. The language control used by the text's author may help the reader to feel comfortable, since the control is familiar. Wordless picture books can be used by teachers to give children the opportunity to use their own language to tell stories; the children's language becomes the language of the book. Composing stories facilitates vocabulary development and helps children to develop a sense of story. Wordless picture books help children to realize that authors are people who talk and then write that talk down to share with others. Alphabet books provide beginning readers with the opportunity to study the letters of the alphabet. Children must know their *ABC*s if they are to learn to read, and these books can help them become familiar with the sound and sight of individual letters.

Texts with repeated syntactic and spelling patterns provide a "built-in rehearsal" system for learning vocabulary. Repeated text patterns help children—particularly those with short-term memory deficits—to retain the language from text, thus facilitating reading ability. Such books provide students with a special sense of security. Youngsters who have had difficulty recalling words in texts can rely on the repetition for recall. This builds vocabulary but also confidence and, therefore, desire to read more.

The following bibliography includes books that are written with repetitive, reliable, and "fun-type" language controls. Youngsters of all ages will gain by listening to and reading these texts. For those who enjoy music, we have included text adapted from songs that repeat and rhyme. This makes reading a "chanting" experience.

WORDLESS BOOKS

AUTHOR	TITLE	PUBLISHER	DESCRIPTION
dePaola, Tomie	Sing, Pierrot, Sing: A Picture Book in Mime	Harcourt Brace Jovanovich, 1983	The French clown Pierrot sets out to win the heart of his beloved Columbine.
Goodall, John	Jacko	Harcourt Brace Jovanovich, 1971	The adventures of an organ grinder's monkey and his friend.
Goodall, John	Paddy to the Rescue	Atheneum, 1985	Paddy the Pig rescues a damsel in distress from a menacing rat.
Keats, Ezra Jack	Skates	Franklin Watts, 1973	Dogs and skates twirl and slide in an adventure that ends with the dogs realizing skating is not for them.
Massie, Diane Redfield	Cocoon	Crowell, 1983	The ordinary emergence of a butterfly from its cocoon produces astonishing consequences.
Mayer Mercer	Ah-Choo!	Dial, 1976	The perils of a simple sneeze fill this book with giggles and fun.
Mayer, Mercer	A Boy, A Dog, and a Frog	Dial, 1967	A boy and a dog attempt to catch a frog.
McCully, Emily Arnold	First Snow	Harper & Row, 1985	A timid little mouse discovers the thrill of sledding in the first snow of the winter.
Spier, Peter	Noah's Ark	Doubleday, 1977	Noah prepares for the Great Flood by gathering animals with which to populate his ark.
Turkle, Brinton	Deep in the Forest	Dutton, 1976	An unusual retelling of the story of "Goldilocks and the Three Bears."
Winter, Paul	The Bear and the Fly	Crown, 1976	Three bears are quietly enjoying their dinner until a fly provokes the father to wreak havoc with a fly-swatter.
Young, Ed	Up a Tree	Harper, 1983	The illustrations present the trials and tribulations of an adventurous cat.

ALPHABET BOOKS TO HELP CHILDREN UNDERSTAND THE RELATIONSHIP BETWEEN ALPHABETIC WRITING AND SPEECH

AUTHOR	TITLE	PUBLISHER	DESCRIPTION
Alda, Arlene	*ABC*	Celestial Arts, 1981	Photographs by the author of things in our environment that resemble alphabet letters.
Craig, Helen	*The Mouse House ABC*	Random, 1979	A book with tiny illustrations which unfolds into a long string of pictures.
Eastman, P. D.	*The Alphabet Book*	Random, 1974	An amusing book with two familiar words for each letter of the alphabet.
Farber, Norma	*As I Was Crossing Boston Common*	Dutton, 1975	A turtle slowly crosses Boston Common, meeting a procession of animals from A to Z.
Lalicki, Barbara, compiler	*If There Were Dreams to Sell*	Lothrop, Lee, & Shepard, 1984	Words by Mother Goose, Longfellow, Coleridge, and others enrich a child's feeling for language.
Lobel, Arnold	*On Market Street*	Greenwillow, 1981	A world of wonders from A to Z is found in the shops on Market Street.
MacDonald, Suse	*Alphabatics*	Bradbury Press, 1986	An acrobatic look at the twenty-six letters of the alphabet; each letter becomes part of a picture that illustrates the letter's sound.
Mayers, Florence	*ABC: Museum of Fine Arts, Boston*	Abrams, 1986	Large red letters are accompanied by fine art reproductions from the Museum of Fine Arts collection.
Pearson, Tracy, illustrator	*A Apple Pie*	Dial, 1976	A spirited new interpretation of a traditional ABC that unfolds into an eighteen-foot-long poster.
Schmiderer, Dorothy	*The Alphabeast Book: An Abecedarium*	Holt, Rinehart & Winston, 1971	Each letter passes through four stages to become a bright-colored animal.
Sendak, Maurice	*Alligators All Around: An Alphabet*	Harper, 1962	Active and silly alligators from A to Z.
Seuss, Dr.	*Dr. Seuss's ABC*	Random, 1963	A short alliterative verse is provided with each letter.

BOOKS TO HELP CHILDREN DEVELOP ORAL AND WRITTEN LANGUAGE FLUENCY USING DIFFERENT FORMS OF LANGUAGE EXPRESSION

Identified language controls used in each book are included in the annotation. These language controls were studied in Chapter 4 of this volume.

AUTHOR	TITLE	PUBLISHER	DESCRIPTION
BOOKS WITH RHYMING LANGUAGE			
Carlstrom, Nancy White	Jesse Bear, What Will You Wear?	Macmillan, 1986	A beguiling rhyme about a young bear's activities throughout the day. *Language Control:* investigative.
dePaola, Tomie	Tomie de Paulo's Mother Goose	Putnam, 1985	A handsome edition of over 200 rhymes provides an opportunity for the youngest listener to hear many rhyming words. *Language Control:* varied.
de Regniers, Beatrice	May I Bring a Friend?	Atheneum, 1964	A repetitive, rhyming text describes a small boy's invitation to tea with the king and queen. *Language Control:* varied.
Frost, Robert	Stopping By Woods on a Snowy Evening	Dutton, 1978	A picture-book version of Robert Frost's poem describing the quiet delights of winter in rhyming verse. *Language Control:* describes the concrete world as well as feelings and emotions.
Gerrard, Roy	Sir Cedric	Farrar Straus Giroux, 1984	A story in rhyming verse of a gentle but bold knight and his search for adventure. *Language Control:* describes the concrete world as well as feelings and emotions.
Langstaff, John	Hot Cross Buns and Other Old Street Cries	Atheneum, 1978	A collection of easy rhymes and rounds. *Language Control:* varied.
Larrick, Nancy	When the Dark Comes Dancing: A Bedtime Poetry Book	Philomel, 1983	Forty-five poems and lullabies designed to soothe a child at bedtime with rhyming and rhythmic language. *Language Control:* varied.

AUTHOR	TITLE	PUBLISHER	DESCRIPTION
Martin, Bill, Jr., and Archambault, John	*Barn Dance!*	Henry Holt, 1986	A cheery rhyming story of a young boy who joins the animals of woodland and farm in a midnight square dance. *Language Control:* varied.
Moore, Clement	*The Night Before Christmas*	Holiday, 1980	Beautiful folkloric motifs illustrate this favorite holiday poem. *Language Control:* describes the concrete world as well as feelings and emotions.
Seuss, Dr.	*The Cat in the Hat*	Random, 1957	A fantastic cat charms two children with his clever rhymes and invented words. *Language Control:* fun, playful.
Silverstein, Shel	*A Giraffe and a Half*	Harper, 1964	Wildly funny rhyming, repetitive language builds a cumulative story about a giraffe "stretched another half" to make "a giraffe and a half." *Language Control:* Playful; describes the real world.
Thomas, Patricia	*There Are Rocks in My Socks Said the Owl to the Fox*	Lothrop, Lee & Shepard, 1979	Zany pictures accompany delightful rhyming nonsense verses. *Language Control:* varied.
Tripp, Wallace	*A Great Big Ugly Man Came Up and Tied His Horse to Me: A Book of Nonsense Verse*	Little, Brown, 1979	Cartoon drawings illustrate rhyming verse that pokes fun at humans and animals alike. *Language Control:* varied.

BOOKS WITH REPETITIVE LANGUAGE

AUTHOR	TITLE	PUBLISHER	DESCRIPTION
Brett, Jan, illustrator	*The Twelve Days of Christmas*	Dodd, 1986	A beautifully executed visual interpretation of the traditional holiday song. *Language Control:* playful; describes the real world.
Eastman, P. D.	*Are You My Mother?*	Random, 1960	A baby bird searches high and low for his mother, repeating the question "Are you my mother?" *Language Control:* investigative.

AUTHOR	TITLE	PUBLISHER	DESCRIPTION
Emberly, Barbara	*Drummer Hoff*	Prentice Hall, 1967	A cumulative, repetitive story about how each member of the militia gets the cannon ready "but Drummer Hoff fires it off." *Language Control:* describes the concrete world.
Hutchins, Pat	*Rosie's Walk*	Macmillan, 1968	Rosie the Hen goes for a walk "across the yard, around the pond, over the haystack . . ." leading the fox pursuing her into one disaster after the other. *Language Control:* describes the concrete world.
Lobel, Arnold	*The Rose in My Garden*	Greenwillow, 1984	A cumulative and repetitive story describing the flowers and insects in a garden. *Language Control:* describes the concrete world.
Martin, Bill, Jr.	*Brown Bear, Brown Bear, What Do You See?*	Holt, Rinehart, & Winston 1967	The reader asks several animals, "What do you see?" *Language Control:* investigative.
Mayer, Mercer	*What Do You Do with a Kangaroo?*	Four Winds Press, 1973	A little girl asks the reader, "What do you do?," as one animal after another upsets her life. *Language Control:* investigative.
Prelutsky, Jack	*The Baby Uggs Are Hatching*	Greenwillow, 1982	Amazing creatures come to life amid repeated and rhyming words. Spelling patterns "ugg" and "atching" stressed. *Language Control:* playful.
Robart, Rose	*The Cake that Mack Ate.*	Little, Brown/Joy Street Books, 1987	A cumulative tale with an amusing ending follows the preparation of a festive birthday cake. *Language Control:* playful; describes the real world.
Sendak, Maurice	*Chicken Soup with Rice: A Book of Months*	Harper, 1962	All months of the year are nice for "eating chicken soup with rice." *Language Control:* playful; describes feelings and emotions.

AUTHOR	TITLE	PUBLISHER	DESCRIPTION
Seuss, Dr.	The Cat in the Hat	Random, 1957	A fantastic cat charms two children with his clever rhymes and invented words. Spelling pattern "at" stressed. *Language Control:* varied with emphasis on playful.
Seuss, Dr.	Fox in Socks	Beginner, 1965	A tricky fox tries to get your tongue in trouble. Spelling patterns "ox," "ick," "ock," and so on are stressed. *Language Control:* playful.
Seuss, Dr.	Green Eggs and Ham	Beginner, 1960	Sam I Am repeatedly tries to convince us to eat green eggs and ham. Spelling patterns "am" and "an" stressed. *Language Control:* playful; describes the real world.
Seuss, Dr.	Hop on Pop	Beginner, 1963	Rhyming, repetitive language stresses spelling patterns "all," "ay," "ent," "other," "ed," "ack," "up," and so on. *Language Control:* playful.
Spier, Peter, illustrator	London Bridge Is Falling Down	Doubleday, 1967	Colorful illustrations detail the construction and collapse of London Bridge ("London Bridge is falling down, falling down, falling down . . ."). *Language Control:* describes the concrete world.
Viorst, Judith	Alexander and the Terrible, Horrible, No Good, Very Bad Day	Atheneum, 1972	Alexander experiences over and over a "terrible, horrible, no good, very bad day" that causes him to consider running away to Australia. *Language Control:* describes feelings and emotions.
Zolotow, Charlotte	Mr. Rabbit and the Lovely Present	Harper, 1962	When a little girl asks Mr. Rabbit for help in finding a birthday present for her mother, they engage in a repetitive dialogue as they search for the perfect gift. *Language Control:* interactive.

BOOKS TO HELP CHILDREN DEVELOP READING COMPREHENSION BY PRESENTING COMMON EXPERIENCES AND/OR IDEAS

Comprehending text means understanding ideas, events, the written code system, the pictures—everything that is on the pages in the wonderful books included in the following. The books listed below are often selected by children over and over again when they find the language enticing, the story interesting, and the solutions to problems satisfying. Children may instinctively select books that include ideas, events, and situations that occur in their lives. These selections can aid diagnosticians in observing how and what children are thinking concerning their self-concepts, their problems with friends, siblings, or adults in their lives, and their interests and loves.

Most important for understanding text is the ability to predict and infer how an author constructs a story. We are concerned with the student's ability to identify the story's central character, plot, setting, time, problems, and resolutions, as well as details as they also relate to character and plot. Well-written books for young children include pictures and story plots that are organized to help develop an image of story structure in the students' minds. When stories are well written, the story maps included in Chapter 6 of this volume can be used spontaneously to develop a sense of story which encourages retention. Oral conversations in small groups and on a one-to-one basis can help students to learn how to recall information from stories and texts.

AUTHOR	TITLE	PUBLISHER	DESCRIPTION
BEGINNING READERS			
Fatio, Louise	*The Happy Lion*	McGraw-Hill, 1964	A happy lion innocently decides to leave his cage with startling results.
Hissey, Jane	*Old Bear*	Putnam/Philomel, 1986	Three stuffed animals set out to rescue Old Bear, who has been left in the attic.
Hoban, Russell	*Bedtime for Frances*	Harper, 1960	A small badger uses her imagination to keep from going to bed.

AUTHOR	TITLE	PUBLISHER	DESCRIPTION
Lionni, Leo	*Alexander Mouse and the Wind-up*	Pantheon, 1969	A little mouse uses a magic wish to make his toy friend real.
Lobel, Arnold	*Frog and Toad Are Friends*	Harper, 1970	An amusing account of the adventures of two best friends.
Marshall, James	*George and Martha*	Houghton Mifflin, 1972	Two funny hippopotamuses teach each other about caring and sharing.
Sendak, Maurice	*Where the Wild Things Are*	Harper, 1963	Max travels from naughty escapades through a dream trip to the land of wild things and back home again.
Seuss, Dr.	*Horton Hears a Who*	Random, 1954	Hugh Horton the elephant helps the teeny, tiny Who's.
Wells, Rosemary	*Benjamin and Tulip*	Dial, 1973	Benjamin is bullied by little Tulip and ends up in all sorts of trouble.
Zelinsky, Paul O.	*Rumpelstiltskin*	Dutton, 1986	A handsome rendering of the classic fairy tale of the girl who must spin straw into gold.

YOUNG READERS

AUTHOR	TITLE	PUBLISHER	DESCRIPTION
Aardema, Verna	*Why Mosquitoes Buzz in People's Ears: A West African Tale*	Dial, 1975	A lively folktale retold with African art motifs examines how rumors begin.
dePaola, Tomie	*Strega Nona*	Prentice Hall, 1975	Big Anthony ignores Strega Nona's warning against using a magic spell to start her pasta pot.
Grahame, Kenneth	*The Wind in the Willows*	Holt, Rinehart & Winston, 1980	A story of the friendship and adventures of Mole, Ratty, Mr. Badger, and Toad.

AUTHOR	TITLE	PUBLISHER	DESCRIPTION
Hodges, Margaret	*Saint George and the Dragon*	Little, Brown, 1984	A retelling of Sir Edmund Spenser's *Faerie Queene* recounting the battle between a brave knight and a dragon.
Hyman, Trina Schart	*Little Red Riding Hood*	Holiday, 1983	Beautiful illustrations complement this retelling of a little girl's encounter with a big, bad wolf.
Jeffers, Susan	*Wild Robin*	Dutton, 1976	Robin, a wild boy who hates doing everyday things, falls under a fairy spell from which only his sister, Janet, can save him.
Kellogg, Steven	*The Island of the Skog*	Dial, 1973	A group of mice learn a lesson about friendship on a mysterious island.
Locker, Thomas	*Sailing with the Wind*	Dial, 1986	Luminous landscape paintings illustrate the story of a young girl who sails to the ocean and back again with her uncle.
Mayer, Marianna	*Beauty and the Beast*	Four Winds Press, 1978	An honorable young girl's life is changed when she accepts responsibility for the actions of her father.
McDermott, Gerald	*Arrow to the Sun: A Pueblo Indian Tale*	Viking, 1974	A native American myth about a young boy's search for his father.
Van Allsburg, Chris	*Jumanji*	Houghton Mifflin, 1981	Two restless children find excitement in a jungle-adventure board game.

AUTHOR	TITLE	PUBLISHER	DESCRIPTION
Yorinks, Arthur	*Hey, Al*	Farrar, Straus Giroux, 1986	A New York City janitor and his dog, Eddie, find that the grass is not always greener on the other side.

MIDDLE READERS

AUTHOR	TITLE	PUBLISHER	DESCRIPTION
Babbitt, Natalie	*Tuck Everlasting*	Farrar, Straus Giroux, 1975	Eleven-year-old Winnie must make some life-and-death decisions after stumbling on a family who has unwittingly drunk from a spring of life.
Bauer, Marion	*On My Honor*	Clarion Books, 1986	Joel comes to understand the power of choice when his daredevil friend drowns in a raging river.
Burnford, Sheila	*The Incredible Journey*	Little, Brown, 1961	Two dogs and a cat travel over 250 miles through the Canadian wilderness in an attempt to return to their home.
Cleaver, Vera and Bill	*Where the Lillies Bloom*	Harper, 1969	A determined fourteen year old keeps her orphaned family together by gathering medicinal herbs in the Appalachian mountains where they live.
Donovan, John	*I'll Get There; It Better Be Worth the Trip*	Harper, 1969	Thirteen-year-old David, stunned by the sudden death of his grandmother, turns to his dog and close friend for help in dealing with his divorced parents.

AUTHOR	TITLE	PUBLISHER	DESCRIPTION
Eckert, Allan	*Incident at Hawk's Hill*	Little, Brown 1971	Ben, a six year old who has trouble communicating with adults, finds himself caught during a storm in a badger's burrow.
Fleischman, Sid	*The Whipping Boy*	Greenwillow, 1986	A young prince learns about friendship and loyalty when he becomes bored with his life and decides to run away with Jemmy, a poor orphan.
Fox, Paula	*One-Eyed Cat*	Bradbury, 1984	Ned disobeys his father and shoots his air rifle; he comes to fear that the shadow at which he aimed may have been an old cat.
Greene, Bette	*Summer of My German Soldier*	Dial, 1973	A Jewish girl aids a German prisoner of war in his escape during World War II in a small southern town.
Langton, Jane	*The Fledgling*	Harper, 1980	Eight-year-old Georgie learns to fly with the help of her friend, a Canadian goose.
L'Engle, Madeleine	*A Wrinkle in Time*	Farrar Straus Giroux, 1962	Meg and Charles Wallace search to find their missing father, accompanied by three extraterrestrials on a journey through time.
Lewis, C. S.	*The Lion, the Witch, and the Wardrobe*	Macmillan, 1951	Four children find adventure when they pass through an old English wardrobe into the magical land of Narnia.

AUTHOR	TITLE	PUBLISHER	DESCRIPTION
O'Dell, Scott	*Island of the Blue Dolphin*	Houghton Mifflin, 1960	A young Indian girl struggles to survive when she is left by her people on a deserted island.
Paterson, Katherine	*The Bridge to Terabithia*	Crowell, 1977	Jess and Leslie share an imagined world until one drowns, leaving the other to cope with the sadness and loss.
Speare, Elizabeth George	*The Witch of Blackbird Pond*	Houghton Mifflin, 1958	On a visit to colonial Connecticut, Kit saves herself from future tragedy in the Salem witchcraft trials when she teaches a young girl to read.
Taylor, Mildred	*Roll of Thunder, Hear My Cry*	Dial, 1976	The story of a strong black family and their struggle to defy southern racism during the Depression.
Taylor, Theodore	*The Cay*	Doubleday, 1969	After the Germans torpedo the freighter on which he and his mother are traveling from wartime Curacao to the United States, Phillip finds himself blind and dependent on an old West Indian when they are cast up on a barren Caribbean island.
YOUNG ADULTS			
Adams, Richard	*Watership Down*	Macmillan, 1974	A band of rabbits threatened by the destruction of their warren sets out to establish a new home on an English down.

AUTHOR	TITLE	PUBLISHER	DESCRIPTION
Baldwin, James	*If Beale Street Could Talk*	Doubleday/Dial, 1974	A young couple support each other in the struggle against injustice and racial oppression in Harlem.
Conrad, Pam	*What I Did for Roman*	Harper, 1987	Darcie, feeling abandoned by her newly remarried mother and a father she has resisted knowing, becomes enthralled by a strange young man while working for the summer at the city zoo.
Davis, Terry	*Vision Quest*	Viking, 1979	The story follows Louden Swain, a gutsy, irrepressible eighteen-year-old champion high school wrestler, as he gears up for a crucial match and the inevitability of manhood.
Demetz, Hannah	*The House on Prague Street*	St. Martin's, 1980	A strongly autobiographical novel concerning a girl's childhood in Czechoslovakia and the tragic circumstances she encounters during the nightmare of World War II.
Gaines, Ernest	*The Autobiography of Miss Jane Pittman*	Doubleday, 1971	The story of a courageous black woman who began life as a slave and lived to take part in the civil rights demonstrations of the 1960s.

AUTHOR	TITLE	PUBLISHER	DESCRIPTION
Guest, Judith	*Ordinary People*	Viking, 1976	A seventeen-year-old boy returns home after a suicide attempt to find he must rebuild his relationship with his parents and learn to cope with the death of his brother.
Hamilton, Virginia	*Sweet Whispers Brother Rush*	Philomel, 1982	A fourteen-year-old girl learns about her family's past from Brother Rush, her uncle's ghost.
Maxwell, William	*The Folded Leaf*	Harper & Brothers, 1945	An unconventional study of adolescent relationships in Chicago and in a middle-western college
McKinley, Robin	*Beauty: A Retelling of the Story of Beauty and the Beast*	Harper & Row, 1978	A young woman, well educated and honorable, accepts responsibility for her father's act and leaves her family to enter the enchanted world of a castle and its Beast.
Oneal, Zibby	*A Formal Feeling*	Viking, 1982	A young girl learns to accept the death of her mother as she adjusts to a new life with her stepmother.
Paterson, Katherine	*Jacob Have I Loved*	Harper, 1980	Plain-looking Louise, feeling eclipsed by her pretty twin sister, finally begins to find her identity.

AUTHOR	TITLE	PUBLISHER	DESCRIPTION
Peck, Robert Newton	*A Day No Pigs Would Die*	Knopf, 1972	A twelve-year-old Shaker farm boy learns to assume responsibilities forced upon him by his father's death in Vermont in the 1920s.
Pierce, Meredith Ann	*The Darkangel*	Little, Brown, 1982	Aeriel is both fascinated and repelled by the "vampyre" as she tries to save her mistress and other "vampyre" bridges.
Rylant, Cynthia	*A Fine White Dust*	Bradbury, 1986	The wrenching story of Pete, a religious young man who is disappointed and betrayed by a traveling tent preacher.
Wharton, William	*Birdy*	Knopf, 1979	The friendship of two Vietnam veterans is tested when one of them is pushed over the edge of reality by his long-time obsession with birds.
Zindel, Paul	*The Pigman*	Harper, 1968	The story of two high school sophomores and their tragic friendship with a lonely old man.

BOOKS DEALING WITH DISABILITIES AND/OR HANDICAPPING CONDITIONS

Current literature for children and young adults is realistic. Many books include plots which address specific physical, emotional, and learning disabilities and the effects of these on daily living. Although some of these disabilities do not directly affect the development of literacy skills, students with these specific problems use a considerable amount of energy dealing with them in their day-to-day existence. The energy used for handling deficits that affect living is the same energy needed for learning.

Books selected specifically to guide children to gain better views of personal and social problems—as they relate to disabilities—can aid them in solving their own problems. This literature, read to students or read by themselves, can encourage them to interact personally with literary characters who face similar deficits. Observing children's reactions as they read or listen—both facial expression and body language—may, along with oral responses, give us some clues to problems they are experiencing that might otherwise go unnoticed. Guided interactions with sensitive plots may lead students to understand the difficulties of others and to apply this understanding in reaching solutions to their own problems and concerns.

The books included in the next section deal with a variety of handicapping difficulties and disabilities. They offer no simple solutions to complex problems. The characters in these books and the plots in which they are engaged should help disabled students to understand that sometimes life itself is, at bottom, problematic. These are books of considerable literary merit—realistic, truthful, and yet hopeful.

Descriptions of the stories' plots and the disability/handicap upon which they focus are included in the bibliography. More extensive lists of books whose stories concern physical, emotional, and intellectual disabilities and their effect on characters' lives are available in *Notes from a Different Drummer: A Guide to Juvenile Fiction Portraying the Handicapped* by Barbara H. Baskin and Karen H. Harris (R. R. Bowker Company, 1977).

AUTHOR	TITLE	PUBLISHER	DESCRIPTION
YOUNGER READERS			
Blue, Rose	Me and Einstein: Breaking Through the Barrier	Human Science Press, 1979	Bobby does not see letters in the way other boys and girls do, but he learns to read and talk about his problem with others who share his difficulty.
Brightman, Alan	Like Me	Little, Brown, 1976	The author uses photographs of retarded children to examine how all people are alike in their need to have friends and to experience success.

AUTHOR	TITLE	PUBLISHER	DESCRIPTION
Fanshawe, Elizabeth	*Rachel*	Bradbury, 1975	Rachel is a young girl who must use a wheelchair but who has a full life, friends who enjoy being with her, and tries to ignore the inconvenience her disability presents.
Jupo, Frank	*Atu, the Silent One*	Holiday, 1967	A young African bushman named Atu cannot speak but is able to communicate vividly the ways of his people through gestures and drawing.
Lasker, Joe	*He's My Brother*	Whitman, 1974	A young boy tells the story of his brother, Jamie, who is learning-disabled and encounters problems and frustrations both academically and socially.
Lenski, Lois	*We Live in the South*	Lippincott, 1952	Evelina's friends are insensitive to her hidden handicap, an enlarged heart, that causes her to complain of chest pains and forces her to withdraw from games and activities.
Montgomery, Elizabeth Rider	*The Mystery of the Boy Next Door*	Garrard, 1978	When a new boy who is deaf moves into their neighborhood, other children are unsure of him until they learn to communicate using sign language.
Powers, Mary Ellen	*Our Teacher's in a Wheelchair*	A. Whitman, 1986	The story of a nursery school teacher who leads an active existence despite a partial paralysis requiring the use of a wheelchair.
Raskin, Ellen	*Spectacles*	Atheneum, 1969	Iris resists getting glasses, fearing they will ruin her appearance, even though her vision is so foggy that she mistakes her grandmother for a dragon.

AUTHOR	TITLE	PUBLISHER	DESCRIPTION
Sobol, Harriet	*My Brother Steven is Retarded*	Macmillan, 1977	Beth has a retarded brother, Steven; she loves him but finds it hard to accept a brother who learns slowly and is not like other children.
Yolen, Jane	*The Seeing Stick*	Crowell, 1977	A wise old man teaches a Chinese emperor's blind daughter to "see" by using her fingers to feel.

MIDDLE READERS

AUTHOR	TITLE	PUBLISHER	DESCRIPTION
Bach, Alice	*Waiting for Johnny Miracle*	Harper, 1980	Becky, a high school student, tries to live a normal life as she struggles with the realities of having cancer.
Brancato, Robin	*Winning*	Knopf, 1977	Gary begins to question his values and his friendships after he is paralyzed in a football accident.
Butler, Beverly Kathleen	*Gift of Gold*	Dodd, 1972	Cathy becomes blind as she is about to enter college and must deal with family and friends who doubt her ability to cope with life.
Butler, Dorothy	*Cushla and Her Books*	Horn Book, 1980	A family uses books to teach and entertain a severely disabled child.
Byars, Betsy	*Summer of the Swans*	Viking, 1970	Sara has a retarded brother, Charlie, whose behavior sometimes tests her love for him and ultimately propels her to new depths of maturity and understanding.
Christopher, Matt	*Long Shot for Paul*	Little, Brown, 1966	Glenn and Judy encounter prejudice and misconceptions as they help and support their thirteen-year-old brother in his effort to learn to play basketball.

AUTHOR	TITLE	PUBLISHER	DESCRIPTION
Cleaver, Vera and Bill	*Me Too*	Harper, 1973	Left to look after her retarded twin for a whole summer, Lydia develops a new understanding about responsibility, love, and success while trying to teach Lornie to be "normal."
DeJong, Meindert	*Journey from Peppermint Street*	Harper, 1968	A young Dutch boy, Siebren, left to stay with a deaf uncle he does not know, learns he has nothing to fear as their friendship develops and deepens.
O'Dell, Scott	*Sing Down the Moon*	Houghton Mifflin, 1970	Tall Boy, a young Navaho, is shot in the arm by white soldiers while trying to protect his people and finds the injury is ruinous to his pride and to his status in the tribe.
Roberts, Willo Davis	*Sugar Isn't Everything*	Atheneum, 1987	Amy, an eleven-year-old diabetic, learns to cope with managing her disease and the strain it places on her relationships with family and friends.
Sutcliff, Rosemary	*The Witch's Brat*	Walck, 1970	A historical tale, set in Norman England, of Lovel, a young boy with a spinal deformity, who gradually comes to believe in himself and his ability to help other people.
Swenson, Judy Harris, and Kunz, Roxanne Brown	*Learning My Way: I'm a Winner!*	Dillon Press, 1986	Dan, a fourth-grader, discusses his learning disability and the positive ways he is trying to deal with the situation.

AUTHOR	TITLE	PUBLISHER	DESCRIPTION
YOUNG ADULTS			
Bradbury, Diana	*The Girl Who Wanted Out*	Scholastic, 1981	Andie must learn to cope with a changed life after she is paralyzed and confined to a wheelchair in a car accident which kills her boyfriend.
Burch, Robert	*Simon and the Game of Chance*	Viking, 1970	Thirteen-year-old Simon learns to look beyond his own needs to those of others when his mother must be hospitalized for depression after the death of her newborn baby.
Corcoran, Barbara	*Axe-Time, Sword-Time*	Atheneum, 1976	Elinor is a high school senior at the beginning of World War II who learns to deal with problems in reading and learning that occur after she suffers a severe concussion.
Corcoran, Barbara	*A Dance to Still Music*	Atheneum, 1974	When fourteen-year-old Margaret becomes deaf, she encounters difficulty in accepting her mother's disinterest, and frustration with her own increasing difficulty in dealing with her disability.
Hunt, Irene	*Up a Road Slowly*	Follett, 1966	After her mother dies, seven-year-old Julia must live with her austere Aunt Cordelia who demands Julia include Agnes Kilpin, an abused retarded girl, in her plans for a birthday party.
L'Engle, Madeleine	*Camilla Dickinson*	Crowell, 1975	Camilla, upset about her parents' troubled marriage, seeks refuge in David, a badly wounded war veteran who lives his life in constant physical and emotional pain.

AUTHOR	TITLE	PUBLISHER	DESCRIPTION
Neufeld, John	*Lisa, Bright and Dark*	Phillips, 1969	Lisa Shilling's behavior becomes increasingly bizarre and uncontrollable, but her parents fail to respond to her pleas for help until she finally attempts suicide.
Neufeld, John	*Touching*	Phillips, 1970	Harry Walsh learns to care about his new stepsister, Twink, who is severely afflicted with cerebral palsy and can barely communicate with him and other family members.
Rabe, Berneice	*Margaret's Moves*	Dutton, 1987	Margaret, a spunky girl, decides her old wheelchair must go and becomes determined to earn enough money to buy herself a new, light-weight model.
Sullivan, Tom, and Gill, Derek	*If You Could See What I Hear*	Harper, 1975	A young blind man recalls his struggle to succeed academically and socially despite his disability.
Walsh, Jill Paton	*Goldengrove*	Farrar, Straus Giroux, 1972	A young girl becomes involved with a blind professor and begins to examine the barriers that interfere with personal relationships.
Webster, Elizabeth	*To Fly a Kite*	St. Martin's, 1987	An eighteen-year-old British girl, Ellie Foster, escapes from a home for the mentally handicapped and encounters a young concert pianist whose career has been cut short by a stroke.

APPENDIX B List of formal tests and informal assessment instruments

Gloria B. Smith, Rider College

Appendix B's list of tests and assessment instruments should be useful to teachers, reading specialists, and other educators. Formal tests are listed first; informal tests, next. The tests are arranged alphabetically by title. For each item, you will find the name of the test given, the author, the date of most recent revision or publication, and the publisher or the company from whom the material is available. A brief description of the test follows the identifying data.

FORMAL TESTS

Intelligence Tests

California Test of Mental Maturity (CTB/McGraw-Hill, 1963). Provides separate IQs for reading and nonreading tasks. Grades K–16, six levels. Group intelligence test.

Cognitive Abilities Test, by Robert Thorndike and Elizabeth Hagen (Riverside Publishing, 1986). Grades K–12. Provides separate scores for verbal, quantitative, and nonverbal reasoning abilities. Individual administration.

Henmon-Nelson Tests of Mental Ability, by Joseph L. French, Tom A. Lamke, and Martin J. Nelson (Riverside Publishing, 1973). A primary-level test (no reading required) for grades 3–12. Provides deviation IQ. Group or individual administration.

Kaufman Assessment Battery for Children, by Alan S. Kaufman and Nadeen L. Kaufman (American Guidance Services, 1983). Five global areas of functioning: sequential processing, simultaneous processing, mental processing, composite (sequential plus simultaneous) achievement, and Nonverbal. Individual administration.

Lorge-Thorndike Intelligence Tests, multilevel edition by Irving Lorge and Robert Thorndike (Riverside Publishing, 1964). Provides verbal, nonverbal, and total scores for grades 3–12.

Otis-Lennon School Ability Test, by Arthur S. Otis and Roger T. Lennon (Psychological Corporation, 1982). Measures abstract thinking, reasoning ability, and abilities emphasized in school learning. Grades K–12. Group administration, two forms.

Raven Progressive Matrices, by J. C. Raven (Psychological Corporation, 1977). Nonverbal intelligence test to measure intellectual capacity to form comparisons and reason by analogy. Three forms, available for ages 5–adult. Group or individual administration.

Slosson Intelligence Test, Richard L. Slosson (Slosson Educational Publications, 1981). Provides IQ, mental age, and an analysis of items for information, arithmetic, similarities and differences, vocabulary, digit span, comprehension. All ages—infant to adult. Individual administration.

Stanford-Binet Intelligence Scale, by Robert L. Thorndike, Elizabeth P. Hagen, and Jerome A. Sattler (Riverside Publishing, 1986). Provides measurement of cognitive abilities and single IQ score for very young child to adult. Individual administration.

Test of Nonverbal Intelligence (Language Free), by Linda Brown, Rita J. Sherbenou, Susan K. Johnsen (Pro-Ed, 1982). Problem solving by identifying relationships among abstract figures. Individual administration.

Wechsler Adult Intelligence Scale, by David Wechsler (Psychological Corporation, 1955). Provides verbal, performance, and full-scale IQ scores. Administered by trained psychologist; individual administration.

Wechsler Intelligence Scale for Children (WISC-R), by David Wechsler (Psychological Corporation, 1974). Intelligence test for children; gives verbal score which includes information, comprehension, arithmetic, similarities, vocabulary, and digit span. Performance score provides picture completion, picture arrangement, block design, object assembly, mazes, and coding. The verbal and performance scores yield full-scale IQ scores. Administered by trained psychologist; individual administration.

Wechsler Preschool and Primary Scale of Intelligence, by David Wechsler (Psychological Corporation, 1963). Provides verbal, performance, and full-scale IQ scores for very young children. Administered by trained psychologist; individual administration.

Reading Tests: Comprehension

California Achievement Test (Reading) (CTB/McGraw-Hill, 1985). Subtests: vocabulary, comprehension, English usage and mechanics, spelling, and mathematics. K–12. Group administration.

Clymer-Barrett Readiness Test, rev. ed. by Theodore Clymer and Thomas C. Barrett (Chapman, Brook & Kent, 1983). Measures visual discrimination (recognizing letters and matching words), auditory discrimination (beginning sounds and ending sounds), and visual–motor coordination (completing shapes and copying sentences). Group administration.

Comprehensive Tests of Basic Skills, Spanish edition, developed by Norwalk-LaMirada Unified School District in Southern California (CTB/McGraw-Hill, 1978). A series of achievement tests to estimate basic skills of Spanish-language students.

Diagnostic Reading Scales, by George d. Spache (American Guidance Service, 1981). Tests of oral reading and silent reading. Individual administration.

Durrell Analysis of Reading Difficulties Test, 3rd ed., by Donald D. Durrell and Jane Catterson (Psychological Corporation, 1980). Provides intensive analysis of reading difficulties: silent reading, oral reading, and listening comprehension. Individual administration.

Gates-MacGinitie Reading Tests, 2nd ed., Forms 1, 2, and 3, by Walter H. MacGinitie (Riverside Publishing, 1978). Provides measures of silent reading comprehension and total reading scores for grades 1–12. Group and individual administration.

Gray Oral Reading Test, by J. Lee Wiederholt and Brian R. Bryant (Psychological Assessment Resources, 1985). Two forms; thirteen levels for oral reading and comprehension; reading passages followed by four literal-meaning questions. Individual administration.

Iowa Test of Basic Skills, Houghton-Mifflin Company, 1982. Achievement battery includes vocabulary, comprehension, work-study-skills. Grades 3–9.

Metropolitan Achievement Test (Reading) by Irving Balow, Roger Farr, Thomas Hogan, and George Prescott (Psychological Corporation, 1979). Eight levels—vocabulary, word analysis, comprehension, spelling; also mathematics, social studies, and science in upper-grade levels. K–12. Group administration.

Nelson-Denny Test, by James I. Brown, J. Michael Bennett, and Gerald S. Hanna (Riverside Publishing, 1981). Silent-reading tests for high school students. Self-administered, individual or group.

Peabody Individual Achievement Test (Subtest: Reading Comprehension), by Lloyd M. Dunn and Frederick C. Markwardt, Jr. (American Guidance Service, 1970). Silent reading, single sentences; pictures provide multiple-choice responses. Individual administration.

Stanford Diagnostic Reading Test, by B. Karlsen, R. Madden, and E. F. Gardner (Harcourt Brace Jovanovich, 1983). Two forms and four levels, for ages 7–19. Complete battery for diagnosis of decoding skills, vocabulary levels, and comprehension. Individual and group administration.

Test of Adult Basic Education (CTB/McGraw-Hill, 1978). Measures adult proficiency in vocabulary and comprehension tests at junior-high level, and upper-elementary and upper-primary levels. Two forms, group administration.

The Test of Early Reading Ability, by D. Kim Reid, Wayne P. Hresko, and Donald D. Hammill, 1981, published by American Guidance Service. Assesses knowledge of the alphabet, comprehension, and conventions of reading. Individual administration.

Woodcock Reading Mastery Tests—Revised (Subtest: Passage Comprehension), by Richard W. Woodcock (American Guidance Service, 1980). Individual administration.

Reading Tests: Word Analysis and Decoding/Word Recognition

Diagnostic Reading Scales, by George D. Spache (American Guidance Service, 1981). Subtests for word recognition lists and twelve phonics and word analysis tests. Individual administration.

Doren Diagnostic Reading Test of Word Recognition Skills, by Margaret Doren (American Guidance Service, 1973). Twelve subtests of word recognition skills, letter recognition, sight vocabulary, phonics, and spelling. Individual or group administration.

Durrell Analysis Reading Difficulties Test, 3rd ed., by Donald D. Durrell and Jane H. Catterson (Psychological Corporation, 1980). Word lists, cardboard tachistoscope, word analysis, phonics, writing, and spelling. Individual administration.

Peabody Individual Achievement Tests (Subtest: Word Recognition), by Lloyd M. Dunn and Frederick C. Markwardt, Jr. (American Guidance Service, 1970). Word lists. Individual administration.

Roswell-Chall Diagnostic Reading Test of Word Analysis Skills, by Florence Roswell and Jeanne S. Chall (Essay Press, 1978). Measures decoding and word recognition skills: grades 1–4. Individual administration.

Slosson Oral Reading Test, by Richard L. Slosson, rev. (Slosson Educational Publications, 1981). Oral reading of word list. Individual administration.

Woodcock Reading Mastery Tests—Revised (Subtests: Word Identification, Letter Identification, Word Attack skills), by Richard W. Woodcock (American Guidance Service, 1987). Individual administration.

Reading Tests: Vocabulary–Semantic

Expressive One-Word Picture Vocabulary Test, by Morrison F. Gardner (Academic Therapy Publications, 1979). For students aged 2–12. Stimulus pictures require response; the test has an "upper extension" for older children. Individual administration.

Gates MacGinitie Reading Tests, 2nd ed., Forms 1, 2, and 3, by Walter H. MacGinitie (Riverside Publishing, 1978). Timed vocabulary tests for grades 1–12. Individual or group administration.

Nelson Denny Reading Test, forms E and F, by James I. Brown, J. Michael Bennett, and Gerald S. Hanna (Riverside Publishing, 1981). Fifteen-minute timed vocabulary test; high-school and college level. Self-administered; individual or group administration.

Peabody Picture Vocabulary Test—Revised, forms L and M, by Lloyd M. and Leota M. Dunn (American Guidance Service, 1981). Measures vocabulary and verbal ability. Individual administration.

Receptive One-Word Picture Vocabulary Test, by Morrison F. Gardner (Academic Therapy Publications, 1985). Child responds to stimulus word by choosing picture from a multiple-choice format. Individual administration.

Woodcock Reading Mastery Tests (Subtest: Word Comprehension), by Richard W. Woodcock (American Guidance Service, 1987). Individual administration.

Spelling Tests

Diagnostic Spelling Potential Test, by John Arena (Slosson Educational Publications, 1978). Four subtests: spelling, word recognition, visual recognition, and auditory–visual recognition. Individual administration.

Doren Diagnostic Reading Test of Word Recognition Skills, by Margaret Doren (American Guidance Service, 1973). Subtest: Spelling, both phonemic and nonphonemic. Group or individual administration.

Peabody Individual Achievement Tests (Subtest: Spelling), Lloyd M. Dunn and Frederick C. Markwardt, Jr. (American Guidance Service, 1970). Multiple-choice format. Individual administration.

Test of Written Spelling, by Stephen Larsen and Donald Hammill (Slosson Educational Publications, 1976). Subtests for spelling of predictable words, unpredictable words, and combined sets of words. Individual or group administration.

Writing Tests

The Picture Story Language Test (PSLT), by Helmer Myklebust (Grune & Stratton, 1965). Measures language disorders—using picture-card stimulus—as well as productivity, syntax, and abstract–concrete language. Individual or group administration.

The Test of Written Language, Donald D. Hamill and Stephen C. Larsen (American Guidance Service, 1983). Six subtests: thematic maturity, spelling, vocabulary, word usage, style and handwriting, and total writing quotient.

Auditory Tests

Audiometer, by Maico. Hearing Instruments (Maico, NA). Individually administered screening for preschool through adult. Using audiometer, can provide information about auditory acuity. Screening only: Evidence of hearing loss should be confirmed by hearing specialists.

Auditory Discrimination Test, by Joseph M. Wepman (Language Research Associates, 1978). Measures child's ability to discriminate between sounds. Individual administration.

Goldman-Fristoe-Woodcock Auditory Skills Test Battery, by Ronald Goldman, Macalyne Fristoe, and Richard W. Woodcock (American Guidance Service, 1976). Five subtests: Auditory Selective Attention Test; Diagnostic Auditory Discrimination Test, Parts 1, 2, and 3; and Auditory Memory Test. Individual administration.

Test of Auditory–Perceptual Skills, by Morrison F. Gardner (Children's Hospital of San Francisco, 1985). Test of auditory number, sentence, and word memory; auditory word discrimination, processing, and interpretation of directions; and includes a hyperactivity scale.

Visual Tests

Bender-Gestalt Test for Young Children, by Elizabeth Koppitz (Grune & Stratton, 1963). Used to assess visual–perceptual skills and perceptual–motor integration. Individual administration.

Keystone Visual Screening Tests, by Keystone View (Keystone View, Division of Mast Development Company, 1969). Visual screening test for preschool through adult levels. Uses a Keystone Telebinocular machine and provides screening tests for far-point and near-point vision and fusion. Individual administration.

Test of Visual–Perceptual Skills, by Morrison F. Gardner (Special Child Publications, 1985). Measures visual discrimination, visual memory, visual–spatial relationships, visual form constancy, visual sequential memory, visual figure–ground perception, and visual closure. Individual administration.

Motor Skills Test

Bruininks-Oseretsky Test of Motor Proficiency, by Robert H. Bruininks (American Guidance Service, 1978). For ages 4–15. Assesses motor performance, and fine and gross motor skills. Individual administration.

Tests for Infants and Preschool Children

Bayley Scales of Infant Development, by Nancy Bayley (Psychological Corporation, 1969). Provides mental scale, motor scale, and infant behavior record. Individual administration.

Gesell Developmental Schedules, by Arnold Gesell and recently revised by Knobloch, Stevens, and Malone (Gesell Institute, 1980). Measures infant responses for motor, language, adaptive, and personal–social behavior. New version distinguishes fine- from gross-motor behavior. Used in medical settings. Individual administration.

McCarthy Scales of Children's Abilities, by Dorothea McCarthy (Psychological Corporation, 1972). Used for preschool children. Measures cognitive abilities, including verbal, perceptual/performance and quantitative, memory index, and motor index. Individual administration.

Learning Disabilities Tests

Slingerland Screening Tests for Identifying Children with Specific Language Disability, by Beth H. Slingerland (Western Psychological Services, 1974). Four forms (A–D) for grades 1–6. Provides information on student's ability to copy from near and far point; tests visual–perception–memory linkage, auditory–perception–memory linkage, and auditory–visual linkage. Group or individual administration.

Oral Language Tests

Assessment of Children's Language Comprehension, Rochana Foster, Jane Giddan, and Joel Stark (Consulting Psychologists Press, 1972). Assesses receptive language disorders in young children. Individual administration.

Carrow Elicited Language Inventory, Elizabeth Carrow-Woolfolk (Teaching Resources, 1974). Measures grammatical structure of child's expressive language. Individual administration.

Cognitive Abilities Test (multilevel edition, form 3), Robert L. Thorndike and Elizabeth P. Hagen (Riverside Publishing, 1978). (Listed also under Intelligence Tests.) Individual administration.

Detroit Tests of Learning Aptitude, rev. ed., by Donald D. Hammill (Pro-Ed, 1985). Tests language proficiency in the following areas: word opposites, sentence imitation, oral directions, word sequences, story construction, object sequences, symbolic relations, word fragments, and letter sequences. Individual administration.

Developmental Sentence Analysis, by Laura L. Lee (Northwestern University Press, 1974). Assesses grammatical structure and syntactic development of young children. Individual administration.

Language Assessment Battery, Spanish-Language Tests, by Staff of the New York City Board of Education (Riverside Publishing, 1977). Provides measure of communication skills for Spanish-speaking students. Individual administration.

Peabody Picture Vocabulary Test, rev. ed., Lloyd M. and Leota M. Dunn (American Guidance Service, 1981). (Listed also under Vocabulary-Semantic.) Individual administration.

Stanford-Binet Intelligence Scale, by Robert L. Thorndike, Elizabeth P. Hagen, and Jerome Satter, Riverside Publishing Co., 1986. (Listed also under Intelligence Tests.)

Test for Auditory Comprehension of Language, by Elizabeth Carrow-Woolfolk (Teaching Resources, 1973). Assesses auditory comprehension of language—both English and Spanish tests available. Individual administration.

Test of Language Development—Primary, by Phyllis L. Newcomer and Donald D. Hammill (Pro-Ed, 1977). Provides information on spoken language, semantics, and receptive and expressive language. Individual administration.

Test of Language Development—Intermediate, by Phyllis L. Newcomer and Donald D. Hammill (Pro-Ed, 1982). Provides information on understanding language (semantics), sentence combining, word ordering, and grammatic comprehension. Individual administration.

Wechsler Intelligence Scale for Children (WISC-R), by David Wechsler (Psychological Corporation, 1974). (Listed also under Intelligence Tests.)

Self-Concept Scales

Coopersmith Self-Esteem Inventories, by Stanley Coopersmith (Consulting Psychologists Press, 1981). For ages 8–15. Shows relationship of academic achievement and personal satisfaction in school. (There is an adult form of this inventory, but there is no normative data for it.) Self-administered; group or individual administration.

Piers-Harris Children's Self-Concept Scale, rev. ed., by Ellen V. Piers and Dale Harris (Western Psychological Services, 1984). Children report on conscious self-perceptions. Six subscales: Behavior, Intellectual and School Status, Physical Appearance and Attributes, Anxiety, Popularity, and Happiness and Satisfaction. Individual or group administration.

The Tennessee Self-Concept Scale, by William H. Fitts (Western Psychological Services, 1965). Two forms—counseling, and clinical and research (both use same test but have different scoring and profiling systems). Used for ages 12 and older (sixth-grade reading level); 100 self-descriptive statements. Self-administered; either individually or group.

INFORMAL TESTS

Reading Tests

Advanced Reading Inventory, by Jerry L. Johns (William C. Brown Publishing, 1981). Vocabulary tests, comprehension tests (either multiple-choice or oral response), and cloze tests. Individual administration.

Basic Reading Inventory (preprimer through grade 8), by Jerry L. Johns (Kendall-Hunt Publishing, 1985). Vocabulary and comprehension tests (oral or written responses). Individual administration.

Botel Reading Inventory, by Morton Botel (Follett, 1978). Word-recognition test, phonemic inventory, and word-opposites test. Individual administration.

Botel Reading Milestone Tests (Foundation Subtests: Decoding/Comprehension), by Morton Botel (Botel/Shepherd Associates, 1981). Grades 1–3. Six subtests of word recognition and decoding.

Botel Reading Milestone Tests (Advanced Subtests), by Morton Botel (Botel/Shepherd Associates, 1981). Grades 4–13. Assesses comprehension and reading skills.

Classroom Reading Inventory, 6th ed., by N. J. Silvaroli (Wm. C. Brown, 1986). Provides diagnostic information, graded word lists and oral reading of graded paragraphs. Individual or group administration.

Decoding Inventory, 2nd ed., by H. D. Jacobs and L. W. Searfoss (Kendall-Hunt Publishing, 1986). Phonics, structural analysis, context clues, readiness for decoding. Grades 1–8. Individual administration.

(Book) *The Early Detection of Reading Difficulties; a Diagnostic Survey with Recovery Procedures,* 2nd ed., by Marie M. Clay (Heinemann, 1979). A diagnostic survey of reading behavior—responses to books, letter identification, concepts about print, word tests, writing tests; and a prescriptive program for use after diagnosing the student's problems.

(Book) *Informal Reading Diagnosis: A Practical Guide for the Classroom Teacher,* by Thomas Potter and Swenneth Rae, 2nd. ed. (Prentice Hall, 1981). Provides informal tests and assessment tools for oral and silent reading, visual memory, auditory memory, etc., which teachers are permitted to duplicate. Excellent source of informal test material.

Johnston Informal Reading Inventory, by M. C. Johnston (Educational Publications, 1982). Silent reading comprehension (reading levels 8–16 years), oral reading, word opposites, and synonyms. Group and individual administration.

Performance Assessment in Reading (PAIR) (CTB/McGraw-Hill, 1981). Minimal-competency test for junior high school students.

Prescriptive Reading Inventory Reading Systems 1 and 2, by Staff of CTB/McGraw-Hill (CTB/McGraw-Hill, 1980). Test of oral language, word-attack skills, comprehension, and study skills. Group and individual administration.

Reading Miscue Inventory, by Yetta Goodman and C. Burke (Macmillan, 1972). Test of comprehension and analysis of "miscues"—substitutions readers make. Oral reading. Individual administration.

Reading Miscue Inventory: Alternative Procedures, by Yetta M. Goodman, Dorothy J. Watson, and Caroline L. Burke (Richard C. Owen Publishers, 1987). Oral reading miscue analysis, individual administration. Apple computer system disk available.

Oral Language

Oral Language Evaluation, 2nd ed., by Nicholas Silvaroli, Jann Skinner, and J. O. "Rocky" Maynes, Jr. EMC (1985). Establishes a beginning oral language level in English or Spanish. Assesses beginning oral language, diagnoses language needs, and prescribes instructional activities.

Record of Oral Language and Biks and Gutches, by Marie Clay, Malcolm Gill, Ted Glynn, Tony McNaughton, and Keith Salmon (Heinemann Publishers, 1983). Contains lists of sentences which children repeat; there are instructions about scoring the oral language.

A Way with Words, by Cecil Kovac and Stephen R. Cahir (Center for Applied Linguistics, 1981). Book and tapes which illustrate functional language—sounds, vocabulary, and grammar—with emphasis on semantics and pragmatic use of language.

Spelling

Spellmaster, by Claire Cohen and Rhoda Abrams (CTB/McGraw-Hill[1], 1976). Tests three categories of words: regularly spelled words, irregularly spelled words, and homonyms.

The Beginnings of Writing, by C. A. Temple, R. G. Nathan, and N. A. Burris (Allyn & Bacon, 1982). Informal measures for prephonemic spelling, early phonemic spelling, letter name spelling, and correct spelling.

Writing

Stanford Writing Assessment Program Guide, by Eric Garder, Robert Callis, Jack Merwin, and Herbert Rudman (Psychological Corporation, 1983). Assesses students' writing, from grade 4 through high school. Four types of informative writing are assessed—describing, narrating, explaining, and reasoning; six dimensions of writing are assessed—general merit, quantity and quality of ideas, organization, wording, syntax, and mechanics. Scoring must be by at least two rating teachers.

Test of Written English, by Velma Andersen and Sheryl Thompson (Slosson Educational Publications, 1979). An informal test for assessing capitalization, punctuation, written expression, and paragraph writing.

Attitudinal Inventory

Dulin-Chester Reading Attitude Scale, Form 1, by K. L. Dulin and R. D. Chester (International Reading Association, 1980). Test of middle- and secondary-school pupils' attitudes toward reading. Group administration.

LIST OF PUBLISHERS AND ADDRESSES

Academic Therapy Publications, 20 Commercial Boulevard, Novato, CA 94947.
Addison-Wesley Publishing Co., 1 Jacob Way, Reading, MA 01867. (Reading tests now available from CTB/McGraw-Hill.)
Allyn & Bacon, 7 Wells Ave., Newton, MA 02159.
American College Testing Program, P. O. Box 168, Iowa City, IA 52240.
American Guidance Service, Inc., Publishers' Building, Circle Pines, MN 55014.
American Testronics, P. O. Box 2270, Iowa City, IA 52244.
William C. Brown Co., 2460 Kerper Blvd., Dubuque, IA 52001. Center for Applied Linguistics, 3520 Prospect St., NW, Washington, DC 10007.
California Test Bureau, CTB/McGraw-Hill, Del Monte Research Park, Monterey, CA 93940.
Center for the Study of Reading, 51 Gerty Dr., University of Illinois, Champaign, IL 61820.
Chapman, Brook & Kent, 1215 De la Vina St., Suite F, P. O. Box 21008 Santa Barbara, CA 93121.
College Reading Asociation, c/o Dr. James Layton, 3340 S. Danbury Ave., Springfield, MO 65807.
Committee on Diagnostic Reading Tests, Mountain Home, NC 28758.
Consulting Psychologists Press, 577 College Avenue, Palo Alto, CA 94306.
Educational and Industrial Testing Service, P. O. Box 7234, San Diego, CA 92107.
Educational Records Bureau, P. O. Box 619, Princeton, NJ 08541-0001.
Educational Testing Service, Princeton, NJ 08541-0001.
Eric Clearinghouse on Tests, Educational Testing Service, Princeton, NJ 08540.
Essay Press, P. O. Box 2323, LaJolla, CA 92037.
Follett Publishing Co., 1010 W. Washington Blvd., Chicago, IL 60607.
Guidance Testing Associates, P. O. Box 28096, San Antonio, TX 78228.
Harcourt Brace Jovanovich (see The Psychological Corporation).
Heinemann Educational Books, 4 Front St., Exeter, NH 03833.
Houghton Mifflin Company (see Riverside Publishing Company).
International Reading Association, 800 Barksdale Rd., Newark, DE 19714.
Kendall/Hunt Publishing Co., 2460 Kerper Blvd., Dubuque, IA 52001.
Keystone View Co., 2212 E. 12th St., Davenport, IA 52803.
Language Research Associates, P. O. Box 2085, Palm Springs, CA 92262.
Macmillan Publishing Co., 866 Third Ave., New York, NY 10022.
Maico Hearing Instruments, 7375 Bush Lake Rd., Minneapolis, MN 55435.
Mast Development Co., 2212 E. 12th St., Davenport, IA 52803.
Charles E. Merrill Publishing Company, 1300 Alum Creek Dr., Columbus, OH 43216. (All Charles E. Merrill tests are now distributed by the Psychological Corporation.)
National Council of Teachers of English, 1111 Kenyon Rd., Urbana, IL 61801.
Northwestern University Press, 1735 Benson Ave., Evanston, IL 60201.
Orton Dyslexia Society, 724 York Rd., Baltimore, MD 21204.
Prentice Hall, Route 9W, Englewood Cliffs, NJ 07632.
Pro-Ed, 5341 Industrial Oaks Boulevard, Austin, TX 78735.
Psychological Assessment Resources, P. O. Box 998, Odessa, FL 33556.
The Psychological Corporation, 555 Academic Court, San Antonio, TX 78204-0952.
Psychologists and Educators, 999 Executive Parkway, Suite 120, St. Louis, MO 63141.
Psychological Test Specialists, Box 9229, Missoula, MT 59807.
Publishers Test Service, 2500 Garden Road, Monterey, CA 93940.
Reading Is Fundamental, 2500 L'Enfant Plaza, Smithsonian Institute, Washington, DC 20560.

Richard C. Owen, Inc., P. O. Box 819, Rockefeller Center, New York, NY 10185.
Riverside Publishing Company, 84209 Bryn Mawr Avenue, Chicago, IL 60631.
Scholastic Book Services, 50 W. 44th St., New York, NY 10036.
Scholastic Testing Service, 480 Meyer Road, Bensenville, IL 60106.
Science Research Associates, 155 North Wacker Drive, Chicago, IL 60606.
Scott, Foresman and Company (see American Testronics).
Slosson Educational Publications, P.O. Box 280, East Aurora, NY 14052.
Special Child Publications, P. O. Box 33548, Seattle, WA 98133.
Stoelting Company, 1350 South Kostner, Chicago, IL 60623.
Teachers College Press, 1234 Amsterdam Ave., New York, NY 10027.
Teaching Resources Corporation, 50 Pond Park Rd., Hingham, MA 02043.
United Educational Services, P. O. Box 357, East Aurora, NY 14052.
Western Psychological Services, 12031 Wilshire Boulevard, Los Angeles, CA 90025.

INDEX

Aardema, V., 366
Abrams, J., 279, *282*
Abuse, drug, 272–74
Acuity, auditory, 18–19, 257–63
Adams, R.S., 34, *43*, 370
Adelman, C., 39, *44*
Adler, S., *282*
Agnew, A.T., 203, *239*
Agraphia, 84
Alcohol abuse, 272–74
Alda, A., 360
Alexia, 21*n*
Allard, H., 113
Allegen, 265
Allen, P.D., *190*
Allergies, 264–69, 303–4
Allington, R.L., 147, 176, *190*, 275–76, *282*
Alphabet books, 360
Altwerger, B., 202, *240*
Alvermann, D.E., 162, *190*
America (Drewry & O'Connor), 338
Anderson, R.C., 206, *240*
Andrews, J.F., 258, 261, *282*
Anomalies syndrome, 83–84
Aparaxia, 84
Archambault, J., 362
Argument text structure, 167
Ashton-Warner, S., 84, *114*, 214, *239*
Assessment of Children's Language Comprehension, 52
Assessment over time, 5
Astigmatism, 248, 256
Attending to task, 19
Attitudes, student, 37–38
Attitudinal inventory, 387
Au, 201
Audience awareness, 104–9
Audiogram, 342
Audiometer, 260
Auditory acuity, 18–19, 257–63, 383–84
Awareness of print, 197, 198–202

Babbitt, N., 368
Bach, A., 376
Baghban, M., 87, *114*, 184, *190*
Baldwin, J., 371
Baldwin, R.S., 147, 167, *193*, 216, 218, *240*, 263, *284*
Barron, R.F., 167, *190*
Basal-reader approach, 263
Basic Reading Inventory (Johns), 234–35
Baskin, B.H., 374
Bates, M., 276, *283*
Bates, R.A., 273, *283*
Bauer, M., 368
Baumann, J.F., 207, 230, *240*
Baxter, D.H., 270, 271, *284*
Bean, T.W., 140, 145, 147, 167, *193*, 216, 218, *240*, 263, *284*

Beck, I.L., 206, *239*, 240
Beck, J., 147, *190*
Beginning writer, 89–90
Behaviors as indicators of physical problems, 251, 260, 273
Bennett, S.N., 37, *43*
Betts, E.A., 128, 130, *190*, 211, *239*
Biddle, B.J., 34, *43*
Biklen, S.K., *43*
Binocular coordination, 248
Bissex, G.L., 87, *114*, 180, *190*
Blakey, J., *241*
Bloom, M.D., 273, *282*
Blue, R., 374
Body language, 31
Bogdan, R.C., *43*
Bond, G.L., 19, *24*, 244, 258, *282*
Books
  alphabet, 360
  children making own, 205–6
  dealing with disabilities or handicapping condition, 373–79
  to guide students to write, 112–13
  to promote reading comprehension, 365–73
  self-selecting, 171–72
  wordless, 359
  See also Literature
Boothby, P.R., 162, *190*
Bormuth, J.R., 59, *79*, 124, *190*, 191
Botel, M., 50, 59, *79*
Botel Reading Milestone Test, 337–38
Bradbury, D., 378
Brain defects, organic, 276–80
Brainstorming, 76–78, 140–41, 160–62, 351
Brancato, R., 376
Brett, J., 362
Bridge, C.A., 146, *191*
Bridwell, L.S., 185, *191*
Brightman, A., 374
Brophy, J.E., 37, *43*
Brown, A., 147, *193*
Brown, A.L., 122, *191*
Brown, C.H., *283*
Brown, D.A., 244, *282*
Brown, J.S., *191*
Bruner, S.J., 47, *79*
Burch, R., 378
Burke, C., *80*, 87, *114*, 180, *192*
Burnford, S., 368
Burningham, J., 113
Burris, N.A., 87, *115*, 223, 226, *241*
Burton, M.R., 113
Butler, B.K., 376
Butler, D., 376
Byars, B., 376

Cahir, S., 50, *80*
Caines, J., 113

391

Calfee, R., 230, *239*
Calkins, L.M., 140, *191*
C-A-L-M (Continuous assessment of language model)
  assessing reading comprehension, 131–80
  ethnographic perspective and, 28
  guide to classroom diagnosis, 289, 290
  informal procedures for assessing oral language, 54–70
  propositions underlying, 4–6, 7
  traditional procedures vs., 6–8, 22–23
Cameron, P., 214, *239*
Camperell, K., 162, *193*
Carey, R.F., 122–24, *191*
Carlsen, J.M., 262, *282*
Carlstrom, N.W., 361
Carpenter, P.A., 58, *80*
Carr, J., 79
Carrara, D.H., 185, *192*
Carroll, J.B., 207, *239*
Carrow Elicited Language Inventory, 52
Carrow-Woolfolk, E., 52, 53
Case reports, sample, 330–54
  long-form, 330–47
  short-form, 348–54
Cause/effect text structure, 167
Central nervous system, gross and severe injury or damage to, 277
Cerebral dominance, 20
Charlton-Seifert, J., *282*
Chemical abuse, 272–74
Chemical pollutants, 265
Chiang, B., 278, *282*
Chomsky, N., 79
Choral drama, 72
Choral reading, 72
Christ, A., 276, *284*
Christopher, M., 376
Clark, R.M., 270, 271, *282*
Classroom
  adjustments
    for auditory acuity problems, 260–62
    for students with allergies, 268–69
    for vision problems, 255–57
  environment, 25–45, 295–96
    aspects of, 32–41
    collecting data and, 41–42
    ethnographic perspective, 27–32
    interactional organization, 35–36
    physical, 34–35
    power and group influence, 36–37
  negotiation in, 26
Classroom diagnosis, 287–306
  C-A-L-M guide to, 289, 290
  identifying and assessing problems
    allergies, 266–68
    nutritional deficiencies, 271–72
    vision in, 248–55
  linking diagnostic questions, variables and procedures, 291–93
  organizing and reporting diagnostic information, 293–306
Clavio, D., 205, *239*
Clay, M.M., 14, 50, *80*, 87, *114*, 180, 184, *191*
Cleary, B., 338
Cleaver, B., 368, 377
Cleaver, V., 368, 377

Clinical ecology, 265
Clinical reading diagnosis, 307–56
  case reports, 330–54
    long-form, 330–47
    short-form, 348–54
  cursory screening, 318–26
  referral system, 308–18
    parent information, 312–16
    school information, 317–18
    telephone interview, 310–12
Cloze procedure, 124, 352
Cockrum, W., 206, *239*
Cognition, interdependence between language and, 47
Cognitive Abilities Test: Multilevel Edition, Form 3, 52
Cognitive processing theory of comprehension, 118
Cohen, A.H., 20, *24*, 254, *282*
Cohn, M., *43*, *239*, 278, *282*
Coleman, E.B., 59, *80*
Colin, 213
Collins, A., 122, *191*
Commercial IRIs, 128
Comparison/contrast text structure, 167
Competence, student, 38–39
Composing in guided writing, 143
Compositions, 226–27, 302
Comprehension
  abilities needed for, 121–22
  defining, 120–22
  formal/standardized tools for analyzing, 122–25
  informal tools for assessing, 126–31
  previous notions about, 117–20
  theories, 117–22
  of written coding system, 17–18
  See also Reading comprehension and retention
Conferencing, 141–42
Conrad, P., 371
Context, 216–20
Continuous assessment of language model. *See* C-A-L-M (Continuous assessment of language model)
Controls, language, 14–15, 56, 57
Convergence ability (vision), 253
Cook, B., 113
Cook-Gumperz, J., 181, *191*
Coopersmith Self-Esteem Inventory, 343
Coordination, binocular, 248
Corcoran, B., 378
Craig, H., 360
Crook, W.G., 264–65, *282*
Cross dominance, 20
Culhane, J.W., 124, *193*
Cunningham, 147, 162
Cursory screening, 318–26
Czilco, G.A., *191*
Czira, 124

Dale, E., 207, *239*
Dale, P., 48, *80*
D'Allesandro, C., *239*
Data
  collecting classroom environment, 41–42
  preobservational, 29
Davies, P., 207, *239*
Davis, T., 371
Dawkins, 50

Deafness, 257–63
Deborah, J., *43*
Decoding, 230–38, 382. *See also* Phonics
Degen, B., 213, *239*
DeJong, M., 377
Delamont, S., 26, 34, 38, *43*, *44*
Delton, J., 113
Demetz, H., 371
Deno, S.L., 278, *282*
Denton, P., 38, *43*
dePaola, T., 359, 361, 366
de Regniers, B., 361
Description, procedures for, 90–91
Desensitization treatment, 266
Designated periods for writing, 109
Developmental Sentence Analysis, 52
Diagnosis
 literature for, 357–79
 purpose of, 3–4
 See also Classroom diagnosis; Clinical reading diagnosis
Diagnostic/prescriptive model, 6
Diagnostic process, 11
Diagnostic propositions, 4–6, 7
Diagnostic variables, 10–24
 differences between C-A-L-M and medical model, 22–23
 effective learning environments, 12–13
 linking questions and procedures and, 291–93
 self-esteem and self-confidence, 21–22
 See also Oral language fluency; Physical factors affecting language learning; Written language fluency
Dialogue journals, 185–89, 353
DiBenedetto, B., 276, *284*
Dictionary of Reading (Abrams), 279
Diet, 20–21, 265, 269–72
Directed reading activity, 351
Directional confusion, 20
Directionality concepts, 202
Direct observation, 29
Disabilities
 books dealing with, 373–79
 tests for learning, 384
Distinct clinical syndromes, 277
Doake, D.B., 184, *191*
Dolch, E.W., 207, *2939*
Dominance, cerebral, 20
Donovan, J., 368
Drama for stimulating oral language, 71–78
Dreher, M.J., *191*, 352, 354
Drewry, H., 338
Drug abuse, 272–74
Drum, P., 230, *239*
Dunkeld, C.B., 131, *193*
Dunn, L.M., 53
Durrell, D.D., 221, 222, *239*
Durrell Analysis of Reading Difficulty Test, 336–37
Dysgraphia, 21*n*, 84
Dyslexia, 21*n*, 279–80
Dyson, 184, *191*

Earle, R.A., 167, *191*
Eastman, P.D., *80*, 113, 213, *239*, 360, 362

Echo reading, 73
Eckert, A., 369
Ecology, clinical, 265
Editing, 144–45
Eeds, M., 233, *239*
Efron, M., 256, *283*
Einsel, W., 214, *239*
Elimination data, 266
Elliott, G., *241*
Elliott, S., *239*
Emas, T.H., 18, *24*
Emberley, E., *80*
Emberly, B., 363
Emergent writer, 90
Environment
 adjusting, 71–76
 classroom. *See* Classroom
 interactive, 180–89
 learning, 12–13
 for learning to write, 87
 natural, 173–74
 reading, 8
 recreational, 172–74, 175
 "work-along-side-of", 182
 See also Settings
Environmental reading, 198
Erickson, F., 35–36, *44*
Ethnographic interview, 31–32, 33
Ethnographic perspective, 27–32, 41
Ethnographic procedures to assess reading comprehension, 137–40
Ewoldt, C., 261, *282*
Expectations, 37, 121
Explanation, procedures for, 94–95
Expository text structures, 167
Eye-focusing problems, 256–57
Eye-teaming problems, 257
Eye-tracking problems, 256

Fagan, W.T., 59, *80*
Fairbanks, 206
Family, alcohol and drug abuse and, 273
Fanshawe, E., 375
Farber, N., 360
Farr, R., 122–24, *191*, 320
Farsightedness, 247, 248, 256
Fatio, L., 365
Fernald, G.M., 214, *239*
Ferrieco, E., 180, *191*
Field notes, 29–31
Fields, P., 124, *191*
Fifteen (Cleary), 338
Fist-full-of-words rule, 171, 172
Fitzgerald, J., 162, *191*
Flake, E., *241*
Fleischman, S., 369
Fleming, J.P., *283*
Flood, J., 224, *239*
Florio, S., 35–36, *44*
Fluency. *See* Oral language fluency; Written language fluency
Formal assessment during cursory screening, 319
Formal assessment tools for analyzing text comprehension, 122–25

Formal interview, 32, 33
Formal tests, 380–86
Form concepts, 202
Forms in written composition, assessing, 90
Foster, 147, 162
Foster, R., 52
Fountoukidis, D., 207, *239*
Fox, P., 369
Francis, W.N., 207, *240*
Frost, R., 361
Fry, E.B., 207, *239*
Fryed, P., *283*
Furlong, V., 36, *43*
Fusion, 247, 248

Gaer, E.P., 58, 59, *80*
Gainer, 124
Gaines, A.S., *191*
Gaines, E., 371
Galdone, P., *80*
Games, word identification, 215
Ganschow, L., 226, *239*
Gardner, R., 86
Gates, A.J., 176, *191*
Genishi, C., 184, *191*
Gentile, L.M., 154, 176, *191*, 280, *282*
Geoffrion, L., *282*
Gerrard, R., 361
Giddan, J., 52
Gill, D., 379
Gill, M., 50, *80*
Gillet, J.W., 4, *8*, 48, *80*, 244, 249, 257, *282*
Glass, G.G., 20, *24*, 237, *239*
Glazer, S.M., 50, 56, 58, *80*, 87, *114*, 117, 154, *191*, 272, *282*
Glines, D., 265, 268, *282*
Glynn, T., 50, *80*
Goffman, E., 38, *43*
Good, T.L., 37, *43*
Goodall, J., 359
Goodman, K.S., 59, *80*, *114*, 120, 131, 181, *192*, 198, *239*
Goodman, Y., 197, 202, *240*
Gormley, K.A., *282*
Gough, P.B., 206, 207, *240*
Grahame, K., 366
Granowsky, A., 50, 59, 79
Graphic organizers, 167–69, 340
Graphophonic cue system, 233
Graves, D.H., 92, *114*, 140–42, *192*
Greene, B., 369
Greene, F.P., *80*, 229, *240*, 733
Greenhalgh, C., 98, *114*
Greenwald, M.S., 273, *282*
Griffin, W.J., 58, 59, *80*
Groff, P., 221, *240*
Group influence in classroom, 36–37
Grune, 86
Guest, J., 372
Guided retelling procedures, 146–53, 338–40, 350
Guided writing procedures, 140–46
Gumperz, J.J., 105, *114*, 181, *191*
Guthrie, L.F., 27, *43*

Hagen, E.P., 52, 53
Haley-James, S., 83, *114*
Hall, M., 263, *282*
Hall, W.S., 27, *43*
Halliday, M.A.K., 47, 48, *80*, 180, *192*
Hallinan, M., 44
Hamill, 86
Hamilton, E., 270, 271, *282*
Hamilton, G., 87, *114*
Hamilton, V., 372
Hammill, D.D., 53
Handicapping conditions, books dealing with, 373–79
Hannan, E., 87, *114*
Harman, S., 279, 280, *283*
Harris, 319
Harris, A.J., 207, 221, *240*, 244, 320
Harris, K.H., 374
Harris, L.A., *283*
Harris, T.L., 19–21, *24*, 258, 279–80, *283*
Harste, J.C., 87, *114*, 180, *192*
Hasenstab, M., *283*
Hearing-impaired students, accommodating, 262–63
Hearing problems, 18–19, 257–63
Heath, S.B., 181, *192*
Heckelman, R.G., 73, *80*
Henderson, L., 207, *240*
Henk, W., 236, *240*
Herman, P.A., 206, *240*
Herndon, J., *43*
Hidden allergies, 265
Hill, D., *240*
Hirsh-Pasek, K., *283*
Hissey, J., 365
Hoban, R., 365
Hodge, R.E., 258
Hodges, M., 367
Hodges, R.E., 19–21, *24*, 279–80, *283*
Hoffman, S., 181, *192*
Holdaway, D., 14
Holistic scoring systems, 97–102
Hooper, M., *80*
Humor, 39
Hunt, I., 378
Hunt, K.W., 56, 58, 59, *80*
Hutchins, P., *80*, 113, 363
Huxley, A., 12, *24*
Hyman, T.S., 367
Hynd, C.R., 279, *283*
Hynd, G.W., 279, *283*
Hyperactivity, 19, 271
Hyperopia, 247, 248
Hypoproteinosis, 270–71
Hypotheses, 27–28

Independence, building, 353–54
Infants, tests for, 384
Inferencing ability, comprehension and, 121
Informal interviews, 31–32
Informal reading inventory (IRI), 128–34
Informal tests and tools for assessment, 386–87
  of comprehension, 126–31
  during cursory screening, 320–25
  of oral language, 50–54
  of vision, 252–55

Information, parent and school, 312–18
Informational reading, 198
Instruction, literature for, 357–79
Instructional change, 3–4
Instructional settings, reading comprehension assessment procedures in, 136–37. *See also* Classroom
Instructional strategies for enhancing oral language, 71–78
Intellectual assessment, sample of, 331–36
Intelligence tests, 319, 380–81
Interaction with others, 323–25
Interactive settings
 assessing oral language in, 66–70
 creating, for diagnosis, 182–89
 organization in classroom, 35–36
 reading comprehension assessment procedures in, 180–89
Interviews
 to assess reading comprehension, 137–38
 during cursory screening, 325–26
 ethnographic, 31–32, 33
 telephone, 310–12
Inventory for assessing print awareness, 199
IRI (informal reading inventory), 128–34
Iron deficiency, 271, 272
Irwin, P.A., 151, 152, *192*

Jackson, P.W., 37, *43*
Jacobs, H.D., 234–36, *240*
Jacobson, M.D., 207, *240*
Jacqui, 213
Jagger, A.M., 185, *192*
James, 34
Jeffers, S., 367
Jewell, M.G., 203, *240*
Johns, J.L., *192*, 208, 234, *240*
Johnson, D.D., 121, *193*, 207, 218, 230, *240*, 263, *283*
Johnson, P.H., *192*
Jordan, J., 37, *43*
Journals
 dialogue, 185–89, 353
 using, with beginning readers, 205
"Junk foods", 265
Jupo, F., 375
Jurich, A.P., *283*
Jurich, J.A., 273, *283*
Just, M.A., 58, *80*

Kaltman, H., 105, *114*
Kamil, M.C., *193*
Kampwirth, T.J., 276, *283*
Karlsen, M., 86
Kaufman, N.L., 278, *283*
Kavale, K., *283*
Keats, E.J., *80*, 359
Kellam, S.G., *283*
Kellogg, S., 113, 367
Keystone Telebinocular Test of Vision, 342
Keystone Visual Survey Tests, 253–54
King, C.M., 258, *283*

King, D., 181, *192*
King, M.L., 184, *192*
Knowledge, student, 38
 prior, comprehension and, 118–20, 121
Kohl, H.R., *43*
Kolers, P.A., 247, *283*
Kovac, C., 50, *80*
Kreeft, J., 105, *114*
Kroll, B.M., 105, *114*
Kucera, H., 207, *240*
Kuhns, C.O., *240*
Kunz, R.B., 377

Labels, nonspecific, 277–78
Lackey, G.H., 256, *283*
Lalicki, B., 360
Langstaff, J., 361
Langton, J., 369
Language
 body, 31
 controls, 14–15, 56, 57
 functions, classifications of, 48
 interdependence between cognition and, 47
 See also Oral language; Physical factors affecting language learning; Written coding system
Language-experience method, 263
Languaging, 48
Lap approach, 73
Larrick, N., 361
Larsen, 86
Lasker, J., 375
Laskin, K.M., 122, *191*
Laterality or lateral dominance, 20
Leadership functions in classroom, 36
Learning behavior checklist, 304–5
Learning disabilities tests, 384
Learning environments, 12–13
Learning to Read Naturally (Jewell and Zintz), 203
Lee, L.L., 52
Leisure reading, 199
L'Engle, M., 369, 378
Lenski, L., 375
Letter-reversal errors, 278–79
Lewis, C.S., 369
Leys, M., 185, *194*
Liberman, S., 254, *282*
Lindfors, J.W., 47, *80*, 184, *192*
Linear notion of comprehension, 118
Lionni, L., 366
List format, books written in, 113
List-making activities, 109–10, 111
List of constructed words, 234. *See also* Word(s)
Literacy, roots of, 197, 202
Literature
 for diagnosis and instruction, 357–79
 guided retellings of, 339–40
 to guide students to write, using, 112–13
Loban, W.D., 53, 58, 59, *80*
Lobel, A., 360, 363, 366
Locker, T., 367
Lojkutz, S., 272, *284*
Long-term memory, 16–17
Lorge, I., 207, *241*
Loughlin, C.E., 34, 35, *43*

McCaslin, F.S., 206, *239*
McCully, E.A., 359
McDermott, G., 367
McDermott, R.P., 39, *43*
MacDonald, S., 360
McGee, L.M., 162, *192*
McGovern, J., 265, 268, *282*
McKenzie, C., *283*
McKeown, M.G., 147, 162, *190*, 206, *239, 240*
McKinley, R., 372
McMillan, M.M., 176, *191*
McNaughton, T., 50, *80*
Main idea maps, 351
Malnutrition, 270–71
Manning, J., *79*
Manual communication, 261
Manzo, A.V., 155, *192*, 350, 354
Maramus, 270
Markle, A., 237, *240*
Marshall, J., 366
Martin, B., Jr., 362, 363
Martin, D., 270, *283*
Martin, M., 270, *283*
Mason, J.M., 197, 201, *240*
Massie, D.R., 359
Maxwell, W., 372
Mayer, M., *80*, 359, 363, 367
Mayers, F., 360
Maynes, R., 50, *81*
Me Book, The, 205–6
Media reading, 73
Medical model, 6, 22–23
Mehan, H., 39, *43*
Memory, 16–17, 222, 230, 232
Mental abilities, observation of, 320, 321
Mezynski, K., 206, *240*
Milz, V., 184, *192*
Minimal brain dysfunction (MBD), 21n
Mitchell, J.M., 151, 152, *192*
Mixed dominance, 20
Modeling, 142
Modified Key Word Method, 208, 214–16
Modified request, 159–60, 299, 338
Modified request/question-answer procedure, 155–59
Moe, A.J., 207, *240*
Moffett, J., 48, 65, *80*, 105–6, *114*, 160, *192*
Montgomery, E.R., 375
Montgomery, R.A., 113
Moore, C., 362
Moore, D.W., 162, *192*, 240
Moore, S.A., *240*
Morris, J.E., 244, *283*
Morrow, L.M., 50, 56, *80*, 147, 153, 154, 178, *193*
Morrow procedure for conducting and evaluating retellings, 153–55
Mosse, H.L., 277, 280, *283*
Most, B., *80*
Motor control, 19–20, 384
Multiple-choice tests, 123
Myklebust, 86
Myopia, 247, 248

Nagy, W.E., 206, *240*
Naour, P., 275, *283*

Narration, procedures for, 91–94
Narrative writing, assessing, 301–2
Nash, R., 37, *43*
Nathan, R.G., 87, *115*, 223, 226, *241*
National Institute on Drug Abuse, 272
Natural environments, 173–74
Natural language interactions, 180–82
Natural pollutants, 265
Nearsightedness, 247, 248, 256
Negotiation in classroom, 26
Nelson, N.W., 36, *43*
Neufeld, J., 379
Neurological deficits, 21, 276–80
Neuropsychology, 280
Newcomer, P.L., 53
New York State Optometric Association (NYSOA) Screening Battery, 254, 255
Nicholson, T., *240*
Nonspecific labels, 277–78
Normative perceptual performance, assumption of, 275
Norris, R.C., 58, 59, *80*
Northman, J.E., 273, *284*
Norwood, G.R., 270, 271, *283*
Notes, field, 29–31
Notes from a Different Drummer: A Guide to Juvenile Fiction Portraying the Handicapped (Baskin and Harris), 374
Nowosad, J., *239*
Nursery rhymes, introducing, 205
Nutrition, 20–21, 265, 269–72

Observation
  assessing spelling ability through, 222–23
  direct, 29
  guide for recreational settings, 297
  in interactive settings, 182, 183
  of mental abilities, 320, 321
  participant, 27–31, 137
  of reading in multiple settings, 5
  for visual problems, 251
Occupational reading, 199
O'Connor, O., *114*
O'Connor, T., 338
Oculomotor coordination, 247
O'Dell, S., 370, 377
O'Donnell, R., 58, 59, *80*
Omanson, R.C., 206, *240*
Oneal, Z., 372
Oral language
  analysis, sample of, 61–66
  assessment in interactive settings, 66–70
  syntax, developmental trends in, 58–59
  tests, 385, 387
Oral Language Evaluation (Silvaroli, Skinner & Maynes), 50, 51–54
Oral language fluency, 13–15, 46–81, 322, 344, 358
  assessing, 49–54
  books to help develop, 361–64
  C-A-L-M informal procedures, 54–70
  classroom assessment checklist, 300–301
  instructional strategies for enhancing, 71–78
  variables, 48–49
Oral reading formats to assess comprehension, 124–25
Oral retellings, unguided, 177

Organic brain defects, 276–80
Organization
 of diagnostic information, 293
 of information, comprehension and, 121–22
 short- and long-term memory and, 16–17
Orientation concepts, 202
O'Rourke, J., 207, *239*
Ortony, A., 117, *193*

Packard, E., 113, 148
Page, W., 124, *193*
Palincsar, A., 147, *193*
Parent information, 312–16
Participant observation, 27–31, 137
Paterson, K., 370, 372
Patricia, T., 362
Pattern Method of word recognition, 211–14
Peabody Picture Vocabulary Test (PPVT), 53, 332
Pearson, D., *79*
Pearson, P.A., 121, *193*
Pearson, P.D., 83, *115*, 117, 118, *193*, *194*, 218, *240*, 263, *283*
Pearson, P.S., 162, *193*
Pearson, T., 360
Peck, R.N., 162, 373
Perception
 comprehension and, 118–20, 121
 defining, 274–76
 language learning and, 274–76
 as predictions, 15
 senses and, 15
 students' self-perceptions, 174–76
Performance, student, 38–39
Perkins, A., *81*
Perkins, E., 214, *240*
Perl, S., 185, *193*
Personal classroom history, 39–41
Personal spelling words, 224–26
Persuasion, procedures for, 95–96, 97
Pertz, D.L., 20, *24*, 271, *283*
Peterson, P., *44*
Phonemic scoring system, 223–24
Phonic Ear Personal FM hearing system, 262
Phonics, 229. *See also* Decoding
Phonograms, 222
Physical environment of classroom, 34–35
Physical factors affecting language learning, 243–86
 alcohol and drug abuse, 272–74
 allergies, 264–69
 auditory factors, 257–63
 in clinical diagnosis, 342–43
 as diagnostic variables, 18–21
 nutrition, 269–72
 perceptual and neurological factors, 274–81
 role of, 244–46
 visual factors, 246–57
 when to assess, 245
Piaget, J., 105, *114*
Picture Story Language Test, The (PSLT), 86
Pierce, M.A., 373
Pipher, J.R., *284*
Pitch, 258
Polk, J.K., 207, *239*
Pollutants, allergies to, 265

Polson, C.J., 273, *283*
Pople, M.T., 206, *240*
Powell, W.R., 131, *193*
Power, classroom, 36–37
Powers, M.E., 375
Predictions, perceptions as, 15
Prelutsky, J., 363
Preobservational data, 29
Preschool children, tests for, 384
Press, M., 276, *284*
Preview in context, 218–19
Prewriting stage, 88
Print. *See* Written coding system
Problem solution, 95
 activities, 110–12
 format, books written in, 113
 text structure, 167
Product notion of comprehension, 118
Pronunciation, spelling ability and, 222
Protein deficiency, 270–71
Psychological factors in drug and alcohol abuse, 273
Publishers, list of, 388
Putnam, L.R., 20, *24*, 271, *283*

Quackenbush, R., *81*
Quandt, I., 71, *81*
Quantification of retellings, 153–56
Quantitative scoring
 of reading passages, 130–33
 of written language, 96–97
Question-answer relationship approach, 155
Questions, 4
 for conducting formal interviews, 138
 diagnostic, linking variables and procedures and, 291–93
 for formal interview, 32, 33
 guided retellings using, 147
 for informal interview, 31
 restating, 5–6
Quigley, S.P., 258, *283*

Rabe, B., 379
Rabin, A.T., *284*
Rankin, E.F., 124, *193*
Raphael, T.E., 155, *193*
Rapp, D.J., 264, *284*
Raskin, E., 375
Rasmussen, B., 264, 265, *284*
Razzi, J., 113
Readence, J.E., 147, 162, 167, *192*, *193*, 214, 216, 218, 220, *240*, *241*, 263, *284*
Reading
 choral, 72
 deficits, stress from, 176
 defined, 2
 echo, 73
 environmental, 198
 environments, 8
 informational, 198
 leisure, 199
 mechanical aspects of, 202–3
 occupational, 199

Reading (*cont.*)
   print awareness and, 198–99
   television or media, 73
   tests, 381–82, 386–87
   uninterrupted sustained silent, 351
Reading comprehension and retention, 15–17, 116–95, 344
   assessment procedures in interactive settings, 180–89
   C-A-L-M procedures, 131–80
      brainstorming procedures, 160–62
      ethnographic procedures, 137–40
      graphic organizers, 167–69, 340
      guided retelling procedures, 146–53, 338–40, 350
      guided writing procedures, 140–46
      in instructional settings, 136–37
      modified request, 159–60, 299, 338
      modified request/question-answer procedure, 155–59
      Morrow procedure for conducting and evaluating retellings, 153–55
      in recreational settings, 172–74, 175
      self-monitoring devices, 169–71
      self-selecting books, 171–72
      story maps, 162–66
      students' self-perceptions, 174–76
      unguided retelling procedures, 177–80, 338–40, 350
   formal/standardized tools for analyzing, 122–25
   informal tools for assessing, 126–31
   literature to promote, 365–73
   overview of comprehension theories, 117–22
   sample assessment case, 336–41
   testing, 321–22, 336–38, 381–82
Reasoning, procedures for, 95–96, 97
Recall, story maps for better, 162
Recomposing, 144
Reconnaissance phase in participant observation, 27
Reconnoitering, 27
Record of Oral Language (Clay, Gill, Glynn, McNaughton & Salmon), 50–51
Recreational settings, 172–74, 175, 176, 297
Referral
   to allergist, 268
   system, 308–18
      parent interview, 312–16
      school information, 317–18
      telephone interview, 310–12
   to vision specialist, 253, 254
Rehearsal in guided writing, 141
Reporting diagnostic information, 293–306
Reports, guidelines for writing, 328–29
Request procedure, 155, 350
   modified, 159–60, 299, 338
Retelling
   assessing story structure and, 298
   guided, 146–53, 338–40, 350
   Morrow procedure for conducting and evaluating, 153–55
   quantification of, 153–56
   unguided, 177–80, 338–40, 350
Retention of text content. *See* Reading comprehension and retention
Reversal tendencies, 278–79
Rhyming activities, 229
Richardson, E., 276, *284*
Richgels, D.J., 162, *192*
Richmond, B., 207, *239*

Ritty, J.M., 254, *282*
Rivers, C., *284*
Robart, R., 363
Roberts, W.D., 377
Robertson, J.E., 59, *81*
Robinson, H.M., 18, 20–21, *24*, 244, *284*
Role playing, 71
Roth, D., *43*
Rouse, M.W., 256, *284*
Rowls, M.D., 256, *283*
Ruddell, R.B., 58, 59, *81*
Rumelhart, D., 117, 118, 120, *193*
Ryan, J.B., 256, *284*
Rylant, C., 373

Salmon, K., 50, *80*
Salus, P.H., 224, *239*
Samples of oral language, 55–61
Samuels, P., *239*
Saur, L.E., 58, *81*
Sawicki, F., *241*
Sawyer, C., 146, *191*
Scales, self-concept, 385–86
Schatell, B., *193*
Schmiderer, D., 360
Schmuck, P.A., *44*
Schmuck, R.A., *44*
School information, 317–18
School's responsibility for drug education, 273–74
Schubert, D.G., 254, *284*
Schultz, J.J., 35–36, *44*
Scoring
   holistic systems of, 97–102
   phonemic, 223–24
   quantitative
      of reading passages, 130–33
      of written language, 96–97
Screening, cursory, 318–26
Searfoss, L.W., 73, *81*, 154, 214, 220, 234–36, *240*, *241*, 263, *284*
Seating positions, 34
Seeing. *See* Vision
Segmentation, terminable or T-unit, 56–61
Seifert, 271
Self-concept scales, 385–86
Self-confidence, 21–22, 353–54
Self-direction, building, 353–54
Self-esteem, 21–22, 343, 344
Self-evaluation in guided writing, 142–43, 145
Self-monitoring devices, 169–72
Self-perceptions, students', 174–76
Self-selecting books, 171–72
Selznick, R., 71, *81*
Sendak, M., 360, 363, 366
Senses, perceptions and, 15
Settings
   instructional, 136–37
   interactive, 66–70, 180–89
   reading comprehension assessment and, 136–37, 172–74, 175, 180–89
   recreational, 172–74, 175, 176, 297
   See also Classroom; Environment
Seuss, Dr., *81*, 213, *241*, 360, 362, 364, 366
Shanahan, T., 124, *193*

Shape Book, The, 205–6
Shearer, E., 20, *24*
Sherman, R.E., 272, *284*
Shiffrin, R.M., *193*
Short-term memory, 16–17
Show and tell, 74
Sight words, 207
Signs, familiarity with, 201–2
Silberman, C., *44*
Silvaroli, N.J., 50, *81*, 208, 234, *241*
Silverstein, S., *81*, 362
Simon, C.S., *44*
Simple listing text structure, 167
Singer, H., *191*, 352, 354
Sipay, E.R., 221, *240*, 244, 320
Skinner, J.T., 50, *81*
Slosson Intelligence Test (SIT), 331
Small group discussion, 75
Smith, C.B., 140, 145, *193*, 283
Smith, F., 16, *24*, *81*, *114*, 117, 120, *194*, 247, *284*
Smith, G.B., 137, 138, *194*
Sobol, D., 113
Sobol, H., 376
Spache, 319
Spache, E.B., 233, *241*
Spache, G.D., 124, *194*, 233, *241*, 244, 246–47, 253, 255, 260, 262, 276, *284*
Speare, E.G., 370
Spelling, 353
    development, 220–30
        assessing spelling ability and, 221–27
        obstruction, 222
        personal spelling words, 224–26
        phonemic scoring system, 223–24
        spelling in compositions, 226–27
    instructional strategies for, 228–30
    tests, 383, 387
Spiegel, D.L., 162, *191*
Spier, P., 359, 364
Spindler, G., 27, *44*
Spiro, R.J., 122, 123, *194*
Spradley, J.P., 27, 41, *44*
Squire, J.R., 83, *114*
Stahl, A., 90, *115*, 206
Stallard, C., 185, *194*
Standardized assessment tools for analyzing text comprehension, 122–25
Stanford-Binet Intelligence Scale, Fourth Edition, 53
Stanford Writing Assessment Program, 86
Stanovich, K.D., 118, *194*
Stark, J., 52
Staton, J., 185, *194*
Steckiewicz, N., 272, *284*
Stern, M., 273, *284*
Stevens, J.J., Jr., 270, 271, *284*
Stolzberg, M., 254, *282*
Stoodt, B., 59, *81*
Story
    maps, 162–66
    structure and retelling, assessing, 298
    structure worksheet, 352
Strange, M., 147, *190*
Stratton, 86
Stratton, B.C., 271, *282*
Stress, reading deficits and, 176
Stricker, G., 278, *282*

Strickland, R., 58, 59, *81*
Stronck, D.R., 264, *284*
Structural analysis skills, 229, 237
Stubbs, M., *44*
Student(s)
    attitudes, 37–38
    expectations of teachers, 37
    knowledge, 38
    performance and competence, 38–39
    self-perceptions, 174–76
Sugar excess, 271
Suina, J.H., 34, 35, *43*
Sullivan, T., 379
Sutcliff, R., 377
Svobodny, L.A., 272, 273, *284*
Swain, C., 176, *191*
Swenson, J.H., 377
Syndromes, distinct clinical, 277
Syntactic Complexity Formula, The (Botal, Dawkins & Granowsky), 50
Syntax, 58–59, 102–4
Systemic allergic reaction, 266

Taylor, M., 370
Taylor, S.J., *43*
Taylor, T., 370
Taylor, W.L., 352, 354
Teacher-made IRIs, 128–30
Teachers
    as classroom ethnographer, 27
    student expectations of, 37
    student knowledge of, 38
Teaching styles, 34
Telephone interview, 310–12
Television reading, 73
Temple, C., 4, *8*, 48, *80*, 87, *115*, 223, 226, *241*, 244, 249, 257, *282*
Terminable or T-unit segmentation, 56–61
Test for Auditory Comprehension of Language, 53
Test of Language Development, 53
Test of Written Language (TOWL), 86, 334
Tests
    auditory, 383–84
    cloze procedure type, 124
    formal, 380–86
    for infants and preschool children, 384
    informal. *See* Informal tests and tools for assessment
    intelligence, 319, 380–81
    learning disabilities, 384
    motor skills, 384
    multiple-choice, 123
    oral language, 50, 52–53, 385, 387
    reading, 381–82, 386–87
        comprehension and retention, 321–22, 336–38, 381–82
    spelling, 383, 387
    visual, 384
    of words in context, 216–18
    writing, 85–87, 241–42, 383, 387
Text structures, expository, 167
Thelen, J.N., 218, *241*
Thorndike, E.L., 207, *241*
Thorndike, R.L., 52, 53
Tierney, R., 83, *115*, 117, 185, *194*

Time, assessment over, 5
Time/order text structure, 167
Tinker, M.A., 19, *24*, 244, 258, *282*
Tobin, A.W., *193*
Tompkins, G.E., 206, *241*
Tools for informal diagnostic procedures, 320–21
TOWL, 86, 334
Townsend, D., 98, *114*
Tracking ability (vision), 253
Tradebooks, 203
Transcription abilities, 84–85
Tripp, W., 362
T-units, 56–61
Turkle, B., 359

Unguided retelling, 177–80, 338–40, 350
Uninterrupted sustained silent reading (USSR), 351

Vacca, R., 147, *194*
Van Allsburg, C., 367
Van Slyck, M.R., 273, *284*
Variables, diagnostic. *See* Diagnostic variables
Vass, M., 264, 265, *284*
Veatch, J., 214, 229, *241*
Viorst, J., 113, 364
Vision, 18. 246–57
 adjusting for student with problems of, 255–57
 checklist, 249–50, 252
 identifying and assessing problems, 248–55
 tests, 384
 vocabulary related to, 248
Visual memory of words, 222, 230, 232
Vocabulary, 206–11, 382–83
Volume, 258

Wagner, B.J., 71, 76, *81*, *192*
Walker, R., 39, *44*
Walsh, J.P., 379
Walton, H.N., 254, *284*
Walton Modified Telebinocular Technique (MIT), 254
Wasson, B.B., 244, 258, *282*
Wasson, J.B., 244, 258, *282*
Watson, P.J., *190*
Way With Words (Kovac & Cahir), 50, 51
Webster, E., 379
Wechsler, D., 53
Wechsler Scales, 53
Weiss, S.E., 185, *192*
Wells, C.A., 124, *194*
Wells, R., 366
Wharton, W., 373
Whitney, E., 270, 271, *282*
Wilkinson, L.C., *44*
Williams, M.C., 271, *282*

Winter, P., 359
Withall, J., 26, *44*
Wolfe, J., 162, *190*
Woodcock, R.W., *241*
Woodcock Reading Mastery Tests, 341–42
Woodward, V., 87, *114*, 180, *192*
Word(s)
 analysis, tests for, 382
 lists, 207–11
 personal spelling, 224–26
 recognition, 206–7, 211–18, 382
 rings, 214
 sight, 207
 visual memory of, 222, 230, 232
Word identification games, 215. *See also* Decoding
Wordless books, 359
"Work-along-side-of" environment, 182
Writing
 activities, 109–12
 without a pencil, 206
 in context, 220
 developmental stages of, 88–90
 dialogue journals, 185–89
 guided, 140–46
 mechanical aspects of, 202–3
 samples, analysis of, 237
 tests, 85–87, 241–42, 383, 387
 workshop, 140, 141
Written coding system, 196–242
 clinical diagnosis and, 341–42
 comprehension of, 17–18
 decoding of word-identification skills, 230–37
 print
  activities for developing concepts about, 205–11
  awareness and comprehension of, 197–205
  concepts about, 197, 202–6
 spelling development, 220–30
 teaching strategies
  for decoding development, 237–38
  for use of context, 218–20
  for word recognition, 211–18
Written language fluency, 15–18, 82–115, 322–23, 344, 358
 assessing, 85–109
 books to help develop, 361–64
 guiding students to improve, 109–12
 quantitative scoring of, 96–97
 using literature to guide students in, 112–13
 variables to measure, 83–85
Written retellings, unguided, 177–80

Yoirinks, A., 368
Yolen, J., 376
Young, E., 359

Zelinsky, P.O., 366

DATE DUE			
OC 11 '89			
OC 3 '96			
OC 14 '97			
FE 25 '98			
MR 19 '98			
AP 20 '98			
GAYLORD			PRINTED IN U.S.A.